INTERNAL COLONIALISM

International Library of Sociology

Founded by Karl Mannheim
Editor: John Rex, University of Warwick

Arbor Scientiae
Arbor Vitae

A catalogue of the books available in the International Library of Sociology and other series of Social Science books published by Routledge & Kegan Paul will be found at the end of this volume.

INTERNAL COLONIALISM

THE CELTIC FRINGE IN BRITISH NATIONAL DEVELOPMENT, 1536–1966

MICHAEL HECHTER

ROUTLEDGE & KEGAN PAUL

London

First published in 1975
by Routledge & Kegan Paul Ltd
Broadway House, 68–74 Carter Lane,
London EC4V 5EL
Set in Monotype Times
and printed in Great Britain by
Butler & Tanner Ltd, Frome and London

ISBN 0 7100 7988 5

TO

GERTRUDE AND OSCAR HECHTER

CONTENTS

PREFACE   xiii

Part I The Problem

1 INTRODUCTION   3

2 TOWARDS A THEORY OF ETHNIC CHANGE   15
Dimensions of national development: an exploratory model   17
Diffusion models of national development   22
An alternative model: the periphery as an internal colony   30
On the cause of cultural differences between collectivities   34
Conclusion: the politics of ethnic change   39

Part II Core and Periphery in the Pre-Industrial Era

3 THE EXPANSION OF THE ENGLISH STATE   47
The role of ecology in British history   49
Territorial expansion and the realization of legitimacy   59
The imposition of English authority   65
English motives behind union   69
Governmental insistence on English cultural superiority   73

4 THE CONSEQUENCES OF POLITICAL INCORPORATION   79
The economic consequences of incorporation   81
    The strain towards regional economic specialization in
    the periphery   81
    The loss of sovereignty and its effects   90
The evolution of regional cultural differences: the
Reformation and its aftermath   95
The cultural consequences of incorporation   109
    The progress of anglicization   109
The political consequences of incorporation   119

CONTENTS

Part III   The Consequences of Industrialization

5 INDUSTRIALIZATION AND REGIONAL ECONOMIC
  INEQUALITY, 1851–1961   127
  The problem of regional economic inequality   130
  Regional economic inequality in the British Isles: the
  nineteenth and twentieth centuries   133
  The spatial diffusion of industrialization, 1851–1961   137
  Structural consequences of development in the periphery:
  the enclave and the hinterland   143
  The interpretation of economic inequality   150
  Conclusion   158
  Appendix: A note on the *per capita* income variable   161

6 THE ANGLICIZATION OF THE CELTIC PERIPHERY,
  1851–1961   164
  The distribution of religious affiliation in the British Isles   167
  The decline of Celtic language speaking in the British Isles   191
  Conclusion   206

7 THE PERSISTENCE OF SECTIONALISM, 1885–1966   208
  The British Isles as a case study   213
  An indirect method of measuring peripheral sectionalism   215
  Findings   223
  Conclusion   233

8 SERVITOR IMPERIALISM AND NATIONAL
  DEVELOPMENT IN AN AGE OF EMPIRE   234
  Theoretical background   237
  Measuring regional political responses   243
  Results: the elimination of structural differences   251
  Estimating the effect of economic diversity   257
  Conclusions   260

9 TWENTIETH-CENTURY CELTIC NATIONALISM   264
  The problem of Irish secession   266
  The inter-war years: solidification of class-based voting   293
  The paradox of Celtic resurgence   298

10 THE POLITICAL ECONOMY OF ETHNIC CHANGE   311
  Ethnicity and culture: problems of definition   311
  Two theories of ethnic change   312
  Testing the functionalist theory: trends in status group
  solidarity   317

CONTENTS

Testing the functionalist theory: the influence of cultural
factors on income   321
Some further considerations   323
On the preconditions of status group solidarity   326
Testing the reactive theory: contextual foundations for
the emergence of status group politics   331
Conclusions   339

11 CONCLUSION   341

INDEX   353

ix

ILLUSTRATIONS

MAPS

1 Great Britain and Ireland xii
2 The stages in the political unification of England by the kings of Wessex 55
3 The spatial diffusion of industrialization, 1861–1961 (Great Britain and Ireland) 140
4 Relatively disadvantaged counties, 1851–1961 (Great Britain) 154
5 Relatively anti-Conservative counties, 1885–1966 (Great Britain and Northern Ireland) 224
6 Relatively Nonconformist counties, 1851–1961 (Great Britain and Northern Ireland) 322

FIGURES

1 Mean regional residuals from multiple regression of *per capita* income on industrialization variables 155
2 Determinants of Welsh speaking 201
3 Distribution of counties, by peripheral sectionalism and voting stability, 1885–1966 227
4 The incidence of peripheral sectionalism in regions of the United Kingdom, 1885–1966. Mean regional residuals from the regression of Conservative voting on seven structural variables 229
5 A typology of counties 329
6 The voting determination model 331

Does the Eagle know what is in the pit?
Or wilt thou go ask the Mole?

WILLIAM BLAKE

Map 1 Great Britain and Ireland

PREFACE

Captain Jack Boyle I ofen looked up at the sky an' assed meself the question—what is the stars, what is the stars?
Joxer Daly Ah, that's the question, that's the question—what is the stars?

SEAN O'CASEY

THE Captain's question might have been asked about ethnicity, as well. This book asks it in his stead; it concerns the social origins of ethnic identification and change. Of necessity, this study delves into historical materials. As will be apparent to some readers, the author's formal training in history is slight. My first encounter with British history came, it happens, in a sociology class. As a student in a course on social change in colonial societies, it was necessary to write a paper on the development of a successful national liberation movement. The lectures were generally concerned with African examples, as were most of the papers. Having admiration for the plays of Sean O'Casey, I suspected that Ireland might well be a suitable case study. Ireland had been colonized, though I knew not when, and, after long struggle, had freed itself from the Black and Tans and British rule. Further study deepened my impression of pre-1921 Ireland as a colonial society. It soon became clear that there were many Irish parallels to the development of nationalism in West Africa; there were also significant differences. However, on reflection, the similarities seemed to be more striking than the differences. Later the fate of Wales and Scotland began to interest me, and the idea for this study was born.

For those concerned with the systematic analysis of social change, European case studies offer several obvious heuristic advantages. European history is longer than the history of most other areas of the world, due to the depth and richness of its written records. Furthermore, most theoretical approaches to social change have come from a consideration of European history, hence, they may be invalidated on the basis of European evidence. Finally, European

xiii

societies offer a wealth of quantitative evidence, some of which is available in time series. With this evidence, it is possible to construct and test simple models deriving from differing theoretical perspectives. Such models can not only cast doubt on particular explanations, but, typically, they raise new questions of old, and familiar materials.

The choice of England and the Celtic fringe for this study was dictated by intellectual, rather than by personal reasons. Autobiography had nothing to do with it: none of my ancestors were English, Welsh, Scottish, or Irish—of either hue. Neither am I of Roman Catholic, Presbyterian, Calvinistic, Methodist, or Anglican descent. I had no particular emotional commitment to the peoples of these lands, and in fact, had never set foot in the British Isles. Finally, it should be confessed, at the outset, that I am not specifically interested in the relationship between England and the Celtic fringe *sui generis*. However, these regions do provide an ideal research site from which to explore some fundamental issues in sociological theory. Perhaps not entirely by coincidence, these issues also relate to problems of social change in contemporary American society.

Since the 1960s, American politics has been preoccupied with the problems of ethnic conflict and assimilation. This overriding concern became reflected in issues such as the movement towards racial integration in public schools; the size of welfare expenditures in central city areas; the spiralling rates of urban crime.

Oppressed 'ethnic' groups, particularly Blacks, had recently become politically mobilized. Initially, Black political organizations, such as the Student Nonviolent Coordinating Committee and the Southern Christian Leadership Conference, were committed to the implementation and extension of Federal civil rights statutes, especially in the South. Their ultimate goal was the integration and assimilation of Blacks in American society on an incremental basis, until full equality might eventually be realized. This goal implied a strategy of establishing broadly based coalitions of Black and white individuals and groups.

By the middle of the decade, a deep split had emerged in the Black community between those traditionalists clinging to assimilation as their ultimate goal, and a younger, more militant group who, instead, argued for a radical separation of Blacks from white society and culture. Malcolm X was perhaps the most impressive of this new generation of 'ethnic leaders.' The goal of this new leadership was to increase the material prosperity and welfare of Black Americans as a separate nation within white society. One of the ways this could be accomplished was to emphasize differences of culture between Black and white Americans, and to argue an American version of *Négritude*: Black is beautiful. The new theory was that Blacks, as a collective group, could begin to assert political power and influence in American society only to the extent that the Black community could be strengthened internally. This theory dictated different organizational strategies, most importantly, the formation of all-Black political organizations.

If the first position was assimilationist, the second came to be known as nationalist. While many white liberals were shocked at this turn of events, which they interpreted as an inverse kind of racism, it is clear that many minorities in history have made a similar voyage, from assimilationism to nationalism, in fighting for greater influence within their societies. A graphic example is provided in Frantz Fanon's intellectual development. In his early book, *Peau noire, masques blancs* (1952), Fanon eloquently argued the case for the assimilation of colonial Blacks to French metropolitan culture. But in his later work, most particularly *Les Damnés de la terre* (1963), the assimilationist position is totally rejected. And it is this book which has become the very Scripture of the Black nationalist movement in the United States.

As these alternative strategies of Black liberation became more clearly defined, they began to emerge as competing theoretical perspectives in the political and scholarly literature on intergroup relations. For a long time, most respectable academics held to the assimilationist view. Hence, many analyses of the fate of the 'ethnic' minorities of the 1960s stress that their position in American society results from the types of norms and values characteristic of ghetto communities which, however, are severely dysfunctional in the wider society. The notion of the 'culture of poverty' is perhaps the most famous example. Ultimately, these groups are poor and frustrated because their communities are isolated from the national culture. In consequence, ghetto children become socialized to failure. The suggestion of a cause leads quickly to a solution: if the government were to invest substantial resources to insure a proper socialization of ghetto children, then the 'culture of poverty' would cease to be significant for future generations. To the extent that the United States government has devoted its resources to aid 'ethnic' minorities, it has adopted this analysis: witness the example of Project Head Start.

Increasingly, the 'ethnic' minorities have, themselves, come to define their situation as that of an 'internal colony.' The structure of the internal colony is maintained by white racism. Third World peoples are used for surplus labor, or cannon fodder in imperial wars, by the institutions of white America. In this view, the position of the disadvantaged 'ethnic' minorities is largely a function of exploitation. Their welfare can best be met by gaining control over their own economic, cultural, and political institutions. Further Black cultural assimilation in white America can only serve to weaken the prospects for the realization of such control.

I saw these issues at first hand as a participant in the Columbia University strike (1968). What had begun as a joint Black and white protest against the university's plan to construct a gymnasium in a Harlem park, soon developed into two separate, but equal, demonstrations. The Black students assumed control of one of the campus buildings, Hamilton Hall, and asked white students to leave and set up their own occupation. Through the course of the strike they made great pains to distinguish their strike from that of the white students.

At this time, it is far from evident which of these analyses—assimilationist or nationalist—has greater merit. Certainly the kinds of changes which must occur to improve intergroup relations in the United States will take some time. Neither perspective can be expected to predict much, in the short run. This, of course, is the great strength of historical case studies: they can be examined over the long run.

To a remarkable degree, these issues are also the subject of this book, though the particular groups and historical conditions are very different from those of twentieth-century America. For one thing, the conflicting 'ethnic' groups in the British Isles, that is to say Anglo-Saxons and Celts, cannot be differentiated by *color*. Despite this, however, racism came to full flower there, as well. I think Americans have come to realize how this is possible by following the recent events in Northern Ireland. The lack of a color difference between Celts and Anglo-Saxons was often noted in Victorian England. Here is Charles Kingsley, a Cambridge University historian of the nineteenth century, describing a visit to Ireland:[1]

But I am haunted by the human chimpanzees I saw along that hundred miles of horrible country. I don't believe they are our fault. I believe there are not only many more of them than of old, but they are happier, better, more comfortably fed and lodged under our rule than they ever were. But

[1] L. P. Curtis, Jr, *Anglo-Saxons and Celts* (Bridgeport, Ct: 1968), p. 84.

to see white chimpanzees is dreadful; if they were black, one would not feel it so much, but their skins, except where tanned by exposure, are as white as ours.

Racism is not the only similarity between the two situations. Many of the same types of arguments about strategies characterized the development of Celtic political thought and action. In the Celtic lands, too, there arose clearly delimited positions for assimilation, on the one hand, and nationalism, on the other. In the early twentieth century, all of the Celtic peoples were torn between these alternatives as solutions to their internal problems: unemployment; poverty; powerlessness in the face of the central government; a sense of cultural inferiority. The Celtic peoples did not react uniformly, but embarked on different courses. The Irish, at least the bulk of them, opted for the nationalist solution, and created a separate, sovereign state, while the Welsh and Scottish remained part of the United Kingdom, and, to a large extent, hoped that the rise of the new Labor Party would solve the severe problems of their respective lands.

Thus, while this problem might initially appear to be far removed from current American issues, I believe this to be a mistaken impression. In examining the interaction of Anglo-Saxon and Celtic peoples over the long run, these alternative strategies for the liberation of oppressed minorities—assimilationism *versus* nationalism—can be elaborated and analyzed in some detail. The consequences of these strategies may then become clarified.

The title of this book indicates which analysis I feel is most useful in describing the historical position of the Celtic fringe in the British Isles. But, in completing this study, I have come to realize that such questions are not resolved by any simple means. The answers which emerge are always based upon assumptions about theoretical and methodological issues. The validity of the answers is ultimately determined by the adequacy of these assumptions. If historical knowledge is to be useful as a guide to political action, these intellectual issues must not be dodged, but met head on.

This book owes its existence to many people and to several institutions. It could not have been completed without the support and encouragement of Immanuel Wallerstein; it would not even have been attempted without his example. The actual work took several years. In addition to Wallerstein, Herman Ausubel, Guenther Roth, and Charles Tilly all read the manuscript in full, and provided valued advice. Both past and present colleagues at the University of Washington, especially William Kornblum, James McCann, and Pier Paolo Giglioli, helped me clarify my ideas repeatedly. Despite his intense skepticism about this enterprise, L. Perry Curtis, Jr, did his best to point out the most obvious of my historical blunders. The errors of fact and interpretation which remain are solely my responsibility. Space does not permit me to thank those who kindly read and criticized individual chapters. Margaret Webber and Richard Honigman did the lion's share of data collection for meager pay, and in the most unfavorable of circumstances. David Baylon helped me to communicate with the computer. Beulah Reddaway and her capable staff had much patience in typing the manuscript. Finally, with great pleasure I record my debt to Joshua Hechter, whose contribution he will, in time, come to appreciate.

Part of the research for this study was supported by a National Science Foundation Dissertation Grant and by a National Institute of Mental Health pre-doctoral fellowship; other funds were provided by two small grants from the Department of Sociology at Columbia University.

Portions of some chapters have previously appeared in *Politics & Society* (chapter 2), the *Journal of Development Studies* (chapter 5), and the *American Journal of Sociology* (chapters 7 and 10). They are reproduced here with the permission of the publishers. Map 2 is reproduced, with permission, from Albert Demangeon's *The British Isles*, published by Heinemann in 1961.

PART I
The Problem

CHAPTER 1

INTRODUCTION

The city was a confederation of groups that had been established before it. . . . We should not lose sight of the excessive difficulty which, in primitive times, opposed the foundation of regular societies. The social tie was not easy to establish between those human beings who were so diverse, so free, so inconstant. To bring them under the rules of a community, to institute commandments and insure obedience, to cause passion to give way to reason, and individual right to public right, there certainly was something necessary, stronger than material force, more respectable than interest, surer than a philosophical theory, more changeable than a convention; something that should dwell equally in all hearts, and should be all-powerful there. This power was a belief.

NUMA DENIS FUSTEL DE COULANGES

HOW do societies pass beyond tribalism? How do they encompass new, culturally divergent groups and yet, in the course of history, emerge to be nations?

Nationalism is often held to be a great, even predominant, social force in the modern world. While in earlier historical eras individuals thought of themselves as members of solidary groups like families, clans, or communities, nowadays almost everyone has a nationality. And nationality clearly has special significance among all of an individual's statuses. For it is in the name of this status alone that individuals are permitted, and at times encouraged, to take the lives of other persons: for example, those having a different nationality. The state of war is considered tolerable only when hostilities occur between social units called nations. Civil wars, or conflicts defined, by at least some participants, as taking place between members of the same nation, are tragic occasions which are quickly put out of mind, and rarely glorified.

In most other types of conflict, the hostile use of the means of violence by ordinary citizens, such as those who are regularly inducted into the military, is strongly sanctioned. In no society are

3

workers encouraged to kill their bosses, or wives their husbands. In no society are the adherents of one religion regarded as justified in committing violence against individuals of another faith. These are all egregious affronts to any social order. When these acts occur with regularity, the social order is seen to be threatened. In this Hobbesian world, society, as such, ceases to exist. The concept of nationality is used to delineate societies, as separate entities, from one another. For the nation, in essence, is a socially constructed boundary which serves to designate societal membership to some groups and not to others. In the modern era, nationality is the concept which best expresses that sense of relatedness which holds between individuals in society.

But what exactly constitutes this sentiment of nationality? The classical sociological answer to this query was framed by Emile Durkheim. Durkheim posited that there is, at the basis of every social order, a set of commonly held values and orientations to social action, or norms, which together make up the *conscience collective*. It is through the action of the *conscience collective* that separate individuals become, in effect, socialized, or made fit for collective life. The *conscience collective* is a primitive in what is loosely termed the culture of any group.

This conception of the social order lies at the heart of much sociological theory and research. But to hold that there is a *conscience collective* at the foundation of every society is necessarily to raise questions for the study of social change.[1] If processes of development are to be understood, the *conscience collective* cannot usefully be conceived to be a static attribute of social groups. It, too, must be a variable; it must have its own dynamics which correspond, in some way, to changes in the social structure. This must be true, since the size and scope of solidary social units has changed greatly in the course of history. To draw the point most forcefully, there are primitive societies not much larger than several extended families. Yet, at the other end of the development continuum, several advanced industrial societies effectively span entire continents.

Most modern states were initially composed of two or more distinct cultural groups. In the course of their development, effective bureaucratic administrations arose in certain regions of the territories later to become the modern States of Western Europe. It was in these *core* regions—Castile in Spain; Île-de-France in France; first

[1] See the excellent discussion in Gianfranco Poggi, *Images of Society* (Stanford: 1972), pp. 249–55.

Wessex, then London and the Home Counties in England—that strong central governments were first established. Each of these small areas had, to varying degrees, distinct cultural practices from those of outlying, *peripheral*, regions.[1] These included differences in language, kinship structures, inheritance systems, modes of agricultural production, patterns of settlement, legal systems or the lack thereof, religious beliefs, and, most generally, styles of life. As the core regions of the developing states advanced economically and technologically, their political influence and control extended outwards to the eventual boundaries of our modern states. National development is a process which may be said to occur when the separate cultural identities of regions begin to lose social significance, and become blurred. In this process, the several local and regional cultures are gradually replaced by the establishment of one *national* culture which cuts across the previous distinctions. The core and peripheral cultures must ultimately merge into one all-encompassing cultural system to which all members of the society have primary identification and loyalty.

It is clear that the assimilation of peripheral cultures has occurred more thoroughly in some societies than in others. The persistence of separatist political movements among groups within such societies as Canada, Belgium and the United Kingdom suggests that the successful incorporation of peripheral groups occurs only under certain conditions. The specification of these conditions is of ultimate concern in this study. Due to the meager body of empirical research in this area, it is even difficult to precisely state the types of conditions —or to use another language, variables—which facilitate national development. Despite this, however, much has been written of a theoretical and speculative nature about national development, and this literature can serve as a starting point for further investigation.

In this book, varying theoretical discussions have been condensed and simplified into two alternative models of national development. I am well aware that this kind of model-building is frowned upon in historical circles. Traditional historiography demands that the facts should tumble forth, free from the artificial constraints imposed by models. Yet, the writing of history itself requires the use of some

---

[1] The core, then, is the region of the *Staatsvolk*. For other definitions of core and periphery, see N. J. G. Pounds and Sue Bell, 'Core areas and the development of the European state system,' *Annals of the American Association of Geographers*, 54, 1 (1964); and Sivert Langholm, 'On the concepts of center and periphery,' *Journal of Peace Research*, nos 3–4 (1971).

kind of intellectual framework, whether implicit or explicit. The historian's decisions about topics, units of analysis, and theories of social action constitute frameworks for the selection and organization of data. Whatever framework is chosen should be appropriate to the problem at hand.

This study seeks to explain the social origins of ethnic solidarity and change, on the basis of aggregated data. These data do not lend themselves to analyses bearing much resemblance to those of the traditional historian. They cannot be used to account for the actions of *specific* individuals, or even *specific* élites. They cannot aid our understanding of why *particular* events occurred when they did. Hence, this study may not pay sufficient attention to microscopic detail for some readers. Rather, it is primarily concerned to account for shifting relationships between large aggregates of people. For this purpose, it makes a good deal of sense to employ explicit models rather than implicit ones. This forces the investigator to express clearly his concepts and explanatory mechanisms. It also helps him extract sets of logically consistent expectations from theoretical discussions which are, too often, vague and logically inconsistent. Given adequate data, these models may then be put to an empirical test.

It is sometimes objected that such models are so crude that only a schoolboy could possibly subscribe to them. The models in this book in no way encompass the complexity of social life. They do not explain everything, nor do they attempt to do so. However, as will become apparent, they do explain some things, to some degree. The great advantage in using models is that they may be falsified, whereas descriptions can only be amended. The models employed here are painfully preliminary. Good models exist that they might later be superseded: in this way, knowledge is cumulated. There is no doubt that these particular models may not appeal to many an historian, but given the purpose of this inquiry, and the quality of available data, I feel they are the best that can be constructed at this point.

What, then, do they look like? The first model is widely held among scholars of political development and modernization. I will refer to it as a *diffusion* model of national development. This model has components derived from the work of the nineteenth-century social theorists, from contemporary structural-functionalists, and from political scientists deeply concerned with communications theory.

The diffusion model is to a certain extent evolutionary. In it there are seen to be three important temporal stages occurring in the process of national development. The first stage is pre-industrial. In this period, the core and peripheral regions exist in virtual isolation from one another. Events in the core have but slight influence in the periphery, and the corollary situation holds as well. A very small proportion of the acts occurring between individuals in each region involves actors from the other region. Not only are the core and the periphery mutually isolated; there are many significant differences in their economic, cultural, and political institutions.

In so far as economic systems are concerned, regional differences may exist with regard to the type of production, for example, arable *versus* pastoral economies; the extent of markets and nucleated settlements; the standard of living; and the type of stratification characteristic of the respective territories. Cultural differences may occur on the dimensions of language, religion, values towards work and leisure, and life-style. In consequence of these variations, socialization practices will differ in core and periphery. Last, political structures may vary from relatively centralized forms of rule, to looser types of political organization and authority.

The second stage in national development occurs after the initiation of more intensive contact between the core and peripheral regions. Often this is assumed to occur at the onset of industrialization. The kernel of the diffusion perspective concerns the consequences of industrialization and the concomitant increase in core–periphery interaction. As a rule, the diffusionist view holds that *from interaction will come commonality.* The type of social structure found in the developing core regions will, after some time, diffuse into the periphery.[1] Since the cultural forms of the periphery were evolved in isolation from the rest of the world, contact with modernizing core regions will transform these cultural forms by updating them, as it were. For a time, it has been argued, the massive social dislocation associated with industrialization and the expansion of core–periphery interaction may heighten the sense of cultural separateness in the periphery. This is because individuals

---

[1] 'Diffusion is the process, usually but not necessarily gradual, by which elements or systems of culture are spread, by which an invention or new institution adopted in one place is adopted in neighboring areas, and in some cases continues to be adopted in adjacent ones, until it may spread over the whole earth.' A. L. Kroeber, 'Diffusionism' in E. R. A. Seligman and Alvin Johnson, eds, *The Encyclopedia of the Social Sciences*, III (1930), reprinted in A. and E. Etzioni, eds, *Social Change: Sources, Patterns, and Consequences* (New York: 1964), p. 142.

and groups in the periphery are, at first, likely to cling to their customary social patterns as a refuge from the chaos of rapid social change. This is an understandable reaction of dismay in the face of an uncertain future.

But such 'traditional' behavior will tend to decline as the new routine of industrial life becomes perceived as more and more satisfactory in promoting the general welfare, and as initial regional differences become muted following industrialization. In the long run, the core and peripheral regions will tend to become culturally homogeneous because the economic, cultural, and political foundations for separate ethnic identification disappear. Many attributes of the regions themselves will converge following industrialization. In the third, and final, stage of national development regional wealth should equilibrate; cultural differences should cease to be socially meaningful; and political processes will occur within a framework of national parties, with luck, in a democratic setting, thereby insuring representation to all significant groups.

These aggregate changes in regional characteristics are mirrored by a profound convergence in the performance of individual roles. Industrialization necessarily involves a change from diffuse role performances and functions to specific roles and functions. That is to say, industrialization causes structural differentiation. Face-to-face interactions are increasingly replaced by social relationships which are largely impersonal. Statuses which are ascribed to individuals become less important than those which are achieved. Individuals are liberated from the constraints of traditional community sanctions, and may therefore develop 'performance-centered' values.[1] All told, the functional requirements of the modern social system cause a breakdown of previous social arrangements. One of the implications of this change is that industrialization favors the inclusion of previously excluded groups into the society.

As a model of social change this is decidedly optimistic: it does not seem to square with much that is happening in the world today. It contrasts in many respects with the expectations of another model, which I will call *internal colonialism*. Despite its current popularity, the concept of internal colonialism is not a new one. V. I. Lenin was, perhaps, the first writer to use this notion in an empirical investigation of national development.[2] Several years thereafter, Antonio

---

[1] Neil J. Smelser, *Social Change in the Industrial Revolution* (Chicago: 1959).
[2] V. I. Lenin, *The Development of Capitalism in Russia* (Moscow: 1956), especially pp. 172–7; 269; and 363ff.

8

Gramsci discussed the Italian *Mezzogiorno* in similar terms.[1] More recently, Latin American sociologists have made use of this concept to describe the Amerindian regions of their societies. At this writing, internal colonialism has also gained wide acceptance in the United States; the term is bandied about in political manifestos and in some scholarly journals. However, neither its proponents nor its detractors have accorded internal colonialism the seriousness which I believe it deserves. It is hoped that this book might contribute to that effort.

Far from maintaining that increased core–periphery contact results in social structural convergence, the internal colonial model posits an altogether different relationship between these regions. The core is seen to dominate the periphery politically and to exploit it materially. The internal colonial model does not predict national development following industrialization, except under exceptional circumstances.

The features of this model may be sketched briefly. The spatially uneven wave of modernization over state territory creates relatively advanced and less advanced groups. As a consequence of this initial fortuitous advantage, there is crystallization of the unequal distribution of resources and power between the two groups. The superordinate group, or core, seeks to stabilize and monopolize its advantages through policies aiming at the institutionalization of the existing stratification system. It attempts to regulate the allocation of social roles such that those roles commonly defined as having high prestige are reserved for its members. Conversely, individuals from the less advanced group are denied access to these roles. This stratification system, which may be termed a cultural division of labor, contributes to the development of distinctive ethnic identification in the two groups. Actors come to categorize themselves and others according to the range of roles each may be expected to play. They are aided in this categorization by the presence of visible signs, or cultural markers, which are seen to characterize both groups. At this stage, acculturation does not occur because it is not in the interests of institutions within the core.

Whereas the core is characterized by a diversified industrial structure, the pattern of development in the periphery is dependent, and complementary to that in the core. Peripheral industrialization, if it occurs at all, is highly specialized and geared for export. The peripheral economy is, therefore, relatively sensitive to price fluctuations

---

[1] Antonio Gramsci, 'The Southern Question' in *The Modern Prince and Other Writings* (New York: 1959).

9

in the international market. Decisions about investment, credit, and wages tend to be made in the core. As a consequence of economic dependence, wealth in the periphery lags behind the core.

To the extent that social stratification in the periphery is based on observable cultural differences, there exists the probability that the disadvantaged group will, in time, reactively assert its own culture as equal or superior to that of the relatively advantaged core. This may help it conceive of itself as a separate 'nation' and seek independence. Hence, in this situation, acculturation and national development may be inhibited by the desires of the peripheral group for independence from a situation perceived to be exploitative.

Given similar initial conditions, the mutual isolation of core and periphery, these models therefore predict different outcomes for national development following the heightening of interaction between these regions. While the diffusion model predicts a lessening of regional economic inequalities, the internal colonial model predicts that these will persist or increase. While the diffusion model suggests the probability of peripheral acculturation, the internal colonial model suggests the likelihood of an assertion of the peripheral culture in reaction to the domination of the core. Finally, while the diffusion model states that functional political cleavages should characterize political behavior in all regions of the society, the internal colonial model states that political cleavages will largely reflect significant cultural differences between groups. It is a welcome situation in social science when two models offer predictions so diametrically opposed, yet so potentially capable of empirical resolution.

This study attempts to evaluate the relative merits of these models in one geographical and historical setting, the British Isles, including Ireland, from the sixteenth to the twentieth centuries. Since early medieval times, the British Isles had been inhabited successively by many separate cultural groups. By the twentieth century, a great majority of the inhabitants of these islands had come to define themselves as being British. Gone were the names and evidences of earlier cultural groups: Picts, Frisians, Angles, Saxons, Danes, and Normans. All of these separate cultural groups have, in history, been amalgamated, and together they make up the British nationality.

That is, all such groups but one, the so-called Celts. In certain regions of the British Isles, large sections of the population continue to define their culture as being 'Celtic' rather than 'British.' These groups have based political movements for regional devolution and self-determination on their claim of a separate culture: they feel themselves to constitute a separate nation. This study concerns the persistence of separate ethnic identity in the Celtic regions of the British Isles, Wales, Scotland, and Ireland, during a century of rapid social change.[1] It seeks to explain the relative failure of national development in the United Kingdom, as indicated not only by the secession of southern Ireland in 1921, but by the existence of a social base for ethnic politics within Wales, Scotland, and Northern Ireland today. The reasons for the existence of separate ethnic identity in the peripheral regions of advanced industrial societies are to a large extent mysterious. In part, this is because the systematic comparative study of national development must be considered to be in its infancy.

There are probably several reasons for this situation. As a thematic concern of social science, apart from the intellectual traditions of natural philosophy or statesmanship, the problem of national development, as formulated in this study, is of recent concern. Many scholars observing the Afro-Asian societies emerging from colonial rule became impressed by the extraordinary difficulties the rulers of the new states encountered following the winning of sovereignty. While initial hopes for material prosperity and political stability in the new states were high, it soon became apparent that there were many constraints on the processes of economic and political development in the Third World setting.[2]

In particular, the anti-colonial united front of different ethnic groups quickly dissolved, to be replaced by ever-growing internal antagonisms. In large part, the basis for this ethnic cleavage was competition between the members of different groups hoping to control the state administration and its resources. Much of this conflict was over issues of *culture*, especially language and religion, since these competing ethnic groups differentiated themselves by their cultural dissimilarities. A rash of case studies documented these conflicts in varying geographical contexts. But, as is explained more fully in chapter 2, the fact that these studies have largely concerned *new* states has inherently limited their generality. Essentially, the new states are inappropriate contexts to study ethnic change because the study of change requires evidence gathered at relatively widely

---

[1] The Channel Islands and the Isle of Man have been excluded from the analysis, as a comparable set of data is not available for them.
[2] A recent example is Michael F. Lofchie, ed., *The State of the Nations: Constraints on Development in Independent Africa* (Berkeley: 1971).

spaced points in time. This heuristic necessity suggests the usefulness of the older, and more developed, European states as suitable cases for consideration.

Unfortunately, there has not been wide appreciation of this point. Few social scientists have wanted to give up the comfort of their disciplinary niches and venture forth into the *terra incognita* of European history. And those few who have begun this journey have not paid sufficient attention to methodological issues.[1] Consequently, the fruit of their labors has rather quickly withered.

This is not to say that it is particularly easy to gather the evidence needed to test these conceptions of national development. For example, it is probably insufficient to rely solely on the syntheses of historians for adequate evidence. Most historical studies have concentrated on events affecting the core areas of the old states, precisely because these sectors were seen to be the most dynamic, and therefore interesting.

How, then, to best proceed? In attempting to address some of these weaknesses I searched for sources of data which might indicate the theoretical model most applicable in the British case. Since these models predict different effects of industrialization on aggregate regional inequalities, I first sought statistics on relative regional social and economic development. The census reports were an obvious starting point, but there is also rich evidence in the so-called Parliamentary Blue Books and Command Papers. An early article reported various statistical time series aggregated for England, Wales, Scotland, and Ireland considered as separate regions.[2] In the course of this research, I discovered that many of the relevant statistics existed for individual counties. While there can be but four (or five, with the separation of north and south Ireland) regions of separate culture, the use of individual counties results in a population of 118 units, thereby allowing for considerably more sophisticated data analysis.

The bulk of the quantitative evidence in the study is composed of demographic, social, and electoral statistics collected for each county at eleven points in time from 1851 to 1966. As a data base, this is unique in the study of national development. It offers detailed evidence for both cross-sectional and longitudinal analyses. Wherever

---

[1] See Karl W. Deutsch *et al.*, *Political Community and the North Atlantic Area* (Princeton: 1957).

[2] Michael Hechter, 'Regional inequality and national integration: the case of the British Isles,' *Journal of Social History*, 5, 1 (1971), pp. 96–117.

possible, I have attempted to supplement this evidence by the use of secondary historical materials. Yet, the adequacy of these ecological data for the purpose of exploring the alternative models of national development is a central problem, as well as a recurrent theme, in this book. Both the diffusion and internal colonial perspectives ultimately rest on assertions about the subjective state of mind of individuals. The diffusion model, in particular, makes reference to discrete changes in individual normative and value orientations. These notions have been criticized, quite rightly in my opinion, for their lack of susceptibility to measurement and subsequent validation. But there are assumptions about social psychological processes lying at the heart of the internal colonial model, as well. Throughout this study I have resisted speculation about these issues, preferring to treat the problem as if it were a black box, in the language of systems analysis.

I have always felt that it is much more profitable in such an endeavor to dwell on the actual behaviors of individuals and groups. However, even in this realm, the difficulties of gathering reliable evidence are manifold. How much more problematic it is to assess this kind of information in historical situations! Bearing in mind a host of qualifications relating to these issues, I have attempted to infer something about the behavior of individuals and groups on the basis of ecological evidence. There has been an intensive scholarly debate concerning the adequacy of ecological inference, and though the complex methodological issues have not been completely resolved, I feel that the sense of this literature is that, when properly analyzed, such data may yield important insights which would be otherwise lost.[1] This is especially true in historical research, which is of necessity limited by the kinds of records previous societies have left behind. Needless to add, I have tried to be as conservative as possible in drawing interpretations from an admittedly shaky empirical base.

The design of the book is quite simple. The second chapter provides an introduction to some of the theoretical issues involved in studying national development, by speculating on some social conditions for ethnic change in peripheral areas. It may be considered to be a prospectus for the study as a whole. Part II considers the historical setting in which England began territorial expansion, as well as some consequences of political incorporation for the Celtic

[1] Mattei Dogan and Stein Rokkan, eds, *Quantitative Ecological Analysis in the Social Sciences* (Cambridge, Mass.: 1969).

13

lands. It is meant to discuss core–periphery relations up to the industrial era.

Part III considers the consequences of industrialization, with its heightened core–periphery interaction, on several processes. It discusses whether industrialization, in fact, led to regional economic equality; whether industrialization facilitated the development of a national culture; and the consequences of industrialization upon the political integration of the Celtic lands as well. The tenth chapter delineates some social structural conditions underlying ethnic solidarity, and is a summary empirical analysis of the variables introduced earlier. The conclusions will not be reported here, as they are discussed, in all of their tentativeness, in the final chapter. Here, also, it will be possible to consider what has been learned and, on this basis, to point to fruitful areas of new research.

CHAPTER 2

TOWARDS A THEORY OF
ETHNIC CHANGE

I have seen, in my time, Frenchmen, Italians, and Russians; I even
know, thanks to Montesquieu, that one may be a Persian; but as for
man, I declare that I have never met him in my life; if he exists, it is
without my knowledge.

JOSEPH DE MAISTRE

Every industrial and commercial center in England now possesses a
working-class *divided* into two *hostile* camps, English proletarians and
Irish proletarians. The ordinary English worker hates the Irish worker
as a competitor who lowers his standard of life. In relation to the Irish
worker he feels himself a member of the ruling nation and so turns
himself into a tool of the aristocrats and capitalists of his country *against
Ireland*, thus strengthening their domination *over himself*. He cherishes
religious, social and national prejudices against the Irish worker. His
attitude towards him is much the same as that of the 'poor whites' to the
'niggers' of the former slave states of the USA. The Irishman pays him
back with interest in his own money. He sees in the English worker at
once the accomplice and the stupid tool of the *English domination in
Ireland*. . . . This antagonism is the *secret of the impotence of the English
working-class*, despite their organization.

KARL MARX

THE persistence of ethnic attachments in complex societies is in
certain respects as vexing today as it was to these two very different
nineteenth-century thinkers. The current flourish of national consciousness among cultural minorities in advanced industrial societies
poses something of a sociological dilemma, for these frequently
territorial conflicts involving language and religion have been
assumed to be endemic to the early stages of national development.[1] Peripheral regions in developing countries have tended to

[1] Clifford Geertz, 'The Integrative Revolution: Primordial Sentiments and
Civic Politics in the New States' in C. Geertz, ed., *Old Societies and New States*
(New York: 1963).

15

resist the incursions of central authorities imposing their omnivorous bureaucracy and haughty culture.

However, the advent of sustained economic and social development presumably serves to undercut the traditional bases of solidarity among extant groups. A familiar list of processes catalogued under the heading of modernization systematically increases the individual's dependence upon and loyalty to the central government. The major foundation of political cleavage in industrial society is then thought to become functional rather than segmental, thereby producing 'alliances of similarly oriented subjects and households over wide ranges of localities.'[1] This provides the nucleus of a very generally held sociological theory of ethnic change. Such a theory predicts that the transformed conditions of industrial society alter the basis on which individuals form political associations. In consequence of modernization, the salience of cultural similarity as a social bond should give way to political alliances between individuals of similar market position, and thus, more generally, social class.

When the Western industrial working class was judged to have been granted the full rights of citizenship following militant trade-union and party organization, some observers relaxed enough to proclaim an end of ideology in the West. It now appears that the Flemings in Belgium, Celts in Britain and France, Slovaks in Czechoslovakia, French in Canada—to say nothing of various minorities in the United States—have not yet received the message.[2] There is a new fear that these phenomena are the rumblings of the eventual dissolution of the Western nation state. In ten years the pendulum has swung far indeed.[3] The specter of class warfare may have subsided only to be replaced by the hoarier aspect of 'racial' conflict. At any rate that state of social harmony sometimes referred to as national integration now seems to many an unexpectedly elusive goal.

In the context of the resurgence of ethnicity as a major political factor in industrial society it may be useful to examine the concept

[1] Seymour M. Lipset and Stein Rokkan, 'Introduction' in S. M. Lipset and S. Rokkan, eds, *Party Systems and Voter Alignments* (New York: 167), p. 10.

[2] E. Allardt and Y. Littunen, eds, *Cleavages, Ideologies, and Party Systems* (Helsinki: 1964); Robert A. Dahl, ed., *Political Oppositions in Western Democracies* (New Haven: 1966); and Stein Rokkan, *Citizens, Elections, and Parties* (New York and Oslo: 1970).

[3] For a graphic demonstration compare two essays written at opposite poles of the past decade by Daniel Bell, 'The End of Ideology in the West' in *The End of Ideology* (New York: 1962), pp. 393–407, and 'Unstable America,' *Encounter*, 34 (1970), pp. 11–26.

of national development and evaluate some of the alternative ways in which it has been used. Accordingly this chapter will have four related foci. First, it will introduce a simplified model for the empirical study of national development. Second, it will review the main currents of previous theory from the perspective of this model, and evaluate its adequacy, in the light of current research. Third, it will define the concept of ethnicity and discuss the social basis of ethnic identification. Finally, it will attempt to sketch some tentative hypotheses about the conditions governing the prospects for ethnic change.

DIMENSIONS OF NATIONAL DEVELOPMENT: AN EXPLORATORY MODEL

Among current concepts of social science, national development must rank high on a scale of ambiguity. One writer has detected five separate senses in which a related term has been used, varying not only in scope but in subject matter as well.[1] Others have denied the utility of this kind of concept outright, particularly in its evolutionary and deterministic form.[2] The general expansion of the size and scope of states since the late Middle Ages is justification enough for the utility of some concept of national development. Clearly the social organization of the Athenian *polis* would be inadequate to maintain a society as large and diverse as the United States, the factor of communications technology aside. The specification of this evolutionary development was the major focus of nineteenth-century social theory. It is by now apparent that the classical social theorists overestimated the extent to which industrialization would lead to a fully national society.

A useful definition of national development would describe a process, the creation of a national society, rather than a particular state of affairs.[3] Here national development will refer to those processes by which a state characterized by sectional, or otherwise competing economies, polities, and cultures, within a given territory, is transformed into a society composed of a single, all-pervasive, and in this sense 'national' economy, polity, and culture. This definition, it

[1] Myron Weiner, 'Political integration and political development,' *Annals of the American Academy of Political Science*, 358 (1965), pp. 52–64.
[2] Randall Collins, 'A Comparative Approach to Political Sociology' in Reinhard Bendix *et al.*, eds, *State and Society* (Boston: 1968), pp. 42–67.
[3] Gunnar Myrdal, *An International Economy* (New York: 1956), pp. 9–11.

should be noted, does not include the analytically distinct problem of the incorporation of excluded social classes into the national society.[1]

It should be understood at once that not much is known about national development in these terms. Since so little systematic empirical work has been done in this area many writers have assumed much about these processes on a purely *a priori* basis. For instance, the relationship between regional economic specialization and interregional political solidarity has never been carefully studied on a comparative basis. Nevertheless, writers will often take sides on this question largely on the basis of theoretical arguments. The difficulty is that a good theoretical case can be made for either side in the dispute.

In the following discussion I shall assume a simple model to illustrate processes of national development in industrial societies. In this model there are two collectivities or objectively distinct cultural groups: (1) the *core*, or dominant cultural group which occupies territory extending from the political center of the society (e.g. the locus of the central government) outward to those territories largely occupied by the subordinate, or (2) *peripheral* cultural group. The model therefore assumes that these respective cultural groups are to a large extent regionally concentrated.[2] For the moment I will assume that these two collectivities are perfectly solidary, and, loosely speaking, possess a group consciousness. Hence, when I conceive of a collectivity as an acting unit, this of course refers to the action of the bulk of its members.

Because the lacunae surrounding the problem of national development are so extensive, it may be wise to proceed initially as if the concept were a black box. Actually, enough is known to separate the problem into three analytically separate black boxes. The first might be labeled the problem of *cultural integration*. The extent to which

---

[1] This problem has received substantially greater attention. See T. H. Marshall, 'Citizenship and Social Class' in *Class, Citizenship, and Social Development* (New York: 1964), pp. 71–134, and Reinhard Bendix, *Nation-Building and Citizenship* (New York: 1964).

[2] This restriction limits the applicability of the model to a subset of the universe of settings for intergroup conflict. However, my central concern in this study is with industrialized societies where this model has wide relevance, except for those societies, like the United States, formed largely from voluntary migration. As R. A. Schermerhorn has argued, 'Studies of ethnic relations based chiefly on data from voluntary immigrations cannot serve as the model or foundation for ethnic relations as a whole.' *Comparative Ethnic Relations* (New York: 1970), p. 156.

groups are objectively differentiated by religion or language, for instance, is easily determinable. Such cultural differences are often invidious and at times contribute to intergroup conflict. Cultural integration includes those processes which lead to the gradual efface-ment of objective cultural differences between groups in contact. In turn, this would encourage the growth of a national identity, providing common access to national symbols and values to each collectivity. The sense of nationality, which entails a feeling of belonging to a corporate group, is likely to be pervasive only in culturally integrated settings. The strength and distribution of this attitude, and related attitudes, has frequently been gauged in survey research.

The second dimension of national development is clearly eco-nomic. *Economic integration* will refer to the evolution of sub-stantially equal rates of social and economic development among the collectivities in a society. It can be measured by the extent to which cultural groups are differentiated by *per capita* income, infant mortality, literacy, and extent of political power. Such trends as the historical tendency towards increasing equality of regional *per capita* income[1] and the extension of citizenship to formerly excluded social groups are included in this dimension.[2]

Last, it is possible to distinguish a separate political dimension to national development. *Political integration* may be said to occur to the extent that the social structural position of a collectivity deter-mines its political behavior, whether electoral or extra-parliamentary. This may be illustrated by an example. If two groups sharing a common occupation (e.g. coal miners), but differing in objective cultural forms (e.g. of different religion), may be shown to have similar general political preferences, this indicates a high level of national political integration. Hence, political integration of this kind implies that objective cultural factors, such as language or religion, cease to have salience in the formation of a collectivity's political demands.

The extent to which a collectivity is politically integrated depends ultimately on its definition of the political situation. At any given time each collectivity may either extend legitimacy to the central

---

[1] Jeffrey Williamson, 'Regional inequality and the process of national develop-ment: a description of the patterns,' *Economic Development and Cultural Change*, 13, 4 (1965), pp. 3–45.   [2] Marshall, *op. cit.*
[3] Obviously this is an extreme simplification. It will be objected that there is an intermediate situation where legitimacy is in fact neither granted nor with-drawn, and the state of affairs is passively accepted as inevitable, though it is

government or it may withdraw it.[3] This grant of legitimacy is given to the government in return for what the collectivity defines as satisfactory societal membership. While this seems analogous to a contractual agreement, there are several key differences. Everything is not written down or specified. There is no way in which this agreement can be legally enforced since cancellation implies the denial of the legitimate authority of the state. Finally, in so far as the reneging collectivity is concerned there may be little or no non-contractual basis to the agreement. The underlying shared values of Durkheim's *conscience collective* may not be presumed to automatically cut across cultural lines in these circumstances. This is precisely the difficulty of the situation.

A collectivity may reassess its sense of societal membership, and hence may withdraw its grant of legitimacy, for essentially two types of reasons. On the one hand it might become aware of measurably unfavorable changes in its situation in the society—such as an outbreak of job discrimination directed against its members, in which case political integration ceases due to a change in the group's social structural position. On the other hand, the collectivity may, in effect, redefine the situation to demand greater rewards from the government in return for its continued support of the régime. In this case there is a subjective reassessment despite little objective social structural change. Tocqueville's notion of the socially disruptive effects of rising expectations among oppressed groups is one example of this phenomenon. Similarly, Marx's idea of the attainment of the true consciousness (*Klasse für sich*) is another attempt at interpretation. It need hardly be emphasized that the conditions under which such reassessments occur are central to the study of political mobilization, and will be briefly considered later in this chapter.

One last caveat. At the risk of repetition, it should be emphasized that at any given time a collectivity's self-definition, or state of consciousness, may or may not be related to objective changes in its relative position within the society. Hence the realization of political integration is a precarious process and an easily reversible one. Since broad economic and cultural changes appear to be very gradual in the history of societies, except in very special circumstances, these

---

negatively evaluated. I will consider this sense of resignation to be support for the state of affairs, since there is no expression of withdrawal of legitimacy, such as through changed voting patterns, or sporadic outbreaks of anti-régime violence.

types of integration are therefore assumed to be much more temporally stable than political integration.

The key empirical question suggested by the model concerns the relationship between intercollectivity economic and cultural differences and the general prospects for political integration. It will be assumed that in the absence of such differences national political integration is a certainty. However, the lack of political integration in the face of economic and cultural differences cannot be presumed, because a collectivity may be resigned to its disadvantaged position in society. It is possible to arrange case studies in a two-by-two matrix bounded by relative levels of cultural and economic integration. At one end of the integration continuum the values assigned to economic and cultural integration are both low. Most societies of the Third World belong here. At the other end of the continuum are 'perfectly integrated' societies where the values given to economic and cultural integration are both high.

It might be interesting to speculate about the politics of the perfectly integrated national society. This type of society would not be immune from political struggle between the members of different cultural groups, but the conflicts generated would be of a specific type, basically between constantly shifting interest groups, each mobilized by the specific political decision at hand more or less in a random order. There would, however, be no permanent constellations of culturally distinct groups such that regular 'ins' and 'outs' could be distinguished. Cultural status would therefore cross-cut all other significant statuses in the social structure. Since both collectivities define the government as legitimate; since they both have equal access to the symbols of nationality, the salience of objective cultural distinctions would quickly fade from the political arena. It is evident that few existing societies approach this ideal to any appreciable extent.[1]

In order to examine such general propositions as whether cultural or economic integration is more significant for the realization of political integration, thereby seeking an elementary causal understanding of the evolution of national development, it must be made clear that *little can be gained from the consideration of case studies clustered at the extreme ends of the integration continuum*. This highlights much of the difficulty with research which has been completed

---

[1] Switzerland is often cited as a developed poly-ethnic society which is politically integrated, but no sufficient qualitative and quantitative evidence exists to support this claim.

on problems of national development. Case studies have been almost exclusively selected from a group of societies having no appreciable prospects for the realization of either economic or cultural integration in the near future.[1]

The critical case studies are those where an *intermediate* level of national development has occurred: either economically integrated societies composed of distinct cultural groups, or—if this is not a null set—culturally integrated societies composed of groups at different levels of economic and social development. By and large such examples may be found among contemporary industrial societies. Cross-national comparisons of societies at these two intermediate stages of integration will help determine the relative dominance of economic or cultural factors for political integration. Only then can the sequences of national development begin to be understood.

In the absence of this systematic body of empirical research, I shall try to sketch and evaluate the relative merits of some alternative theoretical models concerning the processes of national development.

DIFFUSION MODELS OF NATIONAL DEVELOPMENT

Diffusion models of national development ultimately assert that core–periphery malintegration can be maintained only in the absence of sustained mutual contact.[2] Hence, the establishment of regular interaction between the core and the periphery is seen to be crucial for national development. Industrialization is usually conceived to be a necessary condition for intensifying contact between core and peripheral groups. Processes operating at various levels of social organization should reduce much of the diversity characteristic of pre-industrial societies. It may be useful to group diffusionist accounts of the integration of societies[3] into those which emphasize

---

[1] Thus a sample of the most noted case studies includes such societies as Indonesia (Clifford Geertz, *Agricultural Involution*, Berkeley: 1963); Ceylon (W. H. Wriggins, 'Impediments to unity in new nations: the case of Ceylon,' *American Political Science Review*, 55, 2 (1961), pp. 313–20); and Ghana (David Apter, *Ghana in Transition*, Princeton: 1963).

[2] A useful definition of diffusion is A. L. Kroeber, 'Diffusionism' in E. R. A. Seligman and A. Johnson, eds, *The Encyclopedia of the Social Sciences*, III (1930), reprinted in A. and E. Etzioni, eds, *Social Change: Sources, Patterns and Consequences* (New York: 1964).

[3] This discussion does not pretend to offer a review of the literature bearing on these problems, but only on those *general* theoretical images of the mechanism of national development, i.e., a particular problem for the theory of social

22

the dominant importance of cultural elements in the realization of national development and those which essentially seek to explain national development by reference to change in the social structure.

Cultural theories tend to presume a model in which the peripheral group is termed 'traditionally oriented' in contrast to the modernized core group. The most familiar elaboration of this dichotomy is Talcott Parsons's discussion of the pattern variables; they need not be discussed here. Once the peripheral group becomes exposed to the cultural modernity of the core, its values and normative orientations ought to undergo transformation. Frequently, however, this does not seem to occur. In the view of many of the cultural theorists, the maintenance of peripheral cultural forms and customs is an irrational reaction by groups which seek to preserve a backward life-style insulated from the rapid change of contemporary industrial society. The traditional life-style is a comfortable one. Groups tend to resist major change, in any case: there is a collective, if sometimes unstated, desire to optimize short-run interests while prospects for the long range are seriously compromised. The existence of a backward sloping labor supply curve, supposedly endemic to less developed societies, is commonly taken as evidence of a traditional normative orientation.[1]

The cultural theories thus seek to explain differences of values, norms, and life-styles among these collectivities as a function of the relative isolation of the peripheral group from the mainstream culture of the core. If only the choice between tradition and modernity could somehow be placed before individuals of the peripheral group, some have felt, modernity would easily win over. The solution to this problem of persisting cultural differences is, first, to stimulate a wide range of intercollectivity transactions, then, to let time work its inevitable course towards eventual cultural integration. Emile Durkheim presented an early statement of this theory when he discussed the effect of an increase in transactions between cultural

change. There is a vast anthropological literature on Third World societies which categorizes a variety of types of internal ethnic stratification as being more or less 'pluralistic,' without, however, attempting to theoretically account for changes in these situations.

[1] Max Weber is among the many writers who have assumed this to be a defining characteristic of the traditional life-style, *The Protestant Ethic and the Spirit of Capitalism* (New York: 1958), p. 59. See also Wilbert E. Moore and Arnold Feldman, *Labor Commitment and Social Change in Developing Areas* (New York: 1960). For a somewhat skeptical view see Elliot J. Berg, 'Backward sloping labor supply functions in dual economies—the Africa case,' *Quarterly Journal of Economics*, 75, 3 (1961), pp. 468–92.

groups as if it were analogous to the physical process of osmosis.[1] Cultural differences between collectivities would in effect be leveled, presumably according to the relative volumes (magnitudes?) of the respective groups.

This is one of the biological metaphors which Professor Parsons has so rightly disparaged in Durkheim's work. However, the anthropological version of this image, namely the process of *acculturation*, remains a rather current perspective in the study of intergroup relations. Acculturation is thought to occur when 'groups of individuals having different cultures come into continuous first-hand contact, with subsequent changes in the original culture patterns of either or both groups.'[2] Like osmosis, it is often conceived to proceed automatically and irreversibly. Once begun, the diffusion of symbols and institutions from the core to the periphery should lead to a gradual rapprochement, to a stable cultural equilibrium.[3] The proposition that the greater the frequency of interaction between collectivities, the greater the probability they will become more alike is sometimes held to follow from the experimental study of small groups.[4] Since it is not difficult to find evidence that intergroup

[1] 'Some have seen [the increase in national homogeneity] to be a simple consequence of the law of imitation. But it is rather a leveling analogous to that which is produced between liquid masses put into communication. The partitions which separate the various cells of social life, being less thick, are more often broken through. . . . Territorial divisions are thus less and less grounded in the nature of things, and, consequently, lose their significance. We can almost say that a people is as much more advanced as territorial divisions are more superficial.' *The Division of Labor in Society* (New York: 1964), p. 187.

[2] This is the classical definition of acculturation from Robert Redfield *et al.*, 'Outline for the study of acculturation,' *American Anthropologist*, 38, 1 (1936). Since then there have been attempts to specify the types of situations in which contact lessens intergroup conflict. See Gordon W. Allport, *The Nature of Prejudice* (Cambridge, Mass.: 1954); Robin M. Williams, *Strangers Next Door* (New York: 1964); and Thomas F. Pettigrew, 'Racially separate or together?,' *Journal of Social Issues*, 25, 1 (1969).

[3] This is not to deny that acculturative processes occur with some regularity as a result of interaction between collectivities. What is questioned is the simple assertion that acculturation *necessarily* leads to cultural integration under all circumstances. Acculturation studies have failed to describe the nature of the conditions under which assimilation can be expected to occur. 'Although Kroeber's characterization of acculturation as a passing fad was belied it was still true by 1960 that generally accepted propositions about the nature of change under contact conditions were lacking. . . . [Subsequently] the main line of development of acculturation studies continued to be descriptive.' Edward H. Spicer, 'Acculturation,' *International Encyclopedia of the Social Sciences* (New York: 1968) vol. 1, p. 23. It might be added that the large literature on nationalist movements has similarly not yielded a theoretical perspective.

[4] George C. Homans, *The Human Group* (New York: 1950), chapter 5.

contact often leads to hostility rather than mutual accommodation, less inviolable explanations must be sought.

Perhaps the most influential of these is the concept of social mobilization.[1] The social mobilization perspective, as well, assumes that the initiation of cultural contact between collectivities is generally beneficent. But interaction *per se* is seen to be an insufficient condition for the realization of national development. Much emphasis is placed on the power of the central government to coax or coerce the recalcitrant collectivity into acceptance of the core culture. This is best done by the manipulation of cultural symbols and values, especially through the use of communications media.[2] But the deployment of military force is also not ruled out. Social mobilization theorists such as Deutsch do not assume that any mere increase in the rate of intensity of interaction is sufficient to end culture maintenance in the periphery, since they recognize that it may be partially self-imposed. Hence, the active role of the central government is stressed, particularly in the establishment of what is often termed a national 'political culture.'[3] Control of the national information network enables a régime to set national goals, create a national identity, teach needed skills, centralize its power, extend the effective market, confer status on certain groups at the expense of others, and generally manipulate large numbers of individuals through well-developed techniques of mass persuasion.[4] However, with all these tools of behavioral management available, some well-established Western governments are facing ever stronger and more violent challenges to their authority along separatist lines.

Another of the technical means by which a central régime may gain adherents is through an inspiring brand of leadership. The Weberian category of charismatic legitimation has been often invoked to account for specific integration successes.[5] Recently,

[1] Karl W. Deutsch, 'Social mobilization and political development,' *American Political Science Review*, 55, 3 (1961), pp. 493–514. Actually, Deutsch's precise position on this issue shifts from article to article and defies pinning down: see Walker Conner, 'Nation-building or nation-destroying?,' *World Politics*, 24, 3 (1972), pp. 319–55. I feel that, over all, his sympathies lie with the cultural diffusion model.

[2] Lucian Pye, 'Introduction' in *Communications and Political Development* (Princeton: 1963), pp. 3–23.

[3] Gabriel Almond and Sidney Verba, *The Civic Culture* (Princeton: 1963).

[4] Wilbur Schramm, 'Communication Development and the Development Process' in Pye, *op. cit.*, pp. 30–57.

[5] Apter, *op. cit.*, and Seymour M. Lipset, *The First New Nation* (New York: 1963).

however, this explanation has come under criticism for certain theoretical inadequacies,[1] as well as the fact that a host of charismatic leaders in the Third World did not survive as long as their academic observers had anticipated.

Yet another factor which has been cited as having crucial importance for the process of national development is the encouragement of intercollectivity élite participation in shared, especially governmental, activities. It is thought that the experience gained in such activities encourages élite accommodation and mutual understanding, which then 'filters down' to the level of the masses. These so-called 'functional' theories of the political science literature[2] presume, however, a whole host of assumptions about the ability of each collectivity's élite to influence their respective rank-and-file members with the same effectiveness. In fact, there is good reason to believe the results of these filtering down activities to be highly differentiated by collectivity.

The theories of cultural diffusion have several obvious inadequacies. Since most of these hypotheses were derived from considering Third World failures of the integration process, they are not very applicable to the collectivities in developed societies. It is difficult to argue that peripheral groups in industrial societies are economically, politically, and culturally isolated from the core. This is evident from the most casual consideration of the history of Western European societies.

The development of national economies in Western Europe began in the sixteenth and seventeenth centuries with the ascendance of mercantilism.[3] Internal tariffs and other barriers to the free mobility of goods, labor, and capital were substantially eliminated. Weights, measures, and coinage were standardized throughout state territory. The central government succeeded in establishing control over foreign trade, especially in the realm of customs. Attempts to enforce central government control over techniques of production largely failed because of inadequate communications: the center was unable

---

[1] See Claude Ake, *A Theory of Political Integration* (Homewood, Ill.: 1967). It should be pointed out that these are less Weber's difficulties than those of many of his subsequent commentators.

[2] Ernst Haas, *Beyond the Nation State* (Stanford: 1964) and Ernst Haas and Philippe Schmitter, 'Economies and differential pattern of political integration: projections about unity in Latin America,' *International Organization*, 18 (Autumn, 1964), pp. 705–37.

[3] A very useful summary may be found in Eli Heckscher, *Mercantilism* (London: 1955), vol. I.

to carry out these policies because supervision was impossible in remote regions. National economies were basically realized after the Industrial Revolution made possible the proliferation of railway and canal systems throughout state borders.

Similarly, the evolution of strong central administration, begun in the fifteenth and sixteenth centuries,[1] was effectively completed in the nineteenth century, aided by means such as the standing army, which was capable of subduing internal threats to the central régime. Improved communications enabled the center to exert its control into the far reaches of the territory through its cultural influence and military might. Rural–urban migration and the creation of an urban proletariat forced an eventual extension of the suffrage to the working class, which resulted in the formation of mass national parties.[2]

Finally, the Industrial Revolution had direct and indirect effects on cultural isolation. In the late nineteenth century there were dramatic increases in mass literacy.[3] Newspapers reached into the dark corners of the land. Later, radio and television—often operated by the régime in power—penetrated all territorial space, trumpeting the culture of the core. The establishment of national school systems significantly narrowed socialization differences among the youth of separate collectivities. As a consequence of the penetration of the core's cultural institutions into the hinterlands, the maintenance of distinctive languages, and other cultural forms, was severely threatened. These trends indicate that the persistence of a distinctive culture in peripheral areas cannot be explained by the periphery's isolation from the core culture, at least in Western societies. Instead, the persistence of peripheral culture suggests a pattern of resistance to assimilation, a resistance so virile that powerful behavioral management techniques cannot overcome it.

Social structural diffusion theories claim that the malintegration of core and periphery arises from their essential differences of social organization. The 'modern' social organization of the core is characterized by a wide division of labor, high level of urbanization, capital-intensive production, small nuclear family, rationalistic bureaucratic structures, high *per capita* income, and those rational

[1] For England, the first state to undergo such political centralization, see G. R. Elton, *The Tudor Revolution in Government* (Cambridge: 1966).
[2] Moisei Ostrogorski, *Democracy and the Organization of Political Parties* (New York: 1964).
[3] Lawrence Stone, 'Literacy and education in England, 1640–1900,' *Past and Present*, 42 (1969), pp. 69–139.

norms and values which naturally arise in such settings. On the contrary, the 'traditional' social organization of the periphery manifests a narrow division of labor, low level of urbanization, labor-intensive production, large extended family, personalistic and diffuse structures, lower *per capita* income, and traditional norms and values. These are the stereotypical differences between advanced industrial societies and relatively backward agricultural societies and are the stuff of the literature of modernization. What is slightly different in this situation is that this conflict of social systems occurs within the framework of the advanced industrial society. The structural diffusion theories suggest that economic integration precedes, if it does not actually cause, cultural integration and subsequent national development.

How can this survival of traditionalism within a sea of modernity be accounted for? The simplest, and most frequent explanation is that the peripheral collectivity is not, in fact, economically integrated into the society.[1] How, then, can such integration be actively sought? One remedy is to incorporate the peripheral group into the modern industrial economy so that it becomes subject to the strains of structural differentiation. The widening of the division of labor loosens the hold of traditional authorities, creates new social needs and functions, and thus brings pressure for integration. 'Differentiation and upgrading processes may require the inclusion in a status of full membership in the relevant general community system of previously excluded groups which have developed legitimate capacities to "contribute" to the functioning of the system.'[2] As the peripheral collectivity begins to participate in the national economic system, changes in its structural relations should lead to rational, performance-centered, and universalistic values.

A more equivocal response to this problem of integration leans on

---

[1] Erik Allardt, 'A Theory of Solidarity and Legitimacy Conflicts,' in E. Allardt and Y. Littunen, eds, *op. cit.*

[2] Talcott Parsons, *Societies: Evolutionary and Comparative Perspectives* (Englewood Cliffs: 1966), pp. 22–3. This general position has long been held, despite its evident empirical inadequacy. Thus, Max Weber goes to some length to discredit it with respect to the Indian caste system: 'One might believe, for instance, that the ritual caste antagonisms had made impossible the development of 'large-scale enterprises' with a division of labor in the same workshop and might consider this to be decisive. But such is not the case. The law of caste has proved just as elastic in the face of the necessities of the concentration of labor in workshops as it did in the face of a need for concentration of labor and service in the noble household.' Hans Gerth and C. Wright Mills, eds, *From Max Weber: Essays in Sociology* (London: 1948), p. 412.

the tendency towards unbalanced growth in capitalist societies. It is well known that some regional sectors develop faster and more completely than others. Hence the solution to the problem of economic integration is to promote development in the relatively backward regions.[1] Neo-classical economic theory holds that the expansion of efficient capital, labor and commodity markets into regions dominated by traditionally oriented groups should decrease regional economic inequalities in the society as a whole.[2] Once the peripheral region is brought into the national network of commercial flows and transactions, inequality might temporarily increase; but in time an equilibrium will be reached and economic integration will be substantially achieved. This is another osmotic model, only in this case the causal factor is the exchange of material goods and services rather than the interaction of cultural elements *per se*.

Aside from the historical objections to the cultural diffusion theories discussed previously, there is a mounting body of evidence which seems to refute the thesis of peripheral isolation, particularly with respect to economic integration.[3] Thus there are two major difficulties with the structural and cultural diffusion theories. First, the persistence of relative economic backwardness in the periphery cannot satisfactorily be explained by reference to its isolation from the national economy. In effect, peripheral economic development has occurred more slowly than the theory would predict. This has led to analyses which tend to blame peripheral economic sluggishness on the oppressive traditional culture which is maintained.[4] But this points to the second problem: why is traditional culture so enduring in the periphery despite this substantial interaction with the core? Clearly the existence of a distinctive culture in the

---

[1] For a survey, see John Friedmann and William Alonso, eds, *Regional Development and Planning* (Cambridge, Mass.: 1964).

[2] M. Tachi offers an example in 'Regional income disparity and internal migration of population in Japan,' *Economic Development and Cultural Change*, 12, 2 (1964), pp. 186–204.

[3] For example, see Werner Baer, 'Regional inequality and economic growth in Brazil,' *Economic Development and Cultural Change*, 12, 3 (1964); J. R. Lasuén, 'Regional income inequalities and the problems of growth in Spain,' Regional Science Association: *Papers*, no. 8; and J. F. Riegelhaupt and Shepard Forman, 'Bodo was never Brazilian: economic integration and rural development among a contemporary peasantry,' *Journal of Economic History* 30, 1 (1970), pp. 100–16. If the economic isolation of peripheral groups cannot be demonstrated in these societies, then in industrial societies such groups are, *a fortiori*, fully incorporated into the national economy.

[4] Edward C. Banfield, *The Moral Basis of a Backward Society* (New York: 1958).

periphery cannot be taken as a given. The probability of successful acculturation, leading to the cultural homogenization of the two groups, should increase progressively with time. Here as well the diffusion theories present an overly optimistic assessment.

AN ALTERNATIVE MODEL: THE PERIPHERY AS AN INTERNAL COLONY

Common to both the structural and cultural diffusion theories is a unilateral conception of social and economic development. This type of development, as indicated by such measures as labor diversification indices and urbanization statistics, is assumed to spread from one locality to another though the mechanism of this diffusion is somewhat mysterious. However, an important distinction can be made between development which occurs as a result of factors endogenous to a specific society and that which is the result of basically exogenous forces. The second type of development—that usually associated with certain sectors of Third World societies—arose out of what Georges Balandier[1] has termed the 'colonial situation.' Typically this involves domination by a 'racially' and culturally different foreign conquering group, imposed in the name of a dogmatically asserted racial, ethnic, or cultural superiority, on a materially inferior indigenous people. There is contact between the different cultures. The dominated society is condemned to an instrumental role by the metropolis. Finally, there is a recourse not only to force, to maintain political stability, but also to a complex of racial or cultural stereotypes, to legitimate metropolitan superordination.

The pattern of development characterizing the colonial situation is markedly different in these respects from that which emerged from endogenous development in Western Europe and Japan. First, colonial development produces a cultural division of labor: a system of stratification where objective cultural distinctions are superimposed upon class lines. High status occupations tend to be reserved for those of metropolitan culture; while those of indigenous culture cluster at the bottom of the stratification system. The ecological pattern of development differs in the colonial situation, leading to what has been termed economic and social dualism. Since the colony's role is designed to be instrumental, development tends to be complementary to that of the metropolis. The colonial economy often specializes in the production of a narrow range of primary

[1] Georges Balandier, *Sociologie actuelle de l'Afrique noire* (Paris: 1963).

commodities or raw materials for export. Whereas cities arose to fulfill central place functions in societies having had endogenous development, the ecological distribution of cities looks very different in colonies, where they serve as way stations in the trade between colonial hinterlands and metropolitan ports. Hence cities tend to be located on coasts with direct access to the metropolis.[1] Similarly, transportation systems arise not to spur colonial development—they are seldom built to interconnect the various regions of the colony—but to facilitate the movement of commodities from the hinterland to the coastal cities.

Thus, the cultural contact engendered in the colonial situation did not lead to a type of social and economic development in the colony which was recognizably similar to that of the metropolis. Andre Gunder Frank has characterized the fruits of such contact as 'the development of underdevelopment.'[2] It must not, however, be assumed that this colonial type of development is to be found only in those areas subjected to nineteenth-century overseas imperialism.

Simultaneous to the overseas expansion of Western European states in the fifteenth and sixteenth centuries were similar thrusts into peripheral hinterlands:[3]

The prime aim of the new rulers in their expansionist efforts was to bring under sway all territory not already theirs within the 'natural frontiers' dimly coming to be perceived . . . small nationalities which had failed to develop as States were now swallowed up: Brittany (1491), Granada (1492), Navarre (1512), Ireland. Their languages and cultures persisted nevertheless and none of the governments succeeded fully in its program of

[1] Hence Christaller's theory predicting the location of cities in central places (cf. Edward Ullman, 'A theory of location for cities,' *American Journal of Sociology*, 46, 3 (1941), pp. 853–64), and devised from South German data, seems to apply best in Western Europe, or exactly that area which had endogenous development. After the sixteenth century, Eastern Europe experienced extensive refeudalization and came to serve as a major source of primary products for the Western maritime states. Hence these Eastern European societies exhibit many of the characteristics of an area of exogenous development. It has been claimed that this is a significant distinction in the development of feudalism as well. 'A rough general distinction may be drawn between feudalism (in an institutional sense) growing up "naturally" from below, or planted from above. West European feudalism seems to belong in the main to the former type. Peering with due caution into the mists of time and expert witness, one may associate this fact with the long Dark-Age struggle of its region of origin against the pressure of worse barbarism from outside.' V. G. Kiernan, 'State and nation in Western Europe,' *Past and Present*, 31 (1965), pp. 21–2. The defensive nature of Western European feudalism, for Kiernan, led to conditions favoring social solidarity.
[2] Andre Gunder Frank, *Capitalism and Underdevelopment in Latin America* (New York: 1969).　　　　[3] Kiernan, *op. cit.*, p. 33.

31

unification. England strove in vain to absorb Scotland; Spain was only briefly able to absorb a reluctant Portugal. Frontiers thus surviving helped by mutual irritation to generate a corporate sentiment on both sides. By the seventeenth century an Englishman who did not look down on a Scotsman would have been only half an Englishman; a Scotsman who did not hate an Englishman would not have been a Scotsman at all.

These internal campaigns were not in any sense coincidental to overseas colonization. There is reason to believe that both movements were the result of the same social forces in these states, among which the search for new sources of foodstuffs may have been of primary importance. Fernand Braudel has referred to this territorial expansion of the Western European states as a quest for 'internal Americas.'[1]

This bears a striking resemblance to the description of internal colonialism which has emerged from consideration of the situation of Amerindian regions in several Latin American societies. This conception focuses on political conflict between core and peripheral groups as mediated by the central government. From this perspective the 'backwardness' of peripheral groups can only be aggravated by a systematic increase in transactions with the core. The peripheral collectivity is seen to be already suffused with exploitative connections to the core, such that it can be deemed to be an internal colony. The core collectivity practices discrimination against the culturally distinct peoples who have been forced onto less accessible inferior lands.

Some aspects of internal colonialism have been sketched, though not yet systematically demonstrated.[2] These bear many similarities

[1] 'Mediterranean man has always had to fight against the swamps. Far more demanding than the problem of forest and scrubland, this colonization is the distinguishing feature of his rural history. In the same way that northern Europe established itself or at any rate expanded to the detriment of its forest marches so the Mediterranean found its New World, its own Americas in the plains.' *The Mediterranean and the Mediterranean World in the Age of Phillip II* (New York: 1972), p. 67.

[2] Pablo Gonzáles-Casanova, 'Internal colonialism and national development,' *Studies in Comparative International Development*, 1, 4 (1965), pp. 27–37; Rodolpho Stavenhagen, 'Classes, colonialism, and acculturation,' *Studies in Comparative International Development*, 1, 6 (1965). Internal *colonialism*, or the political incorporation of culturally distinct groups by the core, must be distinguished from internal *colonization*, or the settlement of previously unoccupied territories within state borders. An example of the latter process may be cited from twelfth-century France: 'The wild unoccupied spaces belonged almost without exception to the highest nobility, and the attitude of the latter towards these open spaces underwent a change: they now decided to organize their colonization. This choice was frequently dictated by political considerations. It might be a question of securing the safety of a road by settling the forests through

to descriptions of the overseas colonial situation. Commerce and trade among members of the periphery tend to be monopolized by members of the core. Credit is similarly monopolized. When commercial prospects emerge, bankers, managers, and entrepreneurs tend to be recruited from the core. The peripheral economy is forced into complementary development to the core, and thus becomes dependent on external markets. Generally, this economy rests on a single primary export, either agricultural or mineral. The movement of peripheral labor is determined largely by forces exogenous to the periphery. Typically there is great migration and mobility of peripheral workers in response to price fluctuations of exported primary products. Economic dependence is reinforced through juridical, political, and military measures. There is a relative lack of services, lower standard of living and higher level of frustration, measured by such indicators as alcoholism, among members of the peripheral group. There is national discrimination on the basis of language, religion or other cultural forms.[1] Thus the aggregate economic

---

which it passed, or else of asserting control over the frontiers of a principality by establishing strong peasant communities obliged to perform armed service in wooded and deserted marches which had hitherto formed a protective ring round it.' Georges Duby, *Rural Economy and Country Life in the Medieval West* (London: 1968), p. 76.

[1] There does not seem to be a general consensus on a small number of essential defining features of internal colonialism. Since the concept evolved from the study of ethnic conflict in Latin American societies, the above list is particularly applicable to societies with a similar history, especially with regard to Spanish and Portuguese patterns of colonialism. However, with certain modifications, the notion of internal colonialism may be much more general in scope. What if all but one or two conditions seem to be met? The danger, of course, is to so relax the meaning of internal colonialism that almost any instance of stratification may fall somewhere within its boundaries.

Let me give an example. A strict case study of internal colonialism should probably include *administrative differentiation*, such that there are both citizens and subjects, as dictated by the colonial analogy. This qualification is easily met by many Third World societies, but probably by only one developed society, the Republic of South Africa. Are we therefore to conclude that internal colonialism is an inappropriate concept in modern European history? Ireland is a perfect example of an internal colony under the old United Kingdom until 1829, when Catholics were nearly granted full civic and political rights. But it would be folly to consider that this legislation ended the essentially colonial status of the island. Are we then to refer to post-1829 Ireland as an instance of internal neocolonialism?

Similarly, is *territoriality* a necessary condition, or can American Blacks be considered an internal colony as Robert Blauner ('Internal colonization and ghetto revolt,' *Social Problems*, 16, 4 (1969), pp. 393–408) and others have suggested? These are some of the problems that remain to be worked out if internal colonialism is indeed to become a useful concept.

differences between core and periphery are causally linked to their cultural differences.

In this description national development has less to do with automatic social structural or economic processes, and more with the exercise of control over government policies concerning the allocation of resources. Since increased contact between core and periphery does not tend to narrow the economic gap between the groups, national development will best be served by strengthening the political power of the peripheral group so that it may change the distribution of resources to its greater advantage. Ultimately this power must be based on political organization. One of the foundations upon which such organization might rest is, of course, cultural similarity, or the perception of a distinctive *ethnic identity* in the peripheral group. The obstacle to national development suggested by the internal colonial model analogy, therefore, relates not to a failure of peripheral integration with the core but to a malintegration established on terms increasingly regarded as unjust and illegitimate.

Thus the internal colonial model would appear to account for the persistence of backwardness in the midst of industrial society, as well as the apparent volatility of political integration. Further, by linking economic and occupational differences between groups to their cultural differences, this model has an additional advantage in that it suggests an explanation for the resiliency of peripheral culture.

ON THE CAUSE OF CULTURAL DIFFERENCES BETWEEN COLLECTIVITIES

The antecedent causes of cultural differentiation between groups sharing close geographical proximity have seldom been satisfactorily explored by social scientists from a theoretical perspective. Partly this may be due to the extraordinary slipperiness of the concept of culture, which at base must refer to the prism through which groups ascribe meaning to the physical and social world around them. While it is relatively easy to specify the content of a particular culture by observing such phenomena as socialization processes, it is a problem of a different order to ask *why* a child is nursed for five years in one society, or taught to mumble reverences to an inanimate flag in another. The participant's answer to this question will be of the form: 'But that is the way it is customarily done.' The sociologist of Durkheimian persuasion will hasten to illustrate the ways in which such practices simultaneously reflect and contribute to the

34

solidarity of the group. But generally the specific form of the culture —whether it is animist or totemist, Catholic or Protestant—is regarded as of incidental significance when compared with the functions the culture performs towards the maintenance of the social order. It is much simpler to assume that a group's culture is an attribute of the social system rather than a variable to be explained. Thus the group may be defined as having a certain set of cultural traits which, when aggregated, make up its 'ethnicity.'

This may be a valid assumption in those few societies which are largely self-enclosed and have only sporadic contacts with other societies. For instance it is clear that cultural differences between proximate groups may be a function of their mutual isolation. If these groups are suddenly brought into contact they will manifest these cultural differences to a greater or lesser extent. These initial differences may well result in different institutional arrangements in the two groups:[1]

What do we mean by a cultural explanation? When a people has lived together generation after generation, sharing a common history, answering often to a common name, it tends to develop distinctive institutions, a distinctive way of life, adapted of course to its physical environment and technology. When faced with new circumstances, the people may well adjust its institutions to meet them, but the adjustment will start from the old traditions, and a recognizable continuity will be maintained. . . . When we find two people practicing different sets of institutions—even though the differences may not be great, and even though they live in somewhat similar environments and employ a similar technology—we are apt, quite rightly, to explain the facts by saying that the two practice different cultures, the precipitates of different past histories.

For the purpose of cross-sectional analysis at a single point in time the assumption of the givenness of a particular set of cultural traits may well be justified. But if the investigator is interested in the longitudinal process of social change, where the relevant groups are subject to frequent culture contact and exchange, then the maintenance of cultural differences over time may be an important clue as to the nature of their interrelationship, particularly in so far as dominance and subordination are concerned.

The cultural theory is really no theory at all. It merely refers back to an antecedent period when the specific group in question fashioned its culture in an unspecified way. In the attempt to progress beyond 'the fruitless assumption that culture comes from culture,' the notion

[1] George C. Homans, 'The explanation of English regional differences,' *Past and Present*, 42 (1969), p. 29.

of cultural ecology was devised by Julian Steward.[1] For Steward a group's culture emerges from particular characteristics of its social structure, which in turn is adapted to a specific physical environment. Culture, in this view, is largely responsive to changes in a core element of the social structure which is defined as:[2]

the constellation of features which are most closely related to subsistence activities and economic arrangements. The core includes such social, political, and religious patterns as are empirically determined to be closely connected with these arrangements.

While accepting the logic of this search for explanatory variables in cultural differentiation, Clifford Geertz cautions that 'there is no *a priori* reason why the adaptive realities a given sociocultural system faces have greater or lesser control over its general pattern of development than various other realities with which it is also faced.'[3] Geertz's objection seems true *a fortiori* in developed societies, where groups are much less constrained by the purely ecological considerations of how food and shelter are to be provided in the face of a hostile environment. For development typically offers several types of alternative life-styles to individuals. First, there are very many different ways to provide for sustenance through participation in the primary, secondary, or tertiary sectors of the economy. Thus the individual is liberated from crude ecological constraints. But secondarily, in developed societies some individuals are allowed choices about the kind of culture they will adhere to. Individuals may choose to be Protestant or Catholic, Ga or Ashanti, in certain settings.[4] Frederik Barth has emphasized that ethnicity must be considered to be a boundary phenomenon. What ultimately separates one ethnic group from another is that it 'has a membership which identifies itself, and is identified by others, as constituting a category distinguishable from other categories of the same order.'[5] The subjective element in ethnic identity in complex society has been illustrated in a different way by Ernest Gellner:[6]

If a man is not firmly set in a social niche, he is obliged to carry his identity with him, in his whole style of conduct and expression: in other words,

---

[1] Julian Steward, *Theory of Culture Change* (Urbana: 1963), p. 36.

[2] *Ibid.*, p. 37.

[3] Geertz, *Agricultural Involution, op. cit.*, pp. 10–11.

[4] Such subjective 'tribal' re-identification has been described by Immanuel Wallerstein in 'Ethnicity and national integration in West Africa,' *Cahiers d'Études Africaines*, 1, 3 (1960), pp. 129–39.

[5] Frederik Barth, 'Introduction' in F. Barth, ed., *Ethnic Groups and Boundaries* (Boston: 1969), p. 11.

[6] Ernest Gellner, 'Nationalism' in *Thought and Change* (London: 1969), p. 157.

his 'culture' becomes his identity. And the classification of men by 'culture' is of course the classification by 'nationality.' It is for this reason that it now seems inherent in the very nature of things, that to be human means to have some nationality. In our particular social context, it *is* inherent in the nature of things.

In an age of bureaucratic organization and mass literacy, cultural distinctions, particularly those involving language, assume great importance since education has an important place in allocating occupational and social status in the society at large. All of these considerations imply a different type of core element to account for cultural particularity than that which is tied to the ecological situation. *What is problematic in complex society are the social conditions under which individuals band together as members of an ethnic group.*

It is clear that culture maintenance in the periphery can be regarded as a weapon in that it provides the possibility of socialization, as well as political mobilization, contrary to state ends. Max Weber termed those collectivities having distinctive life-styles and cultures status groups (*Stände*), each of which is allocated a different ranking on a hierarchy of social honor, or prestige.[1] In effect, the difference between the type of social solidarity predominating in the core and that in the periphery is akin to the distinction Weber made between classes and status groups. Class solidarity is consonant with a high level of modernization and tends to be organized functionally in occupational groups. Trade unions, for instance, unite men in narrowly defined occupations at the primary, shop level, and confederations of unions tend to be much less solidary than constituent locals. Class solidarity assumes an individual orientation towards the marketplace, whereas status group solidarity involves a group, or collective orientation. The important question, of course, is to come to an understanding of the dynamics between class and status group solidarity. Why does status group solidarity appear to be stronger in the periphery than in the core?

The persistence of objective cultural distinctiveness in the periphery must itself be the function of the maintenance of an unequal distribution of resources between core and peripheral groups. Initially, individuals in the disadvantaged peripheral group are not permitted to become acculturated to the core. For Barth,[2]

the persistence of ethnic groups in contact implies not only criteria and signals for identification, but also a structuring of interaction which

[1] Max Weber, *Economy and Society*, eds Guenther Roth and Claus Wittich (New York: 1968), vol. II, pp. 926–40.   [2] Barth, *op. cit.*, p. 16.

allows the persistence of cultural differences . . . a set of prescriptions governing situations of contact, and allowing for articulation in some sectors or domains of activity, and a set of proscriptions on social situations preventing inter-ethnic interactions in other sectors, and thus insulating parts of the cultures from confrontation and modification.

Such boundaries are maintained by the differential allocation of social roles with the society:[1]

Common to all these systems is the principle that ethnic identity implies a series of constraints on the kinds of roles an individual is allowed to play, and the partners he may choose for different kinds of transaction. . . . The persistence of stratified polyethnic systems thus entails the presence of factors that generate and maintain a categorically different distribution of assets: state controls, as in some modern plural and racist systems; marked differences in evaluation that canalize the efforts of actors in different directions, as in systems with polluting occupations; or differences in culture that generate marked differences in political organization, economic organization, or individual skills.

This system of stratification is, in effect, a *cultural division of labor*.

Gellner sees the initial advantage to one cultural group rather than another as an historical accident caused by the uneven spread of industrialization through territorial space. 'The wave creates acute cleavages of interest between sets of people hit by it at differing times— in other words the more and less advanced.'[2] This accounts for the ability of the superordinate group to impose the kinds of role restraints to which Barth makes reference. However, if the unequal distribution of resources is based on observable cultural differences there is always the possibility that the disadvantaged group in time will reactively assert its own culture as equal or superior to that of the advantaged group:[3]

This cleavage and hostility can express itself with particular sharpness if the more and the less advanced populations can easily distinguish each other, by genetic or rigid cultural traits. These aid discrimination and humiliation, and thus further exacerbate the conflict. If such differentiae are lacking, nothing happens: the 'backward' area becomes depopulated, or a depressed area within a larger unit, or an object of communal charity and assistance. If, however, the differentiating marks are available— whether through distance, 'race,' or cultural traits such as religion, they provide a strong incentive and a means for the backward region or population to start conceiving of itself as a separate 'nation' and to seek independence.

Hence, if at some initial point acculturation did not occur because

---

[1] Barth, *op. cit.*, p. 17.
[2] Gellner, *op. cit.*, p. 171.
[3] *Ibid.*, pp. 171–2.

the advantaged group would not permit it, at a later time acculturation may be inhibited by the desires of the disadvantaged group for independence from a situation increasingly regarded as oppressive. This accounts for the cultural 'rebirths' so characteristic of societies undergoing nationalistic ferment. It is not that these groups actually uncover evidence of their ancient cultural past as an independent people; most often such culture is created contemporaneously to legitimate demands for the present-day goal of independence, or the achievement of economic equality.[1]

CONCLUSION: THE POLITICS OF ETHNIC CHANGE

The internal colonial model would therefore seem to provide a more adequate explanation of the persistence of ethnic identity among peripheral groups in complex societies than do diffusion theories portraying the periphery as culturally and economically isolated from the core. In general, relations between core and peripheral groups may be schematized as follows:

The uneven wave of industrialization over territorial space creates relatively advanced and less advanced groups, and therefore acute cleavages of interest arise between these groups. As a consequence of this initial fortuitous advantage there is a crystallization of the unequal distribution of resources and power between the two groups.

The superordinate group, now ensconced as the core, seeks to stabilize and monopolize its advantages through policies aiming at the institutionalization and perpetuation of the existing stratification system. Ultimately, it seeks to regulate the allocation of social roles such that those roles commonly defined as having high status are generally reserved for its members. Conversely, individuals from the less advanced group tend to be denied access to these roles. Let this stratification system be termed the cultural division of labor: it assigns individuals to specific roles in the social structure on the basis of objective cultural distinctions.

The cultural division of labor may be enforced de jure, when the individual from the disadvantaged collectivity is denied certain roles by the active intervention of the state. This is the racist solution to the maintenance of the status quo. The cultural division of labor may, alternatively, be preserved de facto, through policies providing

[1] David C. Gordon, *History and Self-Determination in the Third World* (Princeton: 1971).

39

differential access to institutions conferring status in the society at large, such as the educational, military, or ecclesiastical systems. This is the institutional racist solution to the maintenance of the *status quo*.[1] Both types of policies insure that the character of the cultural division of labor remains intact.

The existence of a cultural division of labor contributes to the development of distinctive ethnic identity in each of the two cultural groups. Actors come to categorize themselves and others according to the range of roles each may be expected to play. They are aided in this categorization by the presence of visible signs—distinctive life-styles, language, or religious practices—which are seen to characterize both groups. Such visible signals allow for intergroup interaction, necessarily involving a certain commonality of definitions on the part of interacting partners, in the face of objective cultural differences between groups. Acculturation need not occur because each individual can adjust his behavior in accordance with the other's status (which can be perceived visually) even before interaction takes place.[2]

Regarded as a status, ethnic identity is superordinate to most other statuses, and defines the permissible constellations of statuses or social personalities, which an individual with that identity may assume. In this respect ethnic identity is similar to sex and rank, in that it constrains the incumbent in all his activities, not only in some defined social situations.

The political position of the peripheral group within the society is likely to be feeble given this situation. This is so even in the most formally democratic polities since the peripheral collectivity is likely to be resource-poor relative to all other social groups. If the peripheral group is also a numerical minority its political situation is far worse. As a minority group it cannot independently force changes in central government policies, such as those which might provide a reallocation of income from the core group, on the strength of votes alone. This often results in politics of 'stable unrepresentation.'[3]

---

[1] Stokely Carmichael and Charles V. Hamilton, *Black Power* (New York: 1967), pp. 3–4. The failure of national educational institutions to provide equal training for members of all status groups is now well recognized, and has generated an exhaustive literature.

[2] Barth, *op. cit.*, p. 17.

[3] This may be said to occur when the 'political system normally operates to prevent incipient competitors from achieving full entry into the political arena. Far from there being built-in mechanisms which keep the system responsive, such groups win entry only through the breakdown of the normal operation of the

In most developed societies the above considerations hold only in a probabilistic sense. That is to say it is statistically possible for an individual of low ethnic status to achieve, for instance, high-status occupational roles, though of course it is very improbable. The realization of these conventionally forbidden roles makes it possible for statistically deviant individuals to reconsider their ethnic identity. They may have several types of options. By identifying with the advantaged group, these individuals may attempt to 'pass,' and thus undergo a subjective re-identification of their ethnic identity.[1] Alternatively, they may attempt to maximize their individual power by acting as brokers between the two groups. As 'ethnic leaders' they may seek to incrementally narrow the material differences between the groups by appealing to the universalistic norms which many industrial societies aspire to. Or they may reactively assert the equal or superior value of their culture, claim the separateness of their nation and seek independence.

The first option, basically one of selective co-optation, serves to remove potentially divisive leadership from the peripheral group and thereby ensures stabilization of the cultural division of labor. The ultimate consequences of the second choice are somewhat less clear, except for the probability that should any change occur it will be gradual. The slowness of actual economic integration in the face of larger expectations will most likely insure that a more militant group will form in the name of the ethnic nationalist position. In general, the probability of achieving economic integration within the society, as against other outcomes, such as actual secession or relative stasis, will be determined by factors such as the relative numbers of both groups, the indispensability of the periphery's role in the national economy, and the kinds of policies adopted by the central government.

The existence of ethnic solidarity in a given group should therefore be regarded as a special instance of the general phenomenon of political mobilization. Hence, ethnic change facilitating political integration cannot be expected to result in the periphery until there

---

system or through demonstration on the part of challenging groups of a willingness to violate the "rules of the game" by resorting to illegitimate means for carrying on political conflict.' William A. Gamson, 'Stable unrepresentation in American society,' *American Behavioral Scientist*, 12, 2 (1968), p. 18.

[1] It need hardly be added that to the extent that differential ethnicity is symbolized by phenotypical differences between groups such an option is correspondingly limited.

is widespread satisfaction that the cultural division of labor has largely been eliminated. Once placed in this framework, it is easy to see the reason for the frequency of political demands along ethnic grounds in industrial society. The Marxian discussion of political mobilization points to two fundamental conditions for the emergence of group solidarity. Substantial economic inequalities must exist between individuals, such that these individuals may come to see this inequality as part of a pattern of collective oppression.

However, the aggregation of individual perceptions of economic inequality alone is insufficient for the development of collective solidarity. There must be an accompanying social awareness and definition of the situation as being unjust and illegitimate. Oppression by itself can, of course, if severe enough, precipitate random violence against the social system, as in the many instances of peasant *jacqueries* throughout history; but this is not the result of the attainment of group consciousness and hence lacks the organization and purposefulness to achieve effective ends.

Thus another vital condition for the advent of collective solidarity is adequate communication among members of the oppressed group.[1] Communication within collectivities generally occurs within the context of social institutions: neighborhoods, workplaces, schools, churches, social and recreational clubs, and the host of voluntary associations to which individuals may typically belong. To the extent that these contexts for social interaction are limited to members of a group sharing the social definition of an ethnic minority, the possibilities for intercommunication will be maximized. This is so because in the periphery there tends to be not only segregation in the workplace but also residential segregation as well. The concatenation of residential and occupational segregation gives a decisive advantage to the development of ethnic rather than class solidarity. Since the concept of social class seeks to deny the salience of cultural and residential differences among members of similar occupational groups, to the extent that such differences actually exist, class is ultimately more abstracted from the reality of everyday social life than is ethnicity.

Finally, the very economic backwardness of the periphery contributes to the inevitability of such residential and occupational segregation. As an impoverished and culturally alien region there is little incentive for members of the core group to migrate there in

---

[1] Karl Marx, *The Eighteenth Brumaire of Louis Bonaparte* (New York: 1926), p. 109.

force. Typically the periphery has a declining population, an over-abundance of the elderly, and a disproportionate number of females, all of which reflect the lack of adequate employment opportunity which is both a result of peripheral backwardness and a cause of further economic disadvantages.[1]

From these general observations it is possible to make three propositions concerning the prospects for the political integration of peripheral collectivities into the society as a whole:

1 The greater the economic inequalities between collectivities, the greater the probability that the less advantaged collectivity will be status solidary, and hence, will resist political integration.

2 The greater the frequency of intra-collectivity communication, the greater the status solidarity of the peripheral collectivity.

3 The greater the intergroup differences of culture, particularly in so far as identifiability is concerned, the greater the probabilty that the culturally distinct peripheral collectivity will be status solidary. Identifiable cultural differences include: language (accent), distinctive religious practices, and life-style.

It should be underlined that when objective cultural differences are superimposed[2] upon economic inequalities, forming a cultural division of labor, and when adequate communications exist as a facilitating factor, the chances for successful political integration of the peripheral collectivity into the national society are minimized. The internal colonial model predicts, and to some extent explains, the emergence of just such a cultural division in labor.

[1] This vicious circle of regional underdevelopment is lucidly discussed in Gunnar Myrdal, *Rich Lands and Poor* (New York: 1957), pp. 23–38.

[2] For a parallel discussion of the effects of such superimposition on the intensity of class conflict, see Ralf Dahrendorf, *Class and Class Conflict in Industrial Society* (Stanford: 1959), pp. 213–18.

PART II
Core and Periphery in the Pre-Industrial Era

CHAPTER 3

THE EXPANSION
OF THE ENGLISH STATE

To tell the truth, the historian is not unlike the traveller. He tends to linger over the plain, which is the setting for the leading actors of the day, and does not seem eager to approach the high mountains nearby. More than one historian who has never left the towns and their archives would be surprised to discover their existence. And yet how can one ignore these conspicuous actors, the half-wild mountains, where man has taken root like a hardy plant; always semi-deserted, for man is constantly leaving them?

FERNAND BRAUDEL

THE early history of the British Isles may be seen as the record of the successive invasion, and subsequent displacement, of a bewildering number of migrating cultural groups. Celts, Angles, Saxons, Picts, Frisians, Danes, and Normans all came to these islands in search of tribute and land for settlement. With the passing of time the initial cultural differences between conquering and conquered groups all but disappeared. The majority of the inhabitants of these islands came to consider themselves to be 'English,' or less occasionally, 'British.' There is no modern Pict history in Britain; no one speaks of Saxon nationalism; there are no demands on behalf of Frisian home rule in the halls of Westminster; there has never been a Danish National political party in the British Isles. Of all these ancient peoples there remains but one contemporary survivor: the so-called Celts of Wales, Ireland, and parts of Scotland. What is responsible for the peculiar resilience of the Celtic peoples and their culture in the contemporary world?

When separate cultural groups, such as Anglo-Saxons and Celts, enter into sustained contact one of three types of intergroup accommodations may evolve. The first is the complete assimilation of one of the groups: in this example, the Celts might embrace English values and life-styles without reservation. The second is acculturation: here the interaction of the collectivities leads to the establishment of a new culture, which is created by borrowing elements from each of the constituent groups. Both of these cultural changes are thought to occur through diffusion processes.

In this way 'nations,' or large corporate groups amalgamated from smaller, often kin-related units such as families, clans, or tribes, are conceived to be 'built.' Since acculturation is thought to proceed more or less as a function of the rate of intergroup contact, the development of a 'nationality' among groups sharing a thousand years of common history (including almost two hundred years of industrialization), within a sharply delimited territory, is often regarded as a natural outcome rather than one requiring detailed analysis or further explanation. Does this partly explain why there have been no adequate studies of national development in Western European states?

There is also a third possibility: for the separate groups to remain culturally intact despite sustained contact between them. This is sometimes termed segmented pluralism.[1] However, while a name exists for this concept, unfortunately no coherent theory has been advanced to explain why this situation comes about.

From the perspective of the diffusion theories, the apparent persistence of an ancient culture and 'ethnicity' in the British Isles—that of the Celts—should be regarded as remarkable. Why should Frisian or Saxon culture have disappeared if today there is a notable Celtic revival? This problem in its most general formulation is the dominant concern of this book.

One partial explanation of the anomalous persistence of Celtic culture might be that the Celtic groups have been isolated from the course of English history. If there had been no significant interaction between the Celts and the other peoples of the British Isles, acculturation could hardly have occurred. Contemporary Celtic culture could then be regarded as a survival from an earlier period of history, much as the culture of the primitive tribes which have been so thoroughly investigated in the ethnographic literature. While there is some merit to this interpretation, especially prior to the sixteenth century, nevertheless, the history of pre-industrial Britain suggests that the Celts cannot be compared to such culturally enveloped groups as the Ainu of Japan, or the aborigines of the Australian interior.

[1] Val R. Lorwin, 'Segmented Pluralism: ideological cleavages and political cohesion in the smaller European democracies,' *Comparative Politics*, 3, 2 (January, 1971), pp. 141–75.

There have been many instances of cultural, economic, and political interaction between the groups inhabiting the Celtic regions and the peoples of what is now termed England. During the ninth century A.D., in the 'Golden Age' of Irish history—more recent Irish history might properly be termed leaden—Irish monastic scholarship gained wide recognition in England and on the continent. In the eighteenth century the English nobility occasionally sent their sons north to Scotland to be trained in the superior universities of that country. The tradition of cultural interchange between these parts of the British Isles stretches on and off over a thousand years. Of course the evolution of cultural exchange always implies a concomitant interaction in political and economic spheres.

While the Celtic groups were, therefore, not wholly isolated from events occurring elsewhere in the British Isles, it is likely that the Celts were affected qualitatively differently: their history must, in certain respects, diverge from that of the other British peoples. In order to understand the particular historical experience of the Celtic groups it is necessary to begin by considering the ecology of their territories.

THE ROLE OF ECOLOGY IN BRITISH HISTORY

'Geography helps us rediscover the slow unfolding of structural realities, to see things in the perspective of the very long term.'[1] This statement by Fernand Braudel is particularly true in the pre-industrial setting, where geography exercises grave constraints upon the possible forms of social organization in specific territories. In predominantly agricultural societies land is the principal economic resource and factors such as topography, climate, and the chemical composition of the soil have overwhelming significance for production.[2] By the mid-twentieth century a society disadvantaged with respect to these factors can, in principle, develop a relatively diversified economy, given large quantities of imported human resources and capital investment: Israel might serve as an example. By these means the limitations imposed by nature can be minimized. However it was well-nigh impossible for man to outwit nature before the advent of advanced industrial technology. Throughout most of

[1] Fernand Braudel, *The Mediterranean and the Mediterranean World in the Age of Phillip II*, vol. I (New York: 1972), p. 23.
[2] For a discussion of the role of climate in history see Emmanuel Le Roy Ladurie, *Times of Feast, Times of Famine* (New York: 1971).

human history nature has clearly held the upper hand: man has survived in favorable ecological niches, and even then only with the extensive cooperation of the forces of nature.[1]

The constraints of geography upon social organization are universal and therefore cut across cultures. Perhaps the most important common ecological distinction is that which may be drawn between highland and lowland territories.

From one society to another, the differences between the characteristic social organization of highland and lowland zones are remarkably parallel. By and large, highland settlements are relatively pastoral, depopulated, poor, and backward; in contrast, the lowlands tend to be relatively cultivated, populous, wealthy, and culturally advanced.[2]

One thing at least is certain. Whether settled in tiny hamlets or in large villages, the mountain population is generally insignificant in comparison with the vast spaces surrounding it, where travel is difficult; life there is rather like life in the early settlement in the New World, which were also islands set in the middle of wide open spaces, for the most part uncultivable or hostile, and thereby deprived of the contacts and exchanges necessary to civilization. . . . In the mountains, society, civilization, and economy all bear the mark of backwardness and poverty.

Of course there are exceptions to this generalization, but on the whole the highlands are likely to be the poorest region in society, and serve as its proletarian reserves.

Precisely because of their ecology, the highlands tend to be culturally distinctive:[3]

The mountains are as a rule a world apart from civilizations, which are an urban and lowland achievement. Their history is to have none, to remain almost always on the fringe of the great waves of civilization, even the longest and most persistent, which may spread over great distances in the horizontal plane but are powerless to move vertically when faced with an obstacle of a few hundred metres.

Protected by physical inaccessibility, dissident ideas and religions may flourish in highland regions: the Berbers of North Africa could remain Catholic in an Islamic setting, just as the Moors of the Aragon highlands could keep their faith in Muhammed while everywhere surrounded by Catholics.

The inaccessibility of the highlands also means that these regions were among the last to be subject to the central authority of the

---

[1] See Georges Duby, *Rural Economy and Country Life in the Medieval West* (London: 1968).   [2] Braudel, *op. cit.*, pp. 32–3.   [3] *Ibid.*, p. 34.

state. Hence the hills tended to provide refuge not only for cultural dissidents but for outlaws and individualists of all kinds. Remoteness from the agencies of social control made the highlands a land of the free:[1]

For there man can live out of reach of the pressures and tyrannies of civilization: its social and political order, its monetary economy. Here there was no landed nobility with strong and powerful roots. . . . Here there were no rich, well-fed clergy to be envied and mocked; the priest was as poor as his flock. There was no tight urban network so no administration, no towns in the proper sense of the word, and no gendarmes either we might add. It is only in the lowlands that one finds a close-knit, stifling society, a prebendal clergy, a haughty aristocracy, and an efficient system of justice. The hills were the refuge of liberty, democracy, and peasant republics.

The Kurds and Druses in the Levant; the Skafiotes in Crete; the mountain villagers of Greece and Albania; the peoples of the Abruzzi, who remained independent from nearby Papal Rome; these are but a few historical examples of distinctive highland societies.

Despite the obvious barriers to communication imposed by mountainous terrain, highland and lowland regions have usually been in continuous contact, perhaps everywhere but in the Far East. Much of this contact was engendered by economic exchange. The same ecological differences which ultimately separated highland culture from lowland culture also provided incentives for trade, as the economies of these zones developed in complementary directions. Each region was best suited, or had a comparative economic advantage, for the production of different commodities. If conditions in the highlands did not permit of large-scale cultivation, its slopes may have offered the prospect of excellent grazing. In this way elementary exchanges of livestock for, say, cereal crops, were likely to develop between the highland and lowland economies. These typically occurred in market towns which sprang up near the border separating these regions. Further contact may have been caused by the out-migration of the highland population. And in some cases relatively complex institutional arrangements arose in both regions to support transhumance.

These factors have great explanatory power in the case of the British Isles. There is a radical split down the middle of Britain which sharply divides the island into two geographically distinctive areas.[2] The

---

[1] *Ibid.*, pp. 39–40.
[2] This formulation was first made by Halford Mackinder, in *Britain and the British Seas* (Oxford: 1902).

lowland zone, which lies mainly to the south and east, is composed of rich clay and alluvial soils. It is highly suitable for intensive arable cultivation and climatic conditions are mild and moist enough to insure substantial crop regularity. On the other hand, the highlands, generally described as all lands over six hundred feet, cannot sustain much cultivation: the soil tends to be chalky and the climate is too wet and cold. The irregularity of the terrain is by itself a serious hindrance to irrigation, drainage, and large-scale cultivation. At best the highlands can be utilized for grazing and dairying.

The significance of the highland line in the pre-industrial setting can be simply stated as a demarcation of good land from bad. The British highlands were destined to be poor in two respects. First, these regions could not support much population, for it was relatively difficult to eke out a living there. The ratio of men to land was bound to be relatively low. Secondly, there would be little incentive for agricultural improvement, since the general ecological conditions were so unpromising. (This remains true for the twentieth century, where even the most modern techniques have not rescued the highlands for cultivation.) The lowlands, on the contrary, could support a much more dense population. Agricultural improvements would enable these regions to supply a large proportion of the food required by the rapid urbanization of nineteenth-century Britain.

The vast bulk of highland territory in Great Britain falls within the boundaries of Wales and Scotland. Each Celtic region is in fact dominated by highland territory. Given the choice of high land or low, most groups would not hesitate to prefer the latter. So it was for the Celts, who may for these purposes be considered the indigenous people of Britain. Even though the Celtic social organization[1] revolved around a migratory, grazing economy, it was far easier to graze and breed livestock in the lowland valleys and plains than in the mountainous terrain to the north and west. The problem for the Celts was that all the subsequent invaders of Britain shared their preference for land. A great portion of the history of Britain has been a struggle for the control of the fertile lowlands by a series of competing groups.

The fate of the indigenous Celts was essentially to be victims in these invasions. Possibly because of the relatively decentralized nature of traditional Celtic social structure, the invaders invariably triumphed. In theory, this then gave the Celts two options. They

[1] See Sir Henry Maine, *Lectures on the Early History of Institutions* (New York: 1875).

could remain in the lowland areas as a conquered people, subject to whatever indignities their conquerors imposed upon them; or they could flee to refuge in the highlands, where the terrain formed a natural protective barrier, and guerilla tactics could be utilized to insure their autonomy.

So far as individual Celtic tribes were concerned, there was probably no real choice between these alternatives. The fact that the Celts have occupied the highland territories for a thousand years does not necessarily imply they were 'driven' there by other groups. An alternative explanation can account for the highland fate of the Celts. It could be that those Celts who dwelt in the lowlands became eventually assimilated to the conqueror's culture, whereas those Celts who were already in the highlands retained their social organization and traditions because they could not be conquered. Some evidence for this latter position may be found in the consideration of the Roman occupation of Britain.

In 55 B.C. Julius Caesar landed on British shores to prepare for a long military occupation of the islands. The Romans sought to use Britain as a supplier of grain for the support of their continental legions, and to this end they colonized and secured the lowland territories. But the highlands were not conquered, as the Romans could continue to hold these areas only by maintaining a permanent military occupation there. Since it would be very expensive to support a standing army in the highlands, and since the rewards, that is, agricultural produce, would be meager, the Romans withdrew from Scotland and Wales. After retreating they built frontier fortifications, the most notable of which was Hadrian's Wall along the northern English border with Scotland, beyond the areas of occupation. The function of these frontiers was to provide the lowlanders with security from the constant tribal warfare of the highlanders, that there might be an ordered development of economic, social, and even intellectual life in the lowlands. A peaceful and prosperous province was likely to be more profitable than one continually exposed to attacks from outsiders. 'The prosperity of lowland Britain depended as much during the Roman occupation as it did in the Middle Ages upon the imposition of some restraint upon the borderland between the lowland and upland zones.'[1]

Scotland and Wales were hence isolated from the sphere of Roman influence. The effects of the Roman occupation of Britain were considerable. For almost four hundred years, lowland Britain enjoyed

[1] P. H. Blair, *Roman Britain and Early England* (New York: 1963), p. 70.

peace and political stability, and made progress in the development of her natural resources. Before the invasion the native Britons had been mainly a pastoral people; after it Britain became a grain exporter which came to be known as the 'granary of the North.' Some agricultural improvements might have been imported with the Roman colonization, although the evidence on this point is controversial. However, customs of Roman land tenure and estate management took root in Britain, and were more individualistic than the traditional Celtic practices. Lead and tin were mined in Cornwall, iron in parts of England, and coal in Northumberland. Roman military roads stimulated internal trade, and provided an excellent basis for internal communications for the duration of the Middle Ages. Finally, the political connection with the Empire helped develop commerical links to the Continent.[1] Thus, early in their history England and the Celtic regions parted company and pursued different roads in economic and social development, largely on an ecological basis. Later events, particularly the Norman Conquest, further accentuated this difference.

Advances in political development during the Anglo-Saxon period likewise failed to filter through to the inaccessible highlands. The most notable feature of this period was the steady expansion of the kingdom of Wessex, which from 802 to 955 consolidated all the lowland English territories under one rule (see Map 2). The extent of effective centralization should not be overemphasized. Wessex never established a unitary legal system, though at this time the shire system of local government was put into effect. Shires were created around towns which were walled and fortified to protect against Danish invasion. These walled towns provided the only security of the day, not only for individuals but for their investments, which tended to be in kind. The storage of moveable property and the collection and holding of tariffs could occur within the protection of the fortifications. One of the distinguishing marks of English history has been a tradition of strong central government during the medieval period. Although by Renaissance and late medieval standards Anglo-Saxon government was decentralized, nevertheless Wessex was one of the earliest European kingdoms which could successfully collect a national tax, the Danegeld—an impressive testimony to the relative effectiveness of her central rule. Though there were contacts, in the nature of alliances and treaties, between

[1] Arthur Birnie, *An Economic History of the British Isles* (London: 1961), pp. 17–18.

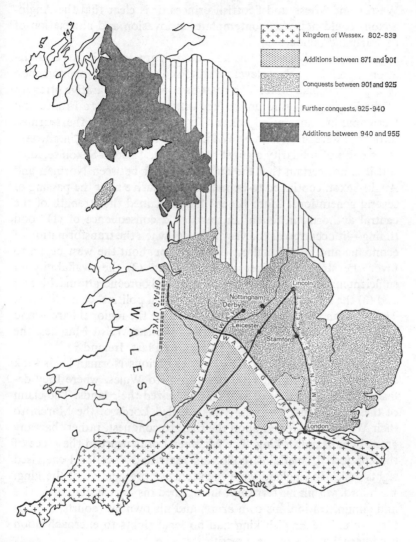

Map 2 The stages in the political unification of England by the kings of Wessex (from Albert Demangeon, *The British Isles*, Heinemann, 1961, after Droysen and Poole)

Wessex and Welsh and Scottish princes, it is clear that the Anglo-Saxons could not even contemplate an invasion and annexation of the highland regions.

The Norman Conquest resulted in much greater political centralization, significant urban development, and the peculiar phenomenon of a protorational state. The reasons for the comparative strength of the English kingship under feudalism, in contrast to France and Germany, are not entirely clear. To a certain extent, the Norman lords who were given land by William, and their ancestors, might have felt a cultural solidarity against their barbaric Anglo-Saxon tenants. But it is not certain that the cultural barrier between Norman and Anglo-Saxon continued to be mutually exclusive after the passing of several generations. Marc Bloch[1] has explained the strength of the central authority in feudal England as a consequence of (1) good timing—'it occurred at the very moment when the transformation of economic and intellectual conditions throughout the west began to favor the struggle against disintegration;' (2) the availability of sufficient numbers of educated personnel and bureaucratic machinery; and (3) the historical legacy of Anglo-Saxon political centralization. The Norman kings succeeded in dominating the regional barons and lords in all sections of Britain save three: the Welsh Marches, the northern counties bordering Scotland, and last, Ireland.[2]

In the eleventh and twelfth centuries various Norman lords took their own private armies on expeditions to Wales, where they defeated certain of the Welsh rulers and seized their lands. The claim of these Normans, who came to be called Lords of the March, to their Welsh lands rested upon the right to conquest, rather than any grant by an English king. The Marcher Lords usurped the place of the conquered chieftains, collecting rents and dues, and exercised rights which in England were the exclusive prerogative of the king. Each lord, within his territory, maintained his own system of justice and administration, his own army, and his own law courts, such as they were. The English king had no legal rights to encroach upon the internal affairs of these territories.

From the twelfth century on, the English kings began to acquire lands in Wales. Simultaneously they attempted to establish the rule of English law there. However, the success of these ventures was limited. The outbreak of the Hundred Years' War in the fourteenth

---

[1] Marc Bloch, *Feudal Society* (Chicago: 1964), pp. 429–31.
[2] Charles Petit-Dutaillis, *The Feudal Monarchy in France and England from the Tenth to the Thirteenth Century* (New York: 1964), pp. 155–6.

century, and the dynastic struggle of the Wars of the Roses in the fifteenth century, rendered the kings of England especially dependent on baronial support and incapable of independent action. 'The Marcher Lordships thus continued as regions of privileged authority and of vested interests, their lords, intensely jealous of the ancient rights, ready to band together to preserve their cherished independence and to check the centralizing policy of the kings.'[1]

Concomitant to their formal political autonomy the Marcher Lords soon were culturally autonomous from the Crown as well, and in effect took on some of the characteristics of their Welsh subjects. With each succeeding penetration of the highlands they increased their own power at the expense both of the traditional Welsh leaders and the Crown. A similar situation had evolved along the Scottish border. Hence there were large blocks of territory at the northern and western extremities of England which were for all practical purposes free from any central control, and therefore vulnerable to extra-national alliances or foreign invasion. Furthermore, these Marches served as sanctuaries for roving bands of cattle thieves and other brigands who would subject the relatively wealthier English border counties to plunder with alarming regularity. Smuggling at Welsh ports enabled enterprising traders to evade paying the Crown duties for customs and excise. The continued existence of these independent principalities threatened England's attempts at national development. With the coming of the Tudor régime, prospects for effective territorial annexation increased markedly.

In sum, prior to the expansion of the English state in the sixteenth century two characteristic types of social organization had evolved in the British Isles, largely, but not totally, based on regional ecological differences. In the main, highland territories had a pastoral economy, whereas the lowlands had an arable or mixed economy. Most land in the pastoral regions was used for grazing livestock and some dairying. Plots of arable were generally small and there was no single distinctive field system.[2] More options were available in the lowlands: there the land could be used for intensive cereal production as well as for grass-growing for livestock. The arable portions were usually very large, characteristically divided into three fields, and held in common by the tenants. There was also much cooperative husbandry. The pastoral regions were dotted with small hamlets or single

[1] W. Rees, *The Union of England and Wales* (Cardiff: 1967), p. 80.
[2] Joan Thirsk, 'The Farming Regions of England' in J. Thirsk, ed., *The Agrarian History of England and Wales*, vol. IV, 1500–1640 (Cambridge: 1967).

farmsteads and were largely free from manorial control. Loyalty to kinsmen, rather than functional relations to the manorial economy, kept these communities solidary. Partible inheritance or *gavelkind* was the rule, and as a result there was a relatively egalitarian distribution of wealth.

On the other hand, the regions of arable land were composed of nucleated villages which were integrated into the highly organized manorial economy. Inheritance tended to occur by primogeniture. This kept the ownership of land relatively concentrated, and there was a greater degree of stratification. Life on the whole was considerably more structured here than in the pastoral regions.

The Celtic territories were predominantly pastoral, while the English regions were usually of the arable or mixed type of social organization (see Table 3.1). Ecological features in England and the

TABLE 3.1 *Two characteristic types of social organization in pre-industrial Britain**

	The 'Celtic system'	The 'English system'
1	*Economies*	
	Pastoral: livestock, dairying	Arable or mixed: cereal *and* grass-growing
2	*Field systems*	
	Small open fields: large wastes	Large common fields: three-field system, cooperative husbandry
3	*Social structures*	
	a small hamlets, or single farmsteads	a nucleated villages
	b little manorial control	b highly organized manorial community
	c loyalty to kinsmen holds community together	c manorial control responsible for social order
4	*Inheritance systems*	
	Partible inheritance	Primogeniture
5	*Extent of stratification*	
	Low	High

* Source: Joan Thirsk, 'The Field Systems of England' in J. Thirsk ed., *The Agrarian History of England and Wales*, vol. IV, 1500–1640 (Cambridge: 1967).

Celtic regions would appear to be related to the development of these social structural differences. In sixteenth century Wales, for instance, in the same locality lowland areas were termed 'Englishries,' whereas the corresponding uplands were known as 'Welshries.'[1] But as George Homans has pointed out, ecological factors alone cannot be assumed to wholly explain these variations in social organization.[2] In fact, during the sixteenth century, aspects of the so-called 'Celtic' field system could be found in many parts of English counties: the fen country of East Anglia, Kent (especially the Weald of Kent), Hertfordshire, Lancashire, and Yorkshire.[3] While *gavelkind* may have persisted in some of these areas due to a woodland ecology, it is also possible that cultural differences among the settlers of these regions had an effect on their social organization.

Undoubtedly, therefore, the differing ecological structures of England and the Celtic regions contributed to the characteristic forms of social organization found in these two parts of the British Isles. However, from the sixteenth century on the English state increasingly strove to bring a certain uniformity to all territories subject to its authority. For example, following the incorporation of Wales (1536) many aspects of the traditional Celtic social structure, especially partible inheritance, were declared illegal. Political factors thus came to supersede much of the influence of geography upon culture in the highlands.

Yet, the union of the Celtic periphery with England, unlike the earlier unification of English counties during the Anglo-Saxon period, did not establish state-wide legitimacy for the government in London. The periphery's weapon of resistance to English authority was the nineteenth-century development which came to be known as 'Celtic culture', though in many ways this had little in common with its ancient counterpart. The renaissance of Celtic culture, the beginnings of Celtic nationalism, and the distinctive electoral behavior of the Celtic territories were all responses to a situation which may usefully be described as colonial.

TERRITORIAL EXPANSION AND THE REALIZATION OF LEGITIMACY

Since the terms state and nation have been defined in many different ways it is advisable to employ a standard vocabulary in discussing them. Here the terminology of Max Weber will be adopted for this

---

[1] Frank Emery, 'The Farming Regions of Wales' in *ibid.*
[2] George C. Homans, 'The explanation of English regional differences,' *Past and Present*, 42 (February, 1969), pp. 18–34.
[3] Thirsk, 'The Field Systems of England.'

purpose. According to Weber 'a compulsory political organization with continuous operations will be called a 'state' in so far as its administrative staff successfully upholds the claim to the monopoly of the legitimate use of physical force in the enforcement of its order.'[1] The state 'claims binding authority, not only over the members of the state, the citizens, most of whom have obtained membership by birth, but also to a very large extent over all action taking place in the area of its jurisdiction.'[2] This definition specifies an organization capable of achieving compliance, with or without the use of physical force, but it implies nothing whatever about the sentiments of those who are subject to its authority. It is the concept of 'nation' which addresses these subjective perceptions:[3]

If the concept 'nation' can in any way be defined unambiguously, it certainly cannot be stated in terms of empirical qualities common to those who count as members. . . . The concept means it is proper to expect from different groups a specific sentiment of solidarity in the face of other groups. Thus the concept belongs to the sphere of values.

Nations, therefore, are created or destroyed independent of formal political events such as annexation or secession.

To the extent that the authority of the state is respected, or perceived to be legitimate, by all its subject social groups and in all its territories, then that state is also a nation, or nation-state.

It follows that two ideal types of territorial expansion may be distinguished. When a state annexes an adjacent territory it may come to be regarded as legitimate or illegitimate by the bulk of the indigenous population. If the conquering régime achieves legitimacy in the course of several generations let this be termed national expansion. On the other hand if this régime fails to become legitimate over the long run let this type of domination be called imperial expansion: 'imperial' because empires are generally concerned to establish political order in the face of social and cultural heterogeneity.[4]

There is a certain sociological tradition which assumes that the imperial political structure tends to be unstable in the long run because its legitimacy is particularly weak.[5] Typically the empire either loses resources and undergoes a process of balkanization, in

---

[1] Max Weber, *Economy and Society*, eds Guenther Roth and Claus Wittich (New York: 1968), p. 54.

[2] *Ibid.*, p. 56. [3] *Ibid.*, p. 922.

[4] Guenther Roth, 'Personal rulership, patrimonialism, and empire-building in the new states,' *World Politics*, 20, 2 (1968), pp. 194–206.

[5] S. N. Eisenstadt, *The Political Systems of Empires* (New York: 1969).

which it is split into its constituent cultural groups, or it develops and evolves into a more cohesive whole. In the latter case, a multinational empire becomes transformed into a relatively solidary nation-state. It has never been clear why some empires have dissolved into small fragments, as did the Habsburg Empire, while others (perhaps thirteenth-century France is a good example) evolved into nation-states. The relative slowness of Austro-Hungarian industrialization has been seen as a contributing factor to the dissolution of the Habsburg Empire.[1]

There is a complementary view that industrialization, in and of itself, leads to structural changes which encourage the inclusion of territorially bound status groups:[2]

As a growing organism changes its structure, as the addition of mass brings structural refinement and diversity, so it is with states. Improvement of communication, population growth, and increased density were the preconditions for an encompassing political organization of our modern societies.

Once included, the newly incorporated group then makes demands which alter the structure of the polity. Otto Hintze argues that the Union of Great Britain and Ireland led to the emancipation of Catholics in both societies, simply because it was necessary to grant Catholics citizenship in order to maintain political stability in Ireland. Thus it is generally assumed that any state, or large culturally heterogeneous social unit, must achieve legitimacy in order to sustain itself.

How does such legitimacy come about, and what function does it serve? Let the centralization of authority in feudal society be taken as an example. The problem here involves the strengthening of the king, the dominant central authority, at the expense of potential rivals distributed throughout a given territory.[3] Initially, there is little need for the development of legitimacy. A powerful lord emerges as king from within an extended kin-related group. To the extent the territory is small, if it may be traversed on horseback in a day or so, the problem of maintaining his authority is rather easily solved. In this case the king, as the most powerful single lord, may simply demand fealty of all other lords in the circumscribed territory at

[1] Oscar Jaszi, *The Dissolution of the Habsburg Monarchy* (Chicago: 1966).
[2] Otto Hintze, 'The State in Historical Perspective' in R. Bendix *et al.*, eds, *State and Society* (Boston: 1968), p. 169.
[3] Joseph R. Strayer, *On the Medieval Origins of the Modern State* (Princeton: 1970).

the pain of invasion. So long as the king remains wealthy, in both crops and retainers, he need not be overly concerned with questions of legitimacy: coercion will do nicely.

However, if there is any desire to increase the scope of the kingdom through reclamation or conquest, certain problems can be expected to arise. The motivation behind such expansion may be regarded as a constant factor in late medieval society. It often involved a desire to increase the prestige of the ruler and members of his immediate political *entourage*. For the lesser lords, increased state power implies greater power for themselves. For the members of the royal court it augurs more official positions, sinecures, and opportunities for advancement. For the feudal vassals such expansion leads to the acquisition of new objects of infeudation as well as more provisions for their progeny. Hence for all the prominent actors in the political structure, state expansion is comparable to a desire to increase their collective social honor.[1]

In the late medieval period the sole means of such aggrandizement was by reclamation or territorial annexation, since the primary economic resource was land, and agricultural technology improved only very slowly before the fifteenth century.[2] For all these reasons there is a natural tendency towards the acquisition of new territories. However, political control becomes much more costly as distance from the center increases. If a ruler wishes to extend his domain he is forced to rely on strategies which aim to augment his influence while not diluting his effective power. In practice this is impossible given the pre-industrial level of communications.

The ruler, in consequence, is forced to settle on alternative tactics. Machiavelli offers some illustrations of such strategies of statecraft in *The Prince*. What any ruler must do in this situation is grant certain individuals limited autonomy in their own internal manorial affairs in return for absolute fealty in state politics:[3] *chacque baron est roi dans sa baronnie*. In return, these individuals—be they traditional nobility or new lieutenants imposed by the ruler—are promised some respite from the eternal violence of medieval life, plus some share in the ruler's moral order. The king, then, gives up some of his

[1] Weber, *op. cit.*, p. 911.
[2] Duby, *op. cit.*
[3] This description probably better fits the situation in France than that in England. In England the King's law prevailed *de jure* on the manors, but in return nobles had relatively greater power at the center than their French counterparts. However my intention is to compare this aspect of feudal society with later societal forms.

formal prerogatives, particularly in so far as manorial questions are concerned, so that his domain can be enlarged and his rule solidified. As a consequence of this grant of internal autonomy the king gains legitimacy. The king's legitimacy in the eyes of the local authorities enables him to rule a relatively large domain by setting up a reciprocal relationship between the crown and the local authorities. This relationship defines the rights and obligations of both. It offers the prospects of mutual support in the event of alien attack, and tends to lead towards a climate favoring negotiation rather than warfare in the settlement of disputes. Legitimacy therefore implies the existence of a kind of feedback loop between ruler and ruled. In a sense this is the gist of S. M. Lipset's notion of the complementarity of legitimacy and effectiveness.[1]

Since the evolution of relations implying a certain degree of reciprocity between the central authority and outlying territorial élites is a necessary condition of successful state expansion in the pre-industrial era, why, then, does not every annexation ultimately come to be regarded as legitimate? The distinction between national and imperial expansion is not only an analytical one: it is deeply grounded in historical experience. All of the present Western European nation-states arose through a complex series of annexations until they reached their present geographical limits and definitions.[2] Most of these ancient annexations have been forgotten by the descendants of the original victims: the central government has long since become regarded as legitimate. Yet the exceptions—Brittany, the Basque country, Slovakia, Macedonia, and others—bear testimony to another pattern of state-building, one whose legitimacy has remained severely in question. What is the origin of this sentiment against legitimation?

[1] S. M. Lipset, *Political Man* (New York: 1966), pp. 38–71.
[2] Yves Renouard argues that the national boundaries of France, England and Spain were effectively determined by the year 1216. See his article, '1212–1216: Comment les traits durables de l'Europe occidentale moderne se sont définis au début du XIIIe siècle,' *Annales de l'Université de Paris*, 28, 1 (1958), pp. 5–21. This process can be usefully compared with later territorial expansion which bore many similarities to overseas colonialism:
'By far the most important [conclusion], and one that I had not realized before going into it, was the continuity of the process of expansion within the [British] islands with that across the oceans, especially the phase of it which is crucial for modern history—Bismarck called it "the decisive fact in the modern world"—that across the Atlantic to the peopling of North America.' A. L. Rowse, 'Tudor expansion: the transition from medieval to modern history,' *William and Mary Quarterly*, 14, 3 (1957), p. 312. Rowse is quite well aware of the fact that his own Cornish origins were indispensable to this view of British history.

In medieval society there are essentially two links to authority which must be legitimated. The first, already discussed at some length, binds the territorial lords to the central authority. However, the second has not yet been mentioned: it is the link between the lord as traditional authority, and his various tenants, freemen or slaves. To the extent that the conquered social group is of a distinct culture, any accommodation made between the central authority and the traditional local authority has the potential of undermining the latter's legitimacy. This is especially so if the traditional ruler alone is permitted to become assimilated to the dominant culture. If the lord becomes identified with the conquering régime, if he begins to speak its words and think its thoughts, the hostility aroused by annexation and its consequences may well descend upon his head, and thus symbolize popular resentment against the central régime.

A defining characteristic of imperial expansion is that the center must disparage the indigenous culture of peripheral groups. To the extent that 'the impingement of the center [is] much weaker than the permeation of the periphery by the center'[1] the periphery will tend to develop a reactive solidarity.[2] This insistence of cultural superiority on the part of the expanding metropolitan state is a characteristic of more recent imperialism as well. The imperial structure is weak because the center is quickly forced to rely on coercion to establish political order, since its legitimacy is frequently in question.

However, if the state conquers a peripheral territory without making the assertion of cultural superiority, assimilation is much easier to achieve. For this reason, not all of the culturally distinctive regions which were subjected by the English state developed into full-fledged internal colonies. Both the Frisian sections of East Anglia and Kent, and the Celtic region of Cornwall became largely assimilated to English culture by the mid-seventeenth century. It was not until the seventeenth century that the English state began to seriously implement policies of cultural intolerance in the peripheral regions. Thus, the relative weakness of Celtic ethnicity in nineteenth and twentieth century Cornwall is due, in part, to the fact that the integration of this region into the English economy has occurred prior to 1600. As early as the fifteenth century, Cornwall had an exceptionally diversified economy—in addition to very prosperous mixed agriculture there were mining, fishing, shipping, textile,

[1] Eisenstadt, *op. cit.*, p. xii.
[2] Frank Young, 'Reactive subsystems,' *American Sociological Review*, 35, 2 (1970), pp. 297–307.

quarrying and shipbuilding industries there.[1] Trade with neighboring English counties was substantial. If intergroup exchange of this type occurs in the relative absence of cultural discrimination, then diffusion processes may be expected to take hold.

This and chapter 4 will argue that the incorporation of the Celtic periphery into England can, with the partial exception of Cornwall, be seen to be imperial in nature, rather than national, and that the renaissance of Celtic nationalism in the nineteenth and twentieth centuries was the logical result of this pattern of state expansion.

THE IMPOSITION OF ENGLISH AUTHORITY

While the overseas expansion of commercial-industrial states has been studied rather extensively in the literature on imperialism, comparatively less attention has been given the problem of conditions for the overland expansion of patrimonial states. In part this neglect may be due to the assumption that the early empires resulting from overland expansion were short-lived and chronically unstable adventures in political organization. Yet any extant nation-state is the survival of an earlier structure which at one time must have been 'imperial' in this sense. Nation-building in its earliest stages might better be thought of as empire-building.[2]

S. N. Eisenstadt,[3] one of the few contemporary writers on this theme, lists several conditions for such imperial expansion: the availability of a ruler with autonomous political goals; the development of different types of groups which are not embedded in the structure of basic, ascriptive territorial or kinship groups; the differentiation of producers from consumers; and the development of a definition of the total community that is wider than any ascriptive group. The kernel of his notion is that there must be the creation of a burgeoning social group, acting as a free-floating resource, which is in some sense functionally autonomous from the feudal social organization. The rise of a commercial class in cities having long-distance

---

[1] Unfortunately, there has never been a detailed study of the anglicization of Cornwall. For some general materials on Cornwall, see John Hatcher, *Rural Economy and Society in the Duchy of Cornwall, 1300–1500* (Cambridge: 1970); A. L. Rowse, *Tudor Cornwall* (London: 1941); Mary Coate, *Cornwall in the Great Civil War and Interregnum, 1642–1660* (Oxford, 1933), especially pp. 1–3; George R. Lewis, *The Stanneries* (Boston: 1908), and John Rowe, *Cornwall in the Age of the Industrial Revolution* (Liverpool: 1953).

[2] Roth, *op. cit.*

[3] Eisenstadt, *op. cit.*, pp. 94–112.

trade is a familiar example of such a group, which can ally with the king against recalcitrant aristocratic élites. Several other elements may be added to this list: the availability of extractable resources; a relatively protected position in time and space; and success in war.[1]

Sixteenth-century England was clearly subject to these peculiar historical conditions.[2] The rise of Thomas Cromwell in the reign of Henry VIII facilitated substantial differentiation in the structure of government: one historian has even claimed these changes amounted to an 'administrative revolution.'[3] Departments of the Crown went out of the court, and yet remained subordinate to the King. Henry could delegate authority to a Wolsey or a Cromwell, and yet still disgrace them with a word. A series of events sharply hurt the territorial barons at the expense of the Crown: the Wars of the Roses thinned their numbers substantially; the wars in France had the same effect; the secularization of the abbeys limited patronage and aristocratic perquisites; the first enclosures drained manpower from their armies. The King could redistribute aristocratic and Church lands to wider sections of the gentry in return for their support against the high nobles.[4]

The Reformation (1534) gave England effective sovereignty from all outside authorities for the first time. Before the Reformation, English kings had to ally with the Pope to control the greater clergy who were privileged landowners and franchise holders. The creation of a national church reduced them to royal servants. The Reformation thus nationalized the Church, prohibited any appeal outside of England, and forbade foreigners to intervene in English affairs on the pretext of religion. Protestantism became synonymous

[1] Charles Tilly, 'Reflections on the History of European Statemaking' in Charles Tilly, ed., *The Formation of National States in Western Europe* (Princeton: forthcoming).

[2] Christopher Hill, 'National Unification' in *Reformation to Industrial Revolution* (London: 1967).

[3] This is the thesis of G. R. Elton, *The Tudor Revolution in Government* (Cambridge: 1953). See also W. C. Richardson, *Tudor Chamber Administration 1485–1547* (New York: 1952).

This view has been attacked as overemphasizing the discontinuity of Tudor history by G. L. Harriss, 'A revolution in Tudor history? Medieval government and statecraft,' *Past and Present*, 25 (1963); and Penry Williams, 'Dr. Elton's interpretation of the age,' and 'The Tudor state,' *Past and Present*, 25 (1965). The debate continues in 'A revolution in Tudor history?,' *Past and Present*, 31 (1965).

[4] Maurice Dobb, *Studies in the Development of Capitalism* (New York: 1963), chapter 5.

with this affirmation of English sovereignty: as Lewis Namier has observed, religion is a sixteenth-century word for nationalism.

The discovery of precious metals in America and the extensive Atlantic-oriented trade which soon followed suddenly placed England in a most geographically strategic position *vis-à-vis* these new routes of international commerce. England's commercial fortunes also soared in response to heightened continental demand for English wool and cloth. Foreign capitalists, who had for centuries managed English trade in London, began to be expelled: in 1532 the Venetians were excluded, in 1578 the privileges to Hanseatic merchants were removed, and in 1597 they were expelled altogether.[1] From 1556 to 1581 the English attempted to set up a commercial connection with the Caspian Sea, circumventing the Turkish-controlled Eastern Mediterranean by an overland route.[2] In 1553 England and Russia established trade through the port of Archangel; the English received whale blubber, furs, timber and other goods in exchange for textiles and money.[3]

Almost concurrently, and on another front, England annexed Wales (1536), attempted to extend English influence beyond the Pale of Dublin in Ireland, and tried to arrange for diplomatic alliance with Scotland through the device of marriage. The Union with Wales imposed English land law, English courts and judges, and the Church of England upon Wales. All Welsh affairs were to be settled in London by the King and Parliament. Only English-speaking Welshmen were permitted to hold administrative office in Wales. Although it is clear that there had been no Welsh state to speak of, the Union with England robbed this territory of potential sovereignty.

Formal political control over the remaining territories of the Celtic fringe was achieved much later. The Union with Scotland (1707), which occurred as a result of negotiation rather than outright conquest, dissolved the separate Scottish Parliament, thus ending independent government for the nation. The Scots were permitted to send a delegation to the English Parliament, but this representation would in normal circumstances be insufficient to determine the outcome of decisions regarding Scotland. Unlike the cases of Wales and Ireland, however, the Union with Scotland permitted the continuation of the Scottish legal system, with its advocates and judges,

---

[1] W. E. Minchinton, ed., *The Growth of English Overseas Trade in the Seventeenth and Eighteenth Centuries* (London: 1969), p. 3.
[2] Braudel, *op. cit.*, pp. 193–4.
[3] *Ibid.*

as well as the Presbyterian Church of Scotland. Thus, while her political sovereignty was sacrificed, Scotland held on to some vestiges of her national culture through these institutional survivals.

The Union with Ireland (1801) dissolved the Irish Parliament at Dublin, which was composed solely of Protestant members. Henceforth, Ireland became part of the United Kingdom. Not only did this result in a loss of sovereignty, but the possibility for the protection of rapidly developing Irish industry from English competition was lost.[1]

The net effect of all three of these unions was to deny to each Celtic territory the exclusive right to determine the policies which would govern it. This is what is usually meant by the term 'sovereignty:' there is no question that the unification of the British Isles represented a loss of Celtic sovereignty. That is not to say that inhabitants of these areas had no voice in the governance of their lands; each of the unions provided for representation from the Celtic lands to Westminster. But except under exceptional circumstances—the case of Ireland in the late nineteenth century being the prime example —such representation tended to have token effects.

The preceding summary has briefly outlined what the Celtic territories lost at the hands of the unions; it has said nothing at all of possible gains from union. By and large, it has been argued that the unions were beneficial because the backward Celts were granted membership in one of Europe's most advanced societies; that all parts of the United Kingdom shared in the development of the first industrial state; that all parts of the United Kingdom gained from overseas empire; and finally, that Celtic devolution would be unrealistic, in terms of size as well as resources, in an industrial age.

In a strict sense the resolution of this argument is impossible. While the size of states has clearly risen over time, it is also evident that very small states, such as Norway, have maintained their sovereignty, and yet managed to prosper economically by sharing common markets with larger and more diversified producers. This study does not aim to decide the case for small states as against large states in the abstract, but merely tries to discover the general significance of the persisting Celtic evocation in the British Isles. The objective gains or losses from union with England have little bearing on the widespread sense in the Celtic lands that these unions were fortunate or unfortunate events. It is that subjective sense which

[1] For an assessment of the state of Irish industry before the Union see L. M. Cullen, *An Economic History of Ireland since 1660* (London: 1972 .

must be put to the analysis, for these sentiments provide the social basis for political action and behavior.

ENGLISH MOTIVES BEHIND UNION

Although there may be no necessary connection between a state's motives in conquest and the form of domination which ultimately occurs in the conquered territory, it may be possible to posit a connection between the two. George Balandier's[1] definition of the colonial situation includes the idea that the metropolis has an instrumental relationship to the colony. This undoubtedly implies that the metropolis tends to use the colony for its own ends. If these ends should co-exist with the best interests of the colony, well and good. Of course the overwhelming suspicion is that they do not.

Although it is far from easy to determine what factors lie behind any specific government decision—most policies are bathed in the self-serving rhetoric of altruism, and often the prominent actors themselves become converted to their own pronouncements—I would like to argue that each of the Celtic regions became politically incorporated at a critical juncture of English history. Largely out of *raisons d'etat* England desired to insure its territorial integrity at all costs, rather than suffer the threat of invasion by hostile Continental neighbors.

This element of protection from foreign invasion is perhaps least important in explaining the Union with Wales, though Welsh support for Kildare's rebellion in Ireland was considered imminent by English authorities.[2] It is also likely that during the sixteenth century English interest in Wales was stimulated by the government's desire to secure a reliable source of foodstuffs. In Europe generally there was a notable increase in the demand for marketed food after 1500. This heightened demand for marketed food resulted from an increase in the urban population, the expansion of landless labor, and the growth of government staffs.[3] Throughout Europe attempts were made to reclaim land which did not naturally support cultivation. These included projects to irrigate the dry lands of the plains and to drain wet marshy expanses.[4] Can it be coincidental that the first plans to drain and reclaim the fenland of East Anglia were made in

---

[1] Georges Balandier, *Sociologie actuelle de l'Afrique noire* (Paris: 1963).
[2] Rees, *op. cit.*, p. 19.
[3] Tilly, *op. cit.*
[4] Braudel, *op. cit.*, pp. 67–70.

the late sixteenth century?[1] By contrast the incorporation of Wales must have seemed an easy task. Charles Tilly has emphasized that securing an adequate and reliable supply of food was a necessity for the building of states.[2] Indeed, one of the initial responsibilities of the Justices of the Peace in England had been to regulate the public food marketing system. The increased demand for food in the sixteenth century encouraged geographic economic specialization and consequently led to regional economic interdependence.[3]

But there were undoubtedly political motives behind the annexation of Wales as well. As discussed earlier Wales represented an obstacle to the full development of the internal security of England since it was a land where law and order was in short supply. Farmers in the English border counties were being continually harassed by highland thieves and brigands; the centralization of political authority was threatened by the presence of the powerful Marcher lords; the Customs could not be enforced. If England were to finally assume a state of internal peace and stability after the chaos of the Wars of the Roses, the situation in Wales had to be improved. The most important consideration was to eliminate the last major obstacle to the development of a central administration. And in this goal the Union with Wales was a conspicuous success: there were no more Welsh challenges to the authority of the Crown. The question of Wales as a separate nation did not arise for three hundred years;

[1] Sir John Clapham, *A Concise Economic History of Britain* (Cambridge: 1949), p. 196.

[2] 'Below the surface raged a long struggle by builders of states to secure the survival of the people most dependent on them and most inclined to serve their ends, a struggle to wrest the means of subsistence from a fiercely reluctant peasantry. It paralleled the struggle to extract labor (most notably via corvees and conscription) and wealth (most notably via taxation). It complemented those struggles. For a long time, the life of the state depended on the success of the battle for food,' Charles Tilly, 'Food Supply and Public Order in Modern Europe,' in Tilly, ed., *op. cit.*

[3] 'A rising population in both town and countryside included the demand for food and the demand for land. Few farmers were so completely self-sufficient on their farms that they could ignore the market entirely. Hence, each half of England found itself exciting greater efforts to produce the food which it could grow well, and which best served the needs of the nearest market. In specializing in one direction, each region gradually placed itself in greater dependence than before upon other regions for some item of food or ingredient of its farming. The whole country was drawn more firmly than ever before into a dovetailed system of agricultural production. The highland farmer bred cattle and sheep, kept some sheep for their wool, but sold most of the rest of his young stock for fattening to the lowland grazier,' Thirsk, 'The Farming Regions of England,' *op. cit.*, pp. 4–5. This argument may be extended to the regional economies of Britain more generally.

once the English succeeded in eliminating the last of the Great Nobles along with the Percies on the northern Marches, very little was at issue politically in Wales. There was no serious attempt to anglicize the population, save during periods of Puritanical fervor under the Cromwellian Protectorate. Wales, to a very real extent, had ceased to exist as a political problem for London.

The Union with Scotland was instrumental in a far different sense. By the late seventeenth century, England had emerged as a power to be reckoned with in European politics. Overseas expansion had begun in earnest, and France had already emerged as England's chief rival to European domination and imperial success. One of the uncertainties in the environment was the political alignment of Scotland. Although since 1603 England and Scotland had entered upon a union of the Crowns, when Scotland's James VI acceded to the English throne as James I of England, the first Stuart King, under the terms of this agreement England could not exert direct political control over her northern neighbor. Furthermore, the Scots had always acted with considerable antipathy toward England. The sole Celtic land to have been politically united—having its own King, Church, and legal system—Scotland had curbed English designs by entering into an alliance with France. At the time of Joan of Arc Scotsmen fought with the French against the occupying English troops. In the sixteenth century Scotland was ruled by Mary of Guise, who imported a French army into Scotland to provide for national defense. The possibility of any resumption of this 'auld alliance' in the eighteenth century was much against English interests.

When the Scots launched an expedition in 1695 to colonize Darien, a Spanish colonial territory in Central America, the English government responded with a fury: its navy in effect scuttled this rather feeble enterprise. But international political stability was threatened by such rash actions. Spain, the major French ally, could declare war on England on just such a pretext. The English government regarded the Scottish action as evidence of a dangerous degree of independence: further, such embarrassments could not be easily tolerated.[1]

The Scots Parliament, angered by English actions at Darien, passed an act stating its determination to make its own foreign policy, even if that be contrary to London's wishes. In retaliation the English Parliament threatened to halt all Scottish exports into England,

[1] T. C. Smout, 'The Anglo-Scottish union of 1707: the economic background,' *Economic History Review*, 2nd ser., 16, 3 (1964), pp. 459–60.

unless Scotland agreed to Union, and to abolish its Parliament. Since exports to England amounted to a major source of Scottish revenues, this constituted grave economic pressure. The Union was finally won—though the English were not above bribing and tricking key members of the Edinburgh Parliament—and afterwards there was little concern with the fate of Scotland within it. The immediate cause of the Union was to neutralize the possibility of an independent Scotland which might align herself with a foreign power and therefore become a staging ground for the conquest of England.

The Irish Union of 1801 has a more complex history, for England's involvement with Ireland was older and more intrusive than with the other Celtic lands. Norman lords had used Wales as a place of departure for their invasion of Ireland in the twelfth century. Around the city of Dublin they maintained lordships which were similar to the Marcher lordships—effectively independent of any other authority. These Norman lords attempted to enlarge their control of the territory around Dublin, which was known as the Pale, at the expense of traditional Irish chieftains. In the sixteenth century, concomitant with the stabilization and expansion of England, there were further actions in Ireland. The English set upon the plan of putting Ireland to plantation as the best means to subdue the island. The most extensive of these plantations was to be that in Londonderry, established in 1608, and roughly contemporaneous to the Virginia Plantation. Englishmen and lowland Scotsmen were lured to Ireland by the promise of free land. Their job was to drive the Irish into the woods and fortify their own villages. For a variety of reasons the plan failed and the native Irish rose up to slaughter the colonists. In retaliation, and again desiring to assert its authority in Ireland, England—now under Cromwell—invaded the island and redistributed the land to new, non-Irish colonists. War between the Catholic indigenes and the Protestant colonists ensued, echoes of which exist to this day in Northern Ireland.

The point is that Irish security was constantly threatened from 1642 to 1801, and never more so in English eyes than by the United Irishmen Movement which instigated a rebellion during the French Revolution (1798), and was supported, albeit insufficiently, by French military aid. The English Parliament decided that its Irish Protestant counterpart was incapable of maintaining any semblance of order and hence tried to arrange for the same kind of union which had so successfully, to that time, integrated both Scotland and Wales. The Irish Parliament was by and large against Union—it feared an end to protection for a thriving Irish cotton industry which would be crushed by competition from Manchester; and it also feared the extension of civil rights to Irish Catholics, which would undermine the Protestant political monopoly—as were certain English interests, but after some complex negotiations the Union passed[1] and the British Isles were formally united. An English explanation of the reasons for Irish union, contained in a letter from an undersecretary to Prime Minister Pitt in 1799 casts light on the government's purpose:[2]

By giving the Irish a hundred members in an Assembly of six hundred and fifty, they will be impotent to operate upon that Assembly, but it will be invested with Irish assent to its authority. . . . The Union is the only answer to preventing Ireland becoming too great and powerful.

The case of Ireland is an almost ideal-typical example of a colonial situation and it provided England with practical experience by which to evaluate later colonial policies.

GOVERNMENTAL INSISTENCE ON ENGLISH CULTURAL SUPERIORITY

One of the defining characteristics of the colonial situation is that it must involve the interaction of at least two cultures—that of the conquering metropolitan élite (cosmopolitan culture) and of the indigenes (native culture)—and that the former is promulgated by the colonial authorities as being vastly superior for the realization of universal ends: salvation in one age; industrialization in another. One of the consequences of this denigration of indigenous culture is to undermine the native's will to resist the colonial régime. If he is defined as barbarian, perhaps he should try to reform himself by becoming more cosmopolitan. Failure to win high position within the colonial structure tends to be blamed on personal inadequacy, rather than any particular shortcomings of the system itself. The native's internalization of the colonist's view of him makes the realization of social control less problematic.[3] Conversely, the renaissance of indigenous culture implies a serious threat to continued colonial domination.

---

[1] These negotiations have been summarized in extensive detail by G. C. Bolton in *The Passing of the Irish Act of Union* (London: 1966).
[2] P. B. Ellis and S. Mac A'Ghobhainn, *The Scottish Insurrection of 1820* (London: 1970), p. 84.
[3] Phillip Mason, *Prospero's Magic* (London: 1962) and Albert Memmi, *The Colonizer and the Colonized* (Boston: 1967).

In this context it is of interest that English political expansion into the Celtic periphery was accompanied by measures designed to suppress Celtic culture. These were most often laws passed to encourage the Celts to embrace English culture in its various forms.

Before the advent of an actual Union with Wales in 1536, the Parliament of Henry IV enacted various Penal Laws[1] against the Welsh which remained in effect from 1410 to 1510. These included the following provisions: in the border areas, Welshmen were forbidden to acquire lands; if stolen goods from a border town were not recovered by one week's time, residents could retaliate on any Welshmen they could seize. In Wales itself, Welshmen were prohibited from acquiring lands within boroughs, nor could they hold any municipal offices. Provisions forbade Welshmen from the carrying of arms, the fortification of any house, or the holding of a responsible office in the service of any English lord. Furthermore, any Englishman who took a Welsh wife was to be legally treated as Welsh. Last, Welshmen were denied freedom of assembly without special permit. The Act of Union itself forbade Welsh-speakers from office-holding, and all judges appointed to the new courts were English.

The Act of Union imposed both English law and English religion on the people of Wales. It thus outlawed *gavelkind* and other traditional customs of the Celtic social organization. The establishment of the Church of England, which continued to hold services in English, became a bitter pill for most Welsh to swallow in the nineteenth century. By that time Nonconformist congregations had attracted the allegiance of the majority of Welsh through policies encouraging services and Sunday schools conducted in the Welsh language. Paying tithes to the Church of England infuriated many Welshmen who resented taxation by an alien church, conducting an alien religion in an alien tongue, while they simultaneously had to support their own Welsh-speaking congregations.

Some evidence for the widespread denigration of Welsh culture can be found in a mid-nineteenth-century report on the state of Welsh education conducted by three English education commissioners for the House of Commons (1846). While this report has had a special place in the history of Wales, it cannot be said to represent an exceptional English view of Welsh or Celtic culture in general. Dispatched to inquire into the causes of social unrest in Wales, the

---

[1] David Williams, *A History of Modern Wales* (London: 1950), pp. 16–17. It should, however, be pointed out that many of these statutes were not enforced.

parliamentary commission returned to Westminster with a stinging indictment of the Welsh language, religion, and national character—the totality of which was reprinted in full as a Blue Book. These are some excerpts on the inadequacy of the Welsh language:[1]

The Welsh language is a vast drawback to Wales and a manifold barrier to the moral progress and commercial prosperity of the people.

It bars the access of improving knowledge to their minds.

Because of their language, the mass of the Welsh people are inferior to the English in every branch of practical knowledge and skill.

The Welsh language distorts the truth, favors fraud and abets perjury.

In sum, Welsh was a 'disastrous barrier to all moral improvement and popular progress in Wales.' Sir Reginald Coupland comments tellingly about the context in which these remarks were made: 'It is not surprising that the Commissioners should have swept aside the ancient language of Wales as ruthlessly as Macaulay, a decade earlier, had swept aside the ancient languages of India.'[2]

The Welsh Nonconformist religion was the butt of the Commission's disdain as well. In effect it was too energetic and zealous. It overemphasized biblical study, such that 'the people were better versed in the geography of Palestine than of Wales.' There was too little interest in the secular stuff of modern life and thought. In general, there was something lacking about the character of the Welsh. Though not an especially murderous people—indeed, they are characterized as warm and open, cheerful and passionate—they none the less were 'lacking in cleanliness and decency,' and had 'a general disregard of temperance, chastity, veracity, and fairdealing.' Sexual incontinency was 'the besetting sin . . . the peculiar vice of the Principality.'[3] The image is not unlike that of the lazy and shiftless plantation nigger, who was really having too much fun for his own, and his people's, good.

Coupland is exactly correct to stress the analogy with the English experience in India and the other colonies: here, too, the natives are seen to be warm and friendly and in desperate need of English help to set them on their feet. Colonial service was a major sphere of employment for the English upper classes, and it is not difficult to understand that they would tend to see 'backwardness' at home as

[1] Reginald Coupland, *Welsh and Scottish Nationalism* (London: 1954), pp. 186–95.
[2] *Ibid.*, p. 190.   [3] *Ibid.*, p. 193.

being fundamentally the same phenomenon as the backwardness they were confronted with—either in person or through extensive written accounts—in the overseas colonies. I have dwelt at some length on this single government report simply because it reveals the attitudes of prominent Englishmen towards Celtic culture rather more fully and completely than most other such documents. Its publication was a political gaffe for precisely this reason: future reports would likely try to hide such an overt bias.

The denigration of Irish culture has a longer and more distinguished history than that of the Welsh. Until the late sixteenth century, English influence had spread hardly beyond the Pale of Dublin. But the development of the Irish plantations, particularly in Ulster, led to a large influx of English (and Scottish) settlers whom the government hoped would subdue the Irish barbarians, in part by driving them off the good arable land:[1]

For the husbandman must first break the land before it be made capable of good seed: and when it is thoroughly broken and manured, if he do not forthwith cast good seed into it, it will grow wild again, and bear nothing but weeds. So a barbarous country must first be broken by a war, before it will be capable of good government; and when it is fully subdued and conquered, if it be not well planted and governed after the conquest, it will often return to the former barbarism.

Sir Francis Bacon, one of the principal architects of the Londonderry plantation (1608) promised King James a time 'when people of barbarous manners are brought to give over and discontinue their customs of revenge and blood and of dissolute life and of theft and rapine.'[2] In Bacon's mind, the Irish were so subversive an element to the possibility of a rational social order that the English settlers must be segregated from them in order to remain free of their taint.

In the centuries subsequent to the planting of Ireland, England never ceased attempting to root out the speaking of Gaelic and the practicing of Roman Catholicism among the Irish. From the early seventeenth century on a steady procession of Penal Laws were passed to this end. The full fruition of these measures came in 1727, when they prohibited Catholics from being members of Parliament; bearing arms, owning horses worth £5 or more; being apprentices to gunsmiths; education abroad; keeping a public school in Ireland; receiving degrees, fellowships, or scholarships at the University of

[1] Sir John Davies, *Historical Tracts* (Dublin: 1787), pp. 3–4.
[2] Sir Francis Bacon, 'Certain Considerations touching the Plantation in Ireland,' in C. Maxwell, *Irish History from Contemporary Sources* (London: 1923), p. 270.

Dublin; being Roman Catholic bishops; practicing law; acquiring land owned by a Protestant; practicing primogeniture; acting as grand jurors; and taking more than two apprentices (save in the linen industry) if they were employers. Finally, Catholics were forbidden to vote. These laws stood for practically the whole period from 1727 to 1829, the year of Catholic Emancipation. While England had passed severely restrictive legislation against her own Catholics during this period, it should be pointed out that in England Catholics were in a tiny minority; in Ireland these laws 'were directed against the majority of the nation by a minority which owned its victory to the armies of England and whose ascendancy depended on English support.'[1]

This massive English pressure failed to convert the Irish to the Anglican religion. It need be mentioned only in passing that the English regarded traditional Irish culture—and its most impressive achievement, the Brehon Laws—with the utmost disdain, as the work of mere barbarians.[2] Gaelic, like Welsh, was not conducive to rational expression. To a certain extent, this Anglo-Saxon distaste and low regard for the Irish can be seen in all of its colonial splendor every year in the Orange Day parades in Northern Ireland:[3]

When the Orange Order and the Apprentice Boys commemorate the victories of 1690, as they do each year in elaborate ceremonies, the message they are conveying is that of their determination to hold for Protestants in Northern Ireland as much as possible of the privileged status which their ancestors won under William of Orange. These are not, as outside observers so easily suppose, comically archaic occasions. The symbols are historical, the iconography old fashioned, but the message is for the here and now. The ritual is one of annual renewal of a stylized act of dominance: 'We are your superiors: we know you hate this demonstrations of that fact: we dare you to say something about it: If you don't you ratify your own inferior status.' That is what the drums say.

The attempt to introduce anglicization into Scotland was far different in character from that in Wales and Ireland. To some extent, the beginnings of anglicization in Scotland are shrouded in

[1] Edmund Curtis, *A History of Ireland* (London: 1961), pp. 280–1. Giovanni Costigan relates that the Irish Parliament passed an ordinance requiring unregistered priests to be branded with a red-hot iron for failing to register. The Irish Privy Council proposed castration as suitable punishment for this offense. See *A History of Modern Ireland* (New York: 1969), p. 92. For a detailed study of the Irish Penal Laws, see Maureen Wall, *The Penal Laws, 1691–1760* (Dundalk: 1961).

[2] See an excellent account of English attitudes towards the Irish found in L. P. Curtis, Jr, *Anglo-Saxons and Celts*, (Bridgeport, Ct: 1968).

[3] Conor Cruise O'Brien, 'Holy war,' *New York Review*, 13, 8 (1969), p. 11.

controversy. It is clear that anglicization began in the thirteenth century, and that it gained ground quickly in the lowlands, where the anglicized dialect came to be known as 'Scots.' Some have suggested that the success of anglicization is related to the fact that the cultural origins of the Scottish lowlanders were Anglo-Saxon or Anglo-Norman, though there is some dispute.[1] In any case from the thirteenth century onward there were three linguistic groups in Scotland: basically English-speaking groups in the lowlands, Gaelic speakers in the highlands and groups of Norwegian descent to the far north. All subsequent attempts at anglicization in Scotland were carried out by the lowlanders, rather than the English government. The implications of this difference will be discussed at greater length in the next chapter.

By recognizing the establishment of the Kirk of Scotland, a Presbyterian body, the English had granted this territory far more cultural autonomy than either Wales or Ireland. However, the existence of the Test and Corporation Acts, which excluded from civil or military office in England all those who refused to take the sacrament according to the usage of the Church of England, was an affront to Scottish sentiments until its repeal in 1828.

Christopher Hill has summarized these developments in similar terms:[2]

The struggle of pious protestants to extend English religion and English civilization, first to the 'dark corners' of England and Wales, then to Ireland and the Highlands of Scotland, was a struggle to extend the values of London, and so to reinforce England's national security.

What remains to be discussed in the following chapter are the consequences of the English conquest, and the general course of the Celtic response to English domination.

[1] Christopher Brooke claims this is the case. See *From Alfred to Henry III* (New York: 1961), p. 198. For another opinion, see T. C. Smout, *A History of the Scottish People, 1560–1830* (New York: 1969), pp. 42–60.

[2] Hill, *op. cit.*, p. 28.

CHAPTER 4

THE CONSEQUENCES OF POLITICAL INCORPORATION

There come times when moral bonds seem to slacken, when the religion, or the patriotic sentiment, that has been the instrument of social cohesion, loses its hold and when the natural healing force, the power to react, fails to operate.

GAETANO MOSCA

DURING the Middle Ages, development in Western Europe had been severely constrained by the inefficiency of agricultural production. From year to year harvests fluctuated considerably due to natural climatic variations. The bulk of the population existed at the margin of subsistence; many were threatened by starvation annually. Demographic pressure, it is true, was kept down by constant warfare and the outbreak of epidemics. But in the long term Western European societies were relatively overpopulated by the late medieval period.

One means of stemming this demographic pressure was by extending, or reclaiming, the amount of arable land. Another, of course, was to improve the efficiency of agricultural production. In fact, both of these measures were taken. From the ninth to the thirteenth century agricultural productivity is estimated to have doubled; even so, it remained highly inefficient. Reclamation went hand in hand with agricultural improvement. The chain of causality appears to have led from agricultural improvement, to demographic growth, to increased migration and, finally, to reclamation. Upon this most delicate balance, Western European civilization rested.

It has become evident that there was already considerable production of grain and other commodities for exchange by the thirteenth and fourteenth centuries. With the growth of the population, food supply became an increasingly critical problem for the medieval social order, demanding a more rational solution.[1] Peasants

[1] Georges Duby, *Rural Economy and Country Life in the Medieval West* (London: 1968), pp. 157–8.

and lords had directly competing interests in determining the forms this production should assume. The peasants desired to preserve their collective rights to pasture, whereas the lords, for their part, sought to restrict access to the uncultivated portions of land.

So long as excess land was available on the frontier, as it were, the feudal social system could be perpetuated without much structural change. It is true that the personal dependency of the peasant labor force did vary throughout this period—from the extremes of bondage at certain times to wage labor at others[1]—but this fluctuation *per se* did not seem to have revolutionary consequences. However, if the supply of excess land were to be used up, then conflicts rooted in class interest between lords and peasants would inevitably emerge. Unless these class conflicts could somehow be averted, the underpinnings of the medieval social system would be torn asunder. Hence, the lords were most anxious to exert their political control over productive resources and territories. While this argument, strictly speaking, accounts for the large landowners' interests in reclamation during the thirteenth and fourteenth centuries, in a very real sense a similar structural imperative lay at the basis of the state's policy toward the Celtic lands during the sixteenth and seventeenth centuries.

The political incorporation of the Celtic territories by the Crown did not end the essentially colonial relationship existing between these lands and England. Quite the reverse. A major premise of this study is that many salient features of the colonial situation have persisted within the very boundaries of the developing metropolitan state. Internal colonialism, therefore, arose out of the same systemic needs which later spawned its more notorious overseas cousin.

It is evident that the mere fact of political incorporation substantially affected the course of development in the Celtic fringe by contributing to its economic, cultural, and political dependence. This can be seen with particular clarity in the economic sphere. Throughout the period, the English market was both relatively larger and wealthier than that of the Celtic regions, taken singly or in the aggregate. This initial difference became greatly magnified over time. Political incorporation also had a decisive effect on the progress of anglicization, which proceeded not only by government

---

[1] For two theoretical accounts of these changes see Evsey Domar, 'The causes of slavery or serfdom: a hypothesis,' *Journal of Economic History*, 30, 1 (1970), and Douglass C. North and Robert Paul Thomas, 'The rise and fall of the manorial system: a theoretical model,' *Journal of Economic History*, 31, 4 (1971).

fiat, but through the voluntary assimilation of peripheral élites. Finally, by removing the locus of authority from the Celtic regions to London, incorporation stimulated apathy and corruption in the peripheral polities.

THE ECONOMIC CONSEQUENCES OF INCORPORATION

In general, political incorporation forced the Celtic territories to develop in a manner which complemented, but did not permit competition with England. This was accomplished in two ways. Incorporation stimulated interregional trade and thereby extended market forces to the Celtic economies. In the periphery, this caused pressures for the evolution of highly specialized export economies. Mass population movements ensued as regional specialization proceeded in each of the Celtic lands. Additionally, from the seventeenth century onwards, England exercised growing dominance over commerce and trade in the Celtic regions and maintained tight control over credit available for investment. Therefore, political incorporation indirectly led to the development of economic dependence in the peripheral regions by facilitating the expansion of production for exchange.

However, it is evident that economic dependence[1] can occur without benefit of political incorporation. Incorporation directly contributed to Celtic economic dependence precisely by prohibiting the existence of states in the Celtic lands, that is to say, agencies of the collective will which might resist English economic domination by taking protectionist measures.

The strain towards regional economic specialization in the periphery

The social organization of the Celtic regions had revolved about a subsistence economy in which tenants sharing common fields engaged in production for themselves, a portion of which went for tribute due the tribal chieftain. Political incorporation had three consequences which in the long run tended to disrupt this social organization. First, it established English inheritance customs and criminal statutes throughout state territory, thereby encouraging the expansion of commerce between England and the peripheral

---

[1] A useful definition of the concept of economic dependency may be found in Theotonio Dos Santos, 'The structure of dependence,' *American Economic Review*, 60, 2 (1970).

regions. Second, increasing interregional contact facilitated the dissemination of English agricultural improvements to the Celtic territories, including new tillage, drainage, and crop rotation techniques. These raised the efficiency of agrarian production in the periphery. Third, increasing demand from English and international markets encouraged landowners in the Celtic regions to engage in commercial agriculture. This combination of new markets and more efficient production sharply increased the value of land relative to labor, giving the Celtic landowner a powerful incentive to clear his common fields.

The incorporation of Wales abolished *gavelkind*, which had led to the proliferation of small units of production, though there is evidence that partible inheritance continued to be practiced until the seventeenth century among smallholders in remote areas.[1] After Union, the prohibition against Welsh office-holding in state and church bureaucracies was lifted. This caused expanded opportunities for individuals to gain wealth and brought into being a class of gentry made up of native Welshmen.[2] Access to the growing English domestic market provided an incentive to regional specialization in livestock and wool by the sixteenth century. Hence, the development of the London food market from the mid-sixteenth century on[3] led some southern Welsh gentry to breed cattle for sale to the metropolis. To further this end they sought to enclose, or restrict tenant access, to common fields. In lowland areas this caused much displacement of peasants and an increase in vagabondage, but in the highlands enclosure did not have such extreme consequences, due to a much lower population density. Peasants who were the victims of enclosure in the highlands could continue to eke out a living, since much waste land remained available there.[4] Welsh

---

[1] T. Jones Pierce, 'Landlords in Wales' in Joan Thirsk, ed., *The Agrarian History of England and Wales*, vol. IV, 1500–1640 (Cambridge: 1967), p. 369.

[2] *Ibid.*, p. 370.

[3] F. J. Fisher, 'The development of the London food market, 1540–1640,' *Economic History Review*, 5, 1 (1935), reprinted in E. M. Carus-Wilson, ed., *Essays in Economic History* (London: 1954), pp. 139–40.

[4] 'The highland zone consisted for the most part of land which was either completely enclosed by the beginning of the sixteenth century, or, if the land was worth enclosing at this time, could and often did undergo painless enclosure. In lowland England where common fields were subject to a system of mixed husbandry, where common grazing rights were highly prized because the pasture steadily diminished as the usable was enlarged, enclosure constituted, at the beginning at least, a painful and socially disturbing reorganization of land and ways of living.' Joan Thirsk, 'The farming regions of England' in Thirsk, *The Agrarian History of England and Wales*, p. 6.

drovers and herds became a common sight in England.[1] Similarly, a sharp increase in the Flemish demand for wool in the sixteenth century encouraged many northern gentry to enclose their lands for sheep-rearing.

The economic situation of the peripheral areas had not changed much by 1707. The Union with Scotland eliminated customs and tariff barriers between the two halves of the island, and reoriented the pattern of Scottish trade from Europe to England.[2] In consequence, cattle production was stimulated, initially in the border counties, and there was some agricultural improvement. As in Wales, the highlands saw an increase in the production of wool.[3] By the eighteenth century, Scotland had a great advantage over England in land available for pasture. Beef was exported not merely to the English cities but, when salted, was used extensively for provisioning the British navy. As a consequence of heightened demand, the price of cattle rose over 300 per cent between 1740 and 1790.[4] Wool prices also gained. This increase in cattle and wool prices, when combined with the importation of English agricultural improvements, led to a situation where the relative value of land surpassed that of labor. In response, the Scottish lairds began encroaching upon the customary rights of their tenants. At this point, *gavelkind* began to give way in the highlands, and there was substantial displacement of peasants. While some of these displaced tenants migrated to lowland farms and cities, others remained in northwest Scotland subsisting on minute pieces of land, and living in very crowded conditions. Extensive potato cultivation enabled this dense rural population to survive until the coming of blight.

While cattle were bred in the highlands, there was no attempt to improve pastures so that they might also be fattened there. To fatten the stock, highland drovers walked the cattle to lowland counties. This was a long journey, and by its end the cattle were not left in the best condition. Nevertheless, the steady increase in cattle prices until 1815 benefited the highland economy, in the short run. In the long

---

[1] Caroline Skeel, 'The cattle trade between Wales and England from the fifteenth to the nineteenth centuries,' *Transactions of the Royal Historical Society*, 4th ser., 9 (1926).

[2] R. H. Campbell, *Scotland Since 1707: The Rise of an Industrial Society* (Oxford: 1965), pp. 3, 41–2.

[3] William Ferguson, *Scotland: 1689 to the Present*, vol. IV of *The Edinburgh History of Scotland* (Edinburgh: 1968), pp. 166–8.

[4] T. C. Smout, *A History of the Scottish People, 1560–1830* (New York: 1969), p. 345.

run, this extremely high demand for cattle worked to the disadvantage of the highlands, since it encouraged landowners to maintain an essentially inefficient economic system.[1] After cattle prices declined in the nineteenth century, the locus of the cattle trade shifted to the northeast lowlands which could both breed and fatten cattle adequately, and the highland droving industry suffered concomitantly.

The case of Ireland illustrates that regional economic specialization may occur in the absence of formal political incorporation. Nevertheless, it would be inaccurate to portray pre-Union Ireland as beyond the political control of England. Ever since Poyning's Law had been enacted in 1494, the Irish Parliament was bound to submit all its pending bills to the English King and Privy Council for prior approval before returning the legislation for Irish consideration.[2] The constitutional dependence of the Irish Parliament was reasserted in 1720 by the Act *Sixth of George the First*.[3] In reality, a semblance of political sovereignty was achieved for only eighteen years in pre-Union Ireland: during Grattan's Parliament lasting from 1782 to 1801.[4]

In 1600, Ireland was largely a woodland society in which there was very little production for export. However, during the seventeenth and eighteenth centuries, English markets penetrated Ireland to much the same effect that they had the economies of Wales and Scotland. While fully one-eighth of Ireland was covered with forests in 1600, a century later the country was virtually cleared. Irish timber was exported to England, and an English-controlled iron industry was also developed.[5] Once the supply of timber ran out, this industry disappeared.

As English demand for marketed food rose, the Irish economy quickly responded by concentrating on cattle-breeding. Seventeenth-century Ireland also exported wool, tallow, hides, and butter.[6] These primary exports were stimulated by the demand for salted beef and other provisions emanating from the sugar islands of the West Indies, as well as from the navies of the Western European maritime powers. Cattle and cattle products remained the backbone

---

[1] Campbell, *op. cit.*, pp. 35–6.

[2] J. C. Beckett, *The Making of Modern Ireland, 1603–1923* (London: 1969), p. 51.

[3] L. M. Cullen, *An Economic History of Ireland Since 1660* (London: 1972), p. 35.

[4] Beckett, *op. cit.*, pp. 221–7.

[5] Eileen McCracken, 'The woodlands of Ireland circa 1600,' *Irish Historical Studies*, 11, 44 (1959), pp. 273, 287, 289.   [6] Cullen, *op. cit.*, p. 18.

of the Irish economy until the late eighteenth century. This economy was very vulnerable to the buoyancy of the English, colonial, and naval markets (when political restrictions were lifted), as well as to the level of animal stocks within Ireland. Abnormal livestock mortality was therefore a critical factor in explaining short-term fluctuations in Irish exports.[1]

Whenever prices for cattle and cattle-products held at a low level tillage was correspondingly expanded.[2] Before the late eighteenth century there was unfortunately no British demand for grain: England was itself a grain-exporter and therefore did not permit the importation of Irish cereal. However, by 1782—in the early stages of the Industrial Revolution—England sought 'a regular and standing supply of corn' and, to that end, passed Foster's Corn Law (1784). Immediately thereafter, tillage in Ireland was vastly extended. Irish grain poured into the British market until the repeal of the British Corn Laws in 1846, when the cattle trade became re-emphasized. Thus the Irish economy was largely transformed from production based on pasture, to tillage, to pasture in the space of a scant seventy years, in adapting to changes in the English demand for agricultural products.

Ireland was also responsible for infusing much capital into England as a result of the rents paid to absentee landlords. After the Cromwellian settlement there had been an upheaval in patterns of Irish land tenure. Englishmen, for the large part absentee, rented their lands to tenants who turned around and rented this land to sub-tenants, the Irish cottiers.[3] The large tenants in Ireland served as middlemen, extracting exorbitant rents from the peasants for their potato patches. The middleman who employed this smallholder received a large part of his income in labor at a low rate and of very low efficiency. But he was in need of a good deal of ready cash—to pay for his own rent as well as personal expenditure. The tendency, therefore, was to subdivide his land into smaller and smaller parcels, while simultaneously increasing his income from the cottiers.

The yearly rental of the country was estimated in 1670 at £800,000 out of a total national income of £4 millions. In 1687 the estimate of rents was £1,200,000.[4] These are estimates of the annual flow of

---

[1] Ibid., pp. 26, 54–5. [2] Beckett, op. cit., pp. 243–4.
[3] For statistics on the extent of absenteeism in Ireland, see Norman D. Palmer, The Irish Land League Crisis (New Haven: 1940), pp. 27–8. A more favorable image of the Irish landlord is presented by John E. Pomfret, The Struggle for Land in Ireland, 1800–1923 (Princeton: 1930), pp. 26–8.
[4] E. Strauss, Irish Nationalism and British Democracy (New York: 1951), p. 11.

money from Ireland to England. The peasant had no means at his disposal of raising capital or improving his land. The process became a vicious cycle. By the mid-eighteenth century, Jonathan Swift estimated that about one third of the produce of Ireland was sent out of the country in payment of rents to these proprietors in England.[1]

After Union, the Irish system of land tenure worsened. It differed from that in the rest of the British Isles in several ways.[2] Improvement and investments in the land, such as drainage, fencing, and the erection of buildings, were not typically assumed by the landlord. Instead, the landlord leased only the soil, and all improvements thereupon were the tenant's responsibility. Further, the pressure of population and concomitant lack of alternative occupations drove land prices up steadily. There was no security of tenure, either for the middleman or his sub-lessee, so that everyone in the system was filled with a pervading fear of eviction, which might be desirable to the landlord as the price of land escalated. After 1826, the practice of sub-leasing was prohibited. Few leases of any kind were, henceforth, made. This general pattern of land tenure was the case for all Ireland except Ulster, where tenants had traditionally been accustomed to greater rights, perhaps evolving out of the original plantation scheme.[3]

The competition for land was such that most prospective tenants were willing to offer rents far greater than the land could reasonably produce under any system of cultivation. In consequence (the tenants) quickly fell into arrears with their payments and continued in occupation under the constant threat of ejectment.

The prolongation of this state of affairs was the basis for the creation of the growth of secret societies such as the 'Whiteboys' and 'Ribbonmen,' which engaged in agrarian terrorism. The structure of the Irish land system was largely upheld by potato cultivation. When this inexpensive sustenance failed, as it did in 1845, disaster struck. The population of Ireland fell by one quarter in the decade after 1845, through mortality and emigration.[4] After the Corn Laws

---

[1] *Ibid.*, p. 11. Strauss regards this estimate as 'not unprobable.'

[2] Barbara L. Solow, *The Land Question and the Irish Economy, 1870–1903* (Cambridge, Mass.: 1971), pp. 4–11 discusses the particulars lucidly. Her analysis suggests that the Irish system of land tenure cannot, however, be blamed for Ireland's economic fate after the Famine.

[3] R. B. Collison-Black, *Economic Thought and the Irish Question, 1817–1870* (Cambridge: 1960), p. 6.

[4] However, the mid-century demographic decline in Ireland cannot be wholly explained by the Famine. See Cullen, *op. cit.*, pp. 132–3.

were repealed, ending Ireland's virtual monopoly of the British grain market, the Irish land system changed radically.[1] The system of rackrents and middlemen disappeared as much land was cleared of tillage for pasture and subsequent livestock production. Large movements of population followed the extension of specialization in all the peripheral regions. Peasants, dispossessed from their customary rights to till common fields, were compelled to migrate in search of alternative means of sustenance. Karl Marx used the term 'forced emigration' in his description of the efflux from the Celtic territories: 'Begin with pauperizing the inhabitants of a country, and when there is no more profit to be ground out of them, when they have grown a burden to the revenue, drive them away, and sum up your Net Revenue!'[2] Celts, particularly those from highland areas, were forced on to the most inaccessible parts of the highlands, into the cities with their growing slums, or overseas. Strictly speaking, the pull of exogenous market forces in the Celtic territories antedated political incorporation. For example, Wales had served, from the thirteenth to fifteenth centuries, as one of the most important recruiting bases for mercenaries in feudal Europe. Archers from South Wales had made the Norman conquest of Ireland feasible; 10,000 of the 12,500 troops in Edward I's campaign to subdue Scotland in the fourteenth century were Welsh.[3] And Irishmen had long engaged in seasonal migration to England and Scotland. Incorporation made these exogenous forces the rule rather than the exception.

The social and economic implications of the Irish situation, with its chaotic land system, were the subject of intensive argument among intellectuals of the day. There was much sentiment in liberal English academic circles to relieve the obvious suffering of the bulk of the Irish rural population. Most observers felt that large capital investments were required to stabilize the Irish economy on a higher level:[4]

The orthodox economists . . . generally took it as axiomatic that increase of capital must be to the general good and so tended to gloss over the disturbances which its introduction might create in a given region. Here

---

[1] R. D. Crotty, *Irish Agricultural Production: Its Volume and Structure* (Cork: 1966), pp. 37–9 argues that livestock production first became re-emphasized in the period following the Battle of Waterloo (1815), rather than after the Famine.

[2] Karl Marx, 'Forced emigration' in *Karl Marx and Frederick Engels on Britain* (Moscow: 1953), pp. 373–4.

[3] V. G. Kiernan, 'Foreign mercenaries and absolute monarchy,' *Past and Present*, 11 (1957), p. 69.

[4] Collison-Black, *op. cit.*, p. 242.

their approach contrasts interestingly with that of Karl Marx, who, concerned always to bring out the contradictory results of capital accumulation, did not fail to note how capital in Ireland had been devoted mainly to livestock production, and to stress the consequent rural depopulation as contributing to the reserve army of labor.

While political incorporation undoubtedly stimulated investment in the Celtic regions, in general, English capital was available only for those investments which could complement existing English industries.[1] The problem of the Irish economy, and of the economies of the Celtic fringe as a whole, lay not so much in the lack of sufficient capital for development, as in the narrowing sectors in which this capital came to be invested.

Nevertheless, indigenous capital was not effectively mobilized to support development in the peripheral regions, with the significant exception of lowland Scotland. In part, this may be demonstrated in considering the fate of the Celtic-owned banks. Banks can play a significant role in economic development by aiding in the accumulation, mobilization and efficient utilization of capital. They may stimulate saving and encourage the introduction of capital from other regions, or from abroad. Financial institutions are also especially critical for regional development in that they 'exercise a large measure of discretion in the selection of investment alternatives.'[2]

It is therefore significant to note that the banks which arose in Ireland and Wales were unable to effectively perform these functions. The Dublin-based Bank of Ireland had never managed to establish itself sufficiently in the Irish countryside, which was, after all, the major site of production on the island. After the Union, Dublin's importance in the Irish economy lessened considerably, and with it the importance of the Bank of Ireland as well: 'Everywhere, there was a growing amount of direct contact between intermediaries in the countryside and business interests in England, and Dublin wholesalers monopolized much less of the country's wholesale business than in the eighteenth century. This was true of external trade, it was also true of internal trade.'[3] Soon goods were being ordered directly from English centers instead of by placing orders with Dublin intermediaries. The Irish economy suffered correspondingly thereby. In similar fashion, the Welsh banks became swallowed in competition

[1] Campbell, *op. cit.*, pp, 57–8.
[2] Rondo Cameron, 'Conclusion' in Rondo Cameron *et al.*, *Banking in the Early Stages of Industrialization* (New York: 1967), p. 292. See also Rondo Cameron, ed., *Banking and Economic Development* (New York: 1972).
[3] Cullen, *op. cit.*, pp. 127–8.

with London institutions. The last Welsh-owned bank, in Cardiff, failed in 1823.[1] Thereafter, English banks had no competition in Wales. Furthermore, the location of branches of the Bank of England were chosen to maximize the bank's profits, rather than out of any concern to stimulate the regional economy.[2]

Interestingly, the situation in Scotland was entirely reversed; at the height of Glasgow's tobacco fortunes in the eighteenth century, a highly advanced and efficient banking system was developed. The reasons for the vitality of Scottish banking are unclear. Rondo Cameron sees the absence of a Scottish central government to be a critical factor in the relative superiority of Scotland's banks to those of England.[3] But, if Scotland is compared not to England, and, instead, to Wales and Ireland, this explanation makes little sense. According to Cameron, the health of the Scottish banks was short-lived because after 1845 Scottish banking policies and practices became assimilated to England's.[4] Can it really be maintained that nineteenth-century England was ultimately so financially inefficient?

Finally, it is likely that the profits which derived from the vastly increased trade between England and the Celtic periphery accrued mostly to England. It is reasonable to suppose that, as early as the seventeenth century, the English took a disproportionately great share of this interregional commerce. The Welsh wool trade may be a model of how this occurred. Thomas Mendenhall has shown, in his detailed examination of the North Welsh wool trade in the sixteenth and seventeenth centuries, that the merchants of the English border town of Shrewsbury effectively monopolized the sizeable profits which accrued to them as middlemen between Welsh sheep rearers and consumers in London. This marketing system lasted until the eighteenth century.[5] The character of this trade was particularly disadvantageous to Wales:[6]

This form of economic domination, of course, was by no means unknown in the English clothing districts, but nowhere did it survive the 'age of monopolies' in so pronounced a form. Moreover, in other regions the

---

[1] T. Mansel Hodges, 'Early banking in Cardiff,' *Economic History Review*, 18, 1 & 2 (1948).

[2] R. O. Roberts, 'Bank of England branch discounting, 1826–59,' *Economica*, 25, 99 (1958).

[3] Rondo Cameron, 'Scotland, 1750–1845' in Cameron *et al.*, *Banking in the Early Stages of Industrialization*, p. 61.

[4] *Ibid.*, pp. 96–7.

[5] Thomas C. Mendenhall, *The Shrewsbury Drapers and the Welsh Wool Trade in the 16th and 17th Centuries* (London: 1953).

[6] A. H. Dodd, *The Industrial Revolution in North Wales* (Cardiff: 1933), p. 13.

dominant market was a local one, whereas here 'the Welsh had the labour, and strangers the profit.' Much of the money gained by sales was spent outside the country, and the road to advancement for the ambitious weaver lay through Shrewsbury in apprenticeship with the all-powerful company, and not at home.

Englishmen also came to occupy high status positions in the social structure of the peripheral regions, mainly as managers, entrepreneurs, and salesmen.[1] In fact, this selective migration was initially responsible for the establishment of a cultural division of labor in the Celtic fringe.[2] Additionally, Englishmen owned most of the ships used in the coastwise trade, and collected large chunks of hidden profits from transportation and insurance expenditures.[3]

The loss of sovereignty and its effects

Looking backward from the perspective of neo-classical economic theory, it is easy to argue that once England entered a phase of rapid and sustained growth, the inescapable destiny of the Celtic lands was to drift into economic dependency. This was bound to occur according to the principle of comparative advantage, if for no other reason. The application of this principle suggests that, whereas the peripheral economies were best suited to supply primary products for export, it was to England's advantage to produce manufactured goods, especially textiles.

But such a passive view of development was not common in seventeenth- and eighteenth-century Europe; nor is it universally held today. Lacking from this perspective is any discussion of the significance of the state's role in fostering economic growth.

[1] Christopher Hill, 'Puritans and the dark corners of the land,' *Transactions of the Royal Historical Society*, 5th ser., 13 (1963), p. 78.

[2] Sometimes the cultural division of labor takes a curious form. In eighteenth-century Ireland, Catholics formed a large proportion of the merchant classes. This occurred because these occupations were generally regarded with low esteem by the aristocratic, and Protestant, landowning class. The Irish Parliament, controlled by landed interests, was content to allow Catholics to amass wealth, because they could subsequently be taxed. Using Catholics as a tax base, it would not be necessary to have high taxes on Protestant-owned land. 'It is easy to see how, in these circumstances, Catholics were permitted to control a large share in the trade of the country. It was a lowly occupation, and it was natural that they should be engaged in it; and since the law did not permit them to buy land, they persevered in it until some of them became quite wealthy.' Maureen Wall, 'The rise of a Catholic middle class in eighteenth-century Ireland,' *Irish Historical Studies*, 11, 42 (1958), p. 97.

[3] Michael Hechter, 'Regional inequality and national integration: the case of the British Isles,' *Journal of Social History*, 5, 1 (1971).

The dominant economic principles of that period may be described as mercantilist.[1] Mercantilism basically held that economies should operate in the service of states, to increase their wealth and power relative to other states in the international system. Accordingly, it was the proper function of government to intervene in the economy to achieve these ends, primarily by manipulating exports and imports in such a way as to nourish native manufactures and bring about a favorable balance of trade.[2] But there was perhaps even more concern to reap the advantages of favorable *terms* of trade.[3] Typically, the mercantilist state intervened in the economy by erecting protective barriers to shield home manufactures from foreign competition in the domestic market. It promoted the establishment of national economies by removing tolls and other restraints on internal trade, and by attempting to secure political stability. It also acted to restrict, as best it could, the number of states exporting manufactured goods for consumption on the international market. For these requirements mercantilist powers sought a particular type of trading partner: namely, colonies.[4] Under the mercantilist system, then, the state was charged with a responsibility to aid in capital accumulation so that society might materially prosper. Whether or not mercantilist policies were successful in this regard is, for the moment, not at issue.

The point here is that the state's responsibility to provide for economic welfare has continued in the *laissez-faire*[5] and modern periods as well. The importance of states in economic development is obvious. They can coerce recalcitrant groups to accept government policies by using the threat of military sanctions. In addition to their

[1] D. C. Coleman, 'Introduction' in D. C. Coleman, ed., *Revisions in Mercantilism* (London: 1969).

[2] Charles Wilson, 'The other face of mercantilism,' *Transactions of the Royal Historical Society*, 5th ser., 9 (1959), reprinted in Coleman, *op. cit.*

[3] Maurice Dobb, *Studies in the Development of Capitalism* (London: 1963), p. 202.

[4] (Mercantilist) 'policy chiefly depended for its success on its application to a system of *colonial* trade, where political influence could be brought to bear to ensure to the parent country some element of monopoly; and it is essentially as applied to the exploitation of a dependent colonial system that mercantilist trade-theories acquire a meaning. . . . For the trade that they evidently had in mind consisted of an exchange between the products of home manufacture and colonial products which consisted chiefly of raw materials and therefore entered as an element into the cost of the former.' *Ibid.*, p. 204.

[5] 'The real executor of mercantilism was *laissez-faire*, which did almost without effort what mercantilism had set out but failed to achieve.' Eli F. Heckscher, 'Mercantilism,' 'Revisions in economic history V,' *Economic History Review*, 7, 1 (1936–7), reprinted in Coleman, *op. cit.*, p. 25.

ability to negotiate the terms of trade, states have the power to legislate against economic rigidities, to alter the rate of involuntary saving through taxation, and to mobilize collective sentiments to ends which they deem necessary.[1] States alone can support large-scale activities which are not in themselves profitable, such as establishing transportation and education systems.

Does it not therefore follow that the state is the greatest weapon in the arsenal of a society determined to struggle against economic dependency? This is not to say that political sovereignty alone is sufficient to the task. Almost everywhere the evidence points in the opposite direction. But in what territory has diversified development occurred without benefit of state protection? It is in this context that the loss of Celtic sovereignty must be considered. By denying these territories political independence, England made their increasing economic dependency inevitable.

The decisiveness of political autonomy for the process of economic development may be summarized simply enough. *Sovereignty might have facilitated and encouraged economic diversification in the Celtic territories.* Here, Ireland perhaps serves as the best example, since its incorporation occurred last. On the eve of the Union (1801) the development prospects of the Irish economy appeared to be very favorable.[2] Prices for agricultural products were rising, but there were also strong signs of industrial diversification. Techniques borrowed from the Industrial Revolution were being rapidly adopted in the textile industries and elsewhere in the 1770s and 1780s. The linen industry was booming. In fact, Ireland's industrial development was so promising that manufacturing interests in Britain violently opposed the establishment of free trade between the islands in 1785. Their fears were that Ireland's lower wages and taxation would enable Irish manufacturers to flood the British market with cheap goods. The result might be a massive migration of British capital and artisans to new industrial centers in Ireland.

By 1801, free trade between Great Britain and Ireland was a reality; however, Irish industry, with one exception—linen, could not withstand English competition. After the Union, Ireland, therefore, became more rural, more agricultural, more economically specialized than it had been previously.[3] But Irish industry might have had a

---

[1] Joseph J. Spengler, 'The state and economic growth: summary and interpretation' in H. J. G. Aitkin, ed., *The State and Economic Growth* (New York: 1959), p. 373.
[2] Cullen, *op. cit.*, p. 97.　　　　　　[3] *Ibid.*, p. 121.

chance to survive if it arose in a state capable of erecting trade barriers for its protection. This industry might have developed solely on the basis of the domestic market: it should be noted that by 1841 the Irish population was over eight million. Similarly, following the Union with Scotland that country's native manufactures, particularly woolen cloth and linen, were crushed after experiencing open competition with English industry.[1] The specific economic consequences of incorporation were very different for Scotland than for Ireland. While Ireland increased its specialization in agricultural products, Scotland specialized in heavy industry, though this too was to its eventual disadvantage.[2]

The English state had itself long resorted to protectionist measures to spur economic growth. The Navigation Acts (begun in 1651), which served to protect English trade and shipping rather than manufactures, were initially passed with the Dutch in mind.[3] These Acts applied with respect to all foreign countries, pre-Union Scotland and Ireland among them. However they were merely among the more notable of England's protectionist policies. Whenever a specific English interest group mobilized enough Parliamentary support it could effectively legislate protection in its behalf.

Frequently, this occurred at the expense of the Celtic lands. The Irish cattle bills may be taken as one instance. It has already been related that during the seventeenth and eighteenth centuries the Irish economy was dominated by the cattle trade. Live cattle were shipped to England where they were fattened and sold for consumption in London. But opposition to this trade arose in English (and Welsh!) cattle-breeding counties, where Irish cattle were regarded as cheap and dangerous competition.[4] By 1681 this opposition had carried the day, and the Irish Cattle Acts were passed, prohibiting the importation of live Irish cattle to the English market. There was strong sentiment to prohibit Scottish cattle as well, but when the Act was passed Scotland remained unscathed.[5] This protectionist

[1] Ferguson, *op. cit.*, p. 180.
[2] See chapter 5.
[3] On the Navigation Acts see Charles Wilson, *England's Apprenticeship, 1603–1763* (London: 1965), pp. 61 *et seq*. According to Christopher Hill, 'The Navigation Act of 1651 represented the victory of a national trading interest over the separate interests and privileges of the companies.' *Reformation to Industrial Revolution* (London: 1968), p. 125.
[4] Carolyn A. Edie, 'The Irish cattle bills: a study in restoration politics,' *Transactions of the American Philosophical Society*, new ser., 60, part 2 (1970) pp. 16–17.
[5] *Ibid.*, p. 29.

legislation, very much to the detriment of the Irish economy, remained in force until 1758; thereafter it was temporarily suspended until 1776, when it was extended in perpetuity.

Other protectionist legislation enacted against Ireland by England included prohibitions against the importation of Irish woolens (1699),[1] colored linens (1699), and glass (1746). Consequently, these industries withered.[2] The Irish brewing industry, which relied on imported continental hops, was set back when Ireland was prohibited from buying hops from any other country but Great Britain (1710). By the late eighteenth century, Ireland's reliance on exporting salted beef to the navies of Europe was jolted when England placed a series of embargoes on these Irish exports to enemy countries.[3]

England's cavalier treatment of the Irish parliament beginning in 1699 was deeply resented by that body and thereby stimulated much interest in lessening the island's economic dependence. Even in its crippled situation, the Irish state did what it could to spur economic development. The state acted to create a Linen Board; to extend tillage; to regulate coal imports; to construct canals for internal trade; to develop collieries; and to construct harbors. Under the relative autonomy of Grattan's Parliament, the state made more lavish grants in support of public works, on behalf of the cotton industry, and for economic development more generally.[4]

But following Union, the Irish state ceased to exist, as had the Scottish state before it.

Previous to the Union of 1707, the Scottish state had enacted several protectionist measures to promote economic diversification.[5] Under James VI, Scotland encouraged the immigration of foreign industrial artisans, including Flemings, Englishmen, and Venetians.[6] James also attempted to increase political stability and internal trade by extending government influence in the remote highlands.[7] Previous to incorporation, Scotland's relatively diversified foreign

---

[1] Cullen, *op. cit.*, p. 34.

[2] Beckett, *op. cit.*, p. 169.

[3] Cullen, *op. cit.*, pp. 56–8.

[4] *Ibid.*, pp. 95–6. However, the effectiveness of these measures has been challenged by Crotty, *op. cit.*, pp. 22–3.

[5] Gordon Donaldson, *Scotland: James V to James VII*, vol. III in *The Edinburgh History of Scotland* (Edinburgh: 1965), pp. 385–6.

[6] T. M. Devine and S. G. E. Lythe, 'The economy of Scotland under James VI; A revision article,' *Scottish Historical Review*, 50, 2 (1971), p. 92.

[7] I. F. Grant, *The Social and Economic Development of Scotland Before 1603* (Edinburgh: 1930), p. 535. See also Maurice Lee, Jr, *John Maitland of Thirlestane and the Foundation of the Stewart Despotism in Scotland* (Princeton: 1959).

trade had allowed the state some maneuverability in international politics. Political and commercial ties to France in the sixteenth century prevented Scotland from coming under the same kind of English overlordship as was suffered by Ireland.[1] However, the Union changed all of this. Scotland's trade became overwhelmingly dependent on the English market. Following incorporation, the English market reigned supreme in the economies of all the peripheral regions.

After political unification, the state continued to exercise great influence upon economic development in the British Isles. By lending its support to the interests of certain sectors of the society as against others—be they regions, social strata or cultural groups— the state could largely determine the winners and losers in any given conflict. It should not come as a surprise that whenever such disputes had regional overtones the state naturally tended to favor the claims of English rather than Celtic regions. Thus, the Celtic periphery was swallowed whole into a state system in which it became economically and demographically only an insignificant part.

THE EVOLUTION OF REGIONAL CULTURAL DIFFERENCES: THE REFORMATION AND ITS AFTERMATH

Now that the persistence, if not the predominance, of status group politics in contemporary Western European societies has come to be widely recognized among scholars, the continuing salience of religious or linguistic factors for political behavior is often ascribed to events surrounding the Reformation and Counter-Reformation.[2] For students of modern politics this may be a particularly attractive explanation, in that it shifts attention from the current situation to that of the dim past, thereby placing this rather sticky problem in someone else's bailiwick: the Reformation historian's. But the Reformation historian has enough difficulties already. To ascribe the present political significance of differential cultural affiliation to events in the sixteenth and seventeenth centuries is, in effect, to sweep any explanation at all under the rug. This is not only because such an explanation fails to deal with the contemporary causes of cultural

---

[1] S. G. E. Lythe, *The Economy of Scotland in its European Setting, 1550–1625* (Edinburgh and London: 1960), p. 168.

[2] For an example of this tendency see Richard Rose and Derek Urwin, 'Social cohesion, political parties and strains in regimes,' *Comparative Political Studies*, 2, 1 (1969), p. 44.

identification, but because it also assumes that Reformation history is coherent and well-understood. Nothing could be further from the truth. In fact, simple hypotheses linking specific social groups with the support of either the Reformation or the Counter-Reformation, either the King or the Country, cannot be adequately tested for some time, if ever, due to a lack of sufficiently discrete evidence. The social history of the sixteenth and seventeenth centuries continues to be seen through a glass darkly. Speculation abounds; this is necessarily and properly so.

The years from 1540 to about 1700 were wrought with massive economic change, religious ferment and political instability, so much so that a 'General Crisis' occurred throughout Europe in this period.[1] The British Isles were affected, in their turn, by powerful international forces: economic changes, represented by a rapid rise in world prices, and political changes, represented by the outbreak of the Reformation.

In 1534, Henry VIII imposed a Protestant Reformation from above, assuming supremacy over the Church of England, and achieved sovereignty from Rome. The immense wealth of the Church was expropriated by the Crown and parcelled out to Henry's political supporters, who were thereafter beholden to him. In effect, this brought into being a new class of landowners, many having large estates. But this was not the only bounty. The offices of the Church, from that of Archbishop on down, reverted to the Crown and were extended to Henry's allies. A layman, Thomas Cromwell, took control of the Church and became Henry's most important tactician. Although the Crown now ruled the Church for its own ends, very little in the way of doctrinal reform occurred in Henry's reign. The form of popular religion, therefore, was not greatly altered by the Henrician Reformation.[2]

In the century following the death of Henry VIII, the official religious doctrine of the Church of England swung dramatically from Henrician Anglicanism, to more puritan strains of Protestant-

[1] See, among others, E. J. Hobsbawm, 'The crisis of the seventeenth century, I, *Past and Present*, 5 (1954); E. J. Hobsbawm, 'The crisis of the seventeenth century, II,' *Past and Present*, 6 (1954); H. R. Trevor-Roper, 'The general crisis of the seventeenth century,' *Past and Present*, 16 (1959). These articles are reprinted in Trevor Aston, ed., *Crisis in Europe, 1560–1660* (London: 1965).

[2] Nevertheless, changes in the ecclesiastical structure greatly affected the position of priests, and they did not hesitate to use their pulpits to attack the Crown. Altogether, their activities posed some threat to the social order. See G. R. Elton, *Policy and Police: The Enforcement of the Reformation in the Age of Thomas Cromwell* (Cambridge: 1972).

ism, exemplified by the Lutheranism of Cranmer's first Prayer-Book (1549) and the Calvinism of his second Prayer-Book (1552), both under the reign of Edward VI; then, to the outright Catholicism of Queen Mary (1553–8); backwards once again, to a compromise Episcopacy of Elizabeth (1558–1603); and finally, to the more Catholic-tinged régimes instituted by James I (1603–25) and Charles I (1625–49). The English Revolution, of course, brought Puritanism into ascendancy, but Catholicism made a comeback during the Restoration. After the Glorious Revolution (1688), the Church of England became an Episcopal institution once and for all.

Along with this remarkable religious fluctuation, England experienced a period of intense political instability which culminated in the Revolution of 1640. But previous to the Revolution, open rebellion had broken out repeatedly: in the northern counties (the Pilgrimage of Grace, 1536–7); in the western counties and Cornwall (the Western Rising, 1549); in Norfolk (Ket's Rebellion, 1549); and in the north once more (the Northern Rebellion, 1569). Essex's Rising of 1600 was the last major outbreak before the onset of the Revolution. Many of these conflicts were instigated by peasant rebellions directed against enclosure and the overstocking of the commons by the gentry, but certain great nobles also lent their support.[1]

Can any order be discerned in the midst of these chaotic events? Here, resort to interpretation is unavoidable. At the risk of much oversimplification, it will be instructive to enumerate four major parties to these struggles. The first group was composed of the old nobility, great magnates such as the Percies and the Dacres, and is often described by Tudor historians as being 'feudalistic'. By this the historians mean that these great landowners felt it necessary, for economic and political reasons, to surround themselves with retainers, that they believed in a tradition of military adventure, and that they deeply resented the encroachments of the Crown into the internal affairs of their domains. Their religious sympathies, like everything else about them, were traditional, harking back to the pre-Henrician era, and, therefore, many among this group remained Catholic, or recusant.

[1] A. G. Dickens, *The English Reformation* (London: 1964), pp. 122–8; A. G. Dickens, 'Secular and Religious Motivation in the Pilgrimage of Grace,' in G. J. Cuming, ed., *Studies in Church History*, IV (Leiden: 1967); C. S. L. Davies, 'The Pilgrimage of Grace reconsidered,' *Past and Present*, 41 (1968); and M. E. James, 'Obedience and dissent in Henrician England: the Lincolnshire rebellion, 1536,' *Past and Present*, 48 (1970).

The second group was capitalist. It was composed of large and not so large landowners, the manufacturers of cloth, and a growing number of urban commercialists, especially wool merchants.[1] The landowners, let them be termed gentry and yeomen, increasingly came to use their land for the production of cattle and, most importantly, wool for sale on domestic and international markets. For this reason, they were likely to resort to enclosure, some, to increase their profits from grazing by restricting peasants from the use of their commons; others, to increase the efficiency of tillage by introducing agricultural improvements. Some of the larger agricultural capitalists had received their lands from the expropriated ecclesiastical property, and hence were loyal to the Crown. Such men played a key role in putting down the regional rebellions mentioned previously. Since the Reformation was, in effect, the harbinger of their newly found fortunes, many in this group were staunch Protestants. The religious affiliation of the manufacturers of woolen cloth, England's most important export, appears to have been more strongly Protestant.

Third, there were the intellectuals, mostly petty benefice holders in the Church; for this group alone matters of Church organization and doctrine were paramount. The clerics felt themselves to be underpaid and otherwise exploited by the ecclesiastical hierarchy, especially by the bishops who held all the power within the Church. For these men the Henrician Reformation had been a reform in name alone, since it left the internal organization of the Church virtually intact, particularly in so far as the power of the bishops was concerned. Hence the militant among them came to champion those forms of Protestantism which were the most radical in *organizational* terms —Calvinism and other types of Puritanism. They sought eradication of the bishops, that is, an end to Episcopacy, and an end to the Crown's use of the church to further its own political goals, as well.

Last, there was the Crown itself, interested, as always, in strengthening its power at the expense of that of any internal rivals. This task

---

[1] This interpretation of the social base of the contending groups in England is partially based on Christopher Hill, 'La révolution anglaise du XVIIe siècle (Essai d'Interprétation),' *Revue Historique*, 221 (1959). The industrial basis for the development of a commercial bourgeoisie is discussed in John U. Nef, *Industry and Government in France and England, 1540–1640* (Ithaca: 1957). Recent research has suggested that none of these groups was as solidary as this brief overview would suggest. Class interests diverged even between the group of London merchants. See Robert Brenner, 'The civil war politics of London's merchant community,' *Past and Present*, 58 (1973).

was made more and more difficult with the precipitous rise in prices. The Crown was forced to hunt for revenues most aggressively, by increasing taxation and by the frequent sale of offices; even then much of its revenue was eaten up by inflation. The revenue-hunger of the Crown was, in itself, a spur to political instability. But even more threatening to the Crown was the developing conflict of interest between the aristocratic and capitalistic landowners. This antagonism between elements of the governing class[1] was basically responsible for the Pilgrimage of Grace and the other regional rebellions of the Tudor period. The Crown apparently wished to avoid open conflict between these groups.[2] Hence it embarked upon ambivalent economic policies which reflected this fence-straddling posture. For instance, under Elizabeth the Crown encouraged the expansion of long-distance trade, and protected native industry. Yet, it ultimately discouraged enclosure and enacted paternalistic welfare legislation, which provided the poor and the evicted with sustenance, thus preventing the development of a free labor market.[3] The ambiguity of the Crown's position was equally evident in its religious policy: under Elizabeth, the Church of England followed a compromise path lying between the demands of the recusants and the Puritans; its adherence to Episcopacy was therefore natural.

But this compromise, like most, could not last forever. As the international economy contracted, the Crown became placed in an increasingly vulnerable position.[4] Even though it ultimately sided with the aristocracy, the Crown's standing among all internal

[1] Perez Zagorin, *The Court and the Country: the Beginning of the English Revolution* (New York: 1970), p. 331.

[2] Here I have relied on the interpretation of Immanuel Wallerstein, *The Modern World-System: Capitalist Agriculture and the Origins of the European World Economy in the Sixteenth Century* (New York and London: 1974), chapter 5.

[3] G. N. Clark summarizes the Tudor economic code in these terms: 'The new legislation accepted and even furthered money economy: it carried forward the limiting of trade, or paying wages in kind. But the general tendency of these enactments was conservative: they aimed at providing an adequate supply of labor first for agriculture, then for the simpler crafts, and at restricting entry into the occupations of higher social standing and into those which were thought to be carried on in unsuitable places ... the Elizabethan code thus aimed at stabilizing the existing class structure, the location of industry and the flow of labour supply by granting privileges and by putting hindrances in the way of mobility and freedom of contract; but it was not the product of a simple doctrinaire economic policy; it reconciled or effected a compromise between conflicting interests.' *The Wealth of England from 1496 to 1760* (London: 1946), pp. 84, 86.

[4] Wallerstein, *op. cit.*

factions eroded and civil war broke out. In this struggle the Crown ultimately relied upon the Celtic fringe to counter Parliament's grip on the majority of Englishmen.

By the end of hostilities in 1688, the capitalist faction of the ruling class had won an important victory.[1] The abolition of feudal tenures and the Court of Wards gave landowners absolute control over their estates, and freed them from dependence upon the Crown. International trade was protected from foreign competition by the establishment of the Navigation Acts; colonial expansion occurred, particularly in India; and England became extensively involved in the slave trade in the new world. In 1641 the central government lost its power to grant monopolies, and to control the administration of poor relief. It also ceased to prohibit the activities of middlemen in industry and agriculture, and London merchants extended their influence throughout the British Isles.

After 1641, the legal monopoly enjoyed by the Established Church, which had previously been a compulsory religious institution, ceased to exist.[2] While Puritanism had initially received much support from the capitalist gentry previous to 1640, the revolutionary temper of the period convinced some of them that Episcopacy, and the monarchy which this implied, was essential to maintain the social order. The Church of England ultimately remained episcopal in form.

If this were the situation in England, things were very different in the Celtic fringe. In these territories there existed no group comparable in strength to the export merchants, wool manufacturers, and capitalist agriculturalists of England. This meant that Wales, Ireland and Scotland all ultimately favored the King as against Parliament during the English revolution. Indeed, the King made special appeals in the Celtic lands to enlist such support. None the less, significant religious differences emerged between the Celtic lands after 1688: Wales accepted Episcopalianism, at least until 1800; Ireland remained Catholic, except in the north; and Scotland emerged with an established Presbyterian church.

Wales was hardly affected by the Henrician Reformation at all; during this period it was among the most docile regions of the British Isles. In so far as popular religious sentiment is concerned, this was undoubtedly the result of the extreme remoteness of the Welsh Church from the lives of the people. The Welsh bishoprics

[1] Hill, *Reformation to Industrial Revolution, op. cit.* pp. 115–16.
[2] *Ibid.*, p. 152.

were very poor and tended to be regarded as stepping stones to more powerful offices elsewhere by those appointed to them.[1] Most of these appointees were English, and they developed little sympathy with the monoglot Welsh clergy.[2] There was, consequently, much absenteeism—a theme which will recur in the following section of this chapter—and resultant neglect. Bishops farmed their dioceses out to others in return for a fixed stipend: one such man had not visited his own diocese in fourteen years. Though the majority of lower clergy were native Welshmen, these priests exploited their benefices as capably as their English superiors: corruption existed up and down the line. Under these circumstances, it is difficult to imagine that the nationalization of the church would cause much popular concern one way or the other. So Wales, as a whole, followed the tortuous path of the Church of England in its zig-zag journey between Catholicism and Puritanism with relative equanimity.

But it is also abundantly clear that reactions to the Reformation need not have been made solely on religious grounds. Probably, the bulk of the population of England cannot have been terribly concerned by the changes within the Church either; yet soon after the Reformation the English countryside was alive with rebellion. Why was there so little resistance to the Reformation in Wales? There appear to be several reasons for this. The destruction of the power of the Marcher Lords, occurring after political incorporation, removed an entire aristocratic class, which would likely have been rebellious and thereby Catholic, from the Welsh scene.[3] This left the gentry as the only politically conscious and articulate class; its loyalty obviously extended to the Crown, since these individuals owed their social elevation to the king. Furthermore, the fact that Henry VIII allocated the confiscated lands to native Welshmen rather than to Englishmen, as was the case in Cornwall,[4] precluded cleavage along cultural lines. The decision to keep the land in the hands of native Welshmen might have been a consequence of Henry's own Welsh origins. This beneficence was repaid a century later in the Revolution when Wales solidly backed the forces of the Crown.

[1] David Williams, *A History of Modern Wales* (London: 1950), p. 49.

[2] One such appointee, Athequa, who became bishop of Llandaff, did not even speak a word of English, a disability, it is true, which he shared with most of the people of his diocese,' *ibid.*

[3] Glanmor Williams, *The Welsh Church from Conquest to Reformation* (Cardiff: 1962), pp. 555–8.

[4] A. L. Rowse, *Tudor Cornwall* (London: 1969), pp. 130–1.

And David Williams explains, 'In Wales there were very few of the "middle sort of men"; the whole trend of the previous century had been towards the rise of the gentry and the consolidation of their estates.'[1] Since the conquest of Wales by England had preceded the Reformation, religion did not immediately become a symbol of Welsh resistance to English domination, as it did both in Ireland and Scotland, until the nineteenth century, when Wales became largely Nonconformist.

While Henry VIII had managed to conquer Wales during the early part of his reign, his designs on Ireland and Scotland were not to be fully realized. Henry claimed the kingship of Ireland, imposed the Reformation, and began a system of government asserting royal supremacy, which was mediated by English deputies. However, recognizing the Crown's weakness in Ireland, Henry attempted to bring both the Anglo-Norman Lords (termed the Old English, and the structural equivalent of the Welsh Marcher Lords), and the native Irish chieftains under his authority by extending to them unlimited autonomy, in return for their pledge of fealty to the Crown. This policy was called 'surrender and regrant,' and it provided Henry with but hollow authority. However, Tudor policy was probably designed for the safety of England rather than the exploitation of Ireland.[2]

The religious changes occurring within the Church of England did not even cause much dissent in Ireland. Neither bishops nor laymen resisted the declaration of royal supremacy over the Church. While the moves towards Puritan doctrine in the reign of Edward VI were unpopular, no serious attempt was made to enforce Irish conformity. During Elizabeth's rule, the bulk of the Anglo-Norman recusants were loyal to the Crown despite their Catholicism. Thus, they were hardly different, in this regard, from their aristocratic counterparts in the north and west country of England—except, perhaps, even more loyal.

But Ireland's geographical situation made it an increasingly sensitive area to the Crown, in a period when armed confrontation with Catholic Spain seemed inevitable. To forestall native Irish collaboration with the Spanish, Elizabeth took measures to tighten royal control in Ireland.[3] Among these was the establishment of an English plantation at Munster (1583), upon lands which had been

---

[1] David Williams, *op. cit.*, p. 95.
[2] Beckett, *op. cit.*, p. 13.
[3] D. B. Quinn, *The Elizabethans and the Irish* (Ithaca: 1966).

expropriated from the native Irish. This naturally caused much resentment and a rebellion soon broke out there, to be defeated by Crown forces in 1585. In that year also the Crown instituted the shire system of government, thereby dividing Ireland into counties. What Elizabeth had begun in a piecemeal fashion James I continued more systematically, by creating a vast plantation in Ulster (1608), which was settled by English and Scottish Protestant colonists on lands confiscated from the native Irish chieftains.[1]

Thus, there were three types of groups which could be mobilized for political action in Stuart Ireland: the native Irish, many of whom had become landless in the face of English confiscation, and who had remained Catholic; the Anglo-Norman aristocracy, also Catholic, but in possession of 60 per cent of Irish land in 1641; and the settlers of the Londonderry Plantation, many of whom were Scottish Presbyterians. This social heterogeneity lent extreme complexity to the political situation on the eve of the English Revolution.

Paradoxically, the Crown's initial fear was caused by the Ulster Scots in 1638–9, sympathizers with the Presbyterian militants of their homeland, who sent an army into England to overthrow Charles I. Meanwhile, both Catholic groups were pressing for religious liberty, and an end to increasing interference by the Crown in their local affairs. In 1641, a group of native Irish in Ulster rebelled, and Ireland was soon plunged into civil war. Peace, of a sort, came with the victory of Cromwell's army in 1649.

It was not until the Cromwellian Settlement that religious difference came to be the dominant political cleavage in Irish society. Cromwell's policies towards the adherents of Catholicism were harsh. For a time Catholic clergy were killed whenever they could be found. Of more lasting import, Catholic landowners, of either Anglo-Norman or Irish descent, were very largely stripped of their land; this expropriated land was then used as payment for Cromwell's military lieutenants in the Irish campaign. By 1688 nearly 80 per cent of Irish land was in the hands of Englishmen and Scottish Protestants.[2] In 1685, Catholic political fortunes seemed to make a recovery;[3] however, six years later, their hopes for power were crushed. After 1691, Catholics were denied political influence, were deprived control of trade, were excluded from the Parliament

[1] T. W. Moody, *The Londonderry Plantation, 1609–1641* (Belfast: 1939).
[2] Karl S. Bottigheimer, *English Money and Irish Land: the 'Adventurers' in the Cromwellian Settlement of Ireland* (Oxford: 1971).
[3] J. G. Simms, *Jacobite Ireland, 1685–91* (London: 1969).

and soon thereafter became subject to the Penal Laws.[1] Adherence to Catholicism had, by this time, become synonomous with resistance to Cromwell's imposition of an English Protestant ruling class on the island.

England and Scotland were the only parts of the British Isles to develop their own Reformations. If events during this period appear in a somewhat murky light in England, in Scotland they seem even more obscure. However, one significant pattern emerges clearly enough. The Scottish Reformation was carried out mainly with the support of the very same type of group which, in England, largely fought to reinstate Catholicism: the non-capitalist aristocracy.[2] This fact alone might dispel speculation about the existence of any inherent relationship between Protestantism and capitalism.[3]

In seeking to incorporate Scotland, unlike Wales or Ireland, Henry VIII had to deal with an independent, if relatively weak, state having several continental connections. His first task was to provide for a marriage between his infant son and heir Prince Edward and the young Queen of the Scots, Mary. The Scottish Parliament saw in this plan, however, a bald attempt toward an English annexation of Scotland; therefore, it was rebuffed. But England's designs on Scotland were not to be so easily dissuaded. Both Henry and his *de facto* successor Protector Somerset carried out military expeditions to subdue the Scots. In the late 1540s, English armies laid waste to the southern Scottish burghs, and, in the process, drove Scotland into a defensive alliance with France. In 1548, France offered military assistance to repel the English invaders, but this was only available at a price: the Scots had to consent to Queen Mary's residence in France and her eventual marriage to the Dauphin. This offer was accepted by Parliament, and soon Scotland became ruled in the interests of France by the Queen Mother, Mary of Guise, in 1554.

Under the rule of Mary of Guise, Frenchmen immediately began to assume high office in the Scottish government, much to the dis-

[1] Maureen Wall, *The Penal Laws, 1691–1760* (Dundalk: 1961).

[2] As I. F. Grant has put it, the Reformation was 'monarchical in England and baronial in Scotland.' *Op. cit.*, p. 234.

[3] It appears that the Polish aristocracy similarly supported a Calvinist Reformation in its initial stages. See Stefan Czarnowski, 'La réaction catholique en Pologne à la fin du XVIe siècle et au début du XVIIe siècle,' *La Pologne au VIIe Congrès International des Sciences Historiques*, vol. II (Warsaw: 1933). This article is discussed at some length in Wallerstein, *op. cit.*, chapter 3. See also H. R. Trevor-Roper, 'Religion, the reformation and social change,' *Historical Studies*, 4 (1961).

pleasure of native Scots.[1] It soon became evident that Scotland had traded a potential dependence upon England for an actual dependence upon France. There were Anglophile as well as Francophile elements within Scottish society, and, ultimately, the Scottish Reformation represented a victory for Anglophiles over Francophiles. But the reasons for this victory are especially illuminating in the light of the English experience.

Patterns of Scottish foreign trade may well provide part of the explanation. In the sixteenth century, Scotland was largely engaged in trade with France, the Flemings, England, the Baltic, and Sweden.[2] The relatively important French trade consisted of an exchange of Scottish fish, skins, wool and cloth for French wine. However, it appears that the terms of trade with France were tending to move against Scotland in this period.[3] Simultaneously, Scotland's trade with England was much more extensive than it has previously been supposed.[4] It is possible that England may have appeared a more attractive trading partner for Scotland, in the long run. A Protestant Scotland, it was reasoned, would also reduce the likelihood of persisting English invasion, and thereby increase the security and prosperity of the southern burghs.[5] Finally, the Scottish lower clergy stood to gain power within a reformed ecclesiastical administration, as did their counterparts in England.

But most important of all, the Scottish Reformation represented a triumph for the old landed aristocracy over the encroaching power of the Crown, and, in this way, it was exactly the opposite of the English Reformation. In England, the Crown had succeeded in crushing much of the power of the old aristocracy, in part, by appropriating Church property and parcelling it out to its supporters. But the Scottish Crown did not require a Reformation for this purpose. Indeed, after losing England to Protestantism, the Pope immediately placed the bulk of the wealth of the Scottish Church in the hands of the Crown so that the monarchy might prosper and remain Catholic, as well.[6] Using this bounty, the Scottish Crown attempted to duplicate the success of the Tudors. It treated the abbeys as part

[1] Donaldson, *op. cit.*, pp. 55–7, 86.
[2] Lythe, *op. cit.*; J. Dow, 'Scottish trade with Sweden, 1512–1580,' *Scottish History Review*, 48, 1 (1969); J. Dow, 'Scottish trade with Sweden, 1580–1622,' *Scottish History Review*, 48, 2 (1969).
[3] Lythe, *op. cit.*, p. 186.
[4] Devine and Lythe, *op. cit.*, p. 102.
[5] Gordon Donaldson, *The Scottish Reformation* (Cambridge: 1960), p. 46.
[6] *Ibid.*, pp. 37–9.

of its own patrimony, and assigned the revenues of bishops to those laymen it chose to nominate. This patronage had occurred at the expense of the ecclesiastical officials. But the consolidation of power in the hands of the Crown was resisted by precisely the same forces which rebelled against Tudor political centralization: that is, the large, and previously autonomous, aristocratic magnates. However, in England since the Crown was Protestant, the rebels found it convenient to remain Catholic. The scenario in Scotland on the other hand was directly reversed: there, a Catholic Crown attempting political centralization faced its challenge from a nobility which had, since French domination, assumed the mantle of Protestantism. It is the same play with only the labels changed. In England, the Crown triumphed, and with it the Reformation persisted; in Scotland the Crown lost, and with it the Reformation occurred.

The success of the Reformation in England and Scotland makes it appear as if the social structures of these two societies had much in common in the sixteenth century, but this impression is largely illusory. In reality, already by the sixteenth century, it is the social structural differences between England and Scotland which have become decisive.[1] The strength of the forces contending for power in each society differed markedly. Political centralization was made possible in England because the Crown, which was itself relatively strong, had the initial support of the indigenous capitalist groups. These elements, capitalist agriculturalists and commercialists in the cities, enabled the Crown to withstand severe challenges to its authority such as those represented by events like the Pilgrimage of Grace. But it was precisely the relative weakness, if not the virtual absence, of comparable capitalist elements within Scotland which sealed the fortunes of the more feeble Scottish Crown.

However, in Scotland as in England, the resolution of this struggle was not to be decided that quickly. When the Scottish Parliament proclaimed its adherence to Protestantism in 1560, upon the death of Mary of Guise, the Crown held out for Episcopacy thereafter, so that it might continue to extend its influence through the bishops. This displeased both the nobility and the clerical intelligentsia, and many within each group embraced the principles of Presbyterianism. For the nobility, Presbyterianism would serve to check the power of

---

[1] The basic structural difference is that England alone was involved in relatively diversified production. None of the Celtic lands could boast of a textile industry to compare with that of England; these textiles were England's primary export. See Nef, *op. cit.* and the previous section of this chapter.

the Scottish Crown by eliminating the existence of bishops. Presbyterian sentiment grew everywhere in Scotland but in the highlands and the northeast. The highlands were infiltrated by Jesuit missionaries from France, perhaps in preparation for an assault on the Protestant monarchy (the last assault ultimately occurred in 1745). The northeast was strongly Episcopal: this may be because it was among the most commercial of regions.[1] According to the logic of the argument concerning Scottish religious affiliation developed above, is it not likely that those Scots most involved in capitalist activities in this period would have adopted the Episcopal religion?

Charles I's plans to restore the old ecclesiastical offices and revenues to the reformed church (1625–35) incensed the Scottish nobility. This antagonism was compounded by their growing perception that the London-based King had become insensitive to their needs and interests.[2] As it happens, a Scottish army was responsible for the onset of the English Revolution. It was sent to England in hopes of toppling the Episcopal régime of Charles I, thereby instituting Presbyterianism in both lands. This army succeeded in its first task but was not so fortunate in its second. Although there was some support in the English Parliament for Presbyterianism, power passed to Cromwell's New Model Army, which was Independent in its religion. During the early stages of the Revolution both English parties appealed for Scottish support. Initially, the Scottish Parliament lent its aid to the forces of its English counterpart. But as the reforms under Cromwell proceeded, Parliament came to regard the régime with fear: after all, the social base of Scottish Presbyterianism was aristocratic. Ultimately, the Scots rejected Cromwell, and installed Charles II as their King, once he had promised to establish the Presbyterian church within Scotland. Charles II's newly acquired base caused Cromwell to invade Scotland.

Hence, in the end, Scotland came to align itself with English royalism, as did the other parts of the Celtic fringe. Appearances notwithstanding, Scotland was structurally much more similar to Wales and Scotland than to England, which alone of the British lands had elevated Cromwell to power.

The effects of the Cromwellian conquest in Scotland were far more benign than in Ireland. Scotland remained occupied by an English standing army which, following a rebellion in 1653, was increased to a total of 18,000 troops. However, Cromwell also

[1] Grant, *op. cit.*, p. 340.
[2] Donaldson, *Scotland: James V to James VII*, p. 300.

instituted reforms which might be conceived to be 'liberating.'[1] Those nobles who had supported military engagement with England forfeited their estates.[2] Cromwell abolished the baronial courts (1654), and in general attempted to break the power of the great magnates by weakening the legal basis of feudal ties. It is, however, unlikely that this goal was substantially reached. Cromwell himself believed that the 'middle sort of people' prospered under his rule,[3] but economic conditions were so unsettled that it is difficult to argue that any group really prospered.

In the years after Restoration, the Catholicism of James VII was resisted almost as much in Scotland as it was in England. The most militant opposition to the Stuart king was from the southwestern counties, traditionally Presbyterian and where there was a large concentration of lesser lairds, who could ill afford paying heavy tithes to any church.[4] Support for James VII, which came to be known as Jacobitism, was confined to the highlands. Political conflict between highland and lowland Scotland, temporarily abated during the period of mutual hostility to French domination, began to re-emerge. This conflict was to be intensified after the Union of 1707. When William of Orange assumed the English crown in 1688, the Scottish Parliament would accept his rule only if a Presbyterian church were to be established there. This was accomplished in 1690.

But it is a mistake to assume that the religious boundaries remained constant in the British Isles after 1690. Following the tumultuous events of the Reformation and the English Revolution, a permanence of religious identification was achieved only in Ireland. There, the Protestant ascendancy, installed by Cromwell, ruled over a population which became ever more self-consciously and militantly Catholic, except in the Protestant-dominated north. The religious composition of the two parts of Ireland has not substantially changed: it is, of course, no accident that the residents of the Shankill Road remember the Battle of the Boyne (1690) to this very day. But religious affiliation continued to shift everywhere else, with great attendant political significance. In England Nonconformity was stimulated by industrialization, while in Wales a different type of religious dissent developed around the symbol of Welsh nationhood

---

[1] Hill, *Reformation to Industrial Revolution*, p. 132.
[2] Donaldson, *Scotland: James V to James VII*, p. 349.
[3] *Ibid.*, pp. 351–2.
[4] Cf. Smout, *op. cit.*, p. 61. Very few Scottish historians have discussed the possibility that social structural distinctiveness in the southwest counties might account for their religious fervor in this period.

in the late eighteenth and early nineteenth century. Finally, in Scotland, religious conflict between the Established Church and the Free Church persisted until 1931; virile antagonism to Irish Catholics is still pervasive there.

THE CULTURAL CONSEQUENCES OF INCORPORATION

Upon their incorporation, the culture of the Celtic lands systematically differed from English culture in several respects. Language and religion were the most visible of these *differentiae*. All of sixteenth-century England, save parts of Cornwall, was English-speaking, but in Wales, highland Scotland, and parts of Ireland the population spoke Celtic languages, Welsh and two Gaelic dialects. In England, Henry VIII had established an Episcopal state church, but the dominant religions of Scotland and Ireland were Presbyterian and Roman Catholic, respectively.

If political incorporation resulted in peripheral economic dependence, it simultaneously gave English cultural forms superordinate status within the societies of the Celtic fringe. Indigenous élites in these regions who sought the increased opportunities afforded by Union began to assimilate by learning the English language, by practicing the Anglican religion, and by intermarriage. But the bulk of the inhabitants of the periphery kept to cultural forms which were non-English.

As the cultural differences between groups in the peripheral regions widened, antagonism between tenants and landlords was correspondingly stimulated. In certain situations, the maintenance of peripheral culture came to be regarded as a threat by the English state as well as by the anglicized peripheral élites. Violence was by no means eschewed on either side. Attempts to forcibly assimilate the population of Celtic fringe significantly raised the level of class conflict in the countryside.

The progress of anglicization

As has been previously related, the Crown attempted to promote English values, religion and language in the Celtic lands to preclude the possibility of regional threats to its hegemony. By and large, its policies were coercive and did not meet with much success. In good part this is due to the spirit with which anglicization proceeded, which forced the individual Celt to admit his cultural inferiority and

109

adopt a more civilized culture. At the same time, few efforts were made by London to insure widespread assimilation by extending ecclesiastical influence or public education to the masses in the periphery. For instance, despite the publication of a Welsh translation of the Bible in 1588,[1] services in the Anglican Church of Wales continued to be given in English. The Calvinistic Methodists were the first sect to preach to the Welsh in their native language. Similarly, when Sunday schools were first set up to teach the poor in Welsh it was the Methodists and not the Anglicans who provided them. In Ireland, most of the effort at anglicization was spent in punishing those who persisted in their Catholicism and Gaelic speaking, rather than in offering these individuals incentives to adopt new cultural forms.

However, one group in the Celtic fringe did not have to be forced, let alone encouraged to adopt the ways and manners of the English; I am referring to the gentry. Among this class were many who obtained wealth and pretension sufficient to consider themselves upper-class Britons; they went to great lengths to dissociate themselves from their rude and barbaric countrymen.

In Wales, the Act of Union had enabled wealthier and more enterprising families to gain great wealth and power by scrambling for spoils after the dissolution of the monasteries, or by becoming representatives in Parliament or office-holders in the government or Church. The removal of the restrictions against Welsh participation in municipal commerce also allowed some Welshmen to accumulate large amounts of capital, which they then invested in land. The illegality and consequent disappearance of *gavelkind*, and its replacement by primogeniture, led to much consolidation of estates in the hands of the wealthy. As a result of these and other statutory changes, the Welsh gentry could acquire much land from the peasants by chicanery in the great confusion of the time. The expansion of foreign commerce under Elizabeth provided an outlet for the younger sons of the gentry to make their fortunes once primogeniture was in effect.[2]

In the late sixteenth century, the gentry showed a tendency to become anglicized in speech, though this was a slow and informal development. Some married Englishwomen; some Welsh heiresses

---

[1] Since most pre-industrial literature was religious, the existence of a Welsh translation of the Scriptures may well have been responsible for the development of Welsh as a literary language.
[2] David Williams, *op. cit.*, p. 85.

married Englishmen, and through these initial contacts the language was passed. As the anglicization of the gentry proceeded, the services of the bards, who had provided a Welsh education in the oral tradition, were no longer required. Furthermore, since the dissolution of the monasteries formal educational institutions had ceased to exist in Wales. Consequently, the gentry began to send their sons off to English schools.[1] Jesus College at Oxford was established in 1571, largely for Welsh students. In later times the lesser gentry sent their sons to the grammar schools of the Principality, which were English in tone, and they, too, ceased to cultivate their native language.

By 1640, the anglicization of the Welsh gentry had reached its final stages.[2] David Williams has aptly summarized some of its consequences:[3]

Thus came about the dichotomy which has marred so much of Welsh life. On the one hand was the Welsh-speaking peasantry, inarticulate but for its bards, who themselves became few through lack of patrons. On the other hand, were the 'natural leaders' of the people who became English in speech, and to this difference in class and in speech there was added, in succeeding centuries, a difference in religion. The position in Wales came to that in Ireland, except that the Welsh gentry were of the same race as their tenantry whereas in Ireland they were of English descent.

Previous to the Revolution, the English state may not have been particularly ill-disposed to Welsh culture, merely indifferent to it. Perhaps this moderate attitude may be explained by the Welsh origins of the Tudor line. It has been noted that the Welsh language was in use in the courts of Wales following the Union.[4] But I think the reason behind this relative cultural tolerance lies elsewhere. England did not seriously attempt to bring the Celtic territories into its geographical division of labor until the seventeenth century. The Cromwellian armies fought for an ideological purpose as well as a strictly military one: to carry the light of English values to the dark corners of the land. English antipathy to the cultures of the Celtic

---

[1] Here is an excerpt from a letter written by a gentleman of Anglesey to his nephew in London during the seventeenth century: 'We heare in Anglesey good commendation of the gentleman you live with and by followinge and observinge of him you may gaine learning, knowledge and experience, for in England curtisie, humanite and civillite doth abound with generosite as far as uncivilitie doth exceed in Wales.' From a manuscript in the University College of North Wales Library, cited by W. Ogwen Williams, 'The survival of the Welsh language after the union of England and Wales: the first phase, 1536–1642,' *Welsh History Review*, 2, 1 (1964), p. 68.

[2] *Ibid.*, p. 86.

[3] David Williams, *op. cit.*, p. 89.

[4] Ogwen Williams, *op. cit.*, p. 73.

fringe developed increasingly in the eighteenth and nineteenth centuries.

The progress of anglicization was entirely different in Scotland in that it was carried out extensively by lowland Scots who received, to be sure, considerable help from the government in London. The cultural origins of the lowland Scots are shrouded in obscurity. One plausible hypothesis is that late in the tenth or early in the eleventh centuries English lands between the Forth and the Tweed, then known as Lothian, became part of the Scottish Kingdom.[1] They had once been part of the northernmost English principality of Northumbria, thoroughly English, and quite distinct from the Celtic and Norse amalgams of northern Scotland. The attachment of this new province, reasonably prosperous, and closely allied in culture and institutions to the English Kingdom, permanently shifted the center of power in Scotland from north to south, and ultimately changed the character of the Kingdom. From then on there ensued sporadic conflict between highlanders and lowlanders.

By the time of the Union, the lowlanders had much in common with their English neighbors to the south. They shared virtually the same language; were Protestant—though many were not Episcopalian; did not live in clans; engaged in extensive tillage; were highly literate; and had many of the other trappings of relatively complex agricultural societies. Unlike the Welsh or Irish, the Scots had developed a political administration with a king who, in theory, commanded the obedience of all Scots; a Parliament, with an attendant legal establishment; and a state Church. Scotland was therefore a fully developed state on the European stage, rather than a mere backwater. Even so, the Scottish kings had never been able to exercise effective administration in the highlands, which were Catholic or Episcopalian in religion; Gaelic in speech; and Celtic in social organization. Bands of highlanders continued to sweep into lowland farms to plunder cattle and other livestock, much as the Welsh had done in England in the sixteenth century. The last pitched battle among highland clans took place in 1680, but the highland plunder of the lowlands continued well beyond this date. The Union of 1707 gave the English government ultimate responsibility for the maintenance of law and order everywhere in Scotland, including the highlands. Dissent in the highlands soon became an English headache: 'From the point of view of London, the main problem (in the highlands) was the Jacobites, whose strongholds in

[1] Christopher Brooke, *From Alfred to Henry III* (New York: 1961), p. 198.

the hills beyond the Tay might yet have proved the Achilles heel of the whole British Protestant establishment.'[1] English fears were heightened by the Civil War in 1689 and the two Highland Risings in 1715 and 1745. There were also abortive attempts at rebellion in 1708 and 1719. Clearly the highlands would have to be controlled. Though this was the golden age of patronage in English administration 'there was not enough of this available for chiefs and leaders who were thinking of abandoning Jacobitism.'[2] What else could be done? To neutralize further disruption in the highlands, the government adopted a three-pronged strategy. First, it aided the Campbell clan's aggrandizement of smaller clans' territories, driving a wedge to any possible highland solidarity. Second, it attempted to 'alter the Highland character by making the clansmen industrious and godly.' Third, it maintained a large standing army in the north, capable of fast movement. Road-building into the highlands was begun to facilitate military mobilization.

The Scottish Society for the Propagation of Christian Knowledge was founded in 1709. Its members decided that 'nothing can be more effectual for reducing these counties to order and making them useful to the Commonwealth than teaching them their duty to God, their King and Country, and rooting out their Irish language.'[3] To this end the SSPCK founded schools in the highlands 'where religion and virtue might be taught to young and old.'

But these efforts were to no avail; a Jacobite rebellion broke out, and was put down in 1745 by an English army having many lowland Scotland troops. The final battle of Culloden was a rout, but the English and Scottish lowlanders pushed on into Inverness, the highland capital, and attacked women and children indiscriminately. Highland troops in prison were tortured so as to provide an example to discourage further rebellion. This participation of lowlanders in the dismemberment of highland society probably marks the nadir of Scottish national unity. After the debacle the government deprived rebel chiefs of their lands, and placed the administration of the alienated property in the control of a committee dominated by Edinburgh lawyers. T. C. Smout describes them: 'Though not in any way vindictive they worked on the assumption that Highland

---

[1] Smout, *op. cit.*, p. 222.
[2] Rosalind Mitchison, 'The Government and the Highlands, 1707–1745' in N. T. Phillipson and Rosalind Mitchison, eds, *Scotland in the Age of Improvement* (Edinburgh: 1970), p. 28. [3] Smout, *op. cit.*, pp. 461–3.

peasants were ignorant, idle, and culturally savage, and they there-fore strove to do all they could to eliminate the mores of the clan.'[1] Clansmen, with the exception of cattle drovers, were forbidden to carry arms, wear the traditional kilt, or play the bagpipes, which were considered potentially subversive and military. Further efforts were made to develop road systems into the highlands.

What caused élites in the periphery to suddenly manifest such concern for the spiritual health of the backward highlanders? In this context, it must be recognized that England served as the major source of capital for investment, and of the extension of credit in the British Isles. Since London had traditionally been the center for all British commercial transaction, its influence as a supplier of investment capital cannot be overemphasized. The political sig-nificance of cultural identification was simple. It is evident that both individual and institutional lenders were willing to invest in the Celtic territories only to the extent they could be assured of con-tinuing political stability in the area. This gave élites in the Celtic fringe a mandate to put their house in order, if they desired to attract English capital. The implications of this investment policy were already clear during the Union with Wales:[2]

The Act of Union of 1536 uniting Wales and England under a common constitution, marked a new stage in Welsh mining. Hitherto the Crown could exercise its right over minerals in Wales only within its own lordships. The Union, however, brought Wales for the first time within the English legal system and extended the prerogative of the Crown over mines Royal —gold, silver, copper and quicksilver—from the more restricted area of the Principality of North and West Wales, to the whole of Wales, this at a critical time in the quest for metals in the national interest, a factor not unimportant in the policy of the Crown in bringing about the Union at this date. The opportunities now presenting themselves for the investment of English capital in Wales and the greater security for the same within the law, . . . had an almost immediate effect on mining in Wales.

England's concern to achieve social control in peripheral regions sometimes had positive consequences. In Ireland, the Union served to protect English investment by taking the administration of the island out of the hands of the often politically intransigent English Protestant landowners, and by placing it in London, where there was a more realistic awareness of the necessity of Catholic emancipa-tion as a minimal concession to realize political stability.

[1] Smout, op. cit., p. 343.
[2] William Rees, Industry Before the Industrial Revolution (Cardiff: 1968) pp. 247–8.

But in Scotland the story is far less pleasant. While some low-landers may have been motivated by altruistic sentiments in their efforts to promote anglicization in the highlands, it is evident that many others desired internal peace so as to attract English capital to Scotland for investment:[1]

A further reason for suppressing Jacobite risings, and cementing the Union (note the action of the lowland Scots against Jacobites in the Battle of Culloden) was to convince English investors that the political climate was safe for their profits. And capital investment from England did not flow to Scotland until well after Union, when such assurances were made.

This provides an explicit link between England's supply of credit and the progress of anglicization in the peripheral regions.

In Scotland, alone, the English had local allies in this process of cultural pacification. When seen from this perspective, England's grant of relative cultural autonomy to Scotland following the Union can be easily understood. In effect, there had already been a large enclave in Scottish society which had only marginal differences from the English. This enclave was ethnically similar to northern England, it was Protestant, and equally anti-Catholic; it could be relied upon to perform much of the dangerous task of controlling and anglicizing the rebellious highlanders. Therefore, it was politically feasible to allow incorporated Scotland its own, autonomous, Church and legal system. The Crown had no comparable allies either in Wales or Ireland.

This is not to argue that the relatively smaller cultural differences between the lowland Scots and the English did not become socially meaningful at a later period. Just as the Union in Wales permitted the local gentry entry into the higher layers of English society, with its greater resources and prestige, similar opportunities arose for the Scottish élite. Some time after Union, various social pressures favoring anglicization acted upon the Scottish gentry. Though English long had been spoken in the lowlands, it was a heavily accented dialect with a distinctively regional flavor. Educated Scots began to be concerned with eliminating obvious Scotticisms in speech and writing. The Scottish lawyers had much difficulty in being understood in the House of Lords. The adjective 'Scottish' tended to be used as a synonym for rudeness in England, and the leading sectors of Scottish society hastened to educate their children south of the

[1] R. H. Campbell, 'The Anglo-Scottish Union of 1707: the economic consequences, II,' *Economic History Review*, 2nd ser., 16, 3 (1964), pp. 475–6.

Tweed so they might pass as Englishmen. In the 1750s textbooks appeared which enabled English to be taught to Scots as if it were a foreign language. Elocutionists visited Edinburgh to give lessons in English pronunciation. English education opened the possibility of a career in England, which was highly significant since employment opportunities were limited in Scotland. As the civil service expanded, particularly in the colonization and administration of India, English education was a definite advantage in enabling a candidate to pass the examination procedure.[1]

By the mid-nineteenth century there arose strong arguments for educational reform. Some Scots wondered why it was necessary to send their sons to England for an education when it was possible to bring the quality and philosophy of the English universities to Scotland. Ranged against this position were traditionalists centered in Edinburgh who clung to the separate cultural heritage of Scotland, and feared that this institutional anglicization would lead to a general belief in the beneficence of anglicization for its own sake. These literary traditionalists provided the basis for a crystallization of Scottish national sentiment. Thus, really for the first time, the concept of a united Scotland—highlander and lowlander, Gael and English-speaker—began to emerge in the 1850s, facilitated by the widespread evidence of increased anglicization plus English attitudes towards the backwardness of Scotland.

In Ireland, the gentry installed by the Cromwellian Settlement were, for the most part, of English origin to begin with. Much conflict focused on the problem of absentee ownership which had become aggravated after Union. In many respects, the 'Irish problem' came to be associated precisely with the widening extent of this absentee ownership, which was popularly thought to have disastrous social consequences. In particular, it was thought to deprive the barbaric Irish peasants from the 'moral benefits' resulting from the residence of their local gentry, thus sharply polarizing the rural stratification system, and contributing to the predictability of discontent and rebellion.

It is possible to extend this argument about absenteeism somewhat metaphorically. The whole process of anglicization can be seen as a progressive estrangement of the gentry from their customary tenants in each of the Celtic lands. This is similar to what Tocqueville termed 'spiritual estrangement' in his discussion of the social consequences of the cosmopolitanization of the gentry in pre-Revolu-

[1] H. J. Hanham, *Scottish Nationalism* (London: 1969), pp. 34–5.

tionary France.[1] Although there was little actual physical removal from the land, anglicization clearly involved a certain effort at mental separation of landlord and tenant. The conscious rationale behind anglicization among the peripheral élite was to dissociate themselves as much as possible from the mass of their countrymen, who were so strongly deprecated by the English culture. Thus, they eagerly learned to speak English in the home, to emulate English manners and attitudes, to style their very lives on the English model. In effect, this was a voluntary renunciation of their national origins.

Associated with spiritual estrangement, in Tocqueville's view, was the tendency for the landlord to begin to objectify his relationship with his tenants. The intimate, if still sometimes conflictful, bonds between landlord and tenant, which were a carryover from the feudal web of mutual obligation, became much more instrumental.[2] The landlord began to think of his socially unacceptable tenants as mere rent-payers. He tended to exact as much as he could from them, either by law or customary right. The result was that the collection of such feudal dues as still existed was apt to seem even more galling to the peasants than it had been in the heyday of feudalism. Under these circumstances, peasants were likely to resist making agricultural improvements. Tocqueville quotes Montesquieu: 'The soil produces less by reason of its natural fertility than because the people tilling it are free.' In sum, the peasants became even more isolated from gentry and bourgeoisie than they were in their previous feudal station. The rural class structure was substantially widened. The peasants lost any remaining stake in the maintenance of the social system. Hence, there followed the extensive rural discontent which helped fuse the French Revolution.

As Tocqueville has argued, political instability may indeed result from the institutionalization of *rentier* capitalism.[3] But if this is a convincing hypothesis in the French case, it must be amended in the case of Britain, since there the peripheral élite was attracted not only

[1] Alexis de Tocqueville, *The Old Regime and the French Revolution* (New York: 1955), part II, chapter 12.
[2] See, for example, E. P. Thompson, 'The moral economy of the English crowd in the eighteenth century,' *Past and Present*, 50 (1971); Louise A. Tilly, 'The food riot as a form of political conflict in France,' *Journal of Interdisciplinary History*, 2 (1971); E. J. Hobsbawm and George Rudé, *Captain Swing* (New York: 1968), part 1; and Elizabeth F. Genovese, 'The many faces of moral economy: a contribution to a debate,' *Past and Present*, 58 (1973).
[3] A similar argument is presented by Arthur Stinchcombe, 'Agricultural enterprise and rural class relations,' *American Journal of Sociology*, 67, 2 (1961), p. 171.

to a cosmopolitan ideal, but an English, and therefore culturally alien ideal, as well.[1] It is evident that the anglicization of the Celtic upper strata, made possible by the incorporation of the periphery into the core state, had profound social effects in the Celtic countryside. The comparison with England along this dimension was marked. 'There was in England no social or religious barrier between landlord and tenant, between large landowner and small, such as there was in Wales and Scotland, so that tenants, however well-to-do, consciously looked to their landlords for political guidance, and almost invariably accepted it when offered.'[2]

It was this cultural barrier which was largely responsible for the different types of rural class relations in England and the Celtic fringe. There were few structural differences between English and Celtic agriculture by the nineteenth century. Following incorporation there were no major English–Celtic variations in either systems of land-tenure (save in Ireland), or in methods of agricultural production, ecological differences aside. The existing evidence also reveals no significant difference in the concentration of landowning, at

[1] Tocqueville was quite sensitive to the implications of this difference. In another work, he refers specifically to Ireland as an example of the most pernicious form of aristocratic domination: 'Imagine an aristocracy that was established by a conquest at a time so recent that the memory and the traces of the event were present in all minds. Place the conquest in a century when the conqueror already had almost all the lights of civilisation and the vanquished was still in a state of half savagery, so that both in moral power and in intelligence the conqueror was as far as possible superior to the conquered. Give to these two, who are already so dissimilar and unequal, a different religion, so that the nobility not only distrusts the people, but also hates them, and the people not only hates the nobles but damns them. Far from giving the aristocracy so constituted any particular reason to unite itself with the people, give it a particular reason not to unite with the people in order to remain similar to the nation whence it came, from which it still draws all its strength, and to resemble which is its pride. Instead of giving it a reason to take care of the people, give it a special motive to oppress them, by placing its trust in this foreign support which provides that it should have nothing to fear from the consequences of its tyranny. Give to this aristocracy the exclusive power of government and of self-enrichment. Forbid the people to join its ranks, or, if you do allow that, impose conditions for that benefit which they cannot accept. So that the people, estranged from the upper classes and the object of their enmity, without a hope of bettering their lot, end up by abandoning themselves and thinking themselves satisfied when by the greatest efforts they can extract from their land enough to prevent themselves from dying; and meanwhile the noble, stripped of all that stimulates man to great and generous actions, slumbers in unenlightened egoism.' From *Journeys to England and Ireland*, ed. by J. P. Mayer, (New York: 1968), pp. 150–1.

[2] H. J. Hanham, *Elections and Party Management: Politics in the Time of Disraeli and Gladstone* (London: 1959), p. 6; also, F. M. L. Thompson, *English Landed Society in the Nineteenth Century* (London: 1963), pp. 203–4.

least between England and Wales respectively during the late nineteenth century (see Table 4.1). The relatively high level of rural class

TABLE 4.1 *Percentage distribution of land holdings by size, England and Wales, 1876**

Region	England (N = 40)	Wales (N = 13)
Peers	0·04	0·05
3,000 acres and above	0·12	0·28
1,000–3,000 acres	0·23	0·75
300–1,000 acres	0·91	2·28
100–300 acres	2·36	5·30
1–100 acres	21·91	29·50
Under 1 acre	72·92	50·61
Public bodies	1·50	1·19

* Source: Calculated from county data in Appendix VI of John Bateman's *The Great Landowners of Great Britain and Ireland*, originally published in 1883, reprinted, New York: 1970, pp. 501–15.

conflict in the Celtic periphery beginning in the seventeenth century arose from the gradually widening cultural identification of landlords and tenants. Therefore, it may be fruitfully seen as a product of the colonial situation.

THE POLITICAL CONSEQUENCES OF INCORPORATION

The loss of sovereignty in the Celtic lands resulted in the development of political dependency upon England. Policies determining the administration of these territories were subsequently to be decided in a larger political arena, one in which the Celts were destined to play only a minor role. The peripheral population, therefore, lost the privilege of determining its own fate. The friction of space in pre-industrial Britain further insulated the London-based government from the consequences of popular disturbances occurring in the Celtic fringe. Altogether, the evolution of political dependence may have encouraged a sense of apathy and despair among potentially active groups in these territories.[1] During the eighteenth and early nineteenth centuries, this probably resulted in a higher than average incidence of political corruption in Wales and Scotland.

[1] For some comparative evidence to this effect see Guiseppe Di Palma, *Apathy and Participation: Mass Politics in Western Societies* (New York: 1970), pp. 184–5. Further support for this position is offered in P. A. Allum, *Politics and Society in Postwar Naples* (Cambridge: 1973).

This is not to argue that English politics during this period was, in any sense, representative. England emerged from the Glorious Revolution of 1688 into a period of great political stability which was achieved under a vastly extended system of spoils and patronage.[1] The last echo of conflict inherited from the Revolution of 1640 was Jacobitism, but its strength was mainly confined to the Celtic fringe. After 1745, there was little organized opposition to the Government of Great Britain for almost a century. How was it possible to so completely mute the great conflicts of the Revolutionary era? Though this subject has not received much detailed analysis, it is evident that the expansion of opportunities in the civil service, in the military forces, and in the colonial administration of India tied diverse élites to the central government.[2] It is certainly not far-fetched to claim that England's political stability in these years was achieved at the expense of much of the rest of the world. Hence, the previous basis of political conflict was dampened and the state was run as if it were a huge, well-oiled political machine.

Nowhere was the extent of machine control greater than in the culturally distinct counties. The management of the Cornish boroughs provided Lewis Namier his best examples of political corruption within England.[3] But it would appear that political activity was even more effectively monopolized in Wales and Scotland.

Eighteenth-century Welsh politics was basically determined by a few families who passed on their seats from generation to generation, as if heirlooms. 'Apart from the intrusion of an occasional interloper the political domination of the Welsh gentry seemed likely to continue as undisturbed as it was undistinguished.'[4] Even the Reform Act of 1832, which widened the franchise considerably,

---

[1] This is the thesis of J. H. Plumb, *The Growth of Political Stability in England, 1675–1725* (London: 1967).

[2] Christopher Hill, *The Century of Revolution, 1603–1714* (New York: 1961), p. 285.

[3] 'There was a peculiar excellence in the Cornish boroughs, an elaborate and quaint machinery for making Members of Parliament, in which irrelevancy reached its acme. ... As an archaic ritual and a pursuit of pleasure and profit Cornish borough elections have the charm inherent in human actions when they are sincere; and there was no humbug about the way in which Cornish boroughs chose their representatives. Thomas Pitt, an old experienced hand, wrote in October 1740: "... there are few (Cornish) boroughs where the common sort of people do not think they have as much right to sell themselves and their votes, as they have to sell their corn and their cattle." The Cornish borough Members were, on the whole, more closely connected with the Government than those in most counties.' Lewis Namier, *The Structure of Politics at the Accession of George III* (London: 1957), p. 299.   [4] David Williams, *op. cit.*, p. 166.

had only minimal effects on the structure of Welsh politics. In the boroughs, Parliamentary seats no longer went to landowners, but to the employers of labor. However, in the countryside, the same families reigned so that in Wales 'the victory of the middle-class reformers in 1832 was more apparent than real.'[1]

Scotland, clearly a potential locus for the crystallization of political dissent, was also controlled almost effortlessly after the Jacobite Rebellion. The government handed out its favors to the leader of the Scottish Parliamentary delegation; he then dispensed patronage as he wished. These circumstances have been ably described by Richard Pares:[2]

Neither the Scottish M.P.s nor the Scottish peers were thought entirely respectable in the eighteenth century. The peers were elected under the thumb of the British government; it promulgated a list of its candidates, and most of the members of this list were duly elected. Perhaps for this reason, the Scottish peers in the house of lords were nearly as subservient to the British government as the English bishops—and one cannot say much more than that. The Scottish M.P.s were no better. They commanded little respect by reason of their method of election: there were few really popular constituencies in England, but none at all in Scotland before 1832. Their behavior after election was no more edifying. They were a by-word for jobbery and bargaining. . . . The Scottish M.P.s traded their votes in return for advantages for Scotland, for their particular constituencies, and for themselves. For Scotland they demanded tax exemptions; for themselves, their friends, and their constituents posts in the customs, posts in the colonies, above all posts in the East India Company's service. These bargains might be made with other sectional interests. Usually, however, they were made with the government, which had most to offer. In return for concessions of these kinds, the Scottish M.P.s voted obediently under the discipline of the lord advocate, a Scottish law officer whose business generally included the management of the Scottish element in the house of commons. There is a story, which may not be true but is a good story to tell, about the Scottish M.P. who complained that the government ought to have appointed a tall man as lord advocate, when Scottish M.P.s did not know how they were expected to vote, they looked to see how the lord advocate voted, and if he was so short that they could not watch him, they were bewildered. By methods such as these, Scotland was managed for the government by one politician after another—. . . above all by Henry Dundas. In the middle of St. Andrew's Square, Edinburgh, stands a column rather like the Nelson column in Trafalgar Square, London. On the top of it stands Dundas; he had certainly deserved well of the British government; whether he deserved so well of Scotland is another matter.

[1] Ibid., p. 176.
[2] Richard Pares, 'A quarter of a millenium of Anglo-Scottish union,' History, new ser., 39, 2 (1954), p. 234.

Patronage was curtailed in the Scottish highlands and Ireland, though the latter country was not incorporated during the eighteenth century. Was this why there was so little patronage for Ireland? J. H. Plumb's answer to this question is that, for some 'accidental' political reason, much of it was cut off to the Anglo-Irish aristocracy, the bulk being dispensed to those defined as politically significant for Westminster.[1] Very largely it appears these were Englishmen. This explanation need not be accepted with the force with which it is made. Ireland's problems could in no way have been significantly eased by the application of more grease to the gears of state: what was required was a complete overhaul. Therefore, while it is true that the popular will was largely absent in English politics as well in this period, the extent of political corruption in the peripheral areas was legend, even by contemporary standards.

However, the docility of late eighteenth-century Wales and Scotland was achieved by the co-optation of regional élites, rather than by the direct intervention of the state. The British government continued to grant extensive autonomy to local authorities. The development of the state's concern with local government had begun in the fourteenth century with the creation of a system of Justices of the Peace.[2] Instead of sending a representative of the central administration to outlying areas to enforce the King's law, as occurred in the French system of *intendants*, the English elected to rely on local gentry for this purpose. In effect, the Office of the Justice of the Peace represented the co-optation of the gentry into the national system of administration. This system was clearly a precursor of Lord Lugard's famed colonial policy of 'indirect rule.' The structural consequence of this policy was to ensure minimal central control over the internal administration of local justice until the 1830s and the passing of the Municipal Reform Law. The gentry had considerable autonomy in the manner and direction of control they asserted. In this arrangement, there was largely private ownership of the means of administration and control. In general, such offices were given to those who already possessed local authority. The Justices tended to execute national policy only when it coincided with their immediate interests. There were limitations to the power

---

[1] Plumb, *op. cit.*, p. 182.
[2] See Sidney and Beatrice Webb, *The Development of English Local Government, 1689–1835* (London: 1963), C. A. Beard, *The Office of the JP in England: Its Origin and Development* (New York: 1904); and Vernon K. Dibble, 'The Organization of Traditional Authority: English County Government, 1558–1640,' in James G. March, ed., *Handbook of Organizations* (Chicago: 1965).

of the JPs—chiefly with regard to strictly local authorities such as the constable, as well as to military organization and policy, which remained tied to the center—but, in the main, they determined the shape and content of social and political life at the county level. Only as urbanization advanced did pressure build for a reform of the system of local government. The immediate cause of concern was the deterioration of health standards in the new industrial cities. Local authorities were unwilling and unable to cope with the manifold problems of rapid urbanization, and the level of capital investment and co-ordinated planning which it required if epidemic conditions were to be avoided.[1]

Since the establishment of a state-wide system of political administration in the United Kingdom was achieved so late, the Celtic territories were only minimally integrated into the dominant political institutions of the society by the early nineteenth century. Until the spread of industrialization, the administration of any given Celtic county had little in common with that of any given English county. Political incorporation, *per se*, resulted in profound structural changes in the Celtic lands. The peripheral economies became heavily commercialized and dependent on extra-regional prices and market fluctuations. Development tended to be on specialized lines. Anglicization resulted in a polarization of the rural stratification system, and also confounded lines of class and culture. The gentry were defined as enemies, not only because of their wealth, but because of their conversion to another culture, that of England. But incorporation did not, in any real way, result in the effective political integration of the Celtic periphery into the United Kingdom. The British political structure on the eve of industrialization continued, in significant respects, to resemble that of a decentralized patrimonial state.[2]

If political and cultural integration were to occur in the British Isles it would be in response to social changes occurring from the mid-nineteenth century on. In Part III, the consequences of industrialization for the integration of the Celtic regions into the United Kingdom will be discussed.

[1] The Webbs, *op. cit.*
[2] Harold Perkin, *The Origins of Modern English Society, 1780–1880* (London: 1969), pp. 40–2.

PART III

The Consequences of
Industrialization

CHAPTER 5

INDUSTRIALIZATION AND REGIONAL ECONOMIC INEQUALITY, 1851–1961

The Celt is often called sensual; but it is not so much the vulgar satis-
factions of sense that attract him as emotion and excitement; he is truly
. . . sentimental—*always ready to react against the despotism of fact.*

MATTHEW ARNOLD

SOCIOLOGICAL theories have long stressed the signal importance of industrialization as the first cause, or *primum mobile*, in a
linked chain of events leading to the eventual creation of the national
state. To be sure there have been some disagreements about the
precise causal connections between industrialization and national
development. Some have tended to see the establishment of the large
nation state as a reflection of the power of the first national ruling
class, the bourgeoisie, in its ceaseless quest for political stability.[1]
Others have stressed the integrative consequences of growing structural differentiation, while a third perspective emphasizes the diffusion of bureaucratic rationality as a unifying moral order in
industrial societies. There is some excellent evidence to support the

[1] Note the following clear statement by Friedrich Engels: 'Since the end of the
Middle Ages, history had been moving towards a Europe made up of large,
national states. Only such national states constitute the normal political framework for the dominant European bourgeois class (*Bürgertum*). . . . The existence
of a mass of petty German states with their many differing commercial and
industrial laws was bound to become an intolerable fetter on this powerfully
developing industry and on the growing commerce with which it was linked—
a different rate of exchange every few miles, different regulations for establishing
a business everywhere, literally everywhere, different kinds of chicanery, bureaucratic and fiscal traps, even in many cases still, guild restrictions against which
not even a license was of any avail. . . . The ability to exploit the massive labor
force of the fatherland in unrestricted fashion was the first condition for industrial
development, but wherever the patriotic manufacturer sought to concentrate
workers from all over Germany, there the police and Poor Law authorities
stepped in against the influx of immigrants.' *The Role of Force in History* (New
York: 1968), pp. 29–32.

127

contention of a link between industrialization and increasing state power: by and large only those states which are industrialized have effective central governments. England is of course the first such example.

Common to these approaches is the tendency to consider economic and social development as automatically snowballing processes which, once under way in a given territory, inevitably 'tear down all Chinese walls,' in Marx's phrase, and revolutionize the nature of political authority as well as the society's mode of production.[1] There would appear to be a strong positive association between economic development and national political integration. If industrial societies have a relatively high degree of political centralization, the societies of the Third World show a notable lack of effective central authority. It is generally acknowledged that the intense regional and ethnic conflicts so characteristic of these new states inhibit their prospects for social and economic development. At the same time it has been felt that in the absence of industrialization, there is little hope of replacing the 'primordial sentiments' of ethnic, religious, or linguistic loyalty by attachments of national scope more conducive to the evolution of political stability.

The consequences of industrialization for national development may presumably be conceptualized on two levels. At the microscopic level industrialization implies great disruption in individual lifestyles. Rapid urbanization, the anomie of city life, and the required adjustment to new modes of production and types of working conditions all are seen to loosen the individual's traditional political attachments. As a result the legitimacy of the central government is thought to be strengthened at the expense of local authorities. At the macroscopic level industrialization stimulates a wide range of transactions which are presumed to significantly narrow differences between regions within state territory. These lead not only to a more homogeneous national culture, but also, it has been argued, to a more equal distribution of regional income in the long run.[2]

It is quite evident that regional variations in income and rates of economic growth can become critical obstacles to the realization of political stability. To the extent that a regional population is self-

[1] A convenient statement may be found in Wilbert E. Moore, *Order and Change* (New York: 1967), pp. 33–48. For England, see Harold Perkin, *The Origins of Modern English Society, 1780–1880* (London: 1969).

[2] Jeffrey G. Williamson, 'Regional inequality and the process of national development: a description of the patterns,' *Economic Development and Cultural Change*, 13, 4 (1965), pp. 3–45.

conscious and perceives itself to be relatively disadvantaged, political opposition to the central régime may become crystallized around the issue. Effective political integration can come about only when regional inequality decreases to a level which can be socially defined to be tolerable. Ideally, economic benefits should be equally shared throughout the society to minimize political disaffection.

However, advanced industrial societies are themselves facing many of the same kinds of political cleavages thought to be characteristic of the new nations. The intensity of ethnic and regional cleavages in these societies suggests that problems of regional inequality may continue to have considerable political salience despite the advent of industrialization. Movements for regional separation are typically based on the twin claims of economic and cultural discrimination against peripheral areas perceived as emanating from the central government. It has become evident that the relationship between industrialization and regional economic inequality is far more complex than had originally been supposed. While industrialization results in a substantial increase in interregional transactions, and hence widens the effective scope of national markets, this cannot automatically be assumed to result in greater welfare in the peripheral regions. What has sometimes been overlooked is that even should industrial development proceed to an appreciable extent, geographical and cultural factors function to spatially confine growth to specific regions for long periods of time.[1] Even in the most developed societies regional growth differentials have tended to persist.

This is the case in the British Isles. Despite centuries of interregional economic transactions, a recent compilation of regional statistics of the United Kingdom ranks Wales and Scotland generally lowest among ten British regions (Northern Ireland is excepted from the data) on a host of indicators of economic and social development, relating to employment, housing, education, health, environment, and personal income.[2]

This chapter will attempt to estimate the extent to which industrialization has affected the economic position of the Celtic fringe

[1] G. K. Zipf, *National Unity and Disunity* (Bloomington: 1941), pp. 5-7; J. R. Hicks, *Essays in World Economics* (Oxford: 1959), p. 163. See also works on location theory in economics, such as W. Alonso, 'Location theory' in J. Friedmann and W. Alonso, eds, *Regional Development and Planning* (Cambridge, Mass.: 1964).

[2] Edwin Hammond, *An Analysis of Regional Economic and Social Statistics* (Durham: University of Durham, Rowntree Research Unit, 1968). The regions are North, East and West Ridings; Northwest; West Midlands; North Midlands; East Anglia; Southeast and Southwest.

relative to England from 1851 to 1961. This will be done by considering several different economic and social indicators of development which have been collected by county units from published government statistics. In general, the conclusion is that the disadvantaged position of the Celtic fringe relative to England has not substantially changed during this period, despite rapid industrialization in parts of Wales and Scotland beginning around 1851. Industrialization *per se* did not, therefore, serve to eliminate the relative economic disadvantages of the Celtic periphery. The *per capita* income of Celtic counties has been consistently lower than that of English counties. Regional income inequality persists even after the level of industrialization is eliminated as a source of variation between regions. Rather, the situation of the Celtic fringe in the British Isles is analogous in several respects to that of the less developed countries in the world system. Development occurred in a largely dependent mode[1] and created dualistic structures within the Celtic periphery. As a consequence the spatial diffusion of industrialization in the Celtic lands was considerably restricted. Further, production in Wales, Scotland, and Ireland was excessively specialized, whereas England alone developed a diversified industrial economy. Finally, it is suggested that the persistence of these systematic disadvantages may partially result from the institutionalization of policies which have the effect of discriminating against the Celtic periphery in a manner similar to that which has been described as institutionalized racism. The perception of a certain Celtic cultural distinctiveness on the part of significant English institutions may serve to discourage prospects for development in these regions.

THE PROBLEM OF REGIONAL ECONOMIC INEQUALITY

There are two independent bases for the development of regional economic inequality at any point in time. In the first place there are causes which are essentially geographical. Regions typically vary with respect to resource base, soil composition, climate, accessibility to navigable waters and other factors potentially bearing on the production and distribution of goods. These factors give advantages to some regions as compared with others. 'Poles of growth' tend to occur in regions with geographical advantages relative to specific

[1] Theotonio Dos Santos, 'The structure of dependence,' *American Economic Review*, 60, 2 (1970), pp. 231–6.

means of production.[1] Once begun, growth may continue in a region even after the loss of a one-time geographical advantage due to the benefits of other external economies, such as the availability of skilled labor, or the presence of a variety of goods and services which need not be imported, or to decision of the central government concerning tariff and investment policies. Thus regional differences may not only persist, they may also increase with time.[2]

Although regional geographic attributes do not undergo objective change in the course of social development, the degree to which a society makes use of its natural resources is a function of the mode of production. It is clear that in pre-industrial times, when agricultural production dominates the economy, that the region richest in topsoil, mildest in climate, smoothest in relief and of appropriate rainfall will be best suited for cultivation and hence will be the most coveted. On the other hand, in an industrial society these attributes are relatively much less valued, as industries tend to be located near sources of minerals or energy, with good natural accessibility to domestic and international markets. This shift in the valuation of land has important consequences for the regional distribution of wealth. A region largely unsuited for efficient arable cultivation in one century may find itself a favored area in the next, with the advent of industrial production. The distribution of comparative geographical advantages may therefore be affected by gross changes in social organization and production. It may also be affected by fluctuations in international demand. The first kind of shift in comparative advantage occurred in Wales and, to a lesser extent, Scotland during the nineteenth century upon the discovery of extremely rich sources of high-quality coal. The second kind of shift followed World War One, when demand for Welsh and Scottish exports dropped off sharply in the face of heightened international competition. Thereafter both Wales and Scotland again became subject to comparative disadvantages in production.

Another major source of regional economic inequality is cultural. In traditional societies there may be major differences in patterns of

[1] François Perroux, 'Note sur la notion de "pole de croissance", matériaux pour une analyse de la croissance économique,' *Cahiers de l'Institut de Science Economique Appliqué*, Série D, 8 (1955).
[2] Werner Baer, 'Regional inequality and economic growth in Brazil,' *Economic Development and Cultural Change*, 12, 3 (1964), pp. 268–85; J. R. Lasuén, 'Regional income inequalities and the problems of growth in Spain,' *Regional Science Association: Papers*, 8 (1962), pp. 169–83.

agricultural production, kinship systems, inheritance customs, and —generally speaking—modes of social organization which affect the level and type of production. Thus in similar geographical environments investigators have found radically different modes of social organization. Explanations of these variations usually rest on theories of group migration. One plausible account of the disparity of agricultural villages in East Anglia from those of the geographically similar Midlands relies on a hypothesis that Frisian migration led to a separate type of social organization in one corner of the British Isles.[1] Therefore, in any investigation of regional inequality both geographical and cultural variables must be weighed as potential differentiating factors.

Once initial economic inequality has evolved, the transmission of growth from dynamic to stagnant regions becomes problematic. The process by which this is thought to occur has been the subject of some controversy. The crux of the debate concerns the role of politics in the regional redistribution of resources. Some writers feel that regional equality will result through the action of economic forces alone.[2] They hold that the diffusion of economic growth is impeded by the constraints of traditionalism in the stagnant regions, and will naturally follow the extension of efficient markets there. With the expansion of the national economy, and consequent heightening of the rate of interregional transactions, disparities in the rates of regional development should decrease.[3]

The alternative argument is pessimistic with regard to the con-

---

[1] G. C. Homans, 'The Frisians in East Anglia,' *Economic History Review*, 2nd ser., 10, 2 (1957-8), pp. 189–206. See also his article, 'The explanation of English regional differences,' *Past and Present*, 42 (1969), pp. 19–34.

[2] M. Tachi, 'Regional income disparity and internal migration of population in Japan,' *Economic Development and Cultural Change*, 12, 2 (1964), pp. 186–204; and Williamson, *op. cit.*

[3] This position tends to be taken by neo-classical economists and by the more sociologically minded political scientists. These economists assume that the market will re-allocate factors of production such that factor prices equilibrate in both regions. While this may not lead to an immediate movement towards regional equalization of *per capita* incomes, in the long run such a trend should emerge, according to this theory. See S. Kuznets, 'Economic growth and income inequality,' *American Economic Review* 45, 1 (1955).

Political scientists such as Karl Deutsch, *Nationalism and Social Communication* (Cambridge, Mass.: 1966) feel that increases in the rates of transaction between regions lead to higher levels of integration, implying more regionally homogeneous levels of social and economic development. The symbolic content of interregional transactions is particularly stressed by the 'political culture' school of comparative politics, led by Gabriel Almond and Sidney Verba, *The Civic Culture* (Princeton: 1963).

sequences of increasing economic penetration of the periphery. These areas are seen to be already suffused with extensive market connections to the dynamic region. In this view the economic inequality of the stagnant regions will tend to be exacerbated by the play of market forces in the absence of intervention by the central government.[1] Hence, since increased economic efficiency between regions can only serve to impoverish the stagnant regions, some form of political action is required to bring about regional parity.

When the periphery is not only economically disadvantaged but culturally distinct as well, the likelihood of increasing regional equality appears to be even more remote. This often occurs in the internal colonial situation.[2] In these circumstances the dynamic region exercises a virtually monopolistic control over production in the peripheral areas. It practices discrimination against the culturally distinct peoples who have been forced on to less accessible, inferior lands, thereby establishing a cultural division of labor. Such cultural discrimination need not be directed against individuals. For example, no one would argue that there is much discrimination against Welshmen as individuals in the United Kingdom today. Nevertheless, the fact that Wales as a region is disadvantaged in terms of income, employment, housing, and education has decisive consequences for the individuals living there. To the extent that the region is materially deprived, the average Welshman competes with the average Englishman at a disadvantage in many free market situations. When such long-term differences in aggregate rates of development are the result of ethnic stereotypes, it is appropriate to speak of institutional racism.[3] This chapter raises the possibility that such processes may be involved in the persistent pattern of economic disadvantages which have characterized the Celtic lands during the past century.

REGIONAL ECONOMIC INEQUALITY IN THE BRITISH ISLES: THE NINETEENTH AND TWENTIETH CENTURIES

It is likely that substantial regional economic inequality existed in pre-industrial Britain though there is little quantitative evidence of

[1] Gunnar Myrdal, *Rich Lands and Poor* (New York: 1957), pp. 23–38; A. O. Hirschman, *The Strategy of Economic Development* (New Haven: 1958), p. 187.
[2] P. Gonzáles-Casanova, 'Internal colonialism and national development,' *Studies in Comparative International Development*, 1, 4 (1965), pp. 27–37.
[3] S. Carmichael and C. V. Hamilton, *Black Power* (New York: 1967), pp. 4–5.

its extent. Wide geographic variations in the British Isles have led to the classic distinction between lowland and highland zones, set apart by a natural boundary, the Highland Line.[1] As discussed in chapter 3, the highlands are beset by a series of comparative disadvantages for agricultural production. The terrain is difficult to plow and drain, the soil chalky, the climate stern, the rainfall too heavy for good cultivation. The regions of Celtic culture are disproportionately clustered in the highland zone. It is reasonable to regard these Celts as a conquered people pushed into these territories by subsequent, more powerful invaders.

The social organization of the Welsh and Scottish highlands and Ireland was substantially different from that of the rest of Britain. Whereas impartible inheritance, primogeniture, was the rule throughout most of the lowland areas, partible inheritance, *gavelkind*, was an integral part of the Celtic social structure. Partible inheritance had two general consequences for agricultural production. There was a marked tendency for large plots of land to be subdivided into small portions in the course of a very few generations. H. L. Gray mentions the example of a 205-acre Irish farm which after the course of only two generations became subdivided into 29 holdings and 422 different lots.[2] The average arable quantity was four acres, while the single largest arable plot owned by any one man was only eight acres. Second, instead of the English pattern of two or three large, commonly worked open fields, the Celtic system led to individual small plots held in widely varying locations, considerably hindering the prospects for efficient cultivation as well as agricultural improvement. This situation often led to early enclosure, with the consequent polarization of the stratification system and proletarianization of the peasantry.[3] All these factors had undoubtedly resulted in differences in regional standards of living before the nineteenth century.

However, even in pre-industrial times it is not possible to argue that the relative povery of the Celtic regions was largely due to their isolation from economic or cultural contacts with England. Great

---

[1] The distinction was first drawn by Halford Mackinder, *Britain and the British Seas* (London: 1902). See also Joan Thirsk, 'The Farming Regions of England,' and F. Emery, 'The Farming Regions of Wales' in Joan Thirsk, ed., *The Agrarian History of England and Wales*, vol. IV (Cambridge: 1967). For another geographer's division of the British Isles, emphasizing north-south conflict in all regions see M. W. Heslinga, *The Irish Border as a Cultural Divide* (Assen, Netherlands: 1962).

[2] H. L. Gray, *English Field Systems* (Cambridge, Mass: 1915), p. 191.

[3] Thirsk, *op. cit.*

Britain was one of the earliest states to achieve a national economy. In large part the foundation of this national economy had been laid very early. England virtually led Europe in eliminating internal barriers to trade such as the random tolls which strangled continental commodity movements during the Middle Ages. By the fourteenth century the state had imposed a uniform toll system on both roads and rivers, and as a general consequence transport costs were much less than elsewhere in Europe, save perhaps Sweden. During the period 1275–1350 a national customs system was evolved under the guidance of the state, without ever being abandoned afterwards.[1] Customs barriers between England and Wales were removed following the annexation of Wales in 1536. The customs barriers between England and Scotland disappeared totally after the Union of 1707, and complete freedom in trade, communication and shipping was established thereafter. Commercial contacts between England and Ireland had existed since the fourteenth century, though the legal status of Ireland *vis-à-vis* England went through several changes until 1801, when free trade was established throughout the British Isles.

Adam Smith, who was otherwise a scathing critic of English mercantilism and the general inefficiency of the economy, was very well placed as Customs Commissioner for Scotland to observe the exceptional extent of British internal trade:[2]

The inland trade is almost perfectly free, the greater part of goods may be carried from one end of the kingdom to the other without requiring any permit or let-pass, without being subject to question, visit, or examination from the revenue officers. There are a few exceptions, but they are such as can give no interruptions to any important branch of inland commerce of the country. Goods carried coastwise, indeed, require certificates or coast cockets. If you except coals, however, the rest are almost duty-free. This freedom of interior commerce, the effect of the uniformity of the system of taxation, is perhaps one of the principal causes of the prosperity of Great Britain; every great country being necessarily the best and most extensive market for the greater part of the production of its own industry.

England was far ahead of her Continental rivals in the realization of central control over local privileges in many other spheres of the economy as well. From the fourteenth century onwards a host of ordinances attempted to establish national, and hence, regionally

---

[1] Eli Heckscher, *Mercantilism* (London: 1962), vol. I, p. 52. The following comments all derive from Heckscher's useful summary.

[2] Adam Smith, *The Wealth of Nations* (London: 1950), part II, article IV, p. 432.

uniform standards of weights and measures. A unified system of coinage was achieved under Henry II in the second half of the twelfth century. The effectiveness of the English central authority by the Elizabethan period can be estimated by the extent to which municipal privilege, an intractable vestige of feudal decentralization on the Continent, was continually eroded in favor of national policies regulating both urban and rural areas.[1]

The establishment of the Justices of the Peace was a much earlier attempt by the Crown to intrude upon regional privileges and ensure national compliance to the law. Though there is doubt as to the effectiveness of the Justices of the Peace in carrying out their prescribed functions, their existence is ample testimony to the desire of the central government to extend its power and authority throughout English territory.

Furthermore, the increasing size of English cities, particularly London, was instrumental in creating a national market for foodstuffs as early as 1600; and production in Wales began to be influenced by this growing demand.[2] Wool was also produced in North Wales for sale in the London market.[3] By the eighteenth century, if not earlier, much of the agricultural production of Ireland and Scotland was similarly bound for England.

In the nineteenth century interregional transactions between Celtic regions and England were substantially increased.[4] The construction of canals and railroads facilitated the expansion of inland trade by significantly lowering transport costs. Interregional economic integration proceeded apace with the growing industrialization of the British Isles. However, this increase in transactions between the Celtic lands and England was not merely confined to commerce. Shifts in the rates of interregional migration also support the thesis

---

[1] 'In two important respects economic legislation was thus less influenced by municipal policy than on the Continent. First, all branches of industry were uniformly regulated throughout the country and great care was taken to maintain a regular supply of labor for agriculture. Secondly, the agents which the law prescribed for the administration of its rules were the same for town and country. . . . Its chief innovation in contrast with the medieval order lay in its uniform and well-planned character, and the monarchy, knowing what it was about, was able to stamp this character on the whole system.' Heckscher, *op. cit.*, p. 233.

[2] F. J. Fisher, 'The Development of the London Food Market, 1540–1640' in E. M. Carus-Wilson, ed., *Essays in Economic History* (London: 1954), I, pp. 135–51.

[3] Thomas C. Mendenhall, *The Shrewsbury Drapers and the Welsh Wool Trade* (London: 1953).

[4] Michael Hechter, 'Regional inequality and national integration: the case of the British Isles,' *Journal of Social History*, 5, 1 (1971), pp. 96–117.

of an increase in the level of more socially diffuse interaction. The decision to migrate from a backward region to an advanced, but culturally alien one is seldom made lightly. Despite the constraint of traditionalism, movements of population between the regions varied throughout the nineteenth century. Massive Irish emigration to Britain after the Great Famine undercut the wages of the British working class and caused it to be divided sharply along cultural lines. The point is not so much that there was a steady secular rise in the rate of interregional migration, but rather that there were fluctuations which demonstrate the increasing permeability of regional boundaries. Similarly, the rates of letters mailed, on a *per capita* basis, increased at about the same degree in Celtic regions as the over-all English rate.

These few examples, which could no doubt be multiplied many times over, serve to illustrate that the Celtic regions were to a considerable extent already tied to the English economy before the Industrial Revolution, and that the advent of the industrial production led to a dramatic heightening of the intensity and quality of the interconnections between British regions. Hence, the proliferation of regional economic inequality following industrialization can in no way be accounted for by reference to the isolation of the Celtic fringe from rapidly developing England. Whatever is responsible for the development of further economic inequality, it is evident that the Celtic regions must, by the mid-nineteenth century, be considered an integral part of the unified economic system of the British Isles of which England was such a conspicuous participant.

THE SPATIAL DIFFUSION OF INDUSTRIALIZATION, 1851–1961

Although Britain was the first society to industrialize, and remains to this day among the most highly industrialized and urbanized of all societies, certain parts of the British Isles almost totally escaped industrialization, while others have been only partially transformed by industrial production. In some ways the United Kingdom is unique in that the great majority of necessary agricultural goods required to sustain her relatively dense population has for the past century come from overseas. If Britain, and more specifically England, were the workshop of the world in the nineteenth century other lands, mostly in the Empire, served as sources not only of primary products for manufacture, but as providers of bread, meat, and dairy products for teeming British cities.

At the beginning of the eighteenth century English industry was not very geographically concentrated. The textile industries, especially wool textiles, were widespread. The iron industry was somewhat less widespread. But perhaps only in mining and the associated smelting industries was there any fairly heavy geographical concentration. By the end of the century, however, this situation was rapidly changing.

The story of the rapid economic take-off of the northwestern counties around the textile industry—and the subsequent redistribution of wealth and, to a lesser extent, political influence from London and the southeast to the provinces—has been told previously, and at great elaboration.[1] Comparatively little attention has been paid to the actual spatial diffusion of industry through the nineteenth and twentieth centuries.[2] In part this neglect is due to the perception that Britain was an industrial society if ever there were one, and that to analyze those areas where industrialization had not taken root was to show a preference for the study of backwardness rather than dynamism. Autopsies have a much grimmer aspect than obstetrical deliveries. For many students of comparative sociology the question of the extent to which the British Isles are industrialized seems very low on any scale of empirical priorities.

But for the purposes of the study of national development the question is a vital one. Dov Friedlander has recently presented a method of distinguishing between industrial and largely rural counties in England and Wales over the period 1851 to 1951.[3] Adopting

[1] For an interesting empirical study of the regional redistribution of wealth following the Industrial Revolution, see E. J. Buckatzsch, 'The geographical distribution of wealth in England, 1086–1843,' *Economic History Review*, 2nd ser., 3, 2 (1950), pp. 180–202. Donald Read's *The English Provinces 1760–1960, A Study in Influence* (London: 1964) provides useful information on the changing influences of the northern cities in English history.

[2] In this context, it is worth noting that the geography of the British Isles provides most British regions with access either to major population centers or to the sea, and thus relatively cheap transportation. Therefore hardly any region is prohibited from industrialization by the constraints of this particular ecological factor. This was not the case, for example, in Spain or in Belgium where the industrial revolution took place in peripheral territories, e.g. Catalonia and Wallonia, which, unlike the core regions, had access to the sea.

[3] Dov Friedlander, 'The spread of urbanization in England and Wales: 1851–1961,' *Population Studies*, 24, 3 (1970). While I have adopted the logic of Friedlander's cut-off points to distinguish between industrial and non-industrial counties, the definition I have used is slightly different from his. Friedlander's

the logic of his method, I have classified British and Irish counties as industrial if their percentage of employed adult males in non-agricultural occupations was equal to or exceeded 85 per cent for the years 1851–81; 87·5 per cent for the years 1891–1921; and 90 per cent from 1931–61. Map 3 shows the spatial distribution of industrial counties in Britain and Ireland in 1861 and 1961. If this map is for the moment merely regarded as an undifferentiated plane divided arbitrarily into counties, then the spatial distribution of the heavily industrialized areas in 1861 is unexceptional. The few industrial counties seem almost randomly distributed on this surface, with the single exception of Ireland where no heavily industrialized location can be seen. By and large these industrial counties are either rich in coal resources (Glamorgan, Durham), loci of the textile industry (Lancaster, Lanark, Renfrew), or large commercial centers (London, and Midlothian, which includes Edinburgh).

The situation in 1961 is strikingly different. A great proportion of the geographical area of England has become heavily industrialized, whereas gains in the Celtic lands are by comparison modest. It appears as if the diffusion of industrial concentration was affected, in some way, by the boundaries of Wales, Scotland, and Ireland.

Shifts in regional economic inequality may be rather quickly scanned by considering the changes in county means for ten indicators of economic and social development in England, Wales, Scotland, Ireland, and Northern Ireland, taken at decennial periods from 1851 to 1961. *Non-agricultural occupations* (Table 5.1) is perhaps the best general indicator of development over time since it does not differentiate between secondary employment, which was the major component of the industrial sector until World War One in Britain, and tertiary employment, which has subsequently increased dramatically. The mean level of non-agricultural occupations is over fifty per cent and virtually identical for England, Wales, and Scotland in 1851, whereas the southern Irish means hover at about 25 per cent, far beneath the rest of the British Isles. Thereafter

---

variable is the percentage of all adult males engaged in non-agricultural occupations, while mine is the percentage of all employed adult males in such occupational categories. This definition is somewhat more stringent, and therefore results in slightly fewer 'industrial counties' than does Friedlander's. Since the *Censuses of England and Wales* and *Scotland* did not publish occupational statistics by county in 1961, Map 3 was constructed for that year with the assumption that the 1951 figures were the best estimates for 1961. Both Ireland and Northern Ireland did publish such statistics.

Map 3 The spatial diffusion of industrialization, 1861–1961 (Great Britain and Ireland)

England develops at a faster rate than all the other regions save Northern Ireland. By 1961 the Welsh mean is only 79 per cent, the Northern Irish 76 per cent, and the Scottish but 57 per cent of England's. Southern Ireland remains untouched by British industrialization, forcefully implying that the diffusion of industrialization throughout state territory is far from an automatic process.

Turning to the secondary sector and the development of *manufacturing occupations*, a somewhat similar pattern emerges. The

TABLE 5.1 *Mean county proportion of employed males engaged in nonagricultural occupations**

	England	Wales	Scotland	N. Ireland	Ireland†
1851	58	57	55	33	22
1861	59	55	49	33	24
1871	66	62	51	33	26
1881	68	61	57	38	30
1891	75	64	53	36	28
1901	76	67	65	39	31
1911	76	67	65	39	31
1921	74	64	64	43	26
1931	78	62	55	42	25
1951	85	67	57	60	32
1961‡	(85)	(67)	(57)	65	39

* Source: *Censuses of England and Wales, Scotland, Ireland* and *Northern Ireland*.
† In this and all following tables 'Ireland' refers only to the 26 Southern Irish counties.
‡ The 1961 *Census of England and Wales and Scotland* did not publish occupation data by Administrative County.

early figures in the series show England, Wales, and Scotland at near parity, while both Irish regions are considerably lower. Thereafter, until about 1931, the first three regions have similar means. In the next thirty years the fall in manufacturing occupations is much greater in Wales and Scotland than England. *Commercial and professional occupations*, in essence comprising the service sector of the economy, are similarly differentiated by region, though in an opposite pattern in the time series. The English advantage is greatest in the earlier periods, and becomes somewhat diminished by 1961.

Regional inequality is most evident when the mean *urban population*, defined as that proportion of a county's population dwelling in cities of 20,000 or over, is considered in British regions. Even by 1961 the average Celtic counties fall between only 20 and 33 per cent of the English statistic. If these peripheral regions were less urbanized, they were also somewhat more prone to *unemployment*, with greater inequality especially noticeable after 1921, *illiteracy* (Scotland is a notable and interesting exception[1]) and *infant mortality* than England. Decennial *population growth* was highest for England throughout most of the period. Southern Ireland lost population at each observation, Northern Ireland in all but the last three decades, and Scottish demographic growth was relatively low. These areas were all plagued by high rates of emigration in the nineteenth and twentieth centuries.

Finally, two indicators of the relative standard of living also give evidence of regional inequality. The crude *marriage rate*, a variable empirically related to industrialization in these data as well as a kind of barometer of economic optimism, is consistently highest in England, though only slightly so by 1961. A measure of *per capita income* constructed from county tax returns (see Appendix) shows hardly any decrease in Welsh and Scottish inequality relative to England over the continuum, while both Irelands made substantial gains, from near starvation and subsistence to something more, perhaps genteel poverty.

On the basis of these data, coupled with the more extensive indicators collected by Hammond, it is evident that substantial regional economic and structural inequality exists today in the British Isles, despite almost two centuries of industrialization. It is slightly more difficult to estimate whether, on the whole, regional inequality has been aggravated or diminished because each measure behaves somewhat differently. I have argued elsewhere[2] that whereas there was in general a tendency towards regional convergence along dimensions similar to these Karl Deutsch has identified as 'social mobilization' variables—perhaps literacy is the outstanding example —the indicators of regional economic development show, at best, slight convergence. Further, the growth of the Celtic lands' de-

[1] The Scottish educational system was the first public institution of its kind in Europe, and for a time, its best. Scotland had, as a consequence, a much higher level of literacy than England throughout the eighteenth century as well (L. Stone, 'Literacy and education in England, 1640–1900,' *Past and Present*, 42 (1969), pp. 69–139). Scotland boasted five universities, two of them outstanding in their day, Edinburgh and Glasgow, at a time when England's two were relatively moribund. The consequence of this was that in the eighteenth century the English aristocracy often sent its sons to backward Scotland for an education. Explanations of Scotland's remarkable educational history tend to fall back on the Calvinistic zealousness of the post-Reformation period, though there has been some question about the moral and intellectual rectitude of the eighteenth-century Kirk.   [2] Hechter, *op. cit.*

pendence on extra-regional markets had certain unfortunate consequences in the twentieth century.

STRUCTURAL CONSEQUENCES OF DEVELOPMENT IN THE PERIPHERY: THE ENCLAVE AND THE HINTERLAND

While the average county data on regional inequalities gives little evidence of a Celtic convergence with England along the several dimensions of development selected, none the less the impression which can be gained is that, at the very worst, the Celtic regions were developing at more or less the same rate as England. And since the rate of English development, particularly in the period 1851 to 1911, was unequaled in all the world, it might be argued that the Celtic regions gained much by association with the premier industrial power of the nineteenth century. In terms of these measures much can be said for this position. However, if the statistical dispersions from the mean rates of development of the Celtic nations and England are considered, it becomes evident that industrialization had somewhat different social consequences in the periphery than in the core. While industrialization became diffused throughout English territory, in Wales, Scotland, and Ireland industrial development was confined to a highly limited and relatively unchanging number of counties. Hence those shaded areas in Wales, Scotland, and Northern Ireland shown in 1961 might be visualized as small industrial enclaves in regions having large non-industrial hinterlands. Industrialization in the Celtic regions created small urbanized enclaves oriented to English and international markets which featured cosmopolitan life-styles. With the passing of time the social and cultural gap between enclave and hinterland areas grew steadily wider. To the extent that southern Irish economy maintained its traditional role as a source of agricultural produce for England—such that its regional specialization was agricultural rather than industrial or extractive—no significant industrial enclave region emerged there outside of Dublin.[1] This relative social and economic

---

[1] Even so, Irish economic historians have begun to distinguish between 'maritime' and 'subsistence' sectors of the nineteenth and twentieth century Irish economy. See F. S. L. Lyons, *Ireland Since the Famine* (New York: 1971), p. 43 *et seq.* for a discussion of this issue. For other materials on sub-regional economic systems see M. Gray, *The Highland Economy, 1750–1850* (Edinburgh: 1957); A. H. Dodd, *The Industrial Revolution in North Wales* (Cardiff: 1933); Christopher S. Davies, 'A Classification of Welsh Regions,' in P. W. English and R. C. Mayfield, eds, *Man, Space and Environment* (New York: 1972); and T. W. Freeman, *Ireland, A General and Regional Geography* (London: 1965).

homogeneity had decisive consequences for the development of a politically cohesive nationalist movement.

One way of looking at the development of enclave-hinterland differences on a regionally comparative basis is through the use of a coefficient of variation within regions, Vw.[1] It is perhaps most instructive to begin with *non-agricultural occupations*, as an overall indicator of industrial development (Table 5.2). In 1851 the levels of

TABLE 5.2 *Coefficients of variation* (Vw) *of non-agricultural occupations**

	England	Wales	Scotland	N. Ireland	Ireland
1851	0·26	0·26	0·36	0·39	0·61
1861	0·27	0·28	0·46	0·36	0·52
1871	0·23	0·22	0·49	0·38	0·53
1881	0·23	0·27	0·43	0·40	0·49
1891	0·22	0·35	0·43	0·46	0·50
1901	0·21	0·29	0·61	0·53	0·58
1911	0·20	0·27	0·34	0·51	0·52
1921	0·26	0·33	0·35	0·51	0·61
1931	0·18	0·39	0·53	0·40	0·65
1951	0·12	0·38	0·53	0·30	0·50
1961	—	—	—	0·30	0·46

* Source: as in Table 5.1.

Vw for England, Wales and—to a lesser extent—Scotland are all comparable. English regional heterogeneity continues at a constant degree until about 1931, when Vw drops beneath 0·20. Welsh heterogeneity fluctuates somewhat above the English level until the same year, when it doubles the English Vw. Scotland's industrial diffusion is more spatially skewed, and in 1931 reaches triple the English level of heterogeneity. By 1951 Welsh and Scottish regional heterogeneity increases substantially relative to England. If absolute rather than relative statistics are examined, English heterogeneity decreases from 0·26 to 0·12 in the 100 years from 1851 to 1951,

[1] The definition of Vw:

$$Vw = \sqrt{\dfrac{\dfrac{\sum\limits_{i}(y_i - \bar{y})^2}{N}}{\bar{y}}}, \text{ where } N = \text{number of counties}$$

A similar measure which is weighted by population has been employed in cross-national studies where the real units for which statistics are selected vary considerably. This is not the case in intra-national comparisons.

while the Welsh and Scottish levels increase significantly—the former, from 0·26 to 0·38; the latter from 0·36 to 0·53. The absolute rate for Northern Ireland looks somewhat curvilinear, while the relatively high levels of Vw attained by Ireland are a function of the over-all extremely low mean of non-agricultural occupations.

Similar absolute increases in regional heterogeneity in the Celtic regions may be found along dimensions of *manufacturing occupations, commercial and professional occupations*, and the *infant mortality* rate. In each of these examples the trend in England was towards homogeneity, while the reverse was true for all Celtic regions. Increasing trends towards regional homogeneity can be found in considering levels of *employment, urbanization, illiteracy, demographic growth*, and *per capita income*. Jeffrey Williamson's hypothesis of the curvilinear path of regional economic inequality over time is incidentally supported in these data.[1] However, this pattern by no means holds within all the various regions of the British Isles. England actually has a higher Vw in 1961 than in 1851 —in other words there is more variation in county incomes with increasing time—though the relationship over time approaches Williamson's expected curvilinear pattern. Wales and Scotland, on the other hand, simultaneously experience a steady decline in county income variation.

Table 5.3 shows the extent of enclave-hinterland differences in all five regions of the British Isles for non-agricultural occupations. It was constructed by subtracting the mean proportion of non-agricultural occupations in non-industrial counties from the industrial (according to the previous definition) county mean. Whereas the extent of enclave–hinterland difference between England, Wales, and Scotland is small in 1851, by 1961 it has stretched out considerably. Similarly, whereas the English statistic falls over the period from 35 to 16, it rises in Wales and Scotland with time. The gaps in the

[1] If the Vws for counties, instead of regions, are considered, the curvilinear relationship holds:

Year	Vw in per capita Income ($N = 86$)
1851	0·36
1861	0·32
1871	0·33
1881	0·34
1891	0·40
1901	0·48
1951	0·30
1961	0·26

145

Irish statistics occur because there is no heavily industrial county, or enclave, in certain years. Table 5.3 thus demonstrates that the higher *Vw*s for Wales and Scotland do not merely represent random county variation, but are systematically related to levels of industrialization. A relatively high *Vw* indicates the necessity of investigating sub-regional phenomena.

Thus in general terms, it is possible to see that development had

TABLE 5.3 *Enclave-hinterland differences: in non-agricultural occupations**

	England	Wales	Scotland	N. Ireland	Ireland
1851	35	(28)	36	(52)	(63)
1861	35	33	43	(52)	(61)
1871	29	30	45	(52)	(59)
1881	28	33	44	(48)	57
1891	25	37	43	(49)	(57)
1901	24	35	55	(51)	(59)
1911	24	33	39	(48)	60
1921	27	37	38	(47)	64
1931	21	39	47	(48)	(65)
1951	16	34	50	(30)	62
1961†	[16]	[34]	[50]	33	59

* In years when there were no industrial counties in a region, the non-industrial mean is subtracted from the minimum level of non-agricultural occupations necessary to define the county as industrial. The result appears in parentheses.
† [ ] indicates estimates from 1951 data.

somewhat different consequences in England than it did in the Celtic periphery. The increasing internal structural differences in Wales and Scotland are reminiscent of the discussions of dualistic or pluralistic economies in the literature of less developed societies, which arose as a function of their colonial mode of development.[1] Metropolitan

[1] 'The third line of expansion of the European industrial economy was towards already inhabited regions, some of which were densely populated, whose old economic systems were of various, but invariably precapitalistic types. The contacts between the vigorous capitalistic economies and these regions of long-standing habitation did not occur in a uniform manner. In some cases interest was limited to the opening up of lines of trade. In others there prevailed right from the start a desire to encourage the production of raw materials for which demand was increasing in the industrial centers. The effect of the impact of capitalist expansion on the archaic structures varied from region to region, being conditioned by local circumstances, the type of capitalistic penetration, and the intensity of the penetration. The result, however, was almost always to create hybrid structures, part tending to behave as a capitalistic system, part perpetuating the features of the previously existing system. The phenomenon of under-development today is precisely a matter of this type of dualistic economy.' Celso

investment in these areas often led to highly specialized export economies. The primary products are obtained in hinterland areas, then passed on to coastal ports for shipment to metropolitan markets or manufacturers. The enclaves in colonial areas are urbanized, Western-oriented, cosmopolitan centers which become highly differentiated from their respective hinterlands, such that they may be considered appendages to the metropolitan economy and— to a lesser extent—culture. The existence of enclave–hinterland conflict in societies of the Third World is an important structural obstacle to the development of a fully national solidarity.

Certain parallels may be drawn between the experience of the typical Third World colony or neo-colony and that of Celtic periphery in the British Isles. Since the colony develops as an appendage to the metropolitan economy, and in this sense is used instrumentally by the metropolis, it most frequently serves as a source for primary or extractive products for metropolitan industrial manufacture and distribution or for food supply. In contrast to the highly specialized nature of Celtic economic structure, the industrial economy of England was diversified—built upon textiles, general manufacturing, steel, coal, and commercial and financial services— and hence, as a whole it was much less vulnerable to international price fluctuations. England also had the advantage of producing mass commodities for the large domestic market, an option not so readily available to Wales, which would have had to compete with Durham and Northumberland in the internal market for coal, and Scotland, which all too quickly saturated the domestic market for ships and locomotives, its most important exports.

Since colonial development occurs as a result of territorially exogenous forces, initiated by conquest, it tends to be dissimilar to that type of development which emerges endogenously in a society, free from external political manipulation or control. In the interest of economic efficiency, and in response to metropolitan demand, there is frequent resort to labor-intensive economies of large scale, effectively reducing the variety of colonial exports, while substantially increasing their quantity, and hence value to the metropolis. The basic distinction is this: there tends to arise a 'national'

Furtado, *Development and Underdevelopment* (Berkeley: 1967), p. 129. These two sectors of the colonial economy are, however, integrally linked together. See Keith Griffin, *Underdevelopment in Spanish America: An Interpretation* (London: 1969), pp. 19–48.

division of labor, such that the majority of manufacturing, processing, and distributing functions in that economic unit formed by the union of the colony and the metropolis are performed in the latter nation, whereas the former is in the subordinate position of supplying materials and cheap labor. The issue is not just that the metropolis 'owns the means of production' for the colony, though in a general sense this tended to occur. Neither is it that the international prices for primary products might be declining relative to those of manufactures.

The structural consequences of colonial development were such that[1]

the country and the people were laid bare and defenseless to the play of the market forces as redirected only by the interests of the foreign metropolitan power. This by itself thwarted individual initiatives, at the same time as it prevented formation of a public policy motivated by the common interests of the people.

There are some significant analogies to economic development in the Celtic periphery in this very general discussion. First, with respect to economic specialization, both Wales and Ireland developed regional economies providing England with primary products. When English demand for primary products shifted, the Celtic economies were forced to respond. Thus from 1770 to 1850 production in southern Ireland went through successive phases emphasizing pasture, then tillage, then pasture once again.[2] Even today the great bulk of Eire's exports are consumed in Britain, and its economy remains but a regional appendage of the United Kingdom. Welsh development in the years after 1851 was dominated by the production of coal in Glamorgan and Monmouthshire. Wales became the world's greatest exporter of coal until World War One. Scotland's development was not nearly so specialized as this, though coal also provided a major source of revenue. The existence of textiles and heavy industry (ship and locomotive construction) in the Clydeside involved much skilled labor, engineering talent, sophisticated organization, none of which are typical of colonial economies. But when domestic and internal markets dried up for the products of Scottish heavy industry, depression affected the entire regional economy, just as it did the more specialized economies of Wales. One consequence

---

[1] Myrdal, *op. cit.*, p. 60.
[2] The central problem of Irish rural society was 'to alter the structure of Irish agriculture in response to the changing pattern of British demand.' Lyons, *op. cit.*, p. 31. See also Raymond D. Crotty, *Irish Agricultural Production: Its Volume and Structure* (Cork: 1969).

of the depression is that Wales and Scotland are no longer so economically specialized.[1] The agricultural hinterland areas of Wales, Scotland, and Ireland were sources of reserve labor for boom periods, and offered the possibility of cash-crop farming during slumps. Much of the activity carried on in the hinterland regions involved mixed farming, with an emphasis on livestock and dairying. In certain areas, notably lowland Scotland, agricultural improvement made great headway. Indeed, by the early nineteenth century the Scottish lowlands became renowned for the practice of progressive agriculture, especially in the application of scientific principles to animal husbandry. But elsewhere mixed farming largely served to meet the subsistence requirements of the rural population.[2]

Despite the existence of significant differences in local traditions separating, for instance, central and northern Wales, northeast and southwest Scotland, and eastern and western Ireland, the hinterlands as a whole became more and more distant, in a social sense, from the industrial enclaves of Wales and Scotland. The industrial cities were far more cosmopolitan, English-oriented in culture, and secular than the rural hinterlands. As this split developed it would have decisive political implications for Wales and Scotland following the evolution of a three-party system following World War One. Welsh and Scottish antipathy to the central government tended to be split up between two opposition groups, the Liberal and Labor parties.[3]

Further, the proliferation of railways as a result of industrialization did not serve to narrow this social distance. Railway development in the Celtic regions followed a very specific pattern. In most cases the rail routes linked the productive centers of the periphery to England. Thus in Wales north-south rail links were late to be constructed, and relatively sparse when compared with routes in the coal-mining areas of Glamorgan and Monmouthshire. Railway extension was much less responsive to population density in Wales, Scotland, and Ireland than in England.[4] Finally, it must be

---

[1] A. J. Brown, *The Framework of Regional Economics in the United Kingdom* (Cambridge: 1972), p. 147.

[2] In certain localities economic diversification failed despite valiant attempts on the part of landowners to promote it. For an interesting case study see E. S. Richards, 'Structural change in a regional economy: Sutherland and the Industrial Revolution, 1780–1830,' *Economic History Review*, 2nd ser., 26, 1 (1973).

[3] See chapter 9.

[4] This has led one writer on Ireland to note that 'before 1850 economic development had been hindered by an underdeveloped transport network. Since

emphasized (in this context) that the major financial institutions in the United Kingdom have always been English, and that London has served as the primary repository of credit and investment capital. Thus, when most individual investment decisions concerning the Celtic lands are made, they are largely decided in London by Englishmen who may be expected to have little knowledge, sympathy, or interest in these peripheral regions.

To this point in this chapter several important differences in Celtic and English patterns of development have been elaborated. Whereas industrialization has become diffused throughout a large proportion of English counties, it was spatially confined to much smaller and relatively compact areas in the Celtic periphery. While the English economy became highly diversified, the peripheral economies were on the contrary extremely specialized, and thus particularly vulnerable to extra-regional price changes. Since industrialization was so geographically widespread in England, it served to dampen traditional sub-regional political and cultural differences, such as those which existed between the northern counties and London and the southeast; whereas in the Celtic periphery (save in southern Ireland where regional specialization had remained agricultural), differences between industrial enclaves and hinterland areas became exaggerated, thereby contributing to the erosion of regional solidarity. Finally, industrialization did not function to narrow systematic patterns of regional economic inequality between England and the Celtic lands.

THE INTERPRETATION OF ECONOMIC INEQUALITY

In the previous sections it has been demonstrated that the spatial diffusion of industrialization was highly skewed in the British Isles, and that large sectors of the Celtic periphery remained non-industrial. The possibility remains that the systematic economic inequalities persisting between the Celtic areas and England are merely a reflection of the rural-urban differences found to some extent in all societies, and that, in and of themselves, little can be inferred about the patterns of regional dominance from these statistics. In part this may be the case because of a downward bias in rural economies on indicators such as *per capita* income, where

---

1850 Ireland has been an underdeveloped economy with a highly developed transport system.' J. Lee, 'The Railways in the Irish Economy' in L. M. Cullen, ed, *The Formation of the Irish Economy* (Cork: 1969), pp. 77–87.

much individual income essentially goes unreported since it is consumed in kind. Clearly differences in occupational categories and the level of urbanization also follow from this essential difference in the mode of production.

The implication, then, is that there can be no *a priori* grounds for believing that industrial development alone is in each region's best interests, and that those areas remaining rural in character are necessarily exploited or otherwise discriminated against by market forces or the actions of the central government. Capital-intensive agricultural production may be a perfectly suitable alternative to industrialization in so far as prospects for capital accumulation are concerned. Indeed, as it becomes evident that industrialization has resulted in greater costs to the environment, in terms of environmental pollution, than had previously been appreciated, the non-industrial path to development—such as that followed in Denmark, New Zealand, and, to an extent, Eire, as well—may well prove the wiser social investment in the long run.[1]

Hence it is difficult to interpret the data on economic inequalities unless the mode of production can satisfactorily be eliminated as a source of variation in these regions. That is to say, the wealth of English industrial counties must be compared to those—admittedly fewer—industrial counties of the Celtic periphery, while simultaneously repeating the process for the non-industrial counties. What is ultimately required is a method for holding the variations in county levels of industrialization constant.

Given the adequacy of available historical data this is no easy task. Since industrialization is a multi-dimensional concept, it is clearly advantageous to employ multiple indicators in its definition. In the attempt to specify significant indicators of industrialization, twenty-seven social and demographic variables were subjected to a principal axis factor analysis for the years 1851, 1861, 1871, 1881, 1891, 1901, 1911, 1921, 1931, and 1951. The factor loadings were rotated to Kaiser's varimax criterion facilitating empirical interpretation.[2] From these ten factor analyses a factor of industrialization was determined, with mean loadings of 0·857 for the percentage of the male labor force engaged in manufacturing occupations, and 0·850 for the percentage of the county's male labor force in

[1] However, a consideration of New Zealand's difficulties during the negotiations on British entry into the Common Market suggests this is an overly optimistic assessment of her economic well-being.
[2] Harry Harman, *Modern Factor Analysis* (Chicago: 1960).

agricultural occupations (Table 5.4). Four other variables were consistently related to this factor over time: proportion of the population aged 65 and over; decennial demographic growth; crude marriage rate per 1,000 inhabitants, and proportion of the county population living in cities over 20,000. A seventh variable, the percentage of employed males in commercial and professional occupations, was included as an indicator of industrialization on the basis of its increasing significance over time. The remaining twenty variables are either not related or are inconsistently loaded on the industrialization factor over the continuum.

Multiple regression analysis was then employed to control for differing levels of industrialization. The indicator of *per capita* income was regressed on these seven variables, empirically related to the industrialization factor, for all counties in England, Wales, and Scotland at all eight points in time where data were available (1851–1901, 1951 and 1961). Data for all thirty-two counties in Ireland, south and north, was available only for 1861, 1871, 1881, and 1961, hence Ireland was not included in this series of regressions.[1] The multiple regression serves, in effect, as a means of holding these seven variables constant, thus enabling a comparison of county results with minute as well as large differences in the level of industrialization accounted for. On the basis of these data taken as a whole, for a given level of industrialization in a particular county in a specific year, the regression equation predicts an estimated level of *per capita* income. Map 4 shows those counties whose mean level of *per capita* income for all eight observations in time was overestimated on the basis of the industrialization variables.[2] In other words, these are counties which are relatively poor given a particular level of industrialization. The preponderance of shaded areas in the Celtic regions is unmistakable, with the single exception of the southern Scottish lowland agricultural counties. Similarly, large areas in England have positive residuals from the regression equation.

[1] The inclusion of Ireland and Northern Ireland in the multiple regression reveals that Northern Ireland is the most disadvantaged of all regions in the British Isles from 1861–81, with roughly twice the negative residual of Wales. Surprisingly, Ireland's income residuals are higher than those of Wales in these years perhaps reflecting the common British complaint of the time that she was proportionally undertaxed.

[2] Since the variability of the *per capita* income variable is greater in 1951 and 1961, when it is based on total county income, than in the preceding years, it was necessary to standardize county income residuals at each observation to avoid a bias in the computation of longitudinal means.

TABLE 5.4 Loadings on the industrialization factor for all counties in England, Wales, Scotland, Northern Ireland, and Southern Ireland (N = 118)

Variable*	1851	1861	1871	1881	1891	1901	1911	1921	1931	1951	Absolute mean over time
(1) Manufacturing occs	0·832	0·852	0·869	0·912	0·936	0·898	0·809	0·754	0·863	0·842	0·857
(2) Agricultural occs	−0·871	−0·845	−0·858	−0·935	−0·929	−0·862	−0·833	−0·620	−0·920	−0·831	0·850
(3) Proportion 65 and over	−0·696	−0·431	−0·666	−0·687	−0·612	−0·766	−0·834	−0·643	−0·679	−0·697	0·671
(4) Decennial pop. growth	0·641	0·667	0·712	0·796	0·747	0·770	0·775	0·176	0·632	0·482	0·640
(5) Marriage rate	0·666	0·588	0·711	0·798	0·811	0·605	0·644	0·468	0·402	0·655	0·635
(6) Urbanization	0·538	0·547	0·556	0·624	0·598	0·626	0·694	0·561	0·772	0·687	0·620
(7) Infant mortality	0·823	0·398	0·661	0·754	0·754	0·802	0·776	0·719	−0·111	−0·119	0·592
(8) Birth rate	0·474	0·709	0·728	0·840	0·334	0·854	0·784	0·798	−0·117	−0·016	0·565
(9) Ethnic diversity	0·609	0·752	0·668	0·598	0·555	0·560	0·452	0·227	0·238	0·160	0·482
(10) Population	0·310	0·263	0·322	0·396	0·404	0·393	0·407	0·353	0·535	0·436	0·383
(11) Comm. and prof. occs	0·402	0·172	0·274	0·509	0·406	0·360	0·397	−0·037	0·613	0·510	0·368
(12) Irish born	−0·331	−0·345	−0·342	−0·514	−0·498	−0·436	−0·444	−0·108	−0·442	−0·219	0·368
(13) Roman Catholic	−0·342	−0·338	−0·328	−0·471	−0·478	−0·397	−0·416	−0·080	−0·399	−0·207	0·346
(14) Established Church	0·236	0·241	0·317	0·502	0·522	0·403	0·440	0·049	0·438	0·203	0·334
(15) Religiosity	−0·166	−0·284	−0·301	−0·408	−0·498	−0·110	−0·465	−0·311	−0·132	−0·361	0·304
(16) English born	0·083	0·056	0·176	0·335	0·401	0·259	0·347	0·006	0·692	0·278	0·263
(17) Foreign born	−0·012	0·259	0·243	0·157	0·244	0·152	0·291	0·117	0·502	0·248	0·223
(18) Celtic speakers	−0·223	−0·192	−0·186	−0·203	−0·167	−0·176	−0·229	−0·184	−0·332	−0·292	0·218
(19) Sex ratio	−0·152	−0·054	−0·117	0·098	0·135	−0·079	−0·018	0·193	−0·307	−0·281	0·143
(20) Female domestics	−0·104	−0·170	−0·136	−0·108	0·032	−0·080	−0·078	−0·365	−0·163	−0·049	0·129
(21) Nonconformity	0·228	0·216	0·107	0·095	0·086	0·130	0·124	0·095	0·043	0·082	0·121
(22) Employment	0·002	0·130	0·269	−0·135	−0·049	0·157	−0·002	0·016	0·328	0·026	0·075
(23) Welsh born	0·125	0·176	0·116	0·148	0·132	−0·110	0·118	0·049	−0·022	−0·002	0·098
(24) Scottish born	0·164	0·169	0·079	0·069	−0·006	−0·095	0·010	0·071	−0·253	−0·057	0·131
(25) City size	0·116	0·073	0·082	0·087	0·073	0·058	0·034	0·031	0·108	0·085	0·075
(26) Civil Service occs	0·104	0·034	−0·057	−0·029	−0·056	0·047	0·002	0·043	0·234	0·104	0·071
(27) Population density	0·074	0·023	0·042	0·054	0·063	0·066	0·059	0·038	0·150	0·134	0·070

* All variables, save (4), (10), (25) and (27), are proportional to county population.

Standardized mean income residuals which are negative for eight observations, 1851–1961

Map 4 Relatively disadvantaged counties, 1851–1961 (Great Britain)

This is a map showing counties which are more or less disadvantaged throughout the whole period. Figure 1 shows residuals from the predicted *per capita* income averaged for counties within England, Wales, and Scotland, at each point in time. It shows trends of income convergence over time which the over-all county means in Map 4 obscure. The most notable feature of Figure 1 is the persistence of Wales and Scotland beneath the English mean residual incomes, save the exceptions of 1891, when the Welsh, and 1951, when the Scottish residual values were highest. In linear regression analysis the residual obtained from the prediction of *per capita*

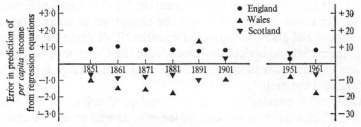

Figure 1   Mean regional residuals from multiple regression of *per capita* income on industrialization variables*

R_s^2: 1851 = 0·275; 1861 = 0·172; 1871 = 0·208; 1881 = 0·119; 1891 = 0·270; 1901 = 0·265; 1951 = 0·448; 1961 = 0·252.

* Manufacturing; agricultural; commercial and professional occupations; decennial population growth; proportion living in cities over 20,000; marriage rate, and proportion of population aged 65 and over.

income from the industrialization variables would usually be conceived as a random error term. However, the consistency of differences among both county and national means obtained in Map 4 and Figure 1 indicate that these residuals do not merely represent random error, but reflect variations between units which have not been specified in the predictive model.[1]

It may be unwise to speculate on the long-term trends towards convergence or divergence shown in Figure 1 because of the spottiness of the twentieth century data. Particularly significant is the absence of county tax returns during the years between the two world wars, when relative levels of unemployment soared in Wales and Scotland with the collapse of their respective economies. Nevertheless, on these somewhat shaky grounds, it may be suggested that there has been little tendency for convergence of these income residuals in the long run, from 1851 to 1961.

[1] One of the missing factors in the determination of county income is cultural: the degree to which given counties are anglicized. See chapter 10.

How can these differentials in average county income be interpreted? One possible explanation is immediately suggested by geographic considerations. Since the English agricultural counties are located in fertile lowland valleys, while large portions of the agricultural areas of the Celtic periphery are highland in character, hence much less potentially productive, it may be that the over-all average income differences between England and Wales and Scotland are due to inequalities among the non-industrial counties of both areas. Regional income differences would then occur even if there were little income variation among the industrial counties of all regions. But Table 5.5 rules out this explanation; the English–Celtic difference in income residuals holds at about the same level of magnitude for both industrial and non-industrial counties. This demonstrates that both industrial and agricultural counties in the Celtic periphery have generally been lower in income than corresponding English counties throughout the period.

Geographic constraints on agricultural productivity in the highlands, which inhibit economies of large scale and extensive capital investment, are probably sufficient to explain differences in income between Celtic and English agricultural counties. The high residuals for the southern Scottish agricultural counties lend support to this supposition. But to what can the differences among industrial counties be ascribed? There are several possibilities. The differential age structure of the respective regions is not one of them, since the income residual already controls for the proportion of elderly in the population. The sex ratio explains some of the difference in income between Scotland and England but it does not reduce the level of disparity of Wales. Hence the best explanation for this inequality of income likely involves factors more directly affecting the gross receipt of wages within each region. Unfortunately existing data do not permit the testing of these alternative explanations in time series.

It might be that the types of industries located in Wales and Scotland paid proportionately lower wages than the aggregate of English industries. However in the late nineteenth century miners and steelworkers were among the highest paid of all industrial workers. Hence in this period such an explanation is unlikely. If there were a greater proportion of skilled workers in English industry than in Welsh or Scottish industry income differentials of this kind would occur. It is also possible that lower wages were paid in Celtic counties than in English ones for comparable employment. While this might have been the case in the years preceding 1921—before

156

TABLE 5.5 Mean residuals from predicted per capita income by multiple regression

	1851	(N)	1861	(N)	1871	(N)	1881	(N)	1891	(N)	1901	(N)	1951	(N)	1961	(N)
Industrial counties in																
England	+1·35	2	−0·67	3	+0·65	4	+1·42	6	+1·09	8	−0·58	10	+2·39	16	+4·82	16
Wales	—		−1·60	1	−2·40	1	−4·10	2	−0·65	2	−3·10	2	−13·30	2	−22·04	2
Scotland	−0·25	2	−1·07	2	−0·20	3	−0·19	7	−0·47	6	+0·07	9	+1·21	8	−4·82	8
All industrial counties	+0·55	4	−0·97	7	−0·05	8	−0·07	15	+0·29	16	−0·54	21	+0·82	26	−0·21	26
Non-industrial counties in																
England	+0·61	38	+1·08	37	+0·75	36	+0·57	34	+0·20	32	+0·56	30	−0·17	24	+11·47	24
Wales	−0·83	13	−1·40	12	−1·55	12	−1·11	11	+1·52	11	−0·76	11	−4·56	11	−19·79	11
Scotland	−0·74	31	−0·52	30	−0·49	30	−0·24	26	−1·03	27	+0·05	24	+1·31	25	−2·09	25
All non-industrial counties	−0·13	82	+0·10	79	−0·08	78	+0·02	71	−0·07	70	+0·15	65	−0·36	60	+0·09	60

the development of strong industrial trade unions—by 1951 and 1961 collective bargaining was carried out on a national basis.

Data from the 1960s indicate that regional variations in economic activity play the major role in accounting for income inequality.[1] A greater proportion of the population is employed, or economically active, in England than in the Celtic fringe. Increasing unemployment following World War One in the Celtic industrial counties and the relative collapse of Celtic industry during the depression could account for the discrepancy in income in more recent years. Unemployment in Wales and Scotland continued to be significantly above the national average at the end of the 1960s.[2]

CONCLUSION

Though it has been determined that regional economic inequalities have persisted—even when taking comparable levels of industrialization into account—for over a century between England and the Celtic periphery, the significance of this fact is not at all clear. Since regional economic equality has not been a natural outcome of the extension of markets into the periphery the central government was urged to take a more active role in redistributing resources to benefit these areas, along with other depressed areas within England. It should be clear that the state has a great deal to say about the extent of regional inequality it will countenance. There are several means by which the state may transfer resources from richer to poorer regions. Taxation is merely one of these. Development in the periphery may also be stimulated by an increase in the level of public expenditure, or by the choice of peripheral sites for capital investments relating to military or administrative activities.

At two stages in recent years, 1945–8, and in the 1960s, the British government has made regional development a high priority in its domestic program, in response to political mobilization in depressed areas.[3] It was recognized that new manufacturing industry should be attracted to the peripheral regions, since basic industry induces an additional 80 per cent of jobs, largely in the service sector. To this end the state extended sizable incentives to industrial firms willing to locate in areas such as South Wales and Scotland. If the results of these policies are evaluated in terms of statistics of the growth in

[1] Brown, op. cit., p. 57.
[2] Hammond, op. cit. The current regional differences in economic activity show up most strikingly not among men, but among women. See Brown, op. cit., pp. 207–10.   [3] Gavin McCrone, Regional Policy in Britain (London: 1969), p. 271.

regional employment it appears that some progress has been made since the early 1960s.[1] Hence there seems no reason to question the fact that state policy may go a long way to redress regional inequalities if sufficient political pressure can be mobilized.

However, despite existing programs for regional development it is indisputable that economic inequality persists in the Celtic fringe. Although the extent of regional inequality in Great Britain is not large when compared with such countries as Italy, it is politically significant none the less. Therefore the need for such development has not subsided. This is a problem of decisive interest because it challenges many of the assumptions inherent in development theory, notably those stressing the inevitably revolutionary consequences of industrialization within territories.

No doubt many additional causes of the persistence of Celtic economic disadvantages in the past century remain to be discovered and analyzed. In the conclusion of this chapter I would like to suggest the possible salience of a social factor, namely ethnocentrism, which may be inferred to be involved, though it is difficult to estimate the extent of its influence.

Writers often distinguish between two types of causes of regional economic differences. Structural disadvantages in a given region may be said to occur when its dominant industry begins to decline because of an inability to compete with more efficient producers in the domestic or international markets. Wales and Scotland have been areas of declining industry, particularly coal and shipbuilding, since the end of World War One. A second source of regional differences lies in locational disadvantages which are thought to characterize specific regions. A firm may, for example, refuse to be located far from its target market, or in an area where labor productivity is supposedly low despite financial incentives from the central government.

Whereas the diagnosis of in industry in decline is relatively objective and therefore not prone to argument among qualified observers, the striking element in the notion of locational disadvantage of its inherently subjective quality.[2] True, transport costs are

---

[1] Brown, *op. cit.*, p. 318.
[2] A. O. Hirschman (*op. cit.*, pp. 184-5) puts this somewhat differently: 'Thus investors spend a long time mopping up all the opportunities around some "growth pole" and neglect those that may have arisen or could be made to arise elsewhere. What appears to happen is that *the external economies due to the poles, though real, are consistently overestimated by the economic operators*. The reason for this tendency . . . must be sought in the realm of social psychology.'

a factor in the decision to locate new industry, though they are far less important now than at any previous time. But the decision to relocate an industry is far more complex than the simple question of transport costs would suggest. There are other considerations, some of which may be subject to ethnocentric bias. A survey of corporate decisions rejecting the establishment of Scottish branches or outright relocation cited the importance of criteria of 'the supposed remoteness of Scotland from the main markets and centers of supply . . . but [there was also] *unwillingness to enter an unfamiliar social environment and the belief that Scottish labor was intractable and not highly productive.*'[1] Hence even the active intrusion of the central government into the marketplace has failed to bring about substantial improvement in redressing regional economic inequality. A. O. Hirschman comments that the mere fact that an ethnically nondistinctive region has been backward for a period of time may create an image of it in dynamic areas which actually serves to preserve and contribute to regional differences by ideological means:[2]

The successful groups and regions will widely and extravagantly proclaim their superiority over the rest of the country and their countrymen. It is interesting to note that to some extent these claims are self-enforcing. Even though the initial success of these groups may often be due to their luck or environmental factors such as resource endowment, matters will not always be left there. Those who have been caught by progress will always maintain that they were the ones who did the catching: they will easily convince themselves, and attempt to convince others, that their accomplishments are primarily owed to their superior moral qualities and conduct.

It has long been recognized that definitions of cultural inferiority have a way of becoming self-fulfilling prophecies, thereby legitimizing the institutionalization of inequality between collectivities.[3] Since most of the investment capital in the British Isles is concentrated in England, it might be asked whether social definitions such as these, when they are tinged with ethnic prejudice against the 'Celts' of the British periphery, might affect the concrete decisions of individual investors. Such ethnic discrimination was characteristic of English attitudes towards the Celtic areas in the nineteenth cen-

---

[1] Cited in A. J. Brown, 'Surveys of applied economics: regional economics, with special reference to the United Kingdom,' *Economic Journal*, 79, 316 (1969), p. 778. Emphasis has been added.

[2] Hirschman, *op. cit.*, p. 185.

[3] The social mechanisms of such institutionalization are very engagingly discussed by Robert K. Merton, 'The Self-Fulfilling Prophecy' in *Social Theory and Social Structure* (New York: 1957).

tury and earlier.[1] Further, actual English decisions to invest in Wales and Scotland were conditional upon the realization of political stability, in practice involving the suppression of Celtic culture in highland areas. While this is a highly inferential suggestion, further analysis lends it some empirical support. Within Welsh and Scottish counties the prevalence of Celtic culture, as indicated by Welsh and Gaelic speaking, and religious nonconformity, is negatively associated with *per capita* income throughout the period.[2] These findings have been demonstrated to be independent of differences in the level of county industrialization.

In fine, continuing Celtic economic backwardness might be seen as an outcome of many individual decisions which affect the Celtic regions directly and indirectly, but which are, in themselves, not part of a planned or even consciously stated policy aiming at the exploitation of the Celtic periphery. The resulting pattern of economic disadvantages in the Celtic lands may in fact be the socially unanticipated result of the aggregate of these individual decisions. In this way the present form and future direction of social life in the Celtic regions may be very largely influenced by market considerations in the United Kingdom as a whole, as well as by the social definitions of significant actors in England with no necessary interest in or commitment to development in the periphery. The phenomenon of Celtic nationalism may be seen in this context as a political response to the persistence of regional inequality.

APPENDIX: A NOTE ON THE PER CAPITA INCOME VARIABLE

Historical estimates of national and regional income accounts are necessarily of doubtful accuracy since the techniques of accounting are of recent vintage, and hence the statistics upon which proper accounts rest were not collected. Despite these limitations there have been two kinds of attempts at national income estimation for nineteenth-century Britain. Estimates for the early part of the century have been garnered from various contemporary writers interested in measuring the growing wealth of the realm.[3]

---

[1] See L. P. Curtis, Jr, *Anglo-Saxons and Celts* (Bridgeport, Ct: 1968); W. R. Jones, 'England against the Celtic fringe: a study in cultural stereotypes,' *Cahiers d'Histoire Mondiale*, 13, 1 (1971); and Edward D. Snyder, 'The Wild Irish: a study of some English satires against the Irish, Scots, and Welsh,' *Modern Philology*, 17, 2 (1920).   [2] See chapter 10.

[3] Phyllis Deane, 'Contemporary estimates of national income in the first half of the nineteenth century,' *Economic History Review*, 2nd ser., 8, 3 (1956).

The second method has relied heavily on income tax statistics supplemented by estimates of the national wage bill, agricultural income and productivity, and other types of income excluded from the tax returns.[1] In the course of a tortuous development the income tax went through many revisions which make the historical series discontinuous and generally incomparable over time.[2] Changes in the exemption limits have to be laboriously calculated if the absolute growth of the national income is desired. If one is interested in the absolute value, in real income, of the tax assessment the net return must be calculated. However, net returns have been published only since the twentieth century. Although the net value for each schedule has been estimated back to 1855 there is no means by which these statistics can be determined for constituent regions.

Since I am not particularly interested in the growth of county incomes over time, but rather in the estimation of the relative shares of national income distributed in counties and regions, the gross measurements are of some value. By holding exemption rates constant for all four regions in given years a crude measure of regional distribution of income at one point in time may be obtained.

There are further difficulties for the period 1851–1911. The income tax was composed of five separate schedules, A through E, corresponding to different sources of income. Only three of these schedules, A, B, and D, relating to income from rents, farms, and industry respectively, were published in county returns. The missing schedules, C and E, refer to income from foreign investment and government salaries. They tend to make up about 15 per cent of the total tax bill through the nineteenth century, and perhaps 20 per cent by 1911. Since there is no way to obtain a county breakdown for these sources of income, I have ignored them in creating the variable, marking the assumption that *per capita* returns for the schedules are equal for all counties and regions. There is abundant reason to question this assumption. London has long been the center of both Britain's administration and finance, hence England's share of schedules C and E should be significantly higher than those in Wales, Scotland, and most especially, Ireland. Thus this indicator probably underestimates English income.

In the construction of the variable, exemption rates were standardized at each decennial period according to the analysis of J. C.

[1] C. H. Feinstein, 'Income and investment in the United Kingdom, 1856–1914,' *Economic Journal*, 71, 282 (1961).
[2] J. C. Stamp, *British Incomes and Property* (London: 1927).

Stamp. Estimates of Ireland's 'true taxability' were taken from Stamp's calculations. It has been assumed that tax evasion for the counties occurred at a constant rate.

The income variable for the years 1951 and 1961 is somewhat different, in that it represents total county net income before taxes. These data were collected and published in county returns by the Board of Inland Revenue, and have been previously used to estimate regional income inequality.[1]

It is possible to gauge the reliability of this indicator of *per capita* income by considering it with reference to a much more elaborate estimate of Gross Regional Product derived for the year 1961 by V. H. Woodward.[2] In comparison with Woodward's results my indicator overestimates Scottish income by about 10 per cent whereas it underestimates that of Northern Ireland by roughly the same margin. The two Welsh statistics are, however, comparable.

[1] Williamson, *op. cit.*
[2] V. H. Woodward, *Regional Social Accounts for the United Kingdom* (Cambridge: 1970), NIESR Regional Papers I.

CHAPTER 6

THE ANGLICIZATION OF THE CELTIC
PERIPHERY, 1851–1961

The language of the conqueror in the mouth of the conquered is ever
the language of the slave.

TACITUS

ONE of the most significant, if least studied, processes in the
development of the modern state has been the emergence of national
cultures. The particularity of localities and regions with respect to
language, 'ethnicity,' and style of life has greatly eroded since
medieval times. The growing strength of the central bureaucracy in
the core areas of the absolutist states—Castile in Spain; Île-de-
France in France, London and the Home Counties in England—
usually established the specific cultural forms of these territories as
standards of highest prestige in their respective societies. The advent
of industrialization seemed to promise that cultural homogenization
would proceed relatively quickly. The nineteenth-century sociologists,
otherwise a fairly contentious lot, were nevertheless in substantial
agreement in predicting the eventual demise of the culture of peripheral areas within the boundaries of the industrializing states.[1]

The evolution of a dominant national culture within a heterogeneous polity has crucial significance for the establishment of
centralized authority. Authority is ultimately legitimated through the
manipulation of symbols. Historically, ecclesiastical and educational
institutions have been established, or appropriated, by states to

---

[1] This is clearly implied in the following passage from *The Communist Manifesto:* 'Independent, or but loosely connected provinces, with separate interests,
laws, governments and systems of taxation, became lumped together into one
nation, with one code of laws, one national class interest, one frontier, and one
customs tariff,' in L. S. Feuer, ed., *Marx and Engels: Basic Writings on Politics
and Philosophy* (New York: 1959), p. 12. Emile Durkheim pointed towards a
similar conclusion. See chapter 2 for an elaboration.

164

serve as disseminators of these symbols, among other things. As a result these institutions have typically enhanced the legitimacy of states. Cultural institutions intrude upon political life in a simple enough fashion. To the extent that individuals and groups embrace cultural institutions identified with the state their political demands will not be couched in cultural terms. For instance, Anglican workers are not likely to attack a British government for its religious particularism; their political demands must generally be framed in class terms. However, Nonconformist workers may challenge the state in the name of a disadvantaged class, on the one hand, and in the name of a cultural minority on the other. The dual basis of this challenge creates a potential for dissent among several different strata. Thus, cultural institutions which develop independent of state sponsorship, and in competition with state-supported institutions, may become nodes for the crystallization of political opposition. Once a cultural institution, such as a church or a voluntary association, perceives that its interests are not congruent with those of the state, it is particularly well adapted to extend its influence in the society, for it can, within variable limits, engage in socialization contrary to the state's ends. When seen from this perspective, it is easy to understand why so many of the political struggles of modernizing societies have been fought over issues of national culture.

It may be suggested that the political significance of cultural distinctions in general tends to increase as industrialization proceeds, unless homogenization has been achieved early. With the extension of formal democracy in polities the state typically removes certain external constraints on individual behavior. The idea of citizenship carries with it the extension of formal political, civil, and social rights. In this setting cultural institutions become even more crucial, since the burden of social control shifts somewhat from the state itself to agencies responsible for the internalization of norms and values, that is, socializing agencies. As literacy increases, ideas subversive of state authority may reach wider audiences. As education becomes a social right, questions concerning secular as against ecclesiastical instruction, and the choice of the language(s) in which such instruction may legally occur become politically charged. In the resolution of these conflicts it is likely that certain distinct cultural groups will lose out, and may consequently be placed at a disadvantage. Linguistic groups provide a familiar example. When states refuse to recognize the legal status of a language, its speakers may be prejudiced in juridical proceedings, in meeting requirements for civil service appointments, and in the allocation of occupational roles more generally. In this way cultural distinctions are perceived to have salience in the system of stratification, and thereby enter the domain of politics.[1]

There is scant evidence concerning the evolution of cultural homogeneity in modern societies, in part because few states have published enumerations of the cultural composition of their populations in successive censuses. Where such data on cultural characteristics are readily available they have been used; however, few historians have attempted to discover alternative statistical sources which might also bear on this phenomenon.

Despite this lack of evidence it is possible to suggest two plausible and alternative theoretical models of cultural dynamics in societies composed of a culturally dominant core, and one or more peripheral regions of distinct culture. The diffusion model of core-periphery relations presumes that the cultural integrity of separate regions can persist only in the absence of sustained interregional contact. The cultural distinctiveness of the periphery is therefore seen to be the result of its isolation from the core. Hence any change in the situation which is responsible for heightening the level of interregional transactions will, in this model, ultimately serve the cause of cultural homogenization, or acculturation. Industrialization causes a transformation in core-periphery relations and ushers in a long series of consequences which are conveniently summarized by the concept of social mobilization. After social mobilization is initiated acculturation proceeds rapidly. The relative cultural dominance of core and peripheral groups will be determined, in part, by the size of the respective collectivities. Furthermore, industrialization is associated with high levels of political centralization; this serves to increase both the prestige and effective scope of the core culture.

Whereas the diffusion model predicts a lessening of cultural differences between the core and the periphery following industrialization, the internal colonial model suggests that cultural convergence between core and peripheral areas is unlikely to occur. This is because the internal colonial model posits the existence of a cultural division of labor. If social stratification in the periphery is based on observable cultural differences, and if residential patterns are correspondingly segregated, then culture maintenance, and not change, is the likely outcome.

[1] R. F. Inglehart and M. Woodward, 'Language conflicts and political community.' *Comparative Studies in Society and History*, 10, 1 (1967).

There is some quantitative evidence which appears to support the diffusion hypothesis, but most of it comes from cross-sectional data in which whole states are taken as units.[1] Unfortunately an evaluation of the relative merits of these models requires observations taken at several points in time, and therefore longitudinal data. Cross-sectional data have no logical bearing on propositions about the consequences of change. But there are other reasons to question the precise nature of the relationship between industrialization and cultural homogeneity. In particular, the salience of nationalist sentiments in the modern world has confounded diffusionist expectations by tending to legitimate culture maintenance in certain peripheral areas. The revival of 'ancient' cultural forms—such as Gaelic speaking in Ireland or Hebrew speaking in Israel—is a frequent characteristic of contemporary nationalist movements. Altogether the problem remains very much open.

This chapter will explore some consequences of industrialization for the evolution of a national culture in the British Isles. The adequacy of these alternative models of core-periphery relations will be discussed with regard to two cultural *differentiae*, religious affiliation and peripheral language maintenance. Towards this end, this chapter presents new data on the distribution of religious affiliation in the counties of the British Isles from 1851 to 1961, as well as considering statistics on the changes in rates of Welsh and Gaelic speaking. These data indicate that industrialization has not led to a convergence of religious affiliation in the core and peripheral areas. While Celtic language maintenance has declined consistently in the periphery, this apparently has not been a direct consequence of industrialization, but rather the result of political intervention by the central government, in providing for compulsory public education on a monoglot basis. At least with reference to the Celtic fringe, these results are less consistent with the diffusion model than with the internal colonial model.

THE DISTRIBUTION OF RELIGIOUS AFFILIATION IN THE BRITISH ISLES

During their long historical association with England, the Celtic lands have been not only economically dissimilar but culturally

[1] Marie R. Haug, 'Social and cultural pluralism as a concept in social system analysis,' *American Journal of Sociology*, 73, 3 (1967), pp. 294–304; and Jonathan Pool, 'National development and language diversity,' *La Monda Lingvo-Problemo*, 1, 3 (1969), pp. 140–55.

distinctive as well. This is especially so with respect to religious and linguistic differences. There had been a great religious transformation in England when Henry VIII instituted the Reformation by cutting ecclesiastical links to the Vatican and established a state church governed by Episcopal principles. Since then the Church of England has been the dominant religious institution in England. But this pattern was not exactly repeated in any of the Celtic regions. Despite the attempts of generations of English rulers in Ireland, the adherence of the population to Roman Catholicism could not be swayed and a Reformation never occurred there. In Wales Protestantism triumphed as a consequence of events in England. But by the early nineteenth century the popular appeal of the Church of Wales (Anglican) eroded relative to that of various Nonconformist sects which swept the country on a tide of evangelism. Subsequently the separate cultural identity of Wales was prominently identified with Nonconformity. Last, because Scotland was a sovereign land in the sixteenth century, the Scottish Reformation came under the influence of John Knox rather than Henry Tudor. The organization of the Church of Scotland became Presbyterian, with significant Calvinist influences, rather than Episcopalian. Upon incorporation Scotland was allowed to keep her church intact.

These regional religious differences were to an extent superimposed upon linguistic differences in Wales, Scotland, and Ireland. One of the legacies of the Celtic social organization was the persistence of the Celtic languages Gaelic and Welsh among certain groups in the periphery. By the beginning of the nineteenth century most of Wales was Welsh speaking. A smaller proportion of Irish spoke Gaelic, and in Scotland Gaelic speaking was confined largely to the highlands.

What is generally known about the distribution of religious affiliation of the population of England and Wales in the nineteenth century comes largely from one historical source. In 1851 a religious census was conducted on a single Sunday, which tabulated church attendance by various denominations in each county. These data have frequently been used to indicate the relative strength of Anglicanism and Nonconformity in nineteenth-century Britain. Some attention has been devoted to the question of the geographical distribution of religious affiliation.[1] However, no similar source of religious statis-

---

[1] J. L. and Barbara Hammond, *The Town Laborer: The New Civilization, 1760–1832* (New York: 1968); E. J. Hobsbawm, 'Methodism and the Threat of Revolution' in *Laboring Men: Studies in the History of Labor* (New York: 1967); and John D. Gay, *The Geography of Religion in England* (London: 1971).

tics exists to which the 1851 data may be compared. Consequently much of the discussion of changes in the strength of Protestant denominations in the late nineteenth and early twentieth centuries has remained speculative and inferential. The problem itself has been regarded as of decisive interest if only because of Elie Halévy's claim that Methodism was responsible for inhibiting a social revolution in nineteenth-century England.[1]

This chapter introduces a different indicator of religious affiliation in an attempt to describe changes in religious affiliation in England and the Celtic periphery. The indicator has been taken from marriage registers compiled by the office of the Registrar of Births, Deaths, and Marriages. As a source of data these statistics have several obvious advantages over the 1851 census material.

An analysis of marriage registers by county has been published annually since 1851 (exceptions for Wales in 1851 and 1891 must be noted), which is the beginning of many other county statistical series on occupational and demographic variables. This makes comparisons over time feasible. Additionally, the indicator is behavioral. It was constructed in the following way. For every year, in each county, the marriage register records the total number of registered marriages. This total is then disaggregated according to the type of ceremony by which the marriage rites were performed. Denominations are specified in considerable detail—for instance, there are separate data on Quakers, several types of Methodists and even Jews—but for the purposes of this study were classified in three broad categories: Established Church marriages (Church of England —England, Church of Wales—Wales, Church of Scotland—Scotland [Note that the Church of Scotland is Presbyterian and not in any way affiliated with the others which are Episcopalian], Church of Ireland—Ireland); Nonconformist marriages (all varieties of Methodists, Baptists, Congregationalists, Unitarians, etc.); and Roman Catholic marriages. The religious variables corresponding to these categories were established by taking the respective proportions of total marriages contributed by each religious grouping within counties. One other variable was created as well. Information is also available on marriages performed under secular auspices by civil authorities. This number was then calculated as a proportion of the total number of marriages to provide a crude indicator of each county's religiosity, here defined in opposition to secularism.

[1] Elie Halévy, *History of the English People in the Nineteenth Century*, vol. I (London: 1965).

169

The reliability of these indicators is initially dependent upon two major assumptions. The first assumption is that the propensity to marry does not vary significantly within the different religious categories. There appears no reason to doubt this, except in the case of Ireland.[1] The second assumption is that the age structure of British and Irish counties is comparable with respect to the ages of highest marriageability. These are the ages twenty to twenty-nine. I have no direct means of testing this assumption. It should be noted, however, that the greatest variations in age structure between populations seem to occur in groups either younger or older than twenty to twenty-nine.[2] It has previously been determined that the crude marriage rate is positively correlated with the level of county industrialization in Great Britain and Ireland.[3] Therefore, it is likely that these indicators will be biased by the differential concentration of religious groups in industrial and non-industrial areas. For example, if Nonconformity is predominantly an urban phenomenon in the British Isles, while Anglicanism is largely rural, then the incidence of Nonconformist adherence may be overrepresented in these data.

Even if these assumptions are granted the data are questionable on other grounds. It is likely that the statistics on Established Church marriages overstate the actual allegiance of the population to the

[1] The marriage rate in post-Famine Ireland has been outstandingly low, and therefore the subject of considerable demographic interest. See K. H. Connell's articles, 'Marriage in Ireland after the famine: the diffusion of the match,' *Journal of the Statistical and Social Inquiry Society of Ireland*, 19, 1 (1955–6); 'The land legislation and Irish social life,' *Economic History Review*, 2nd Ser., 11, 1 (1958); and 'Peasant Marriage in Ireland: its structure and development since the famine,' *Economic History Review*, 2nd Ser., 14, 3 (1962). See also Robert E. Kennedy, Jr, *The Irish: Emigration, Marriage and Fertility* (Berkeley: 1973). However, since the population of the twenty-six counties is so overwhelmingly Roman Catholic, this source of error is of little concern in the regional comparisons.

[2] Consider the following statistics:

Per cent of population aged 20–9*

	1921		1968
England and Wales	15·4	England and Wales (urban)	14·3
Southern Ireland	15·4	England and Wales (rural)	13·6
		Scotland†	13·0
		Northern Ireland	14·8
		Southern Ireland	14·3

*Sources: 1921: N. Keyfitz and W. Flieger, *World Population* (Chicago: 1968).
1968: N. Keyfitz and W. Flieger, *Population: Facts and Methods of Demography* (San Francisco: 1971).
† 1963 statistics.
[3] Chapter 5, Table 5.4.

Anglican religion.[1] In nineteenth-century England marriages in non-Anglican surroundings were far from socially respectable. Further, since the parish church is usually the most impressive religious edifice in the community, it is often chosen as the site of marriage even by committed Nonconformists. Finally, the indicator of religiosity cannot be interpreted to reflect secular influence alone. Couples might choose a civil ceremony because it costs less; because of pre-marital conception; because of religious intermarriage, or because either party has previously been divorced. Most divorced persons are remarried in Registry Offices. However, none of these sources of error, save perhaps the first, should seriously bias the regional comparisons. Even so, the limitations of these data must constantly be kept in mind in the following analysis.

Why should such imperfect indicators be used at all? The answer is that they are the best possible systematic source of information on religious change in Great Britain and Ireland. The accuracy of the 1851 census data is itself subject to serious qualification on sampling grounds. No claim can be made that the census offers a true representation of religious affiliations among the population of an individual county as a whole. At best, it might indicate the distribution of denominational strength of a particular sub-sample, the church-going populations of the respective counties. However, very little is known if the relationship of this sub-sample to the study universe, the county population as a whole. Conceivably, it too might vary between denominations. To take a hypothetical example, it could be argued that Nonconformists as a group are more likely to attend religious services on a regular basis than Anglicans. Perhaps the norms regarding church attendance in both groups are quite different. Nonconformists, to momentarily accept the arguments of Weber and Tawney, may be more compulsively pious than Anglicans. If this were so, the religious census of 1851 would tend to overstate the extent of Nonconformist support in each county. Thus, there is no *a priori* reason to choose between these respective indicators of religious affiliation.[2] While neither can confidently be regarded as

[1] Gay, *op. cit.*, pp. 39–41.
[2] For other defects in the religious census, see W. S. F. Pickering, 'The 1851 religious census—a useless experiment?,' *British Journal of Sociology*, 18, 4 (1967), pp. 383–407. K. S. Inglis, 'Patterns of religious worship in 1851,' *Journal of Ecclesiastical History*, 11, 1 (1960) provides a discussion of the results of this census. Inglis's book on the subject, *Churches and the Working Classes in Victorian England* (London: 1963), does not treat the Celtic fringe. See Henry Pelling's criticism, 'Religion and the nineteenth-century British working class,' *Past and Present*, 27 (1964).

being without error, the indicator based on marriage statistics has much to recommend it in the study of religious change.

Following the Restoration, the social structure of English religion resembled a sandwich in that Anglicans were generally at the top and bottom and Dissenters in the middle.[1] During the eighteenth century Nonconformist sects made substantial inroads among the lowest strata. These new religious variables yield the following information in the period 1851–1961. English county means are overwhelmingly high for Established Church affiliation (Table 6.1) though there is a steady secular decline from a mean of 91 per cent in 1851 to 73 per cent by 1961. Wales shows a much smaller adherence to the Church of Wales, though very surprisingly the county means exceed 50 per cent for six of the nine observations when data are available. Anglicanism appears weakest in Wales in the period between 1901 and 1931. Ireland is conspicuously low in Anglicanism throughout the whole period, a reflection of its overwhelmingly Catholic population.

In Scotland, the cultural situation was qualitatively different than that in Ireland or Wales. For the national church in Scotland was established as a condition of the Union of 1707. In Ireland and Wales the Established Churches were regarded as an imposition of illegitimate English authority; in Scotland the Established Church could be held to be a repository of the national heritage. The cultural autonomy of Scotland thus defused much potential anti-English sentiment. Even so, there was much concern about encroaching anglicization. This can be seen in the repeated attempts to revive a Scots literary language, the first of which was made immediately following the Union.[2] But, on the whole, the internecine religious controversies between the Church of Scotland and the various dissenting sects never took on the nationalistic color which characterized such struggles in Ireland and Wales.

Variations in Scottish Protestant statistics largely indicate the respective fortunes of the Church of Scotland and the Free Church, which has been coded as Nonconformist for the purpose of this analysis. These two churches ultimately merged in 1931. In so far as this chapter is primarily concerned with the implications of religious differences for the evolution of a national culture, there will be relatively little discussion of the religious peculiarities of Scotland in this

[1] Harold Perkin, *The Origins of Modern English Society, 1780–1880* (London: 1969), p. 34.
[2] H. J. Hanham, *Scottish Nationalism* (London: 1969), pp. 33–49.

TABLE 6.1 *The incidence of Established Church adherence: county means in percentages**

	1851	1861	1871	1881	1891	1901	1911	1921	1931	1951	1961
England											
All counties	91	88	86	84	84	83	82	82	83	77	73
Industrial counties	88	84	84	84	83	79	79	78	80	74	68
Non-industrial counties	91	89	86	84	84	84	83	84	84	78	77
Wales											
All counties	na	71	63	54	na	47	45	49	54	50	53
Industrial counties	na	62	67	63	na	56	55	59	61	57	56
Non-industrial counties	na	72	63	53	na	45	44	47	53	49	52
Scotland											
All counties	48	49	50	50	51	54	55	54	80	78	78
Industrial counties	40	39	43	47	46	50	48	48	71	70	69
Non-industrial counties	49	50	50	51	52	55	57	56	82	80	81
Northern Ireland											
All counties	na	36	29	30	30	29	30	28	na	na	na
Industrial counties	na	—	—	—	—	—	—	—	na	na	na
Non-industrial counties	na	36	29	30	30	29	30	28	na	na	na
Southern Ireland											
All counties	na	11	9	10	9	7	6	6	5	5	3
Industrial counties	na	—	—	21	—	—	15	15	—	4	3
Non-industrial counties	na	11	9	10	9	7	6	6	5	5	3

* Source: compiled from the *Annual Reports* of the Registrar of Births, Deaths and Marriages for England and Wales, Scotland, and Ireland.

TABLE 6.2 *The incidence of Nonconformity: county means in percentages**

	1851	1861	1871	1881	1891	1901	1911	1921	1931	1951	1961
England											
All counties	7	9	11	13	13	14	15	14	12	13	14
Industrial counties	4	6	8	9	11	15	16	15	12	13	15
Non-industrial counties	7	9	12	14	14	14	15	14	13	13	13
Wales											
All counties	na	27	35	43	na	50	52	48	42	45	39
Industrial counties	na	31	23	29	na	38	39	34	32	33	31
Non-industrial counties	na	27	36	46	na	53	54	51	44	47	41
Scotland											
All counties	47	46	46	45	44	41	39	39	13	14	11
Industrial counties	47	48	48	41	41	38	38	37	11	12	10
Non-industrial counties	47	46	45	46	45	43	40	40	13	14	11
Northern Ireland											
All counties	na	30	32	31	29	30	27	31	na	na	na
Industrial counties	na	—	—	—	—	—	—	—	na	na	na
Non-industrial counties	na	30	32	31	29	30	27	31	na	na	na
Southern Ireland											
All counties	na	2	2	2	2	2	2	2	0	0	0
Industrial counties	na	—	—	2	—	—	2	3	—	0	0
Non-industrial counties	na	2	2	2	2	2	2	2	0	0	0

* Source: As in Table 6.1.

TABLE 6.3 *The incidence of religiosity:* * county means in percentages†

	1851	1861	1871	1881	1891	1901	1911	1921	1931	1951	1961
England											
All counties	95	93	91	88	88	87	82	80	84	71	71
Industrial counties	98	91	90	88	85	85	79	75	83	70	69
Non-industrial counties	95	93	91	88	88	88	83	82	85	71	72
Wales											
All counties	na	87	77	74	na	72	73	72	76	75	76
Industrial counties	na	74	43	62	na	63	62	66	67	71	70
Non-industrial counties	na	88	80	77	na	73	75	73	77	76	77
Scotland											
All counties	99	99	99	99	99	99	98	94	95	88	87
Industrial counties	100	99	96	99	97	99	95	90	92	86	84
Non-industrial counties	99	99	99	99	99	99	98	95	95	88	88
Northern Ireland											
All counties	na	91	95	95	97	97	97	97	na	na	na
Industrial counties	na	—	—	—	—	—	—	—	na	na	na
Non-industrial counties	na	91	95	95	97	97	97	97	na	na	na
Southern Ireland											
All counties	na	99	99	99	99	99	99	99	98	99	99
Industrial counties	na	—	—	95	—	—	96	73	—	99	99
Non-industrial counties	na	91	95	95	97	97	97	97	na	na	na

* Source: As in Table 6.1.
† Defined as the proportion of total marriages performed under the auspices of religious authorities.

section. Suffice it to say that neither the Free Church nor the Church of Scotland was doctrinally or organizationally tied to the Church of England in this period.

Mean county data on Nonconformity (Table 6.2) show a slow increase in England from 7 to 14 per cent from 1851 to 1961. The Welsh data are curvilinear, with 1911 being the year of highest Nonconformist popularity. Thereafter there is a slight decrease in support, but the average county level of Nonconformity is considerably higher in 1961 (39 per cent) than 1861 (27 per cent). Again, the Irish figures are near zero. The data on religiosity (Table 6.3) are somewhat surprising, since the 1851 census suggests a negative association between religious attendance and industrialization. England, by far the most industrialized part of the British Isles, has consistently higher levels of religiosity than Wales. Scotland appears very pious indeed by this measure, as do both parts of Ireland.

One of the most fruitful findings of the 1851 census for subsequent historical research was the apparent concentration of Nonconformity in heavily industrial areas. Halévy seized upon this fact in assigning Nonconformity its counterrevolutionary role. More recent research has further specified the nature of Nonconformity's appeal to the industrial working class. It is evident that the vast social disruption accompanying the process of industrialization was reflected by a major religious transformation in Britain. Large-scale internal migration had taken individuals from a relatively secure pastoral environment to burgeoning cities where mere survival had suddenly become problematic. These cities were ill-prepared for the pulsating waves of immigrants. Housing was inadequate; sanitation facilities overtaxed, and epidemic conditions were rife. Agricultural laborers became transformed into factory operatives. Families were dismembered, and in nearly every conceivable way life-styles came to be revolutionized. Little solace was to be found in the anomie and deprivation which characterized early capitalist urban life.[1] It was precisely in this kind of environment that Nonconformity took hold with an evangelistic fury. The kind of religious service which appealed to the urban underclasses—and also, somewhat paradoxically, to the rising bourgeoisie—was wildly messianic and highly emotional.[2]

---

[1] One of the classic studies of industrial life in this period remains Friedrich Engels's *The Condition of the Working Class in 1844* (Stanford: 1968).

[2] This religious alliance of bourgeoisie and proletariat was subsequently to be mirrored in the political coalition known as the Liberal Party, *circa* 1885–1921. For useful studies of the appeal of millenarian religion to groups engaged in struggle see Ronald Knox, *Enthusiasm: A Chapter in the History of Religion*

Many of the Methodist sects, though not all, were also politically conservative.

E. P. Thompson argues compellingly that Nonconformity was instrumental in providing the industrial proletariat with an inner compulsion to self discipline, so necessary for the success of factory production in the early period of industrialization.[1] In his account, workers submitted to the 'physic exploitation' of Methodism for essentially three reasons. Methodist Sunday Schools not only served the educational needs of the proletariat, but they also engaged in direct indoctrination to which most succumbed. Second, the Nonconformist chapels performed an integrative function by providing solidarity and a sense of community in the otherwise chaotic and anomic cities. And last, enthusiastic Methodism provided chiliastic outlets for despair and hopelessness.

In contrast, Anglicanism had little to offer the urban underclass. It did not provide any educational equivalent to the Sunday School. Its services were typically less emotionally charged and devoid of millenarian content. After all, its greatest patrons, the state and the landed upper class, were *arrivés* of the first order. Little could be gained among this group by insisting upon the imminence of a New Jerusalem. Further, the upper-class aura of the parish church could hardly have been a congenial setting for intermingling among the working classes.

So goes the general argument. But did industrialization have a similar effect throughout the British Isles? One means of testing this hypothetical affinity of Nonconformity with industrialization is to break down the regional means on the religious variables by recomputing them separately for industrial and non-industrial counties.[2] Table 6.2 presents these data for Nonconformity and is significant in several respects. With respect to England, differences between industrial and non-industrial counties are relatively slight, and

---

(New York: 1961); Karl Mannheim, *Ideology and Utopia* (New York: 1940); Vittorio Lanternari, *The Religions of the Oppressed* (New York: 1963); and E. J. Hobsbawm, 'The Labor Sects' in *Primitive Rebels* (New York: 1959), pp. 126–150.

[1] E. P. Thompson, *The Making of the English Working Class* (New York: 1963), pp. 351–400. For a criticism of these conclusions see R. M. Hartwell, *The Industrial Revolution and Economic Growth* (London: 1971), pp. 370–2.

[2] Counties are defined as *industrial* if their percentage of employed adult males in non-agricultural occupations was equal to or exceeded 85 per cent from 1851 to 1891; 87·5 per cent for the years 1891 to 1931, and 90 per cent from 1931 to 1961. See chapter 5.

confirm the expected relationship between Nonconformity and industrialization only from 1901 to 1921 and in 1961. In all other years the non-industrial counties have comparable or stronger Nonconformist support. But notice the statistics for Wales. There, the differences are larger, but all in an unexpected direction. That is to say, in Wales the non-industrial counties appear to far exceed industrial counties in the extent of their Nonconformity. However, Nonconformity in both kinds of Welsh counties is much greater than that in either English industrial or non-industrial counties. A similar difference between England and Wales can be seen in Table 6.1 concerning Established Church affiliation. Greatest support for the Established Church in Wales is in the industrial counties, whereas in general the reverse is true in England. Secondarily, there appears to be only slight convergence between England and Wales over time. These religious differences have remained quite constant in both settings. The only variable which shows any tendency towards convergence in England and Wales is religiosity.

It is possible to further specify the relationship between industrialization and religious affiliation by calculating the statistical association between an indicator of industrialization, and the religious variables. The measure of association best suited for these comparisons is the unstandardized regression coefficient, b, of each of the religious categories on the manufacturing variable.[1] The association between Nonconformity and industrialization (Table 6.4) reveals a difference in the direction of the relationship in England and Wales. In England b is positive after 1891, whereas it is negative throughout the period investigated in Wales. The differences are about equally large in 1911 and 1961. Only in 1931 does the nature of the association converge in England and Wales. Since the absolute magnitude of the association expressed by b is somewhat difficult to interpret since it is unstandardized, an idea of the strength of the relationship may be gained by examining the respective English and Welsh zero-order correlation coefficients. In 1911, the year when English–Welsh differences are greatest, the English r is 0.371, while the Welsh r is -0.390. The degree of association is therefore moderate in both cases. On the other hand, the association between

---

[1] Conventionally, the correlation coefficient r is used to indicate the strength of an association between two variables, but r cannot reliably be employed in comparisons between samples, or of the same sample at different points in time. See Hubert M. Blalock, Jr, 'Causal inferences, closed populations and measures of association,' *American Political Science Review*, 61, 1 (1967), pp. 130–6.

TABLE 6.4 *The association between religious affiliation and industrialization. Unstandardized b coefficients from the regression of religious affiliation on manufacturing occupations*

	1851	1861	1871	1881	1891	1901	1911	1921	1931	1951	1961
England											
Nonconformist	−0·128	−0·073	−0·065	−0·023	0·015	0·109	0·127	0·078	0·026	0·017	0·097
Church of England	−0·035	−0·074	−0·047	−0·153	−0·151	−0·211	−0·241	−0·208	−0·172	−0·201	0·347
Wales											
Nonconformist	na	−0·071	−0·273	−0·231	na	−0·081	−0·251	−0·181	−0·027	0·220	−0·162
Church of Wales	na	−0·035	0·109	0·073	na	−0·005	0·190	0·095	−0·052	0·120	0·042
Scotland											
Nonconformist	0·209	−0·055	−0·127	−0·163	−0·195	−0·180	−0·016	−0·164	−0·022	−0·043	−0·024
Church of Scotland	−0·297	−0·106	0·033	0·033	0·045	0·054	−0·101	−0·079	−0·156	−0·107	−0·129
Northern Ireland											
Nonconformist	na	1·177	1·1181	0·816	0·677	0·432	0·472	0·707	na	na	na
Church of Ireland	na	−0·163	0·062	0·162	0·063	0·194	0·177	0·153	na	na	na
Southern Ireland											
Nonconformist	na	−0·023	−0·028	−0·088	−0·066	−0·072	−0·062	−0·074	−0·003	−0·004	−0·027
Church of Ireland	na	0·406	0·290	0·144	0·148	0·103	0·163	0·213	−0·030	0·044	−0·050

industrialization and Nonconformity is much larger and subject to fluctuation in Northern Ireland. This is because Catholics were heavily concentrated in the rural parts of Northern Ireland, while Protestants of all varieties were clustered in industrial areas. In Ireland, however, there is virtually no relationship throughout the period.

These data suggest that the social base of Nonconformity varied in the English and Welsh contexts. The conventional explanation of the rise of Nonconformity in Britain will clearly not serve for Wales. Although the industrialization and proletarianization of South Wales occurred largely within the scope of these time series, Welsh Nonconformity, in contrast to English, appears to be a predominantly rural phenomenon.

The nature of the relationship between industrialization and Established Church affiliation is also different in England and Wales. In England the association is a negative one throughout the period, indeed increasingly so over time. In Wales the association is almost continuously positive. In 1911 for instance, the English r is -0.579, while that for Wales is 0.293. The strength of the relationship is somewhat weaker in Wales than in England, but again the major importance is the difference in the direction of the association in the two contexts. There is a strong positive association between these variables in both Ireland and Northern Ireland.

In summary, then, the differences may be described as follows. In England and Northern Ireland Nonconformity's strength is in the industrial counties; in Wales, it is in the non-industrial counties. On the other hand, in Wales, Ireland, and Northern Ireland affiliation with the Established Church is positively related to a county's industrialization; in England the reverse is true. Given these data it is apparent that no simple hypothesis about the social structural underpinnings of Nonconformity or Anglicanism can be tenable for all the regions of the British Isles. One is forced to suspect that the category 'Nonconformist,' which was derived from coding marriage rites by recorded denominations, has a different social meaning in Wales, for example, than in England despite the formal similarity in doctrine or ritual. What can account for these striking differences?

There seems no reason to dispute arguments about the appeal of Nonconformity to the English working class. What then was the situation in the countryside? In that much more intimate setting, the squire could, if he so desired, strongly influence the church-going habits of each of his tenants. E. P. Thompson suggests that the

Anglicanism of the countryside was less a matter of belief than a consequence of the power of the squire:[1]

For centuries the Established Church had preached to the poor the duties of obedience. But it was so distanced from them . . . that its homilies had ceased to have much effect. The deference of the countryside was rooted in bitter experience of the power of the squire rather than in any inward conviction.

And W. G. Hoskins's study of Wigston, a village with an 1871 population of 2,638 and the site of a small hosiery industry, provides confirming evidence of Methodist strength in an English semi-rural setting:[2]

The church was too closely linked with the masters in the nineteenth century; the wage-earners filled the chapels. Nonconformity had grown strong in Wigston all through the Georgian era. . . . In 1676 they had been about 4 per cent of the total population; by the 1720s about 16 per cent; and a hundred years later they were fully 40 per cent. . . . So in 1870 the empty Sunday streets would suddenly resound with the loud defiant singing of the chapels from one end of the village to the other, while from the parish church came the more subdued murmur of 'the Conservative Party at prayer.'

In smaller rural settlements, Nonconformity was presumably less tolerable to the ruling establishment:[3]

There was one other context in which Methodism of *any* variety necessarily assumed a more class-conscious form: in the rural areas. The chapel in the agricultural village was inevitably an affront to the vicar and the squire, and a center in which the laborer gained independence and self-respect.

The squire presumably felt that Nonconformity represented a challenge to his authority and traditionally paternalistic role in 'his' village.[4] This might lead to the conclusion that Nonconformity could exist comfortably only in those rural settlements exceeding some threshold of absolute size, perhaps 1,000 inhabitants or more, where

---

[1] Thompson, *op. cit.*, p. 351.
[2] W. G. Hoskins, *The Midland Peasant: The Economic and Social History of a Leicestershire Village* (London: 1957), pp. 278–9.
[3] Thompson, *op. cit.*, p. 397.
[4] It should, however, be pointed out that there was a certain degree of religious toleration in England. 'In a world of personal dependency any breach of "the great law of subordination," between master and servant, squire and villager, husband and wife, father and child, was a sort of petty treason, to be ruthlessly suppressed. Resentment had therefore to be swallowed, or sublimated in religious dissent, or, when pressed beyond endurance, it exploded in outbursts of desperate violence.' Perkin, *op. cit.*, p. 37.

is was not practicable for the squire to exert his will against his tenants' religious convictions.

However, it is very clear that England had many more villages of this size than Wales, where nucleated settlements had been much rarer owing to the absence of feudalism throughout most of the Principality.[1] Thus, if anything, English rural Nonconformity should exceed that in Wales if these were the major causal factors. That they are not the sole causal factors is obvious. Part of the difficulty here is that the descriptions previously referred to have emphasized the salience of stratification in the English countryside. But the extent of rural class struggle in these accounts was not presented in a regionally comparative context within Britain. There was a qualitative difference between the rural stratification systems in England and the Celtic periphery. In England, even when class interest separated landlord and tenant, they still shared a common bond as English nationals. In the periphery, however, in addition to clashes of interest rooted in class, landlord and tenant tended to conflict on issues of culture as well. The landed classes in Ireland, for instance, were literally of English origin in the main; in Wales and parts of Scotland, however, they were anglicized, that is to say they regarded themselves, and behaved, as if they were English. But why should this matter? What force or importance did issues of culture have on landlord-tenant relations in nineteenth- and twentieth-century Britain?

First there is the matter of language. Most of Wales was Welsh speaking in the year 1800. The anglicization of the Welsh gentry tended to increase the social distance between landlord and tenant, much as if there had been actual absenteeism. This, in turn, was generally associated with increased exploitation of the tenants and agricultural laborers. In this situation cultural differences worked to complement class distinctions. Since the Welsh gentry had ultimately chosen to abandon their Welsh culture, thereby heightening their social status both in Wales and in England, they were not anxious to devalue this privilege by democratizing access to English culture among the Welsh masses. The value of English culture and most particularly of English speaking in Wales, was a direct function of

---

[1] 'The native way of life in upland Wales has retarded the growth of nucleated settlements. . . . Wales has no civic heritage. The essentially rural culture of Wales, like that of the Balkans, had crystallized before the introduction of towns by aliens, and after the conquest the distinction between country and town became largely a distinction between English and Welsh.' Alwyn D. Rees, *Life in a Welsh Countryside* (Cardiff: 1968), p. 108.

its very exclusivity. This situation led to the proliferation of Nonconformity in the Welsh countryside in two ways. The Anglican church, for its part, was basically uninterested in acculturating the Welsh masses. The Church of Wales, organizationally tied to Canterbury, held its services largely in English, and thereby did not welcome those monolingual Welsh-speakers who might be in search of salvation. The Nonconformist sects gained spectacularly in the late eighteenth century because they actually ministered to the religious needs of the great majority of Welsh people.[1] Services were offered in Welsh, and Welsh-language Sunday Schools were established, providing the first exposure to formal education for the bulk of the populace. Hence, the failure of the Church of Wales to accept the responsibility for the religious affairs of Wales through its monoglot predilections was one factor spurring the growth of Nonconformity in the rural setting.

But there was another major consideration in the Welsh countryside. Whereas tenant Nonconformity might have been an affront to the English squire, leading to some efforts at its suppression, it was probably often a blessing to his Welsh counterpart. For it was through the maintenance, even the proliferation, of cultural distance that the Welsh squire preserved his domestic privilege. Every interaction with common Welshmen on a basis of equality threatened the squire's own precarious ethnic identity.

Once ensconced in the countryside the Nonconformist sects took great pains to emphasize and promote the indigenous culture—this was, after all, Nonconformity's organizational *raison d'être* in Wales—in religious services and publications as well, lending it dignity and legitimacy in the eyes of its adherents.[2] This linkage of Nonconformity with Welsh nationality was already evident in the early 1800s. When the Education Commissioners leveled their attack on the Welsh language and popular religions, Nonconformity's appeal could only be intensified.[3]

The Irish case, however, illustrates that language difference is hardly a necessary condition for the salience of cultural distinctions in landlord–tenant relations. The persistence of Roman Catholicism

[1] 'Above all it was the Welsh character of nonconformity in its services and Sunday schools which ensured its dominance, a marked contrast to the inadequate attention paid by the Church to the linguistic question for over a century.' Kenneth Morgan, *Wales in British Politics, 1868–1922* (Cardiff: 1963), pp. 11–12.
[2] *Ibid.*, pp. 8, 9.
[3] Reginald Coupland, *Welsh and Scottish Nationalism* (London: 1954), pp. 186–95.

in the Irish countryside was not tied to Gaelic speaking. As early as 1851 the average Irish county was only 22 per cent Gaelic speaking—and this statistic includes bilingual Gaelic speakers. In contrast, the average Irish county was 91 per cent Roman Catholic. Neither the Anglo-Irish aristocracy nor the English government had ever invested much effort to induce the Irish to Protestantism. There were, however, times when the English government had great reason to be concerned about Catholicism in Ireland.

In the sixteenth and seventeenth centuries there was widespread fear in England that Irish Catholicism might provide a foothold for the great Catholic continental rivals of England, Spain and France, to launch an invasion in the British Isles. The English knew there was much sympathy for these Catholic powers among the Irish. The plantations of Munster, Offaly, and Londonderry were all conceived, in part, to be solutions to the problem of securing Ireland from possible foreign invasion. As such the plantations were designed to pacify the native Irish and achieve security of the island by military means.[1]

There was no sustained attempt to proselytize the Irish. Instead the English authorities drove the native Irish off their customary lands, and established fortresses of Protestant military power.

In Londonderry there were strict inhibitions against social intercourse with 'mere Irish.'[2] When it became evident that the plantation policy had failed, following the massacre of thousands of English and Scottish settlers in Londonderry in 1642, the English authorities concluded that more coercion was necessary to dissuade the Irish from their Catholicism. They burned Irish abbeys; destroyed sacred relics; and attempted to root out the Papacy by every possible means.[3] Once England's power in the international arena had been secured, Ireland represented less a threat than an opportunity for investment. Still there were actions taken against Catholicism, most notably the Penal Laws, which were enforced until 1829. But their rationale had changed somewhat. A prominent Irish historian has described these ordinances as a kind of apartheid whose purpose was 'not to destroy Roman Catholicism but to make sure that its adherents were left in a position of social, economic, and political inferiority.'[4] As a consequence of these policies generation after

[1] T. W. Moody, *The Londonderry Plantation 1609–1641* (Belfast: 1939).
[2] Walter Harris, ed., *Hibernica* (Dublin: 1770).
[3] Edmund Curtis, *A History of Ireland* (London: 1966), pp. 165–6.
[4] J. C. Beckett, *The Making of Modern Ireland, 1603–1923* (London: 1966), p. 159. L. P. Curtis, Jr, makes a similar point: 'What some Englishmen described

generation of Irish were confirmed in their Catholicism, which came to be symbolically representative of their status within Irish society.

Hence, despite the fact that conflict between landlord and tenant was greater in Wales and Ireland than England, in the periphery tenants, ironically, had much more autonomy to develop their own cultural institutions than in the English countryside. Therefore the strength of dissenting religion in the Welsh and Irish countryside was itself a reflection of the social gulf separating classes and freely acknowledged and countenanced by both groups. In the relative intimacy of the rural setting, the maintenance of cultural differences between landlord and tenant indicated that the landlord had reneged the paternalistic sense of obligation to his tenants which was a carry-over from the medieval pattern in favor of a more modern style of interaction. What induced the landlord to renege this role as village *paterfamilias*? In the periphery there were basically two types of inducement; in England, only one. The common link was that of commercial gain. In both England and the periphery landlords did not hesitate to attempt to clear their lands when it became commercially profitable to do so. Enclosure and engrossing invariably led to a sharp break in the nature of landlord–tenant relations. But in Wales and most of Ireland landlords were also motivated to abandon their paternalism by their differential ethnic identity.

If this might account for the greater prevalence of dissenting religion in the peripheral countryside, what can explain the positive association between Anglicanism and industrialization in Wales, Ireland and Northern Ireland? In England there is substantial agreement that Nonconformity took hold among both bourgeois and proletarian elements. Evidently the situation in the peripheral areas was somewhat different.

In chapter 5 I have shown that some of the structural consequences of industrialization were dissimilar in England and in the peripheral areas. To a certain extent development in Wales, Scotland, and Ireland conformed to the internal colonial model. When English

---

as a process of Anglicization in Ireland amounted in practice to a policy of enforced acculturation with the object of converting the 'Irishry' into docile hewers of wood and efficient drawers of water for the old and new English settlers. The goal of Mountjoy and other Lord Deputies was not just to suppress Irish rebellions, but to make the native Irish conform as much as possible to the English working classes in respect of manners, dress, religion, and, above all, obedience to English law, and the penalties for nonconformity.' *Anglo-Saxons and Celts* (Bridgeport, Ct: 1968), p. 202.

markets penetrated the peripheral regions, differences between industrial enclaves and agricultural hinterlands developed. In England, the spatial distribution of industrialization was more complete than in the periphery. The distinction between enclave and hinterland expressly does not imply a division into 'modern' and 'traditional' sectors of the economy. Instead, both sub-regions of the peripheral areas were seen to be closely integrated into the national economy. The economy of the peripheral regions depended on a narrow range of exports, either foodstuffs, raw materials or industrial commodities.

The sites of the export enclaves in Scotland, Ireland, and Northern Ireland were, by and large, culturally anglicized prior to the Industrial Revolution.[1] The lowland industrial belt of Scotland centered around the English speaking cities of Glasgow and Edinburgh. The antipathy between Scottish lowlanders and highlanders has previously been recounted. Dublin had since the twelfth century been an Anglo-Norman settlement; the Pale of Dublin marked the boundary between civilization and the barbarism of the 'mere Irish.' And the growth of Belfast was ultimately the result of large-scale Scottish and English emigration which began in the seventeenth century with the establishment of the Londonderry plantation. However, by comparison, nineteenth-century Wales had remained a largely Celtic society. Monmouthshire, to be sure, was often regarded as an English, rather than a Welsh county, even in the nineteenth century. But the most rapid expansion of the coal and steel industries occurred in Glamorganshire, which prior to 1850 or so, was a rather typical Welsh county both economically and culturally.

From 1850 on the industrial enclaves in the periphery experienced continual demographic expansion, while the absolute population size of the hinterland counties either stabilized, as in Scotland, or actually declined, as in Wales, Ireland, and Northern Ireland (Table 6.5). Much of the migration from hinterland to industrial areas occurred within regions. Some, however, also was between regions.[2] In general, the periphery fed the core. After 1846, for instance, there was massive Irish emigration to industrial areas in Scotland and England. Scotland itself had been faced with serious emigration

[1] Gordon Donaldson, *Scotland: James V to James VII*, vol. III of the *Edinburgh History of Scotland* (Edinburgh: 1965), p. 259; and Maureen Wall, 'The decline of the Irish Language' in Brian Ó Cuív, ed., *A View of the Irish Language* (Dublin: 1969).

[2] P. Friedlander and R. J. Roshier, 'A study of internal migration in England and Wales: part I,' *Population Studies*, 19, 3 (1966), pp. 239–79.

TABLE 6.5 *Mean county population by region and level of industrialization, 1851–1961**

	1851	1861	1871	1881	1891	1901	1911	1921	1931	1951	1961
Industrial counties in											
England	2215	1937	1931	1716	1925	1859	1718	1899	2214	1934	1980
Wales	—	326	406	376	484	579	759	852	831	814	838
Scotland	395	361	437	259	340	314	383	383	406	411	423
Northern Ireland											690
Ireland				419			477	506		693	
Non-industrial counties in											
England	324	350	377	415	369	397	416	448	507	442	491
Wales	91	82	85	75	74	79	82	87	85	88	88
Scotland	68	66	68	74	73	68	80	73	76	72	72
Northern Ireland	240	233	226	218	203	207	209	210	214	229	147
Ireland	197	169	156	138	133	124	107	99	114	91	84

* For the definition of 'industrial' and 'non-industrial' counties see note 2, p. 177.

problems since the eighteenth century.[1] But there was also a movement of population, albeit smaller, from England to the periphery
following industrialization there. This can be seen with especial clarity
in Wales. Table 6.6 gives an indication of these trends by presenting
the respective proportion of individuals of English birth in each of the
peripheral enclave regions. The mode of this distribution occurs in
1911, when a full 22 per cent of the enumerated population in the

TABLE 6.6 *Percentage of English-born enumerated in the peripheral
enclaves*

	Wales	Scotland	Northern Ireland (Antrim county)	Ireland (Dublin county)
1851	—	3	1	3
1861	11	3	1	4
1871	9	3	1	4
1881	15	2	2	5
1891	19	3	2	5
1901	18	3	3	5
1911	22	4	3	5
1921	15	4	3	3
1931	15	3	3	3
1951	13	4	3	2
1961	12	5	3	3

industrial counties of Wales was of English birth. This rate of
English migration is not approached in any other peripheral region.
The proportion of English-born in Wales roughly corresponds to
the period of the coal boom in South Wales.[2] In general, there is no
statistical information about the kinds of jobs Englishmen assumed
in the peripheral enclaves: birth-place data were not cross-tabulated
by occupational status. However, it is likely that they had a disproportionate share of jobs in managerial and commercial categories.[3]

[1] Gordon Donaldson, *The Scots Overseas* (London: 1966).
[2] Brinley Thomas, 'The migration of labour into the Glamorganshire coalfield
(1861–1911),' *Economica*, 10, 3 (1930), p. 281.
[3] 'Many of the early industrial entrepreneurs were English immigrants, and
English was unmistakably the language of commerce and industry at these higher
levels.' Glanmor Williams, 'Language, literacy and nationality in Wales,' *History*,
56, 186 (1971), p. 11.
    Nationalists in Scotland made much of the fact of increasing English immigra-
tion, which was considered 'a special menace because of their habit of acquiring
desirable and remunerative positions such as those of managers, agents and so
forth.' G. S. Pryde, 'The development of nationalism in Scotland,' *Sociological
Review*, 27 (1935), p. 277. This impression is confirmed in the comments of a
contemporary: 'it was rather curious to observe how few of the inhabitants of

There were, of course, also working-class English migrants, especially in Wales, where much of the influx came from miners in south-western English counties.

The cultural implications of these demographic shifts are of central concern. In Scotland, Ireland, and Northern Ireland the enclave areas were already substantially anglicized. Presumably the English migrants found the social milieu relatively familiar. But in Wales, the enclave was initially culturally Welsh. The linguistic evidence is indisputable here. Given this fundamentally alien social environment the early English migrants to Wales identified with anglophile elements. In practice, this of course meant the Welsh landed gentry. But, in the course of this identification, the English migrants found their own identities undergoing change. In England, many of these migrants had been middle and working-class Nonconformists. Upon coming to Wales, they apparently felt an elevation in status relative to the general population. For here they were, by virtue of their English culture, suddenly transformed into an élite:[1]

In the industrial areas the iron-masters, many of whom had their origins in English middle-class dissent, became allied through marriage and association, with the gentry, and adopted their anglicanism. Seldom did Welsh workmen attain to high administrative posts. 'In the works,' says a government investigator, in 1847, 'the Welsh workman never finds his way into the office. He never becomes either clerk or agent. He may become an overseer or contractor, but this does not take him out of the labouring and into the administering class.' The English-speaking land-owner and the iron-master were anglicans; the Welsh-speaking tenant and industrial worker became increasingly nonconformist.

To be English-speaking in nineteenth-century industrial Wales was to be culturally privileged—just as it is today in neo-colonial cities like Accra or Lagos. It was a mark of status and an entrance to

---

South Wales have benefited from the extraordinary wealth their country contains and that the Saxon race of men should have been almost the sole adventurers which have in latter times brought this wealth into action, and by their ingenuity, perseverance and adventurous spirit have raised many a noble fortune and laid the foundation of many more.' C. Hassall, *General View of Agriculture in the County of Monmouth* (London: 1812), cited in A. H. John, *The Industrial Development of South Wales, 1750–1850* (Cardiff: 1950), p. 24.

Though most of the industrialization of Wales was accomplished with English capital and managerial expertise (*ibid.*, pp. 23–57), the development of the steam coal industry was a notable exception: see E. D. Lewis, *The Rhondda Valley* (London: 1959). The consistently low numbers of English-born in Ireland provides further support for this general thesis.

[1] David Williams, *A History of Modern Wales* (London: 1969), p. 246.

privileged company. Englishmen in Wales were in this sense akin to a colonial élite. Their cultural identification, of itself, determined many aspects of their behavior. This is evident in the following complaint of a prominent Welsh Nonconformist writing in 1865:[1]

Numbers of educated persons in the middle class come, year after year from England to occupy positions of respectability and influence in the Principality. We find that many of these gentlemen were members of Congregational churches in England, but on their arrival in Wales, they, almost without exception, renounce their Nonconformity. After reaching the places of their destination, for a few Sabbaths they will go about and visit the Independent, the Baptist, and the Wesleyan chapels; but, finding neither chapels, ministers, nor congregations, up to their mark in point of respectability, they make their home at the parish church, where the presence of a few country squires, lawyers, and surgeons, will feed their pride.

There is little reason to suspect that this pattern was different in the industrial enclaves of Scotland, Ireland, and Northern Ireland. In each of these settings English migrants would probably identify with the most anglophile elements in the population, and hence, perforce, the Established Church (save in Scotland, where they would most likely be Episcopalian). This would then account for the positive association between Established Church affiliation and industrialization in the periphery. Once the tide of English emigration to the periphery stopped (in Wales this occurred in the period 1911–31), the Established Church remained a symbol of high prestige among English-speakers in general.

In this sense it is likely that the social meaning of religious affiliations differed in the core and peripheral contexts. However valid it is to lump together all of the Nonconformist sects in a single category, it is evident that regional comparisons must be performed with care:[2]

Nonconformity in Wales was, and is, one with English Nonconformity in its theology and polity; with the exception of the Calvinistic Methodists, Nonconformity was an importation from England into Wales. But there can be no doubt that it took on a Welsh dress and found its expression through the medium of the Welsh language; it had a homespun quality which made it essentially Welsh in texture. Events were to show by the end of the century that it was losing its distinctive character by the decline of the Welsh language and that, consequently, its hold on the industrial areas was weakening. It might have been expected that the decline in Welsh

[1] Thomas Rees, *Miscellaneous Papers on Subjects relating to Wales* (London: 1867), p. 89, quoted in E. T. Davies, *Religion in the Industrial Revolution in South Wales* (Cardiff: 1965).   [2] *Ibid.*, p. 74.

Nonconformity would have led to a corresponding strength of the 'English cause' in the same denomination. But this has not been so: the change in language meant the loss of a distinctive quality from which English Nonconformity in these parts did not ultimately benefit.

In sum, these data indicate that there was no significant convergence in the religious affiliations of England and the Celtic regions in the course of British industrialization. Indeed, it would appear that the effects of industrialization on religious affiliation were quite different in the core and the periphery. While industrialization did stimulate increased contact between Englishmen and natives of the periphery as a result of heightened levels of interregional migration, such contacts tended to emphasize cultural differences between the interacting groups rather than mute them. Even where Englishmen in the periphery might have originally shared the religious status of Nonconformity with most Welshmen, contact between individuals of different nationality often led to religious re-identification on the part of Englishmen, so that the mutual statuses between the two groups were minimized. This, in turn, created antipathy to the English migrants, and was probably a stimulus to the development of nationalist sentiment in the Celtic periphery. But it cannot be argued on this basis alone that industrialization did not contribute to the cultural integration of the British Isles. While each of the peripheral lands maintained its religious distinctiveness from England despite the vast social disruptions of the nineteenth century, nevertheless in one sphere, that of language, anglicization made significant headway everywhere.

THE DECLINE OF CELTIC LANGUAGE SPEAKING IN THE BRITISH ISLES

Language conflict is a dominant political feature of many societies: some, like India and Nigeria, relatively non-industrial; others, like Belgium and Canada, highly industrial and modernized. Sociological interest in language conflict and change is of relatively recent vintage, and the field as of yet lacks a general theoretical perspective.[1] Early work in language change has been dominated by the diffusion perspective of social change, particularly by the literature on

[1] For three surveys, see Joshua A. Fishman, C. A. Ferguson, and J. Das Gupta, eds, *Language Problems of Developing Nations* (New York: 1968); Pier Paolo Giglioli, ed., *Language and Social Context* (London: 1972); and John J. Gumperz and Dell Hymes, eds, *Directions in Sociolinguistics: The Ethnography of Communication* (New York: 1972).

acculturation processes, but there are significant exceptions.[1] That is to say, it is for the most part assumed that there is a strong correlation between intergroup interaction and linguistic assimilation. There has been much discussion of language change and industrialization which stresses the liberating effect of the urban environment on the traditional mores of hinterland residents.

Karl Deutsch has argued that language change in the 'traditional' group will ultimately proceed in direct proportion to the extent of interaction with the mobilized population.[2] Similarly, A. Tabouret-Keller claims that language maintenance among a minority is likely only in a rural setting when 'rural life assures living conditions that are not too precarious.'[3] Urban life, on the contrary, is not conducive to such language maintenance. One of the effects of the social disruption following rural–urban migration is a weakening of ties to the rural culture. Torn from the comfort of a secure and comprehensible environment, the new migrant is forced to recognize the value of the majority language to his potential social and economic opportunities. To read these authors is sometimes to gather the impression that many of the ancient languages of the peripheral areas of the world are inevitably doomed. There is also some disconfirming evidence which complicates these simple notions of acculturation. A study of bilingualism in Montreal suggests that French speaking has remained much more prevalent than would be predicted on the basis of the level of interaction between English and French groups.[4] Such tendencies are indicative of a phenomenon which might be termed language nationalism.[5] The success of the rejuvenation of Hebrew in

[1] Jan-Petter Blom and John J. Gumperz, 'Social meaning in linguistic structure: code-switching in Norway' in Gumperz and Hymes, *op. cit.*; Einar Haugen, 'The curse of Babel,' *Daedalus*, 102, 3 (1973).

[2] Deutsch discusses the decline of Gaelic speaking in Scotland according to this model in *Nationalism and Social Communication* (Cambridge, Mass.: 1966).

[3] A. Tabouret-Keller, 'Sociological Factors of Language Maintenance and Language Shift: A Methodological Approach Based on European and African Examples,' in Fishman *et al.*, *op. cit.*, pp. 116–17.

[4] Stanley Lieberson, 'Bilingualism in Montreal: a demographic analysis,' *American Journal of Sociology*, 71, 1 (1965), pp. 10–25.

[5] The phenomenon of language maintenance among cultural minorities was even evident to early nineteenth-century observers of intergroup relations. Here is a fascinating example. In a paper, 'On the language and character best suited to the education of the people' published in 1837, the Honorable Frederick John Shore, Judge of the Civil Court and Criminal Sessions of Farrukhabad and an official representative of the British Imperial presence in India, came to reflect on the persistence of Welsh in the British Isles:
'When one nation, which, to say the most, was only advancing in the march of civilization, had conquered another, the conquerors conceived, that it would be

Israel, and much less conclusively, Gaelic in Eire, illustrates that formally dead, or at the least dying languages can be reborn given suitable political control over status-conferring institutions.[1]

To the extent that monolingual groups speaking different languages interact in society, it is clear that there will be powerful incentives for a solution to the system problem of allowing for communication between these groups. However, there are several ways for such inter-communication to be facilitated. Group A and group B might, as in some African societies, communicate through a 'neutral' language, C; in which case both become bilingual with respect to C. Conversely, both groups can become mutually bilingual, such that an A learns B in the course of his education, while Bs are simultaneously gaining proficiency in A. Alternatively, only one group need become bilingual for intercommunication to proceed. If all Bs speak A, there is not much incentive for all As to learn B. While the first two solutions are essentially symmetrical in so far as the two groups are concerned, the third alternative is asymmetrical, and generally reflects the dominance of the monolingual group in the national society. This is so because there is considerable individual cost involved in the

---

less trouble to compel the conquered to adopt the language of the former than for themselves to acquire that of their new subjects. The plan has never yet succeeded, except where the original race has been entirely or nearly exterminated. It is needless enumerating the various countries in which the experiment has been made and failed. They have been so often alluded to of late, that even those who were previously ignorant on the subject, must be familiar with the instances: one, how-ever, which, perhaps, furnishes the strongest example of any, seems hitherto to have escaped observation—I allude to that of Wales. This small portion of terri-tory has been closely connected with Saxon England for nearly eight centuries; it has formed an integral part of the kingdom for six and a half. Travellers in-numerable, from each, have visited the other, and the closest communication has existed between them. Yet, to this day, Welsh is the vernacular language of the majority of the people, so much so, that in the churches service is performed once a day in Welsh; and even in some of the inns, on the high roads, which are chiefly frequented by English, servants will be found, whose language is Welsh, and who understand no more of English than the mere names of the articles which a traveller is likely to call for. Yet it might, with some reason, have been expected that, in such a case as this, the language of the smaller, weaker, and conquered province would gradually disappear, by the constant intercourse, and the repeated attempts that have been made to introduce that of its most powerful neighbour and conqueror. This may, perhaps, ultimately be the result; but more than six cen-turies have not been sufficient to accomplish it, and how much longer it may be before the object will be attained, it remains for time to show.' From F. J. Shore, *Notes on Indian Affairs* (London: 1837), vol. I, p. 433. I am indebted to Paul R. Brass for bringing this passage to my attention.

[1] J. Macnamara, ed., *Problems in Bilingualism*, special issue of the *Journal of Social Issues*, 23, 2 (1967).

learning of a new language. Furthermore, these considerations of dominance become all the more critical in developed societies, where mass literacy is a requirement of participation in the bureaucratic order. In practice, literacy is obtained through participation in a national educational system. The language in which training will proceed is a matter of great political significance in that it tends to give certain groups, native speakers of the language in question, a distinct advantage in the realization of skills at the expense of others, those who learn this language as a second tongue. The administration of examinations on a universalistic basis for the allocation of occupational roles will tend to 'institutionalize' these advantages.

Whether or not language differences between groups in contact are always mirrored by corresponding economic differences is not of concern in this chapter. English language dominance is clearly present in this case study. To the extent that language change occurred it was the Celtic speakers, and not the English speakers who initially submitted to bilingualism. With time most actually became monolingual English speakers. The most important determinant of the relative dominance of a specific cultural, or linguistic, group is the extent to which it exercises control over the apparatus of the central government. In this way, national cultural policies, such as those legitimating the use of particular religions or languages in national cultural institutions, are ultimately political in origin. In formal democracies much of this political power, in turn, is a function of the relative demographic strength of respective cultural groups. Presumably the higher the proportion of the population speaking a minority language, the greater the likelihood the group will maintain its language. The group may self-consciously hope to some day overtake the present majority by the strength of its numbers, and thereby have its language and culture become dominant, or at the least co-equal. The case of the Flemings in Belgium illustrates that such strategies are in fact practicable.[1]

However, industrialization and mass literacy have introduced a new demographic calculus with respect to the cultural autonomy of minorities. Prior to the age of mass literacy, a minority cultural group need merely to have been heavily concentrated in a given region of the national territory to ensure that its language would likely be maintained. To the extent that skills and education could be acquired

[1] Val R. Lorwin, 'Linguistic Pluralism and Political Tension in Modern Belgium' in Joshua A. Fishman, ed., *Advances in the Sociology of Language*, vol. 2 (The Hague: 1972).

informally, or through affiliation to voluntary associations, such as the Nonconformist church in Wales, which sponsored education in Welsh, there need be little threat to the persistence of a minority language. For, in this example, while Welsh speakers might have been a minority in the United Kingdom, they were an overwhelming majority in Wales. In the preceding section it was shown that regional religious differences between England and the Celtic periphery had long historical roots and were not diminished with the advent of industrialization. However, when universal education under governmental regulation becomes compulsory (in Britain this occurred in 1918) the regional concentration of a minority cultural group loses much of its salience. Decisions involving the institutionalization of language are made by a national polity. Thus the relative size of interacting language groups really does not become critical for the issue of language maintenance until the twentieth century.

The word Celtic technically classifies a family of formally similar languages. There are two distinct Celtic languages in Britain: q-Celtic (Irish, Manx and Scottish Gaelic) and p-Celtic (Welsh, Cornish, and in France, Breton).[1] These languages are not mutually understandable. For the purpose of this analysis I will resort to the term 'Celtic speaker' to represent individuals speaking either Welsh or any version of Gaelic though no such language actually exists. Since 1891 British censuses have recorded the prevalence of Welsh and Gaelic speaking among the county populations of Wales and Scotland; comparable data for Ireland exist from 1851 to 1961, and for Northern Ireland from 1851 until 1921, the date of the Partition.

The census is not an ideal source from which to determine language distribution.[2] It is most effective when the enumerated population is highly educated. However, it tends to obscure socially significant differences in dialect. The names for many local forms of speech vary. Further, if the respondent's language is of low prestige he may prefer to list himself as a speaker of the high prestige language. But these objections aside, the census return provides the only empirical basis for the study of language shift in the British Isles.

With the exception of Ireland, the mean county proportion of Celtic speakers has declined everywhere in the British Isles (Table

[1] Ó Cuív, op. cit.; M. W. Heslinga, The Irish Border as a Cultural Divide (Assen, Netherlands: 1962), pp. 108 et seq.
[2] John J. Gumperz, 'Some Remarks on Regional and Social Language Differences in India' in John J. Gumperz, Language in Social Groups (Stanford: 1972), pp. 2–3.

6.7). In Wales the decline has been from 57 to 39 per cent; in Scotland, from 11 to 3 per cent; in Northern Ireland Gaelic speaking hovered at 3 per cent throughout the period. In Ireland the statistics fell from 22 to 14 per cent from 1851 to 1911; thereafter, with governmental stimulus, Gaelic speaking rose to 26 per cent. All of these statistics include mono- and bilingual Celtic language speakers.

It is readily apparent that the population of the Celtic periphery relative to England has steadily declined from 1801 to 1951. In 1801 England contained 53 per cent of the population of the British Isles; in 1851 this proportion had increased to 61 per cent. By 1921 the English percentage was 75, and in 1951 it was 79. In contrast the contributions of Wales and Scotland were remarkably consistent— Wales providing about 4 per cent and Scotland 10 per cent. Chronic emigration from Ireland is indicated by the fact that in 1801 the island composed fully one-third of the population of the British Isles; by 1951 this had declined to 8 per cent. However, these figures become especially important for this scheme after 1918. In 1921, then, even if the Celtic periphery were totally Celtic speaking, the national proportion of Celtic language speakers could only approach 25 per cent. This assumes that those migrants to England from the Celtic periphery who might have been minority language speakers gave up their Gaelic or Welsh tongues. A study of language loyalty in the United States, which may be compared to this example, indicates that language shift among immigrants occurred after two or three generations.[1] However, as has been related, the actual proportion of Celtic language speakers by 1891 was very small except in Wales, where a majority were either mono- or bilingual speakers of Welsh. In reality, then, the actual national proportion of Celtic speakers was considerably less than 25 per cent.

Was industrialization basically responsible for the decline in peripheral language maintenance? Table 6.7 shows that the incidence of Celtic speaking was greater in the peripheral hinterlands than in the industrial enclaves. In Wales there is a difference of thirty-two percentage points in 1891; by 1961 this has increased to a thirty-five point difference. Thus the rate of change in both contexts was about the same. In Scotland the enclave is barely Gaelic speaking by 1891, and not at all by 1961; the hinterland declines from 13 to 10 per cent. In the two largest counties of Ireland, Dublin and Antrim (including

---

[1] Joshua A. Fishman, *Language Loyalty in the United States: The Maintenance and Perpetuation of Non-English Mother Tongues by American Ethnic and Religious Groups* (The Hague: 1966), pp. 396–8.

TABLE 6.7 *The decline of Celtic language speaking: county means in percentages**

	1891	1901	1911	1921	1931	1951	1961
Wales							
All-counties	57	54	51	50	50	41	39
Industrial counties	30	26	22	19	18	11	10
Non-industrial counties	62	60	57	55	56	47	45
Scotland							
All counties	11	9	8	7	6	4	3
Industrial counties	2	2	1	1	1	0	0
Non-industrial counties	13	11	10	9	7	5	4
Northern Ireland							
All counties	2		3	na	na	na	na
Industrial counties			—	na	na	na	na
Non-industrial counties	2	2	3	na	na	na	na
Southern Ireland							
All counties	14	14	14	16	21	19	26
Industrial counties	—	—	4	8	—	13	20
Non-industrial counties	14	14	14	17	21	20	26

* Source: *Censuses of England and Wales, Scotland, Ireland, and Eire* (1931–61).

Belfast) as early as 1851 only 1 per cent of the population spoke Gaelic. The reason behind the low incidence of Celtic language speaking in all but the Welsh enclave has been previously sketched. Ultimately it reflects the fact that these had been culturally anglicized contexts for some time. Therefore, the relationship between industrialization and the decline of Celtic language speaking can be studied best in Wales, for Wales alone has a reasonably large proportion of Celtic speakers in its industrial enclave in 1891.

Table 6.8 presents the degree of association between manufacturing occupations and Celtic language speaking in each of the peripheral contexts over time. As is evident, for most of the observations the direction of the association is negative, save for Wales in 1891 and 1901, when it is weakly positive. The relationship is most negative in Ireland over all seven observations, then next so in Scotland, and least in Wales—at any rate until 1961. On the whole the direction of the Welsh statistics over time is weakly negative, and there is a slight resurgence of Welsh speakers in the industrial areas during 1931 and 1951. Both the Scottish and Irish statistics, on the contrary, gain in strength, though it must be emphasized that the actual proportion of Gaelic speakers in Scottish counties is very small. The data indicate that the distribution of this tiny minority is changing; there is apparently movement of Gaelic speakers from agricultural areas towards industrial sites. A similar movement is evident in Ireland. But a reverse process has occurred in Wales. How can this difference in trends be interpreted?

While the industrial enclave was culturally very Welsh in the mid-nineteenth century, it was becoming successively more anglicized through the late nineteenth and early twentieth century.[1] If for no other reason, this was a consequence of the rate of English immigration during the period from 1861 to 1911 (see Table 6.6). A very great proportion of this current of English migration went to Glamorganshire, which was the center for the expanding coal industry. Brinley Thomas has estimated that of the five decades between 1861 and 1911, four had greater numbers of English migrants to Glamorganshire than Welsh migrants from hinterland counties.[2] Thus a major part of the decline in the proportion of Welsh speakers

---

[1] The process of anglicization in Wales began in the sixteenth century. For a discussion of its beginnings see W. Ogwen Williams, 'The survival of the Welsh language after the Union of England and Wales: the first phase: 1536–1642,' *Welsh History Review*, 2, 1 (1964).

[2] Thomas, *op. cit.*

TABLE 6.8 *The association between Celtic speaking and industrialization. Unstandardized b coefficients from the regression of Celtic speaking on manufacturing occupations*

	1891	1901	1911	1921	1931	1951	1961
Wales	0·066	0·022	−0·290	−0·175	−0·022	−0·035	−0·412
Scotland	−0·467	−0·246	−0·308	−0·265	−0·153	−0·089	−0·071
Northern Ireland	−0·055	−0·034	−0·055	na	na	na	na
Southern Ireland	−0·577	−0·695	−0·662	−0·511	−0·452	−0·529	−0·270

in the enclave might be attributed solely to this influx of English-speaking migrants.

Additionally, the literature on language change often stresses that there is something in the industrialized environment *per se* which loosens the ties of the recent rural immigrant to his customary language. High population density and industrial organization are assumed to signal abrupt changes in life-style, means of survival, patterns of social interaction, and ultimately individual values. To the recent immigrant from the hinterlands this environment might seem to be almost in Brownian Motion.[1] The complex individual readjustments required to perceive meaning and social order in this apparently chaotic milieu also might be hypothesized to encourage language shift. These structural changes, apart from the exogenous factor of the level of English migration to Wales, might be the major cause of the decline of Welsh speaking in the Principality.

In comparing which of these two factors had the greatest independent effect on the fall-off of Welsh speaking, certain problems immediately arise. The cause of English migration to Wales in the period 1861–1911 was very clearly the expansion of the coal industry. The great bulk of such migrants therefore went to the industrial enclave. To estimate the independent effect of English migration on the decline in Welsh speaking the effect of industrialization must be controlled. Alternatively, to estimate the independent effect of industrialization on Celtic-speaking, the level of English migration must be controlled. This dilemma suggests a series of multiple regressions arranged in a path model.[2] There is no difficulty in specifying the causal order of the variables; industrialization clearly causes both

---

[1] 'The psychological basis of the metropolitan type of individuality consists in the intensification of nervous stimulation which results from the swift and uninterrupted change of outer and inner stimuli. Man is a differentiating creature. His mind is stimulated by the difference between momentary impression and the one which preceded. Lasting impressions, impressions which differ only slightly from one another, impressions which take a regular and habitual course and show regular and habitual contrasts—all these use up, so to speak, less consciousness than does the rapid crowding of changing images, the sharp discontinuity in the grasp of a single glance, and the unexpectedness of onrushing impressions. These are the psychological conditions which the metropolis creates. With each crossing of the street, with the tempo and multiplicity of economic, occupational, and social life, the city sets up a deep contrast with small town and rural life with reference to the sensory foundations of psychic life.' Georg Simmel, 'The Metropolis and Mental Life' in K. Wolff, ed., *The Sociology of Georg Simmel* (New York: 1964), pp. 409–10.

[2] A good introduction to path analysis may be found in Otis Dudley Duncan, 'Path analysis: sociological examples,' *American Journal of Sociology*, 72, 1 (1966), pp. 1–16.

the English migration as well as any changes in language. However, since the data are assembled from the county units, there are only thirteen cases at each point in time. This requires an absolute minimum of independent variables in order to achieve significant results. The county proportion of adult males in manufacturing occupations will serve as an indicator of industrialization. The degree of English migration will be represented by the proportion of English-born to total county population. The dependent variable is the proportion of Welsh speakers. The model may be represented in Figure 2:

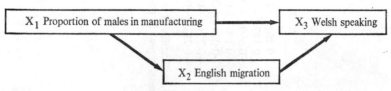

Figure 2 Determinants of Welsh speaking

The estimate of the independent effect of industrialization on Welsh speaking is the standardized regression coefficient, or path coefficient, linking X_1 and X_3. Table 6.9 represents path coefficients, with their respective levels of significance, for each of the seven decades from 1891 to 1961. In 1891 alone both independent effects are statistically significant. The path weight of the English migration factor is very strongly negative (-0.894). However, the effect of industrialization on Welsh speaking is in the opposite direction, at a weight of 0.376. Thereafter the only significant influence on Welsh speaking in the model is from English migration. After 1931 this model is unable to explain most of the variation in Welsh speaking, thereby indicating that entirely different social processes begin to account for the continued decline of Welsh speaking in the Principality.

Very little is known about the type of social interaction which occurred between the English migrants and the native Welsh in the industrial context.[1] There is some evidence that the mining valleys remained culturally Welsh—but little can be said about the tendency for English workers to embrace this Welsh culture. What must ultimately cause language change in the subordinate cultural group (at least from monolingualism to bilingualism) is the opportunity to escape from cultural restrictions on the performance of certain roles

[1] A. H. Dodd claims that there was much sectarian strife between English and Welsh laborers. This was heightened by the fact that when workers had to be laid off, Anglican foreman would see that Welsh Dissenters went first. See *The Industrial Revolution in North Wales* (Cardiff: 1933), p. 399.

TABLE 6.9 Determinants of Welsh speaking from path models

| Year | Determinant | | $R^2(3.12)$ |
	Manufacturing	English-born	$r(12)$	
1891	0·376 (+0·544)*	−0·894 (−4·642)*	0·452 (+0·103)	0·692
1901	0·134 (+0·210)	−0·818 (−3·299)*	0·147 (+0·057)	0·654
1911	0·318 (+0·475)	−0·915 (−4·413)*	0·560 (+0·173)*	0·613
1921	−0·232 (−0·310)	−0·533 (−2·405)*	−0·190 (−0·056)	0·291
1931	0·016 (+0·022)	−0·570 (−3·213)*	0·058 (+0·014)	0·324
1951	−0·388 (−0·519)	−0·363 (−1·608)	−0·224 (−0·068)	0·050
1961	−0·376 (−0·489)	−0·278 (−1·219)	−0·212 (−0·063)	0·045

* Significant at 0·10 (2-tailed test). Numbers not in parentheses are standardized path coefficients. These are appropriate for comparing the independent effects on Welsh speaking at each point in time. Unstandardized coefficients appear in parentheses. These are appropriate for comparisons of the effects of the same variables at different points in time.

in the social structure. To the extent that the great majority of Welshmen in the industrial context were locked in the least skilled occupational categories there would be little necessity or incentive to learn English. This would entail no difficulties for industrial production so long as supervisory personnel were bilingual, and could thus interpret instructions and commands to the workers in their native tongue.

Thus no firm conclusions can be drawn about the character and quality of social interaction between culturally different groups in the industrial context. Such patterns of social contact might be highly structured according to mutual expectations of different behaviors among two hierarchically stratified groups. Typically, the subordinated cultural groups might employ English to address their status superiors, but maintain Welsh for use in social interaction among equals. This type of situation would be much less conducive to the disappearance of the socially inferior language than the loose interaction theories would predict. Instead, a stable pattern of bilingualism might result.

Given the fact that the major flow of English immigrants to Wales began in 1861, the persistence of Welsh speaking in the industrial enclave, when English migration is accounted for, gives evidence that at this time (1891) many Welshmen were subject to asymmetric interaction with English speakers. This most likely was associated with differential stratification between the two cultural groups, and might also suggest the possibility of residential segregation. But here the lack of detailed and systematic evidence about the interaction of cultural groups in Wales is most unfortunate.

After 1891, however, the path data seems to indicate that the high level of English migration came to have general significance for the anglicization of the area. This was noted in a government commission report from 1917:[1]

During the last 50 years or so the rapid development of the coal mining industry, as also, to a less extent, of steel and tinplate manufactures, and transport service, has attracted to this district exceptionally large numbers of immigrants from all parts of the United Kingdom.... The resultant mixture of people in any particular district often presents great differences in their traditions and antecedents, in their speech, habits and temperament, in their mental and moral make-up generally. Until some 15 to 20 years ago, the native inhabitants had, in many respects, shown a marked

---

[1] *Commission of Enquiry into Industrial Unrest* (*Wales, including Monmouthshire*), Parliamentary Papers, 1917–18, XV, Cd 8668, p. 15.

capacity for stamping their own impress on all newcomers, and communicating to them a large measure of their own characteristics. In more recent years the process of assimilation has been unable to keep pace with the continuing influx of immigrants.

It is possible to estimate the change in the independent effects of industrialization and English migration on Welsh speaking by comparing the unstandardized path coefficients of each relationship separately over time. Table 6.9 shows that the independent effect of industrialization changes continuously in a negative direction, save in 1931. That is, the industrial context begins from 1921 on to explain increasingly more of the decline in Welsh speaking with time. On the other hand, the effect of English migration tends to be muted over time. By 1951, industrialization explains relatively more of the decline in Welsh speaking than does English migration. After 1911, the large scale English migration to Welsh industrial areas ceases. In 1951 and 1961, to the extent that English migrants settle in Wales it is more likely to be in hinterland counties. This change in flow is most probably connected with the industrial depression which occurred in Wales after World War One. As a consequence, Welsh speakers are more likely to be found in the enclave in 1931.

Hence, at least on the basis of this evidence, there is nothing in the industrial context which initially encourages language shift from Welsh to English.[1] Not until 1921 is the independent effect of industrialization associated with a decline in Welsh speaking. This is a significant time for two different reasons. First, by this time the universal education act had been passed for Britain, ensuring that free education would be carried on in English and English alone.[2]

---

[1] 'Industrialization was ... transforming the potentialities of Welsh social and cultural life. It gave rise to a phenomenal internal migration ... most of the inhabitants of the industrial areas were Welsh by origin, speech and culture. In this context there was a marked difference between them and Irish and Gaelic speakers. ... The Welsh in their search for industrial employment were not obliged to abandon their language along with their rural homes. They could take Welsh with them to new industrial towns and villages—they even contrived to do so very successfully in London or Liverpool or Manchester as well as in Wales,' Glanmor Williams, 'Language, literacy and nationality in Wales,' op. cit., p. 11.

[2] In the 1911 Census, for example, the highest proportion of non-Welsh speakers is found among those aged twenty-five and younger. 'The chief reason for this ignorance of Welsh among the lower age groups was undoubtedly the ... language policy adopted in the schools of Rhondda (as elsewhere in Wales) during the last quarter of the nineteenth century. In the Colliery Schools, and British and National Schools, as well as in the schools controlled by the different School Boards, the only official medium of instruction was English. Perusal of the Log Books of the Early Head teachers read as if these schools were situated in the heart of Somerset.' Lewis, op. cit., p. 242.

A stable pattern of bilingualism requires the existence of at least two functionally distinct domains of social life, each corresponding to a particular language.[1] The two domains of great importance, of course, are the home and the workplace. In this example, the Welsh language could survive despite the dominance of English in the workplace only so long as it continued to be spoken in the home. Monolingual education (particularly elementary education) in English, however, tended to subvert the use of Welsh in the home in the course of several generations. In this respect, the influence of state policy in the process of acculturation can be considerable.

Second, by this date a great majority of Welsh workers in the enclave had become affiliated to national industrial trade unions rather than the regional associations which had characterized the early period, whose leaders, headquarters and directives emanated from England. This period further coincides with the triumph of the Labor Party in all subsequent Welsh elections and the waning of Welsh nationalism. As national cultural institutions further penetrated the periphery, both in the enclave and the hinterland, anglicization proceeded apace. Language shift occurred at virtually the same rate in both sub-regions.

Whereas in Scotland and Ireland the decline of Gaelic speaking largely preceded the Industrial Revolution, it is clear that industrialization played some role in the weakening incidence of Welsh-speaking in contemporary Wales. However the evidence indicates that the nature of this effect was not exactly as might have been anticipated on the basis of the expectations of the diffusion model. Urban industrial life was not apparently antithetical to Welsh language maintenance. As late as 1911 it has been estimated that the effect of the industrial context on Welsh speaking was, indeed, positive: most of the recorded fall-off in Welsh speaking was due to the immigration of large numbers of English speakers to industrial Wales.[2] There is little evidence that anything in the industrial context *per se* reduced the hold of the language on the lives of most Welshmen. But the growing penetration of the central government into the everyday lives of all citizens, initially felt through legislation on public education, did lead to subsequent language shift. Only after its existence

[1] Joshua A. Fishman, 'The Sociology of Language,' in Giglioli, *op. cit.*, pp. 51–4.
[2] The decline of Welsh speaking may of course have been facilitated by other factors, such as differential fertility among Welsh and English speakers in the enclave cities. This is a promising field of inquiry which, however, has never been adequately investigated.

was not recognized by the political authority of the state did Welsh begin to be abandoned in both the enclave and the hinterland.

Of course, many dialectical differences continue to distinguish English speaking in England from English speaking in each of the Celtic regions, just as linguistic regionalism within England itself is quite notable. There is every reason to believe that these dialectical differences serve as cultural markers.[1] The existence of cultural markers has been observed in the face of extremely minute morphological differences in languages.[2] So long as the speech community recognizes these dialectical differences and endows them with social significance, ethnic boundaries may persist.

CONCLUSION

The data presented in this chapter indicate that, during the period of industrialization from 1851 to 1961, there was no convergence of religious affiliation between England and the Celtic periphery. There was, however, significant language shift in the peripheral areas. Since but two dimensions of regional cultural identity have been discussed, the role of industrialization in the evolution of national cultural homogeneity would appear to be cloudy. In addition, much detailed evidence about intergroup social relations in the peripheral areas does not exist. In these circumstances it is difficult to choose between the diffusion and internal colonial models of cultural integration without resort to speculation.

The evidence with respect to religion is at variance with the diffusion perspective, if it can be demonstrated that the difference between Nonconformity and Anglicanism has remained socially significant following industrialization. Historical accounts of the religious re-identification of English migrants to Wales is powerful testimony of such social significance. Further data analysis has demonstrated that Nonconformity explains more of the variance in

[1] For attempts to measure differences in dialect, and to relate them to various groups in the social structure see William Labov, 'The study of language in its social context,' *Studium Generale*, 23, 1 (1970), reprinted in Giglioli, *op. cit.*, and William Labov, 'On the mechanisms of linguistic change,' *Georgetown University Monograph Series on Languages and Linguistics*, No. 18, reprinted in Gumperz and Hymes, *op. cit.*

[2] John J. Gumperz, 'The Measurement of Bilingualism in Social Groups' in L. G. Kelley, ed., *The Description and Measurement of Bilingualism* (Toronto: 1969).

county voting behavior than any social structural variable in the peripheral regions, though not in England.[1]

On the other hand, the census evidence also points towards eventual linguistic homogeneity, save in Eire. This might appear to weigh against the internal colonial model, which predicts the maintenance of indigenous cultural identity in the periphery despite heightened exposure to the core culture. However, the establishment of compulsory public education in the English language introduces a new element to the analysis, namely a legal sanction against Welsh speaking in school. The active intervention of the state on behalf of this English cultural form was not easily resisted in the Celtic lands. The internal colonial thesis need not insist on maintenance of the peripheral culture in all its forms, but in at least one. It is the existence of a social boundary which defines the peripheral group, and not the particular cultural stuff that it encloses.[2] This chapter suggests that religion continues to serve this purpose rather more than does language in the Celtic lands. Of course, there are many more subtle cultural *differentiae* (customs, folklore, sports activities, dialects, and so forth) which cannot, unfortunately, be analyzed in a systematic fashion. They remain extremely important none the less. In conclusion, the persistence of cultural boundaries in the Celtic regions cannot be easily reconciled with the diffusion model of core-periphery relations.

[1] See chapter 10.
[2] Frederik Barth, 'Introduction' in F. Barth, ed., *Ethnic Groups and Boundaries* (Boston: 1969), p. 15.

CHAPTER 7

THE PERSISTENCE OF SECTIONALISM, 1885–1966

The sea, O the sea, *a ghrádh-gheal mo chroí,*
Long may it roll between England and me;
God help the poor Scotsmen, they'll never be free
But we are surrounded by water!

TRADITIONAL IRISH SONG

SPATIAL factors have seldom received primary attention in political science or in the related disciplines of economics and sociology. In consequence the study of regional politics has largely suffered from neglect. By *region*, I refer initially only to a large and indefinite part of the territory of a state. Much of what is known about the social bases of regional politics is descriptive and highly derivative of nineteenth-century sociological insight. This is clearly the case in considering the effects of industrialization on regional political differences.

Throughout modern history, political differences between regions of states have occurred with some regularity. They have been regarded with especial alarm by central rulers, for secession always lurks as a possible outcome of territorially-based political cleavages. Few states have countenanced regional secession as a resolution of political conflict. But the definition of regionalism as a meaningful concept in social science must involve more than an empirical demonstration of political differences between regions of a state. This is because it is necessary to distinguish between two analytically separate social bases of regional political distinctiveness. Regions may differ according to (1) their *social structural composition* and (2) their *cultural composition*.

It has long been held that in pre-industrial societies individuals are communally solidary and have political commitment to local authorities, whereas in industrial societies individuals are likely to be class solidary and have political commitment to a particular social class

208

and its representatives. The first base of solidarity is territorial and can ultimately be perceived to be cultural; the second is often described as functional. The regional political distinctiveness can reflect the existence of both cultural-territorial and functional cleavages, but the differences between the two are significant. In the first case, the cause of political differences results from what is socially defined to be the specific culture of the region; in the second, political distinctiveness is ecologically determined and therefore ultimately is due to the social structural composition of the territory. In one case all political actors, whatever their class or occupational position, tend to unite behind the common elements of a regional culture, for instance, a distinctive language or religion. In the other, class or occupational position determines the actor's political alignment, but certain strata, for instance, peasants or industrial workers, are disproportionately located in particular regions.

It is often assumed that the cultural basis of regional political distinctiveness has decreased *pari passu* with the growth of central administration and its subsequent incursions upon the traditional prerogatives of regional authorities. However, simultaneous with the expansion of internal markets, regional economic specialization tends to arise on the basis of comparative geographic advantage. So while the cultural causes of regional political distinctiveness are presumed to be declining, the strictly social structural causes gain steadily in importance. The net effect of these countervailing tendencies is that regional political differences can be expected to occur at different stages of societal development.

Since both types of regionalism can be measured by the same variables, the degree to which a region differs from the rest of the society with respect to aggregate political behavior, it becomes crucial to introduce a terminological distinction between them.

When a region's political distinctiveness occurs as the result of what may broadly be termed cultural factors, this bespeaks a failure of national integration, and hence will be termed *peripheral sectionalism*. In many instances, regional secession is advocated as a means to realize self-determination, especially in the more culturally distinctive, peripheral regions. On the other hand, regional political differences resulting from variations in social structural composition will be simply termed *functional sectionalism*. The types of conditions leading to the salience of cultural as against structural factors in the political behavior of groups are largely unknown.[1]

[1] These are discussed in chapter 10.

In advanced industrial societies the most threatening type of political regionalism is that which cannot be explained by purely social structural factors. This is the case because functional sectionalism can, in the short run, be bought off by appropriate actions of the central government. A wheat-producing region, to give an example, may be guaranteed subsidies in the face of declining international grain prices by a central government anxious to avoid political challenge.[1] However the issues raised by peripheral sectionalist movements—often involving religion, language, or 'ethnicity'—appear to be more nearly zero-sum in nature, and therefore do not lend themselves to easy short-run resolution.[2]

There is some question about the incidence of these types of regionalism at different stages of national development. The diffusion model of social change regards peripheral sectionalism as a feature of pre-industrial societies, while functional sectionalism is expected to increase following industrialization. Alternatively, the internal colonial model suggests that peripheral sectionalism arises reactively, despite the advent of industrialization, in situations where there is a cultural division of labor in peripheral regions.

The diffusion model of social change predicts an inverse relationship between industrialization and the maintenance of the type of regional culture which sustains peripheral sectionalism.[3] In this model it is assumed that the persistent identification of regional actors with a specific, differential set of cultural forms is retrograde and may therefore be considered as 'traditionalistic.'

In the industrial setting, processes operating at various levels of social organization are thought to coverage in reducing much of the

---

[1] S. M. Lipset, *Agrarian Socialism* (New York: 1968), pp. xv, xvi.

[2] Attempts to further specify these kinds of conflicts, according to the unique nature of the dimensions along which the cleavage has developed or whether 'ideological' elements are attached to it, will be misleading for reasons to be explored below.

[3] In the past several years research in comparative politics has indicated that religious and linguistic differences between groups are frequently of greater significance in the politics of developed societies than differences of social class. These findings have been used to cast doubt on sociological theories of modernization, and what I have labelled the diffusion theory of regional interaction. While many have been willing to cast this theory to the winds, no plausible alternative theoretical schemes have been advanced to explain these phenomena. A recent influential paper ascribes the significance of religious distinctions in contemporary European politics somewhat nebulously to 'events surrounding the Reformation and counter-Reformation' (Richard Rose and Derek Urwin, 'Social cohesion, political parties and strains in regimes,' *Comparative Political Studies*, 2, 1 (1969), p. 44). Why such historical events continue to intrude upon a radically different social reality is conveniently left unexplained.

regional diversity of less complex societies. *Industrialization should promote political centralization by strengthening the central state apparatus at the expense of regional and local authorities.* Max Weber noted that the tempo of business communication in the industrial economy requires a public legal order which functions promptly and predictably.[1] The expansion of markets which follows industrial development tends to destroy traditionally monopolistic economic organizations. This favors the concentration of all legitimate coercive power in one universalist institution, the state. In consequence, tradition-determined relationships decline in politics as well as other spheres.

Regional differences should, in general, decline as a function of the growth of interregional transactions. This is especially so with regard to differences in regional wealth and culture. Since industrialization is associated with increasing interregional factor mobility, it has been argued that, in the long run, this results in the equilibration of *per capita* income among regions.[2] Similarly, the intensification of cultural contact (an inevitable consequence of what Karl Deutsch has termed social mobilization), should ultimately lead to the assimilation of peripheral regions.[3] The peripheral culture, in effect, becomes merged into a territorially inclusive 'national' culture. This process is facilitated by the establishment of national educational systems, generally on a monolingual basis.

At the level of individual orientations towards political action, industrialization should encourage class rather than status group identification. The allocation of social roles on universalistic grounds, thereby eliminating particularistic and ascriptive criteria in the stratification system, undermines status group solidarity. Structural differentiation forces individuals into association on the basis of functional rather than cultural affinities.[4] At the same time, class

[1] Max Weber, *Economy and Society* (New York: 1968), pp. 336–7.
[2] Jeffrey G. Williamson, 'Regional inequality and the process of national development: A description of the patterns,' *Economic Development and Cultural Change*, 13, 4 (1965), pp. 3–45.
[3] Karl Deutsch, *Nationalism and Social Communications* (Cambridge, Mass: 1966); and Karl Deutsch, 'Social mobilization and political development,' *American Political Science Review*, 55, 3 (1961), pp. 493–514.
[4] This conception is integral to modern sociological theory. Talcott Parsons has contributed perhaps more to the development of this theory than anyone. His conception of the pattern variables lies at the basis of much work on political development. See T. Parsons and E. Shils, eds, *Towards a General Theory of Action* (New York: 1962), pp. 76–91. A later notion, adaptive upgrading, adds considerable detail to this formulation. See T. Parsons, *Societies: Comparative and Evolutionary Perspectives* (Englewood Cliffs: 1966), pp. 22–3. Political

interests become more sharply divergent following industrialization.[1] The extension of the franchise to the mass of working people (often with the temporary exclusion of women) leads to a change in the structure of party systems. Political parties are required to maximize votes from among the most disadvantaged sectors of the population, which initially comprise a majority. Despite the development of mass parties, however, political cleavages are not expected to occur strictly along class lines at first. Only after industrialization has firmly taken root in a society will class politics come to predominate. What results is a 'democratic translation of the class struggle.'[2] In contrast to the situation in pre-industrial societies, the most important predictor of an individual's party preference in an advanced industrial setting should be his class position.

However, the internal colonial model, as discussed in previous chapters, suggests that status group political orientations will persist in peripheral regions given the existence of a cultural division of labor. Just as groups in the periphery have resisted cultural assimilation, they should resist political integration with the core. Since the stratification system appears to discriminate against individuals of the peripheral culture, the development of functional political cleavages is impeded. The internal colonial model of national development predicts the emergence of peripheral sectionalism in reaction to the salience of cultural distinctions in the stratification system.

These models therefore predict entirely different outcomes for peripheral secionalism given similar initial conditions. This chapter will present systematic evidence of the extent to which the Celtic lands have become politically integrated in the United Kingdom since the late nineteenth century. In order to empirically differentiate the two types of regionalism, a quantitative measure of peripheral sectionalism, derived from multiple regression analysis of aggregate electoral statistics has been constructed for British counties in the period 1885–1966. The results appear to challenge the diffusion hypothesis— that industrialization necessarily leads to a decline in the level of peripheral sectionalism. The effects of industrialization on national integration in the British Isles have evidently not been unidimensional.

---

sociologists who have been influenced by these ideas include T. H. Marshall, 'Citizenship and Social Class' in *Class, Citizenship, and Social Development* (Garden City: 1964), pp. 71–134; and S. M. Lipset, *Political Man* (New York: 1963), pp. 230–303; S. M. Lipset, *The First New Nation* (New York: 1963).
[1] Weber, *op. cit.*, pp. 336–7.
[2] Lipset, *Political Man*, p. 230.

THE PERSISTENCE OF SECTIONALISM, 1885–1966

Whereas industrialization may be associated with the waning of territorial cleavages within England, no such pattern can be discerned in the Celtic regions and Northern Ireland.

THE BRITISH ISLES AS A CASE STUDY

Whereas regionalism was endemic in pre-industrial times, when centralized authority was threatened by shifting alliances of outlying magnates, the modern industrial age has witnessed the solidification of the central state apparatus. It is generally assumed that there has been a significant reduction in the level of political violence. Nowhere has this been an earlier and more thorough development than in England. The relatively impressive record of successive British governments has led many writers to emphasize the consensual elements in British political history to the exclusion of all others as explanatory variables.[1] Concomitantly, regionalism is often considered to be of minor significance in contemporary British politics.[2]

However, this view overlooks the somewhat less tidy political history of Wales, Scotland, and Ireland. It has largely been left to historians of the Celtic periphery to recount the divergent paths taken in these regions' reactions to English economic, political and cultural domination. Such efforts have included the establishment of

[1] 'Unfortunately many who write about British politics confuse England, the largest part, with the whole of the United Kingdom, or ignore any possibility of differences within it. For instance, Bagehot's study of *The English Constitution*, published in 1867, gives no hint of the constitutional problems that followed the Fenian Rising in Ireland in the same year. Latter-day writers have also ignored differences between English and the United Kingdom politics. L. S. Amery, an active politician during the Irish troubles, gave careful attention in his *Thoughts on the Constitution* (1953) to the integration of colonies into the British Empire and Commonwealth, but none to the problems of the integration and disintegration of parts of the United Kingdom. Samuel Beer's study of *Modern British Politics* (1965), although concentrating upon the historical evolution of the political culture, contains no index references to Scotland, Wales, or Ireland. For Harry Eckstein, the terms England and Britain are also interchangeable. He can thus write of a period when Scotland had its own king and Ireland was unsettled: "Britain emerged from the Middle Ages with a consensus upon the most basic of all elements of political culture." Recognition is sometimes given to differences of peoples within the United Kingdom, but these are then treated as of little or no significance. For instance Jean Blondel begins a discussion of social structure by asserting, "Britain is probably the most homogeneous of all industrial countries," and S. E. Finer, after reviewing differences between the parts of the United Kingdom, concludes by listing regional differences as the first of "factors that assist consensus." ' Richard Rose, *Governing Without Consensus: An Irish Perspective* (Boston: 1971), pp. 42–3.

[2] Robert Alford, *Party and Society* (Chicago: 1963).

separatist, 'nationalist,' voluntary associations, both legal and illegal, and political parties advocating Home Rule in various forms. The secession of the twenty-six counties of Ireland from the United Kingdom in 1921 has been the culmination to date of these movements for Celtic self-determination.

It is the timing of these events which is of concern here. Has regional political distinctiveness declined throughout Britain following industrialization? The answer for England is, by all accounts, affirmative. However, British industrialization did not prevent the secession of southern Ireland in 1921, though the notable lack of industrial development within the twenty-six counties might well explain this.[1] The role of industrialization in the political integration of Wales and Scotland is more ambiguous, since the incidence of nationalism in these regions has fluctuated considerably in the nineteenth and twentieth centuries. Most historians[2] suggest that nationalist sentiment in Wales and Scotland became intensified in the period 1850 to 1921; thereafter, it declined precipitously until the mid 1960s, when a nationalist resurgence occurred, catching most observers by surprise. Scattered evidence indicates that each of the peripheral regions remaining in the United Kingdom continues to manifest distinctive political behavior.[3] These impressions are based upon the revival of the fortunes of the Scottish National Party, Plaid Cymru (The Party of Wales), and the outbreak of new troubles in Northern Ireland.

The apparent vacillation in the strength of Welsh and Scottish nationalism is puzzling. How can a social movement, such as

[1] Michael Hechter, 'Regional inequality and national integration: the case of the British Isles,' *Journal of Social History*, 5, 1 (1971); Eric J. Hobsbawm, 'The attitude of popular classes towards national movements for independence: the Celtic parties of Great Britain' in *Mouvements nationaux d'indépendance et classes populaires aux XIXe et XXe siècles en occident et en orient* (Paris: 1971).

[2] For example see Reginald Coupland, *Welsh and Scottish Nationalism* (London: 1954); Otis Dudley Edwards et al., *Celtic Nationalism* (London: 1968); Kenneth O. Morgan, *Wales in British Politics, 1868–1922* (Cardiff: 1963); Glanmor Williams, 'Language, literacy, and nationality in Wales,' *History*, 56, 1 (1971); J. P. Mackintosh, 'Scottish nationalism,' *Political Quarterly*, 38 (1967); H. J. Hanham, *Scottish Nationalism* (London: 1969); and F. S. L. Lyons, *Ireland Since the Famine* (London: 1971).

[3] For the United Kingdom as a whole see: David Butler and Donald Stokes, *Political Change in Britain* (New York: 1969), chapter 6; for Wales, Scotland, and Northern Ireland see: Kevin R. Cox, 'Geography, Social Contexts, and Voting Behavior in Wales, 1861–1951' in Erik Allardt and Stein Rokkan, eds, *Mass Politics: Studies in Political Sociology* (New York: 1970); Ian Budge and D. W. Urwin, *Scottish Political Behavior: A Case Study in British Homogeneity* (New York: 1966); and Rose .op. cit.

nationalism, 'die' after 1921, then suddenly 'reappear' forty years later? Nationalist movements take root because the issues they raise have salience for political actors. This salience apparently disappeared after 1921. How can this be explained? Did circumstances in Wales and Scotland change so drastically that these needs were eclipsed by others, of totally opposite direction? Or did political actors take their nationalism, and place it in the hands of candidates of national parties? Questions of this nature suggest there might be a more systematic, and general, means of measuring the degree to which groups do not feel themselves to be integrated in the national society.

AN INDIRECT METHOD OF MEASURING PERIPHERAL SECTIONALISM

In this section I will present an indirect method of estimating the salience of cultural factors for aggregate voting behavior. The method is indirect in that it does not employ direct measurement of cultural variables but estimates their significance inferentially. Such an indirect method is important because statistics enumerating the cultural composition of the population are not readily available for many Western European societies (France is a major example). Hence, estimates of the salience of cultural composition for voting behavior must, in these cases, be made indirectly. The method is very simply summarized:

$$V_T = V_S + V_C + \varepsilon \qquad (1)$$

where V_T is the total variance in the aggregate vote for a specific party; V_S is the amount of that variance explained by social structural composition; V_C is the amount of variance explained by cultural composition; and ε is the amount of unexplained variance. When measures of C are unavailable, (1) may be written in the form,

$$V_C + \varepsilon = V_T - V_S \qquad (2)$$

Since C is unknown, interaction effects, if any, cannot be estimated. It is assumed that there is no significant interaction between S and C. In the following discussion the term $(V_C + \varepsilon)$ will be taken as a crude indicator of the salience of cultural composition for aggregate voting. This can be justified only if it is assumed that ε is not correlated with any other unmeasured variables, or that it is a trivial component of the term $(V_C + \varepsilon)$. This assumption in part depends on the extent to which S is adequately measured. Fortunately, direct measures of cultural variables are available for the United Kingdom,[1] and can be employed to test these assumptions. The justification for this method is theoretical and somewhat complex. Inherent in the concept of national integration is the idea that individuals of diverse ascriptive, or primordial, statuses come to recognize that they are primarily members of a corporate group, the nation, which is territorially inclusive in scope.[2] In consequence, loyalties to their tribal, ethnic, religious, linguistic, or regional group are correspondingly diminished. How might such a concept be operationally defined and measured over time?

At the crudest level, measurement is hardly difficult or problematic. A society beset by civil war, as distinct from social revolution, is by definition not nationally integrated. Similarly, the development of a strong, well-organized peripheral sectionalist movement provides evidence of relatively low national integration. If the sectionalist movement is legal, it may well be led by a separatist political party. It might be said that a society having a significant separatist party is somewhat more integrated than one where the corresponding movement is forced underground.[3] Finally, both of the preceding societies are probably more nationally integrated than the first example, the society facing outright civil war. The concept of national integration seems, therefore, to imply differences in degree or level. A good measure of such integration, it follows, would be a variable with scalar qualities, such that 'high,' 'medium' and 'low' levels of integration could be distinguished from one another. In societies having substantial intergroup political cleavage such a crude measure is probably sufficient for analysis. However, the more subtle these cleavages are, the more discriminating the measure must become.

National integration as a concept used by many writers implies that individual political actors behave according to universalistic and achieved statuses in the national society, rather than in response

---

[1] See chapter 6.

[2] For a bibliography on problems of national integration, see Karl Deutsch and William Foltz, eds, *Nation-Building* (New York: 1966). It is important to note that *both* problems of class and status group integration are potential sources of political instability. National integration hence in no way implies political stability—since it must be kept analytically separate from class integration. A society may have a high level of national integration as well as intense, potentially revolutionary class conflict.

[3] This is so because a legal political party, no matter how revolutionary, is always potentially subject to co-optation in the manner described by Robert Michels in *Political Parties* (New York: 1962).

to particularistic and ascriptive statuses. Universalism has been defined as 'the normative pattern which obliges an actor in a given situation to be oriented toward objects in the light of *general standards* rather than in the light of the objects' possession of properties which have a particular relation to the actor's own properties.'[1]

These general standards must be impersonally and non-subjectively applied. The type of social mechanism which can best serve to generate these standards is the *free market*. The free market is universalistic because it exemplifies a type of social relationship which has been termed *open*.[2] Such relationships do not deny participation to anyone wishing to join, and in a position to do so. *Closed* relationships, on the other hand, exclude individuals from full participation on the basis of various criteria.

Associations vary between the extremes of being open and closed according to members' definitions of expediency in given situations. In general the relationship will be closed if members' expectations are of improving their position by monopolistic tactics. The relationship will tend to be open 'if the participants expect that the admission of others will lead to an improvement of their situation, an improvement in degree, in kind, in the security or the value of the satisfaction.'[3]

The outstanding example of the closed association is the medieval guild, whereas the free market typifies the open association. Max Weber's use of the terms 'class' and 'status group' as alternative types of stratification units closely mirrors this discussion of open and closed social relationships. In the famous exposition on 'Class, status, and party' it is important to note that the defining characteristic of class position is an individual's relationship to the marketplace.[4]

Status groups, however, 'hinder the strict carrying through of the sheer market principle.' They thereby act to enforce a certain degree of closure upon the otherwise free social interaction inherent in market relations. The notion of a status group, for Weber, is purposely vague, for he used the word 'amorphous' in describing it. One of the distinctive marks of status group stratification is a specific style of life. This is a functional means of introducing closure into the social relations of a group. Endogamy is a common example. The formulation of the status group tends to be very much like a residual category: it includes attempts to introduce closure in groups on any specific basis—religious, linguistic, 'ethnic,' and so forth.

[1] Parsons and Shils, *op. cit.*, p. 82.
[2] Weber, *op. cit.*, p. 43.
[3] *Ibid.*, p. 43.
[4] *Ibid.*, p. 927.

Whenever a number of individuals collectively withdraw in some respect from the formal openness of market relations, they become a status group.[1] The market relation is impersonal; the status relation just the opposite. Here the antimony between class and status group orientations is made clear. The individual's class orientation in action is always towards the market—he is always 'looking out for number one,' always trying to improve his relative position. However, to the extent that an individual feels himself part of a status group, his actions towards the market place will be constrained in one way or another. He may, in certain situations, be led to act against his particular class interests. Hence, in so far as these terms denote different orientations or proclivities to action, *an individual acts as a member of a status group when he feels socially constrained from fully pursuing his class interest in a specific situation.* All socially meaningful behavior which cannot be accounted for in terms of the social structural situation of actors hence falls into this residual category.

It therefore follows that a society is nationally integrated to the extent that individual, or group, orientations towards political action are made on the basis of class, or social structural, rather than status, or non-structural considerations. Hence, by definition, a group's political integration can be estimated by the extent to which social structural factors determine its voting patterns.[2] As a corollary, a

[1] The third type of solidarity in Weber's scheme is, of course, that of *party*. If status solidarity is defined as the residual of class solidarity, it might be well asked how party solidarity fits this scheme. In my view, to the extent that a party persists in the long run, it will tend to be either on a class or status basis. I am therefore arguing that party solidarity, unlike the former types, is inherently a transitional category, subject to decomposition in much the same way that charismatic authority is temporarily unstable, and, thus, is subject to routinization.

[2] One attempt to measure the deviation from structurally explained voting behavior is Robert Alford's index of class voting, which was constructed from sample surveys. In *Party and Society* (Chicago: 1963) Alford conducted a comparative analysis of class voting in four Anglo-American societies of roughly comparative cultural traditions and level of political stability. On the basis of his evidence, Alford determined that: 'Class polarization of the support for national parties seems to be most evident in the countries where a national political identity has replaced political identities centered on regional or religious loyalties. The aspects of modernization ... favor the emergence of national political identities and thus favor class polarization of the parties—up to a certain point. These societies may all be moving toward a common level of structurally based class cleavages—cleavages which remain while traditional political identities dwindle in importance' (p. 310). This index was applied to British regions on the basis of survey data collected between the years 1957 and 1962, and Wales and Scotland had distinctive voting patterns among British regions. But there are serious drawbacks in his method. The use of survey data as a measure of national integration is of virtually no utility if one is interested in long-term

group is malintegrated to the extent that the voting behavior of its members cannot be explained by reference to its social structural composition.

The only means of measuring levels of national integration historically is through the ecological analysis of electoral returns.[1] Historians and sociologists have more and more frequently employed areal statistics as a means of following political trends over time, with full cognizance of the limitations of such analyses. To construct a measure of structually explained voting from ecological data, it is necessary to obtain both electoral and social structural data for the same geographical units. The constituency[2] is inadequate in this regard because British electoral and social statistics were collected for different areal units. Election results are tabulated by constituencies defined by population, which vary in size from small parts of large cities to entire counties and, occasionally, pairs of counties. On the other hand, social, economic, and demographic statistics have been until recently collected for Administrative Counties, which are geographical units. While it is impossible to compress the social statistics into constituency units, the aggregation of constituencies within county boundaries is feasible, and has been done in this study.

According to the previous analysis the salience of class orientations towards voting may be estimated by *the degree to which social structural variables account for the variance in party choice in a specific county*. Each county has, at a given period, a specific structural composition, including a distribution of social classes. Inherent

---

historical trends. The earliest British survey to which Alford can refer was conducted as recently as 1943. Second, by constructing the index of class voting in Britain on differential support for the Labor party among manual and non-manual occupations, Alford's measure implicitly lumps the Conservative and Liberal party supporters together. This sharply distorts the regional comparisons since the Liberal party has traditionally been a regional opposition force to the center in both Wales and Scotland, but has served a different role within England. From my perspective both objections are critical.

[1] There is little question that information about individuals is generally lost in turning to ecological data. Nevertheless, if properly analyzed, ecological data can yield extremely accurate estimates of group voting patterns, when compared with survey results. See E. Terrence Jones, 'Ecological inference and electoral analysis,' *Journal of Interdisciplinary History*, 2, 3 (1972).

[2] Partly in reaction to the fundamentally impressionistic methodology of many historians, Henry Pelling set out to collect relevant electoral data by constituencies in order to be able to analyze British politics on a regional basis. In *The Social Geography of British Elections* (New York: 1967) he presented percentages of the constituency poll received of each party at successive General Elections from 1885 through 1910 for thirteen English regions plus Wales and England.

in this structural composition are tendencies, or propensities, towards the differential support of particular parties. It is possible to estimate these propensities at each point in time by performing a regression of the proportion of X party support on social structural variables for all counties in the United Kingdom. The regression equation establishes these propensities on the basis of data from all the counties in the population in a given year. It may predict, for instance, that in 1966 the average British industrial county will give 50 per cent of its votes to the Labor Party. Turning from the hypothetical 'average' county to the real behavior of specific counties, it should be clear that the estimate obtained from the regression equation 'fits' some counties better than others. The fit is close if there is very little difference, or residual, between the estimated party support obtained through the regression analysis and the actual support received in a specific election. If this residual value is low it may be inferred that the social structural variables accounted for almost all of the variance of the county's voting behavior, and further, that these structural factors virtually 'explained' the county's voting behavior in this election. On the other hand, a relatively large residual from the county's expected vote indicates that other, non-structural, factors are interfering with structurally predicted voting behavior. In other words, the residual from structurally predicted voting is an indicator of the degree to which, by definition, status group solidarity of one kind or another is inherent in the county. Hence this residual may be taken as an indicator of peripheral sectionalism. It varies inversely to the extent a particular county may be said to be nationally integrated.

What kinds of structural variables can be taken as sufficient for these purposes? The stratification system in industrial societies is so complex that relatively discrete distinctions—which have political significance—can be made between related occupations.[1] At the very least, a primitive labor diversification index should probably be employed. To determine the voting residuals in this study, seven variables which have been previously determined through factor analysis to be indicators of industrialization were employed.[2] These variables include three broad occupational categories which correspond to the primary, secondary, and tertiary sectors of economic

[1] Harold Wilensky, 'Mass Society and Mass Culture' in Bernard Berelson and Morris Janowitz, eds, *Reader in Public Opinion and Communication* (New York: 1966), pp. 317–18.
[2] See chapter 5.

activity—agricultural, manufacturing, and professional and commercial occupations—as well as four contextual measures of industrialization: decennial population growth, proportion of the population aged sixty-five and over, the marriage rate, and level of urbanization. Voting residuals were generated by regressing the proportion of the county's Conservative vote on these seven structural variables. The Conservative vote was chosen as the dependent variable, rather than the Labor vote, because this party has since the nineteenth century been closely identified with the traditional political leadership of London and the Home Counties, as well as the Crown and the Church of England itself. Thus, its traditional role has been to represent the core against any possibility of regional devolution or autonomy. On the other hand, both the Labor and Liberal parties have consistently catered, to varying degrees, to voters in the Celtic regions, and have successfully co-opted regional dissent into their formally national parties. General Election data come from eight specific polls, those of 1885, 1892, 1900, December 1910, 1924, 1931, 1951, and 1966.[1] These data are meant to correspond to the structural variables from census and other sources, taken each decade from 1881 through 1961, with the single exception of 1941 when no census was published.[2] Unopposed candidacies were coded as representing 100 per cent of the vote.

This measure of peripheral sectionalism has one other important feature. There are essentially two ways that a county might not fit its predicted Conservative vote. The actual vote might either be higher than the expectation on the basis of the regression equation, or be lower. The first situation is one where the social structural variables underestimate the Conservative vote; in the second, these variables overestimate the county's Conservatism. In other words residuals from structurally explained voting can be either toward or away from the Conservative Party. Presumably those counties whose residuals

[1] The data from 1885–1910 were calculated from constituency results published in *The Constitutional Yearbook* (London: 1919) and Dod's *Parliamentary Companion* (London: various years) for elections thereafter. For the sake of simplicity it has been assumed that the eight elections are comparable in so far as voter eligibility is concerned. The most important change in this regard occurred with the extension of female suffrage in 1918. Turnout, another complicating factor, is difficult to estimate in the early elections for reasons discussed by Pelling, *Social Geography of British Elections*, pp. 7, 8. The analysis proceeds as if there were no significant regional variations in eligibility and turnout, though by conservative assumptions this is unlikely.

[2] Southern Ireland has been excluded from these regressions because after the formation of the Irish Free State in 1921 its political parties are not comparable to those in the United Kingdom. Northern Ireland, however, is included.

TABLE 7.1 *Zero-order correlations ($P < 0.05$) of structural and cultural variables with the voting residual ($N = 92$)*

Variable	1885	1892	1900	1910	1924	1931	1951	1966
(1) Population growth								
(2) Aged 65 and over								
(3) Sex ratio								
(4) Population density								
(5) Marriage rate								0·219
(6) *Per capita income*	0·228				*	*		
(7) Agricultural occupations								
(8) Manufacturing occupations								
(9) Commercial and professional occupations								
(10) Civil Service occupations	0·239			−0·243				
(11) Female domestics								
(12) Employment								
(13) Urban population								
(14) Average city size					−0·246			
(15) Ethnic diversity	*	−0·391	−0·507	−0·283	−0·593	−0·371	−0·425	−0·352
(16) Celtic speakers	0·346	0·246	0·347	−0·464	0·219			−0·535
(17) Established Church				0·321				
(18) Non-Conformity	−0·438	−0·306	−0·525	−0·498	−0·502	−0·307	−0·361	−0·389
(19) Roman Catholic		0·337	0·242		0·384			
(20) Literacy	0·231	0·257	0·338		0·364			
(21) Religiosity	0·286	0·241	0·291	0·266	0·272			
(22) English-born								
(23) Welsh-born		−0·329	−0·448	−0·376	−0·447	−0·337	−0·487	−0·435
(24) Scottish-born								
(25) Irish-born								
(26) Foreign-born								
(27) Birth rate	0·392		0·262	0·279	0·450	0·271	0·260	0·281
(28) Infant mortality	*							0·290

* Missing data.

are the result of a structural overestimation of the Conservative vote are most likely to support a nationalist movement.

In multiple regression analysis this residual is usually conceived to be an error term, since it represents the error in prediction of the dependent variable from the set of independent variables. Such error terms are expected to occur with regularity in social statistics and are conceived to be random with respect to other variables in the system.[1] Table 7.1, however, indicates that the voting residual is not merely composed of random error, as it is generally correlated with English and Celtic cultural variables. Similarly, it is positively associated with residence in Wales and Scotland and negatively correlated with residence in England, as indicated by the birthplace variables. The strength of these associations is only moderate: r varies from around 0·3 to 0·6. The correlation matrix provides evidence that the voting residual is only partly an estimation of the strength of peripheral sectionalism. It is quite likely that the residual is also error-laden, and therefore it should be merely regarded as a crude indicator of peripheral sectionalism.

FINDINGS

Map 5 shows the geographic distribution of counties having mean voting residuals which are negative for all eight elections. In general, the Celtic lands have the highest concentration of such counties. Every county in Wales but one manifests high negative residuals (Table 7.2). Similarly, the intensity of negative residuals in Scotland is notable, though there is much geographical clustering. In Map 5 it is possible to distinguish three separate political territories in Scotland. To the north and northwest are the highlands, with the highest negative residuals. Then there is a curving strip of counties also shaded from Banff through Lanark and Renfrew, most of which are part of the industrial belt of Scotland. The intensity of structurally unexplained anti-Conservative voting in this area is somewhat smaller than in the highlands. Finally, there are several Scottish pro-Conservative counties which are to be found mainly in the lowlands. This spatial clustering demonstrates the efficacy of two important cleavages in Scotland: that between industrial and non-industrial counties, and that between Celtic (highland) and

[1] These issues are discussed in J. Johnston, *Econometric Methods* (New York: 1962), pp. 3–29.

Map 5   Relatively anti-Conservative counties, 1885–1966 (Great Britain
and Northern Ireland)

TABLE 7.2   *Peripheral sectionalism in counties, 1885–1966**

England		Wales		Scotland		Northern Ireland	
Rutland	23						
Shropshire	21						
Westmorland	19						
Worcester	14						
Berkshire	12						
Buckingham	12						
Hereford	12						
Sussex	12						
Suffolk	11						
Warwick	11						
Hertford	10						
Somerset	10			Bute	20		
Surrey	8			Wigtown	20		
Oxford	7			Peebles	17		
Kent	7			Ayr	11		
Middlesex	5			Kirkcudbright	10		
Stafford	5			Kinross	7		
Dorset	4			West Lothian	7		
Nottingham	4			Argyll	6		
Cambridge	3			Roxburgh	6		
Cumberland	3			Nairn	5	Down	32
Derby	3			Perth	5	Antrim	30
Cheshire	2			Selkirk	3	Armagh	29
Huntingdon	2			Dumbarton	2	Londonderry	15
Northampton	2			Moray	1	Tyrone	7
Wiltshire	0			East Lothian	0	Fermanagh	0
Lincoln	0	Radnor	0	Kincardine	0		
Lancaster	—1	Monmouth	—7	Lanark	—2		
Gloucester	—2	Flint	—7	Renfrew	—2		
Durham	—3	Brecknock	—8	Clakmannan	—3		
Hampshire	—3	Pembroke	—10	Berwick	—4		
Yorkshire	—3	Caernarvon	—18	Stirling	—5		
Cornwall	—4	Denbigh	—18	Aberdeen	—6		
Essex	—4	Anglesey	—19	Banff	—8		
Norfolk	—4	Montgomery	—19	Dumfries	—8		
Bedford	—5	Glamorgan	—22	Angus	—11		
Devon	—5	Cardigan	—23	Midlothian	—11		
London	—5	Carmarthen	—24	Fife	—14		
Northumber-land	—5	Merioneth	—28	Shetland	—16		
Leicester	—6			Sutherland	—16		
				Caithness	—18		
				Orkney	—19		
				Inverness	—24		
				Ross and Cromarty —28			
Mean	4·3	Mean	—15·6	Mean	—2·3	Mean	18·8

* Longitudinal mean voting residuals.

non-Celtic (border) counties.[1] In England several northern and south-western counties have negative residuals—including Cornwall, which

[1] For a discussion of the significance of these cultural distinctions within Scotland see D. Daiches, *The Paradox of Scottish Culture* (London: 1964).

was the first Celtic territory to be incorporated. Northerners have traditionally resented the domination of London in the governance of the realm.[1]

However, there are also some anomalous results. If resentment of London's dominance is one of the dimensions of a negative residual score, it is disconcerting to find London itself numbered among such dissenting counties. It will be wise to recall previous reservations about the reliability of this measure. Probably the most fruitful comparisons between counties may be made only when there are substantial differences in the individual county residual scores. For example, in Table 7.2 the less integrated counties in Wales and Scotland have considerably greater negative scores than those in England. Similarly, all six Northern Irish counties have large residuals, denoting their political distinctiveness, but these are in a positive, pro-Conservative, direction.

Northern Ireland is interesting in that it is a weakly integrated region—clearly shown by the magnitude of its residual scores—which has habitually supported the political center and its culture in hopes of maintaining its autonomy from the Irish Republic. The consequences of the disestablishment of the Stormont Parliament suggest that such support is likely to be highly unstable. Following a redefinition of the political situation by the center, regions such as Northern Ireland may quickly swing from a position backing the center to one of outright political challenge. It might be inferred that the relative instability of voting patterns over time is characteristic of a lack of political integration.

The data lend weight to this conclusion. Figure 3 shows the relationship between the temporal stability of voting patterns and the overall degree of peripheral sectionalism in counties. Temporal voting stability is indicated by the standard deviation of the longitudinal mean voting residual, whereas the actual value of the longitudinal mean indicates the extent of peripheral sectionalism. The great majority (79 per cent) of counties having low peripheral sectionalism scores are stable over time. Of the counties with high positive voting residuals, 64 per cent fall into the stable category. But the relationship changes for the counties having negative residuals, those most likely to support nationalist movements. Of these, 74 per cent are quite unstable. Table 7.3 indicates that most of the Welsh counties are in this category. The English counties, on the other hand, are

[1] Donald Read, *The English Provinces, 1790–1960: A Study in Influence* (London: 1964).

Degree of peripheral sectionalism[+]

		High negative (−8·0−)	Low (−7·9→7·9)	High positive (8·0+)
Temporal voting stability *	Stable (0−14·9)	6	37	14
	Unstable (15·0+)	17	10	8

Figure 3 Distribution of counties, by peripheral sectionalism and voting stability, 1885-1966

* Standard deviation of longitudinal mean voting residual
† Longitudinal mean voting residual

predominantly temporally stable and politically integrated. The Northern Irish counties are largely stable and show high positive sectionalism. The diversity of the Scottish counties is once more evident in this table. Many of the counties with high mean voting

TABLE 7.3 Percentage of counties in each region, by degree of peripheral sectionalism and voting stability, 1885-1966

	Degree of peripheral sectionalism		
	High negative	Low	High positive
Temporally stable counties			
England	0	65	20
Wales	31	7	0
Scotland	6	30	9
Northern Ireland	0	0	50
Temporally unstable counties			
England	0	2	13
Wales	62	0	0
Scotland	27	21	6
Northern Ireland	0	33	17

residuals have at least one instance of an unopposed candidacy, which necessarily results in a high residual value (Table. 7.4). In proportion to counties in the periphery, English counties have (1) fewer unopposed electoral contests in this sample of elections (save Northern Ireland) (2) fewer consistently malintegrated counties (in fact, only one: Rutland), and (3) fewer fluctuations in county political integration.

TABLE 7.4 *Counties having unopposed candidacies in eight General Elections, 1885–1966*

County	General Election
England (N = 40)	
Suffolk	1892
Hereford	1900
Wales (N = 13)	
Anglesey	1900, 1910
Brecknock	1900
Montgomery	1931
Scotland (N = 33)	
Argyll	1931
Banff	1910, 1931
Clackmannan	1885, 1910
Kincardine	1892
Kinross	1885, 1892, 1910, 1966
Moray	1910, 1931
Nairn	1885, 1910, 1931
Selkirk	1885, 1910
Sutherland	1900, 1924, 1931

The analysis therefore indicates that English counties are more nationally integrated and have more stable voting patterns over time than the peripheral counties. Such findings are reasonable and fully consistent with the historical evidence. These results would appear to further validate the utility of the voting residual as an indicator of peripheral sectionalism. However, as the industrialization of the periphery occurred somewhat later than in England, these data should not be interpreted to suggest that the Celtic lands continue to remain politically distinctive. The higher mean levels of peripheral sectionalism in these regions might merely reflect large political differences which occurred in the early decades following 1885, when regional inequalities between England and the Celtic lands were presumably at a peak.

To determine the effect of industrialization on the political integration of the Celtic periphery in the United Kingdom, the data must be considered in time series (Figure 4). When this is done, the evidence clearly indicates that peripheral sectionalism has not declined as a function of industrialization in the United Kingdom as a whole. The amount of variance in voting explained by the structural variables in the eight regressions (as indicated by the coefficient of determination, R^2) does not consistently increase from 1885 to 1966, despite the progress of industrialization during this period.[1]

There appears to be a pattern of increasing political integration among English and Scottish counties, but this is not the case in Wales and Northern Ireland. It is, however, likely that the Scottish

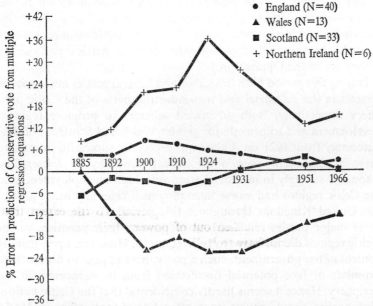

Figure 4   The incidence of peripheral sectionalism in regions of the United Kingdom, 1885–1966. Mean regional residuals from the regresssion of Conservative voting on seven structural variables*

R_s^2: 1885 = 0·279; 1892 = 0·178; 1900 = 0·277; 1910 = 0·285; 1924 = 0·147; 1931 = 0·091; 1951 = 0·250; 1966 = 0·155.

* From regression of industrialization variables on Conservative vote.

means hide much variability between highland and border counties. Wales and Northern Ireland have similarly high mean scores in 1892 and 1966 and the pattern of their means over time is curvilinear. The highest residual means occur in 1924 and 1931, though the Welsh are relatively anti-Conservative and Northern Irish pro-Conservative.

[1] The low R^2 for the 1931 election is striking. In 1931 Ramsay MacDonald supported a National Coalition ticket to secure a maximally cohesive government (see Henry Pelling, *Modern Britain, 1885–1955* (New York: 1966), pp. 120–2). Neither structural nor cultural variables explains as much variance in voting in 1931 as in the other elections.

The implication that there was a high level of peripheral sectionalism in Wales, and parts of Scotland, from 1924 through 1951 appears in one sense paradoxical. For in the previous section it has been noted that after 1921 the nationalist movement waned sharply in both Wales and Scotland. How can this be reconciled with the results in Figure 3? The answer is that *there need be no one-to-one correspondence between the persistence of regional cultural identity and support for a separatist party*. Peripheral sectionalist sentiments may also be appealed to by statewide political parties, particularly if they are in the Opposition.[1]

During this period both the Labor and Liberal parties made special appeals in the industrial and non-industrial parts of the Celtic periphery respectively. Both advocated schemes to promote regional development and to provide for greater Welsh and Scottish political autonomy from 1921 on. Labor was especially successful in making these appeals. The party's ideological antipathy to *laissez-faire* resonated strongly in industrial areas with high unemployment, and the Celtic regions had worse unemployment than any other part of the United Kingdom throughout this period. To the extent that these major parties remained out of power, their promises to the Celtic regions did not have to be lived up to. However, upon gaining control of the government, such a party must appear to honor these promises or face potential disaffection from its supporters in the periphery. Hence it seems hardly coincidental that the Celtic nationalist parties should revive soon after Labor took office in 1964.[2]

This apparent persistence of peripheral sectionalism in a highly industrialized society poses a dilemma for the diffusion theory. How is it to be explained? One interpretation consistent with the diffusion perspective stresses that this occurs when the periphery remains dominated by traditionalism.[3] But this is most unsatisfactory in that this unexpected political behavior is explained by a concept—the holding of 'traditional values'—inherently difficult to measure and hence verify. Furthermore, the argument is tautological: peripheral areas are different because they are different. The critical question is

---

[1] This point is elaborated in chapter 9.

[2] Since this chapter was written, a similar interpretation has been supported by J. M. Bochel and D. T. Denver, 'The decline of the SNP—an alternate view,' *Political Studies*, 20, 3 (1972). There was no comparable nationalist support in Wales and Scotland after 1945 because the welfare and nationalization policies of the Attlee government (especially in the coal industry) seemed to offer new hope for the development of these depressed regions.

[3] Lipset, *Political Man*, 274.

why do individuals in the periphery hold 'traditional values'—though the distinction between modern and traditional values has itself come under sharp attack.[1] Under what objective conditions does the periphery become nationalistic?

Another diffusionist interpretation conceives peripheral sectionalism to be the product of a regionally distinctive culture which defines itself in active opposition to the culture of the core, rather than as a passive residue of tradition-bound individuals. Hypothesized conditions for the emergence of territorial counter-cultures include: the peripheral group must have a territory which facilitates intercollectivity communication; the periphery must be culturally and economically isolated from the national core, and oriented to some extra-national center; and the periphery *must not engage in extensive trade*, or other economic transactions, with the core.[2] Such conditions are likely to be found in relatively non-industrial parts of developed societies, if anywhere.

In these data the consequences of industrialization for the development of political integration might still be regarded as inconclusive. This is because the United Kingdom, taken as a geographical space, is not uniformly industrialized. Since England is disproportionately industrial among British regions, the high mean residual scores in Wales and Northern Ireland might reflect voting behavior in dominantly rural counties. Welsh, Scottish, and Northern Irish industrial counties, on the other hand, might be fundamentally similar to English industrial counties in terms of their political behavior.

However, Table 7.6 discounts this possibility. Industrial counties in all three peripheral regions continue to manifest peripheral sectionalist voting patterns, even as late as 1966. While the English industrial counties appear to be characterized by functional political cleavages from 1892 through 1966, Welsh industrial counties have high levels of peripheral sectionalism throughout the period. Those in Scotland have somewhat intermediate levels of peripheral sectionalism. Antrim (including Belfast) is coded as industrial only in 1966, and it shows very high peripheral sectionalism in that year. These regional relationships are quite similar to those among non-industrial counties: Wales and Northern Ireland have high peripheral sectionalism, England and Scotland low. The Scottish non-

---

[1] Reinhard Bendix, 'Tradition and modernity reconsidered,' *Comparative Studies in Society and History*, 9, 3 (1967), pp. 292–346.
[2] S. M. Lipset and Stein Rokkan, 'Introduction' in S. M. Lipset and S. Rokkan, eds, *Party Systems and Voter Alignments* (New York: 1967), p. 42.

TABLE 7.5 *Peripheral sectionalism in industrial and non-industrial counties, by region**

	1885	1892	1900	1910	1924	1931	1951	1966
Industrial counties in								
England	+6 (6)	+1 (8)	+1 (10)	+1 (13)	+1 (12)	+2 (10)	−2 (16)	+1 (16)
Wales	−16 (2)	−10 (2)	−3 (2)	−17 (2)	−18 (2)	−30 (2)	−9 (2)	−9 (2)
Scotland	−19 (7)	−3 (6)	+4 (9)	−6 (7)	−6 (8)	+4 (6)	0 (8)	−7 (8)
Northern Ireland								
All regions	−2 (15)	−2 (16)	+2 (21)	−3 (22)	−3 (22)	−1 (18)	−2 (26)	−2 (27)
Non-industrial counties in								
England	+4 (34)	+5 (32)	+10 (30)	+10 (27)	+7 (28)	+4 (30)	+2 (24)	+3 (24)
Wales	+3 (11)	−13 (11)	−26 (11)	−19 (11)	−24 (11)	−21 (11)	−16 (11)	−13 (11)
Scotland	−8 (26)	−2 (27)	−6 (24)	−5 (26)	−3 (25)	−2 (27)	+4 (25)	+3 (25)
Northern Ireland	+8 (6)	+11 (6)	+21 (6)	+22 (6)	+36 (6)	+27 (6)	+12 (6)	+13 (5)
All regions	0 (77)	0 (76)	0 (71)	1 (70)	1 (70)	0 (74)	1 (66)	1 (65)

* Counties are defined as industrial if their percentage of employed adult males in non-agricultural occupations was equal to or exceeded 85 per cent for the year 1885, 87·5 per cent for the years 1891–1924, and 90 per cent from 1931 to 1966.

industrial means are low because scores in the highland (negative) and border (positive) counties tend to offset each other.

CONCLUSION

The results indicate that industrialization cannot be considered a sufficient cause of national integration in the United Kingdom. Some case might be made for its explanatory power in this regard within England alone. But the thesis that industrialization leads to a decline of peripheral sectionalism has not been demonstrated for the Celtic fringe. Evidently the persistence of regional cultural identity, which underlies peripheral sectionalism, must in some way mediate the structural consequences of industrialization where political behavior is concerned.

The fact that groups in the peripheral regions continue to define themselves in cultural terms—as being 'Welsh' or 'Scottish' as against 'British'[1]—challenges the generality of the diffusionist model of core-periphery interaction. While these data are insufficient to validate the internal colonialism thesis, they do suggest the necessity of a reactive model to explain peripheral sectionalism in the industrial setting. The diffusion model is quite inadequate in its failure to consider the utility of the maintenance of peripheral cultural identity as a form of political mobilization among groups perceiving themselves to be disadvantaged.[2]

[1] This generalization is supported by the meager survey evidence on the perceived nationality of residents of Wales and Scotland. In 1968, 67 per cent of a Scottish sample defined themselves as 'Scottish' rather than 'British,' while 69 per cent of a Welsh sample correspondingly described their nationality as 'Welsh.' See Rose, *op. cit.*, chapter 6.

[2] See chapter 10.

CHAPTER 8

SERVITOR IMPERIALISM AND
NATIONAL DEVELOPMENT IN AN
AGE OF EMPIRE

No Vietnamese ever called me Nigger!

SLOGAN FROM THE WAR IN INDOCHINA

THERE is a natural tendency to consider the relations between
England and the Celtic regions as the result of an interplay of factors
located solely within the British polity. The pattern of Celtic history
may then be conceived to be insulated from events occurring elsewhere in the world. However this tendency must be resisted. All
modern states participate to varying degrees in a world system which
impinges upon many of their internal processes.[1] For instance, there
is ample evidence of a series of systematic expansions and contrac-
tions in the international economy which have beset the European
states at least since the fifteenth century.[2] These international economic fluctuations have had important consequences for patterns
of production, consumption, and relations between various strata
in these societies.[3]

In the long run changes in the international context have significance upon the internal dynamics of states in another respect as
well. For these changes in the world system do not affect all societies
in equal measure, but tend to favor some states at the expense of

[1] Immanuel Wallerstein, *The Modern World-System: Capitalist Agriculture
and the Origins of the European World Economy in the Sixteenth Century* (New
York and London: 1974).
[2] For a summary and synthesis of his literature see F. P. Braudel and F.
Spooner, 'Prices in Europe from 1450 to 1750' in E. E. Rich, ed., *The Economy
of Expanding Europe in the Sixteenth and Seventeenth Centuries*, Vol. IV of the
Cambridge Economic History of Europe (Cambridge: 1967), pp. 378–486.
[3] Charles Tilly, 'Food Supply and Public Order in Modern Europe' in Charles
Tilly, ed., *The Formation of National States in Western Europe* (Princeton, N.J.:
forthcoming).

others. It may be useful to think of the world system as being hierarchically ordered and composed of whole states as individual units. At certain times the structure of this hierarchy is disturbed and formerly peripheral states come to assume centrality and, hence, high rank in the world system. In fact this is precisely what happened to England between the sixteenth and the nineteenth centuries. In the early sixteenth century England had itself been a relatively peripheral region in the world-system.[1] Its forays into the dark corners of the British Isles were the aggressive actions of an immature state bureaucracy attempting to centralize. This state apparatus had little in terms of material benefits to offer its allies in the Celtic periphery. By the nineteenth century, however, England had achieved virtual hegemony among the nations of the world. The British Empire came to be symbolic of this pre-eminence both at home and abroad.

Much of the difficult task of tracing the consequences of shifts in the international context for developments within Britain remains to be done, and is generally beyond the scope of this study. However, this chapter will discuss one specific question which is related to this general theme: how did British imperialism of the late nineteenth and early twentieth century affect the political integration of the Celtic regions?

As has been previously related, a major problem in the establishment of the modern state involved the attempt to attract the political allegiance of individuals of differing classes and statuses from local and particular institutions to those emanating from a dominant central authority. There has been general agreement that the development of the status of citizenship, particularly the extension of the franchise to the industrial working class, was one of the significant means by which the state achieved legitimacy. Furthermore, this gain in political rights was not accompanied by the continued immiseration of disadvantaged groups. On the contrary, the absolute standard of living increased for all groups in the developing state, and it became evident that prospects for violent revolution had been averted by the end of the nineteenth century.

For those who held that the interests of capital and labor within the industrial state were of necessity mutually antagonistic the apparent softening of class conflict came as a phenomenon which cried for explanation. The germ of this explanation focused on the idea that the imperial expansion of the Western European states in

[1] Fernand Braudel, *The Mediterranean and The Mediterranean World in the Age of Phillip II* (New York: 1972), pp. 228-9.

the late nineteenth century benefited their working classes and encouraged them to hold patriotic attitudes.

The brunt of scholarly research on overseas imperialism has sought to determine the extent to which the acquisition of colonies was in the interest of the metropolitan states. In particular, two questions have frequently been raised. The first has been termed the problem of economic imperialism: was more wealth generated for the metropolis than lost in imperial ventures? The second—how did imperial expansion alter the balance of power in the world system?—has been the keystone of the study of political imperialism. But relatively little is known of the role of imperialism as a doctrine in the internal politics of the metropolis, especially as a possible source of increased legitimation among discontented groups.

This is all the more surprising since many writers have long called attention to the possible integrative function imperial expansion might serve in the creation of national solidarity. The Marxian notion of the 'aristocracy of labor,' as discussed by Engels, Lenin, and Gramsci, and the nationalistic theory of social-imperialism, as developed by Cunningham, Ashley and others in this sense share a common sociological perspective. The meager evidence which has been collected suggests that European socialist and labor parties displayed but slight resistance to the expansionist policies of their respective governments.[1]

This chapter considers the role imperialism can play in the integration of excluded status groups, particularly cultural minorities, into the national society. It is quite possible that minority groups might embrace imperialist policies enthusiastically as a means of improving their standing in the society as a whole and compensating for their lack of political and cultural autonomy. I have used the phrase 'servitor imperialism'—the imperialism of second-class citizens—to describe this reaction; it forms a kind of counterpoise to the phrase 'labor aristocracy.'

It is evident that imperialism might appeal to lower status groups in the metropolis on basically two different grounds. A concern for economic advantage may lead to favorable attitudes towards imperialism among those groups directly benefiting from such policies. This would include individuals in certain export sectors, as well as those who might take advantage of employment opportunities in the colonial civil service or military establishment. Secondly, imperialism

---

[1] For one of few studies in this area see Horace B. Davis's survey: *Nationalism and Socialism* (New York: 1967), chapter 5.

may serve indirectly to expiate some of the inferiority associated with peripheral social origins; it may give individuals from disadvantaged groups the first opportunity to escape from a self-assessment as victim to one as conqueror.[1] On the other hand, peripheral groups may adopt militantly anti-imperialistic attitudes in empathy with the plight of other submerged nations.

An attempt will be made to illustrate these themes in the Celtic territories using previously introduced data for the years 1885–1924 supplemented by materials from secondary sources. On the whole, the evidence suggests that appeals on behalf of imperialist policies were far more effective in muting class consciousness in England than cultural consciousness in the Celtic periphery.

THEORETICAL BACKGROUND

The notion that the acquisition of new territory, accompanied by a subsequent increase in state wealth, is a means of mediating internal conflict is hardly a new one in modern history. In 1608, Francis Bacon, counselor to James I, argued that the colonization of Ireland would relieve English over-population, reduce the risk of internal rebellion due to food shortages, and simultaneously strengthen the authority of the Crown.[2]

Two centuries later James Madison advocated American expansion on the Western frontier as a solution to the growing conflict between differentiating regions representing sectoral interests in the economy.[3]

The smaller the society, the fewer probably will be the distinct parties and interests composing it; the fewer the distinct parties and interests, the more frequently will a majority be found in the same party; and the smaller the number of individuals composing a majority, and the smaller the compass within which they are placed, the more easily will they concert and execute their plans of oppression. Extend the sphere and you take in a greater variety of parties and interests; you make it less probable that a majority of the whole will have a common motive to invade the rights of

---

[1] 'The narcissistic satisfaction provided by the cultural ideal is also one of the forces that effectively counteract the hostility to culture within the cultural group. It can be shared not only by the favored classes, which enjoy the benefits of this culture, but also by the suppressed, since the right to despise those that are outside it compensates them for the wrongs they suffer in their own group.' Sigmund Freud, *The Future of an Illusion* (New York: n.d.), p. 18.

[2] Francis Bacon, 'Some Considerations . . ., in Constantia Maxwell, ed., *Irish History from Contemporary Sources* (London: 1923), p. 270.

[3] James Madison, *The Federalist*, No. 10 (New York: n.d.), pp. 60, 61.

other citizens; or if such a common motive exists, it will be more difficult for all who feel it to discover their own strength and to act in unison with each other.

This constitutes the same kind of argument that F. J. Turner formulated a century later in his frontier thesis.[1] Both writers saw territorial expansion as having favorable democratic consequences for the society as a whole.

In the nineteenth and twentieth centuries both socialists and capitalists alike suggested that imperial expansion might enable the metropolitan industrial proletariat to escape immiseration through an absolute increase in wages and standard of living. Engels commented that the English workers were in some respects turning into a bourgeoisie:[2]

The English proletariat is becoming more and more bourgeois, so that this most bourgeois of all nations is apparently aiming ultimately at the possession of a bourgeois aristocracy and a bourgeois proletariat *as well* as a bourgeoisie. For a nation which exploits the whole world this is, of course, to a certain extent justifiable.

Lenin elaborated on this theme by claiming that the monopolistically high profits received by the capitalists[3]

makes it economically possible for them to corrupt certain sections of the working-class, and for a time, a fairly considerable minority, and win them to the side of the bourgeoisie of a given industry or nation against all the others. The intensification of antagonisms between imperialist nations for the division of the world increases this striving.

In this way, the notion of the 'aristocracy of labor'—originally referring to the privileged minority of top-stratum metropolitan workers—came to be used in a more general sense to indicate status differentials within the international proletariat.[4]

[1] William A. Williams, *The Tragedy of American Diplomacy* (New York: 1962), p. 20.

[2] Marx-Engels: *Selected Correspondence* (1934), quoted in E. J. Hobsbawm, 'The Labor Aristocracy in Nineteenth-Century Britain' in *Laboring Men* (New York: 1967), p. 356.

[3] V. I. Lenin, 'Imperialism, The Highest Stage of Capitalism' in H. M. Christman, ed., *Essential Works of Lenin* (New York: 1966), p. 268.

[4] Karl Polanyi saw the main advantage to the metropolitan worker in the protection his governments offered from the anarchy of the free market. 'The revolt against Imperialism was mainly an attempt on the part of exotic peoples to achieve the political status necessary to shelter themselves from the social dislocations caused by European trade policies. The protection that the white man could easily secure for himself through the sovereign status of his communities was out of reach of the colored man as long as he lacked the prerequisite, political government.' *The Great Transformation* (Boston: 1957), p. 183.

Whereas this apparent preference of the working class in expansionist states for short-run, nationalist interests over long-run international interests was regarded with increasing gloom by such socialists as Lenin, Michels[1] and Gramsci,[2] some capitalists of the period saw in imperialism the only possible salvation from an otherwise inevitable class war. Cecil Rhodes has been cited as having remarked in 1895,[3]

I was in the East End of London yesterday and attended a meeting of the unemployed. I listened to the wild speeches, which were just a cry for 'bread,' and on my way home I pondered over the scene and I became more than ever convinced of the importance of imperialism. . . . My cherished idea is a solution for the social problem, i.e., in order to save the 40,000,000 inhabitants of the United Kingdom from a bloody civil war, we colonial statesmen must acquire new lands to settle the surplus population, to provide new markets for the goods produced by them in factories and mines. The Empire, as I have always said, is a bread and butter question. If you want to avoid civil war you must become imperialists.

Rhodes was one of many contemporary British proponents of a policy combining imperial expansion with social welfare legislation for the working class. Later this practice came to be known as 'social-imperialism' which[4]

was designed to draw all classes together in defence of the nation and empire and aimed to prove to the least well-to-do class that its interests were inseparable from those of the nation. It aimed at undermining the argument of the socialists and demonstrating that, contrary to the Marxist allegation, the workers had more to lose than their chains.

These twin concepts, the international 'aristocracy of labor' in the Marxian literature and social-imperialism in the nationalist literature,

---

[1] 'While...this view of a community of interests in the national sphere between the bourgeoisie and the proletariat has a basis of reality, there can be no doubt that not only is it absolutely antagonistic to the *idealism* of class, that is to say, to the fraternal affection which denies national solidarity in order to affirm with enthusiasm the international solidarity of the proletariat, tending and aiming at speedy class emancipation, but further that it undermines the very *concept* of class.'

'The social-democratic concept of class aims at aggrandizement of the fatherland and at the prosperity of the proletariat and of the bourgeoisie therein, through the ruin of the proletariat of other lands.' Robert Michels, *Political Parties* (New York: 1968), p. 360.

[2] Gramsci's description of the Southern Italian soldier acting as a strikebreaker in the North who justifies his participation by saying that Northern workers are—to his eyes—gentry, is illustrative. See 'The Southern Question' in *The Modern Prince* (New York: 1959), p. 35.

[3] Quoted by Lenin, *op. cit.*, p. 229.

[4] Bernard Semmel, *Imperialism and Social Reform* (New York: 1968), p. 12.

are strikingly similar save in their evaluative aspects. While the sociological theory underlying them seems intuitively straightforward, closer examination reveals that it rests upon an analogy which itself implies several questionable assumptions.

There are two senses in which the privileged sector of the working class can be defined as being 'aristocratic.' Along one dimension these workers can have certain material advantages *vis-à-vis* the mass of the proletariat. Hence such factors as the level and regularity of the worker's earnings, his prospects for social security, the general conditions of his labor, particularly the manner in which his superiors treat him, and the prospects of future advancement for him and his children are all objective bases for differentiating workers into higher and lower groups.[1] The worker presumably can sort himself out on these dimensions relative to other workers in his environment and thereby determine if he is relatively advantaged or not. But it is by no means clear that when the horizon is shifted from the local to the national or international level—that is, when the worker is assumed to compare his own position with that of individuals in localities to which he has never been, or even imagined—that this analogy will hold. Indeed, one has to postulate that entirely different social processes must occur in the latter situation.

The second possibility is that the aristocratic worker sees himself as the recipient of greater prestige—irrespective of material rewards —than the bulk of his working-class associates, and that he comes to act on the perception and appreciation of this differential rank. This might occur in certain industries which may be socially defined as particularly glamorous relative to most. Some so-called white-collar jobs are exemplary in this regard. It might also operate where the working class is ethnically heterogeneous, when high ethnic status in the workplace of itself may lead to a separate, élitist consciousness. However, here too when the analogy is shifted from a local to a fundamentally macroscopic setting, it is difficult to see the concrete satisfaction an English worker might gain from the belief that he has higher status than a laborer in Accra, Madras, or Santiago. This knowledge can intrude upon his everyday life only indirectly, through newspapers and popular literature in the nineteenth century, and movies and television in the twentieth. He has no opportunity to engage in the superordinate-subordinate interaction with this Third World worker which it must be assumed provides much of the

---

[1] See Hobsbawm, *op. cit.*, p. 322 for these formulations of the initial concept of the aristocracy of labor.

gratification of status differentiation. In fact, this part of the argument requires that the metropolitan worker, in effect, recognizes the Platonic ideal of an international stratification system which develops alongside the burgeoning international economy, and that his relatively high position in this system is a continuing source of satisfaction to him.

For it is not clear that his objective social position relative to the metropolitan bourgeoisie is substantially altered. Weber[1] and Schumpeter[2] actually have argued the inverse: that it becomes worsened. Thus for the differential prestige argument to be fully convincing the metropolitan proletariat must be possessed of rich fantasy-lives. The workers' perceptions of status must not be derived from their immediate life experience; and in this perhaps limited sense, they may be considered to be acting irrationally. Bagehot, for one, had no doubt this kind of behavior was to be expected among the masses:[3]

No orator ever made an impression by appealing to men as to their plainest physical wants. . . . But thousands have made the greatest impression by appealing to some vague dream of glory, or empire, or nationality. The ruder sort of men . . . will sacrifice all they hope for, all they have themselves, for what is called an idea—for some attraction which seems to transcend reality, which aspires to elevate man by an interest higher, deeper, wider than that of ordinary life.

Appeals to the subconscious, according to Schumpeter, were strong enough to outweigh the class interests of English workers and lead to the near-hysterical advocacy of empire known as jingoism.[4]

The plan was calculated to divert the attention of the people from social problems at home. But the main thing, before which all arguments stemming from calculating self-interest must recede into the background, was the unfailing power of the appeal to national sentiment. No other appeal is as effective, except at a time when people happen to be caught in the midst of flaming social struggle. All other appeals are rooted in interests

---

[1] Max Weber, *Economy and Society* (New York: 1968), vol. II, p. 920.

[2] 'If we may speak of impoverishment of the workers anywhere within the world of capitalism, then a tendency to such impoverishment is apparent (in a system of export monopolism), at least in a relative sense. . . . If it is ever true that there is not a trace of parallelism of economic interests between entrepreneurs and workers, but instead only a sharp economic conflict—and usually there is much exaggeration in such statements—then this is true here.' See Joseph Schumpeter, 'Imperialism,' *Imperialism and Social Classes* (Cleveland: 1955), p. 87, for the argument, which is too detailed to summarize here.

[3] Walter Bagehot, *The English Constitution* (New York: n.d.), p. 66.

[4] Schumpeter, *op. cit.*, p. 12.

that must be grasped in reason. This one alone arouses the dark powers of the subconscious, calls into play instincts that carry over from the life habits of the dim past. Nationalism satisfied the need for surrender to a concrete and familiar superpersonal cause, the need for self-glorification and violent self-assertion.

Hence there are two kinds of arguments offered to explain the alleged patriotism of the metropolitan working class, and by extension, that of disadvantaged groups in general. The subjectivist position predicts that, whatever the economic situation, the group can be won to the imperial cause given the proper quantum of political education, that is to say propaganda. It does not, however, specify the conditions under which such a strategy will succeed and therefore is somewhat of a residual explanation.

The materialist argument, on the other hand, rests on three propositions which are potentially subject to empirical verification.

The first basis for the argument must be that along with imperialism (though not necessarily as its effect) went a significant increase in national wealth, as measured by the Gross National Product or its indicators.

The second is that part of this increment in national wealth went, in some form or another, to disadvantaged groups, and that this was perceived by an appreciable heightening of their material well-being (higher wages, better conditions of labor, or some combination of both, etc.).

The third assumption is that the disadvantaged groups attributed their higher standard of living to their country's imperialism, that they believed imperialism to be its cause, directly or indirectly. This in effect takes some of the credit for the amelioration of living conditions away from the actions of the specific groups themselves—for instance, they must not feel that 'things got better' solely because of their own efforts at political or trade-union organization—and places it firmly in the hands of the leaders of the central government.

However, when the focus shifts from classes to peripheral status groups within the metropolis another factor is introduced. To the extent that imperial expansion tends to redefine the status of individuals in the periphery as being part of the greater nation, this might result in a relative increment in prestige. Overseas imperialism may encourage the peripheral group to be included in the metropolitan task of civilizing the native peoples of the world.

This is in essence a meliorist view of how the consciousness of the peripheral group might be changed: its attitudes toward the core become increasingly favorable with incremental changes in its material welfare. On the other hand, the internal colonial model of core-periphery relations suggests that ethnic change in the peripheral group does not occur merely as a function of increases in the standard of living. The internal colonial situation cannot be so easily remedied. Instead, this model asks fundamentally different questions: did overseas imperialism alter the economic and political dependency of the periphery on the core? Did overseas imperialism contribute to substantial change in the cultural division of labor in peripheral areas? There are no *a priori* reasons to expect overseas imperialism to be related to structural changes of any magnitude.

However, it is important to note that any attempt to determine the meaning of imperialism to different groups must be kept analytically separate from analyses of the 'objective benefits' of imperial policies to these groups carried out according to some theoretical scheme.[1] The social definitions of each group must be taken into account since they ultimately emerge in political behavior.

MEASURING REGIONAL POLITICAL RESPONSES

How can the collective political response of the Celtic lands to British imperialist policies be gauged, if at all? One traditional approach would be to derive a general estimate of the direction and intensity of this response by considering specific historical events where pro- and anti-imperialist forces met and competed for influence among the particular groups. By aggregating many discrete and local events the historian attempts to create an image of the macroscopic situation. This tends to involve the use of evidence which is not strictly comparable from one locality or period to another. Since there are necessarily few situations where the same evidence can be used to compare the political response of different localities, historical interpretations based on such evidence are subject to serious qualification.

Let me give two examples which deal with Celtic lands and attitudes towards British imperial policy. In 1876 Turkey, then a client state of

---

[1] Thus for the purposes of understanding the significance of imperialism from the actor's point of view, theoretical discussions such as Arghiri Emmanuel, *Unequal Exchange* (New York: 1972), and the various rejoinders by Charles Bettelheim are essentially reifications since they refer to a battery of academic theories beyond the grasp of most political actors, unless disseminated in popularized forms. For a summary of their debate, see *Monthly Review*, 22, 2 (1970), pp. 13–23.

the United Kingdom, brutally suppressed a nationalist rebellion by the Bulgarians, who, as it happens, were Christian. The Turkish troops used to restore order in Bulgaria were Muslims, and the British press made much of the torture which they perpetrated against a Christian people with the sanction of the London Foreign Office. A rash of protests were filed with various government agencies from all over the British Isles. R. T. Shannon has analyzed the regional origins of these protests against the Turkish atrocities.[1] He found that Wales was the second of seven regions in the intensity of anti-Turkish, and hence anti-government, sentiment, However, Scotland was a distant sixth, and Ireland sent virtually no protests at all. The results are somewhat equivocal, and I should think difficult to interpret. However Shannon is not daunted. Wales protests strongly because of her Nonconformity, excellent 'campaign leadership,' and extensive newspaper coverage. Scotland's poor anti-Turkish reaction is taken at face value; it attests to the Scots' lack of sympathy with the fate of subject nationalities in general. The reason the Irish do not respond is because they feel the English are in no position to criticize the Turks in Bulgaria since they commit the same crimes in Ireland: why appeal to the morality of thieves and bandits? Shannon's *ex post facto* interpretation is quite plausible, but hardly convincing.

One of the major, if not the dominant, national political issues in the 1900 election involved the role of the United Kingdom in the Boer War. Several writers have made assessments of the regional reactions to the United Kingdom's attempt to crush the self-determination of the Boers.

Reginald Coupland, for instance, argues in *Welsh and Scottish Nationalism* that Wales, as a whole, was much more inclined to militant anti-imperialism than was Scotland, where support for the war in South Africa was strong. 'There was a Welsh color to [Lloyd George's opposition to the Boer War]; for Wales was a small nation, with an historic tradition of fighting for freedom, and Wales, like the little Boer Republics, was a land of farmers.'[2] He cites the election of Liberal MPs as evidence for this position. But a Scottish historian, W. Ferguson, firmly disagrees with this assessment of the Scottish climate of opinion:[3]

[1] R. T. Shannon, *Gladstone and the Bulgarian Agitation of 1876* (London: 1963), pp. 147–60.
[2] Reginald Coupland, *Welsh and Scottish Nationalism* (London: 1954), pp. 268–9.
[3] W. Ferguson, *Scotland—1689 to the Present* (New York: 1968), p. 333.

In Scotland the Imperialists found a difficult field for their labors. There, in spite of the hysterical trumpetings of the press, existed a core of radical 'little Englandism' and a cynical refusal to plaster needs with moral whitewash. For many of the Scots the Empire denoted objects rather than ideas—places to go, to explore, to exploit, proselytize or settle. Except among the anglicized upper class the empire had little of the quasi-religious significance which seemed to appeal to all classes in England.

And K. O. Morgan, in his excellent study *Wales in British Politics, 1868–1922*, challenges Coupland's description of Wales:[1]

One of the many myths of modern Welsh history is that Wales, with its fellow-feeling for small nations, was ardent in support of the Boers. In fact, the pro-Boers were in a minority in Wales as everywhere else.

For evidence he cites the defeat of slates of local pro-Boer candidates, particularly in South Wales; Welsh pride in her colonial fighting units; and records of pro-British victory celebrations in several localities. In another work, however, Morgan claims 'the pacifist tradition of Henry Richard was still abroad in the land, and many Welsh people felt disengaged in a war waged by English generals and capitalists of unidentifiable race in a remote country.'[2] How can these contradictory assessments be reconciled? The basic difficulty is that Coupland's generalization explicitly compares Wales to Scotland, while Morgan's and Ferguson's sights are trained exclusively upon one region.[3] Actually, there is not enough solid evidence to support the speculations of any of these writers on this question.

Such evidence is of course not easy to come by. Before the rise of public opinion polling the best source of attitudinal data on political issues are electoral returns which can be analyzed ecologically.[4] In this case the best is, admittedly, none too good. Electoral data can

---

[1] K. O. Morgan, *Wales and British Politics, 1868–1922* (Cardiff: 1963), p. 179. This argument is amplified in K. O. Morgan, 'Wales and the Boer War—a reply,' *Welsh History Review*, 4, 4 (December, 1969), pp. 367–80.

[2] K. O. Morgan, 'The Merthyr of Keir Hardie' in *Merthyr Politics* ed. by Glanmor Williams, 1968–9, cited in Goronwy J. Jones, *Wales and the Quest for Peace* (Cardiff: 1969), pp. 84, 85.

[3] This lack of a regionally comparative perspective also mars Richard Price's *An Imperial War and the British Working Class* (London: 1972). In this book the author disputes the claim that the English working class supported South African intervention, but never manages to mention the reaction of the working class in either Wales or Scotland.

[4] Great strides in ecological analysis have occurred subsequent to the elucidation of the ecological fallacy of inferring individual characteristics from aggregate statistics, discussed by Robinson in 1950. See Mattei Dogan and Stein Rokkan, eds, *Quantitative Ecological Analysis in the Social Sciences* (Cambridge, Mass.: 1969), for a discussion of the limits and advantages of ecological analysis.

only be used in this manner if the major political parties have taken opposing stands on clearly dominant national issues. It can be maintained that this was the case with regard to the Boer War in the General Election of 1900.

In that election the Conservative (Unionist) party was the proponent of British intercession in South Africa,[1] whereas the Liberal party became divided on the issue. A group of renegades from the Liberal party calling themselves Liberal Imperialists supported British intervention, whereas the pure Liberals advocated the idea of 'Little Englandism' (sic!) which minimized the importance of actual colonial takeovers and insisted, instead, upon the primacy of free trade. As Gallagher and Robinson have pointed out, both formal and informal empire were part and parcel of British imperial practice during the entire nineteenth century, and that objectively speaking, both policies were equally imperialist in intent and outcome.[2] However, this position was not commonly held at the time and cannot be presumed to be present in the minds of the voters. Pro-imperialism, in the public eye, was generally regarded as the exclusive property of the Tories and the Liberal Imperialist dissidents; it became identified with the political career of Joseph Chamberlain in his later years. The intensity of the Conservative and Liberal Imperialist vote in a given locality has previously been used to indicate favorable popular attitudes towards British intervention in South Africa. On the basis of a regional analysis of electoral results by constituency, Henry Pelling made this assessment of attitudes towards the war in Wales and Scotland:[3]

In 1900 the South African War seems to have influenced Welsh and Scottish voters in contrary ways. The Scots, who felt they had a share in the British imperial commitment, moved more strongly to Unionism; the Welsh, who sympathized with those whom they regarded (like themselves) as the victims of exploitation, became more Liberal than before.

[1] 'The election [of 1900] took place in September of that year, at a time when the South African War, after initial reverses, appeared to have turned decisively in favour of British arms. The leaders of the Unionist government, and particularly Joseph Chamberlain, sought to focus the campaign on the question of the war, and Chamberlain branded all the Liberals as "pro-Boers," implying that a seat won by the Opposition was a seat won by President Kruger.' From Henry Pelling, 'Wales and the Boer War,' *Welsh History Review*, 4, 4 (December 1969), pp. 363–5.

[2] John Gallagher and Ronald Robinson, 'The imperialism of free trade,' *Economic History Review*, 2nd Ser. 6, 1 (1953), p. 1.

[3] Henry Pelling, *The Social Geography of British Elections* (New York: 1967), pp. 416–17. See also Pelling, 'Wales and the Boer War.'

In principle this represents some improvement over the method of Morgan and Coupland. But here, too, it may well be objected that the raw percentages of votes received by political parties cannot be precisely correlated with mass attitudes towards specific political issues.

There is a serious methodological pitfall in attempting to infer collective attitudes towards specific issues from aggregate electoral statistics which may be expressed as the problem of the meaningfulness of election results. How can it be assumed that diverse individuals let alone social groups, vote for a particular party on the basis of similar intentions? And if this assumption is not justified, in what sense can variations in party support between different groups be interpreted? In this chapter it will be argued that such meanings can be at least partially rescued from this ambiguity inherent in electoral statistics. This is most feasible in circumstances where one overriding political issue dominates a national election.

How does the rescue operation proceed? There seems to be no empirical basis for the assumption that electoral results in different collectivities may be similarly interpreted. However, it is well established that such results are in fact generally comparable within a given group. The notion of contextual effects on individual political behavior has gained wide currency.[1] The thrust of this idea is that some aspect of an individual's context—perhaps the 'climate of opinion' or 'definition of the situation' characterizing a group of which he is a member—actually serves to constrain his political choices. In this way the context acts to minimize differences in voting intentions among individuals. But what constitutes such contexts? Presumably they vary in size as well as saliency, from microscopic units, such as families, to large aggregates, such as regions or nations. It might be expected that the effectiveness of the context as a constraint on individual attitudes varies inversely with its relative size. In this sense an individual may consider himself a member of many overlapping groups. As an example, one may be a member of a specific family, e.g., a Redford, but simultaneously one

---

[1] The literature on contextual effects is vast. See P. L. Kendall and P. F. Lazarsfeld, eds, 'Studies in the Scope and Method of *The American Soldier* (Glencoe: 1955); P. M. Blau, 'Formal organization: dimensions of analysis,' *American Journal of Sociology*, 63, 1 (1957), and Raymond Boudon, 'Propriétés individuelles et propriétés collectives,' *Revue Française de Sociologie*, 4, 3 (1963). The discussion by P. F. Lazarsfeld and H. Menzel 'On the relation between individual and collective proprieties' in A. Etzioni, ed., *Complex Organizations* (New York: 1961), is also useful in this regard.

is a Mancunian, a professor, a Northerner, a bourgeois, an English-man, a Briton, an English-language speaker, and so forth. Each widening circle introduces more social heterogeneity, and therefore allows for greater 'individualistic' behavior. Yet it is known that even such highly abstract collectivities as nations have salience for individual behavior in countless ways.[1]

The strategy adopted here will be to eliminate, so far as is possible, the effects of potential contextual differences between political units such that any variations in voting results may be attributed to the effect of regional differences alone. The smallest units for which this can be done in Britain are counties. In this chapter constituency electoral returns have been aggregated within counties, so that they may be compared with social and cultural variables collected for the same geographical units. Since counties have boundaries which are somewhat arbitrary in so far as social groups are concerned, it may be objected that the task is well-nigh impossible. But it is generally acknowledged that some types of differences between groups (e.g., social class), tend to have more political significance than others (e.g., hair color). These may roughly be summarized as group differences with respect to party loyalty, social structural composi-tion, economic diversification, and 'ethnic' or cultural composition. The indicator of peripheral sectionalism introduced in the previous chapter is a crude but, I will argue, adequate means to control for the most important of these contextual differences.

In the course of many election studies it has often been determined that certain constituencies or aggregations of them, such as regions, regularly support the same political party in the face of changing circumstances.[2] This apparent loyalty to party has been regarded as taking precedence over parameters such as the attractiveness of individual candidates or the party's ideology and platform as a whole. To explain the regularity of these voting patterns it was inferred that individuals define themselves in political terms as members of specific parties, rather than as proponents of specific policies or ideologies. Such party loyalty is then transmitted across generations through

---

[1] This is presumably what is referred to by the widely used concept 'political culture.'

[2] For statements of the efficacy of party loyalty see V. O. Key and Frank Munger, 'Social determination and electoral decision: the case of Indiana,' in E. Burdick and A. J. Brodbeck, eds, *American Voting Behavior* (Glencoe: 1959); and the work of various members of the Michigan school of election analysis. For a representative example cf. Angus Campbell, *et al.*, ed., *Elections and the Political Order* (New York: 1966).

socialization processes. But there are also organizational supports for the dominance of the party in a given place. Opposing parties may in effect come to recognize their spheres of firm support and tend to reserve major party resources for competition in those relatively uncommitted areas which are regarded as marginal. Thus single party dominance in given localities is ensured by the actions of both parties in the political system. Hence a vote for Labor in South Wales, a Labor stronghold, may have a very different meaning than a comparable vote in Rutlandshire, a Conservative stronghold.

A second contextual difference which generally has political significance is the relative level of industrialization in given localities. This affects the distribution of social classes. Highly industrial areas have large proportions of workers in manufacturing and service occupations. Non-industrial regions, alternatively, have high concentrations of workers in agriculture. If voters are at all class conscious these social structural differences will account for some of the variance in voting.[1] To give an elementary example, industrial workers often have different interests with regard to food prices than agricultural workers. Industrial workers tend to want the price of foodstuffs kept at a minimum, while farmers typically desire stable high prices for these commodities. In general it might be expected that the political interests of groups will coalesce around their respective situations relative to markets of capital, labor, and commodities. To the extent that counties or regions have different concentrations of workers in the primary, secondary, or tertiary sectors of the economy, voting differences between these units may reflect these structural differentials. This is particularly so if tariff policies which differentially affect workers in these sectors are a major issue in the political situation, as they were in this historical situation. From 1903 to 1922 the Conservative Party supported policies of imperial protection (Tariff Reform) which were acknowledged to have the result of raising food prices in the domestic market.[2] Much of the working-class antipathy to the Tories in this period has been thought to derive from its protectionist tendencies.

---

[1] S. M. Lipset, *Agrarian Socialism* (Berkeley: 1950).

[2] 'The Tariff Reformers appealed for working-class support on the grounds that the condition of the working man was dependent upon the prosperity of British industry which required tariff protection against foreign rivals and that only imperial preference could prevent the disintegration of the empire, whose unity, strength and markets were essential to the welfare of the working class.' Semmel, *op. cit.*, p. 14.

These broad social structural categories are not sufficient to distinguish between even finer structural differences between localities. For example, within industrialized regions localities may differ according to their specific economic interests in national and international markets. Prices in these markets are determined for specific commodities. The price of coal may rise simultaneous to a general decline in the price of textile goods. Alternatively, the target markets for specific commodities may be more or less diversified. Using the same example, a coal-producing region generally exports to industrial areas, while a locality specializing in textile production has much greater flexibility in the marketing of its exports. Basically, textiles can be profitably marketed in both industrial and non-industrial societies. This distinction assumes great importance during periods when protective tariffs are under consideration in a national election. To the extent that these regional sectoral interests coincide with well-organized constituencies, such as labor unions or trade associations, they will be pursued all the more vigorously.

Last, localities may differ according to their 'ethnic' or cultural composition. The sense of cultural distinctiveness may predispose a region to antipathy towards a central government if it is perceived as being in the control of a dominant cultural group. Celtic nationalism is just such a phenomenon, but a regional sense of separateness need not be linked specifically to 'ethnic' factors.[1]

Since the problem at hand is to estimate the nature of collective responses to imperialist appeals in England and the Celtic lands, not all of these potentially salient contextual differences need to be held constant. It is of particular interest to determine the effect of 'ethnic' and cultural differences on a group's receptiveness to imperialist politics. By analyzing electoral results by region, that is in England, Wales, Scotland, and Northern Ireland, it will be possible to estimate the effect of the Celtic context on voting differences, if the influence of structural variables is largely controlled. It should, however, be noted that regional differences in party loyalty need not be accounted for in the creation of these estimates.

This is because it cannot be conceded that party loyalty has the status of an independent variable *in the long run*. The existence of party loyalty does not serve as an adequate explanation of differential voting patterns between regions.[2] Rather it must be assumed to be

---

[1] The case of the American South is exemplary here.
[2] Pelling, *Social Geography*, p. 15 expresses this somewhat more cautiously: 'Then, as today, large numbers of electors tended to develop a loyalty to one or

problematic in any given situation. Party loyalty is itself an outcome of the interaction of other factors, either structural or cultural, operating within each context. The areas of high party loyalty are not randomly distributed across states. The Conservative Party does notoriously badly in Wales in election after election, and notoriously well in the Southeast. This circumstance cannot be regarded as accidental: there are both historical and contemporary reasons to account for it. The example of recent electoral trends in the American South is highly illustrative in this respect. In past years the South has appeared to be the private preserve of the Democratic Party. But recently the Republicans have made strong inroads in this region. Obviously something in the contemporary situation has caused party loyalty to decline as a basis for electoral choice among Southerners. Conceding party loyalty the status of a causal variable might be very useful for the prediction of electoral processes. As an explanation of political behavior party loyalty can only serve to obscure deeper issues in political sociology. By confusing an effect with a cause, the significant determining factors in regional political behavior will surely go unnoticed.

RESULTS: THE ELIMINATION OF STRUCTURAL DIFFERENCES

Structural differences between the regions may be accounted for by the procedures outlined in the preceding chapter. To reiterate, the proportion of Conservative and Liberal Imperialist votes in each county was regressed on seven variables previously determined to be indicators of industrialization.[1] Three of these indicators include broad occupational categories corresponding to the primary, secondary, and tertiary sectors of economic activity—the proportion of employed males in agricultural, manufacturing, and commercial and professional occupations. The remaining four indicators are

---

the other of the political parties which was of so habitual a character that it was not easily shaken by novel controversies. If there is one thing research into voting behaviour appears to have established, it is that there is no reality to the concept of the "mandate"—that is to say, the supposed commitment of the electorate to support of a particular measure because the party advocating it had secured a parliamentary majority. Yet some issues clearly had the effect of making some electors change their allegiance and others abstain, and these alterations of the voting pattern, although perhaps only affecting a small minority of voters, were nevertheless important determinants of the outcome of elections.'

[1] See chapter 5.

decennial population growth; proportion of the population aged 65 and over; the crude marriage rate; and the degree of urbanization in counties. In this way regional voting results can be compared with the assurance that the effect of these structural factors as sources of contextual variations has been eliminated. On the basis of these data taken as a whole, for a given level of industrialization in a particular county in a specific year each regression equation predicts an estimated proportion of Conservative votes. Table 8.1 shows the

TABLE 8.1 *Mean residuals from multiple regression of Conservative vote on structural variables**

	1885	1892	1900	1910	1924
England	4	4	8	7	5
Wales	0	−12	−22	−19	−23
Scotland	−7	−2	−3	−5	−3
Northern Ireland	8	11	21	22	36
R^2s	0·279	0·178	0·277	0·285	0·147

* Source: Figure 7.1.

extent to which the prediction of Conservative voting on the basis of industrialization variables corresponds to the actual voting results in English, Welsh, Scottish, and Northern Irish counties.

The residuals represent the proportional difference between actual and expected levels of Conservative voting. Hence a positive residual indicates underestimation of the Conservative vote from the set of structural variables. In this case a given county is relatively more Conservative than the average British county of comparable structural composition. By the same token, a negative voting residual describes overestimation of Conservativism from the structural variables. Such a county is relatively anti-Conservative given its level of industrialization.

Mean Conservative (including Liberal Imperialist) voting residuals in England, Wales, Scotland, and Northern Ireland are presented for five elections from 1885 to 1924 (Table 8.1).[1] Especially noteworthy

[1] In so far as the comparability of these elections are concerned, the constituencies and qualifications for voting were virtually identical for the period 1885 through 1910. See Neal Blewett, 'The franchise in the United Kingdom, 1885–1918,' *Past and Present*, 32 (1965), pp. 27–56 for a complete discussion. In 1918 the Representation of the People Act caused some redistribution of constituencies, allowed female suffrage, and eliminated plural voting. The data presented here

in this regard are two elections. The election of 1900, the so-called Khaki election, tested opinions about the necessity of British intervention in the Boer War. The election of December 1910 saw Chamberlain's Tariff reform *cum* imperial protection plan hotly debated as the overriding national political issue.[1] Throughout this period English mean voting residuals are consistently positive. Relative to all British and Northern Irish counties English counties were therefore somewhat pro-Conservative in these years. Further, in the 1900 election English counties became increasingly Conservative relative to the average county in the sample.

Scotland as a whole, just as consistently, deviated from the Conservatives and towards the opposition. Neither of the key elections of 1900 and 1910 served to alter Scottish voting patterns relative to England's. Thus there is no evidence of the phenomenon of servitor imperialism among the Scots, though there was apparently no strong reaction against imperialism either.

---

do not include the University franchise, a major component of plural voting The 1918 redistribution did, however, do away with the freeman franchise allowing plural votes especially in four English counties. Pelling, *Social Geography* (p. 8) does not feel this is a major problem in comparability. It has been estimated that the Conservatives *gained* a net total of 33 seats as a consequence of the 1918 redistribution. See Michael Kinnear, *The British Voter: An Atlas and Survey. Since 1885* (London: 1968), p. 72. Turnout, another complicating factor, is difficult to estimate in these elections for reasons discussed by Pelling, *ibid.*, pp. 7 and 8. Table 8.1 is made with the assumption that there are no significant regional variations in turnout, though there is some reason to doubt this.

[1] In the attempt to survey the climate of opinion surrounding these General Elections I am forced to rely on the assessments of historians. The elections at the beginning and end of this period, that is in 1885 and 1924, are most difficult to associate with one dominant, national issue. See Pelling, *Social Geography of British Elections*, p. 17, for 1885, and Pelling, *Modern Britain, 1885–1955* (New York: 1966), pp. 99–100, for the 1924 election.

The dominant issue in the 1892 election was the question of Home Rule for Ireland and Church disestablishment in Wales and Scotland, all of which were supported by the Liberal Party and opposed by the Conservatives. See Pelling, *Social Geography of British Elections*, p. 17.

For 1900, the question of 'the responsibility of the government for the outbreak of the war . . . was the principal issue of the election, and for the rest the issues of previous elections remained in the background as continuing matters of concern' (*Ibid.*, p. 18).

In the election of December, 1910, the parties made fever-pitched appeals to the electorate on the basis of support for rival trade policies—Free Trade for the Liberals, and imperial preference with tariff reform for the Conservatives. 'Imperial preference was presented to the electorate as a means of maintaining a colonial market essential for employment and a protective tariff was pictured as a device for providing revenues for social reform'. (Semmel, *op. cit.*, p. 16.) Again, Irish Home Rule and Welsh Disestablishment divided the parties, Pelling, *Social Geography of British Elections*, p. 21–2.

In Wales and Northern Ireland there are strong, and mutually opposing, reactions to the Conservative Party. Welsh voting patterns were strongly anti-Conservative from 1891 on and ultimately much greater than Scotland's. The 'myth' of Welsh sympathy for the self-determination of subject peoples may well have empirical support when considered in a British context.

On the other hand, Northern Ireland, a settler colony established by lower-class Scots and Englishmen in the seventeenth century, and much poorer than any other region of the British Isles,[1] shows itself to have a clear servitor imperialist response, voting disproportionately Conservative through the whole period, especially in 1910 and 1924.

Thus it has been demonstrated that while holding these structural factors constant each part of the British Isles differentially supported the Conservative Party in the years 1885 through 1924. If Conservative and Liberal Imperialist Party support is used as an indicator of popular attitudes towards imperialist policies, this evidence suggests that among British regions Wales and Scotland were against such policies, while England and Northern Ireland were for them. However this interpretation of these responses remains unconvincing. What could account for the apparent pro-Conservative tendencies of English counties?

Certainly one possibility is that the English working class adopted, to some extent, the pro-imperial politics characteristic of an international aristocracy of labor. Whether or not English imperialism spurred on national wealth in the period from 1850 to 1922 is not of concern here. British national income, variously calculated, was rising steadily in the late nineteenth century.[2] Further, British real wages likewise rose during the whole period, though at different rates: from 1850–75 at 36 per cent, from 1875–1900 at 35 per cent, and from 1889–1914 at about 10 per cent.[3] In the early part of the nineteenth century, as Eric Hobsbawm argues, there were large masses of workers who did not gain from Britain's imperial hegemony. However,[4]

---

[1] Using an indicator of regional wealth based on *per capita* income tax returns by county, in 1881 if England were 100, Wales was 77, Scotland 84, Southern Ireland 55, and Northern Ireland only 48.

[2] Phyllis Deane and W. Cole, *British Economic Growth, 1688–1959* (Cambridge: 1967), p. 284.

[3] *Ibid.*, pp. 27–8.

[4] Eric Hobsbawm, 'Trends in the British Labor Movement Since 1850' in *Laboring Men*, pp. 380–1.

the further we progress into the imperialist era, the more difficult does it become to put one's finger on groups of workers which did not, in one way or another, draw some advantage from Britain's position; who were not able to live rather better than they would have done in a country whose bourgeoisie possessed fewer accumulated claims to profits and dividends abroad, or power to dictate the terms of trade with backward areas. Or, since there is no simple correlation between the standard of living and political moderation, on workers who could not be made to feel that their interests depended on the continuance of imperialism.

This subjective linking of imperialism with a higher standard of living apparently occurred despite the uneven distribution of the imperial spoils. This is because, 'for the utter pariahs of the mid-nineteenth century slums, even modest improvements seemed absolute gains.'[1]

The rapid rise of the professional labor movement provided an excellent site in which certain working-class leaders could be imbued in the imperialist ideology: labor politicians, union officials, and others in high organizational positions were all susceptible to these persuasions. Similarly, the growth of the white-collar occupations hastened the process of ideological cross-fertilization. Elie Halévy, noting the sharp drop in industrial strikes between the years 1894 and 1900, explains:[2]

A wave of imperialism was sweeping over the country, and, as hatred of the foreigner—the German, the Russian, the Frenchman—prevailed over hatred of the domestic enemy, and racial hostility thrust the conflict of the classes into the background, the situation became unfavourable to labour agitation . . . the imagination of the middle class, and even of the proletariat, was pre-occupied.

Hence, all three of the assumptions lying behind the meliorist notion of the international aristocracy of labor are apparently fulfilled in the English case: rapid economic growth enabled the industrial working class to gain material advantages and increase its standard of living. Simultaneously, the development of the organized labor movement provided an institutional basis for the co-optation of masses of workers in the manner in which Michels has illustrated. Last, the growth of white-collar occupations provided an objective measure of upward status mobility for those whose social horizons had previously been limited to factory work. All these favorable developments were occurring at the height of the Empire, and attempts to infer causal links between imperialism and these greater benefits

---

[1] *Ibid.*, pp. 383.
[2] Elie Halévy, *Labour and the Rise of Imperialism* (London: 1965), pp. 258–9.

have plausibility to recommend them. Under these circumstances a jingoistic appeal to the masses for patriotic commitment is well received and further stimulates imperialist sentiments in the working class.

This line of analysis would then imply that the working classes of Wales and Scotland were much less prone to pro-imperial politics for some reason. Why should this be the case? Clearly it was not so in an earlier era. In the eighteenth century, just preceding the Scottish–English Union of the Parliaments (1707), the major argument which swayed the Scots towards acceptance of Union was that political incorporation would enable Scotland to engage in England's prosperous colonial trade, otherwise prohibited by the Navigation Acts.[1] Similarly, the Scots had historically taken great advantage of employment in the burgeoning British colonial administrations and corporations, first in India, later, the world over.[2] There has never been any record of Welsh or Scottish protest against 'old' imperialism, but then again, Celtic nationalism is largely a mid-nineteenth century phenomenon, save in Ireland.

Victor Bérard, one of the earliest writers to take up this question, felt that Welsh and Scottish anti-Conservatism in this period was opposition, not to imperialism, but to the tariff protection which went along with it in the Chamberlain program.[3] Hence, the reasons for the opposition voting patterns were not empathetic, or cultural in any sense, but essentially economically rational. His argument is that the major exports of Wales and Scotland, coal and ships, could best be purchased by industrializing countries and not by newly-developing colonies, whereas markets for English industrial exports were highly diversified. Although in the early part of the nineteenth century England herself was the best market for these commodities, by the end of the century English demand fell off rapidly and was insufficient to absorb production in Wales and Scotland.

[1] For an excellent discussion of the context in which Union occurred see T. C. Smout, 'The Anglo-Scottish Union of 1707—the economic background,' *Economic History Review*, 2nd ser., 16, 3 (1964), pp. 455–67.

[2] For a general treatment, see Gordon Donaldson, *The Scots Overseas* (London: 1966). For evidence of the prevalence of Scots in high positions in the East India Company see C. H. Phillips, *The East India Company, 1784–1834* (Manchester: 1961), pp. 35–6. Data on the regional origins of higher civil servants in Australia are presented in R. S. Neale, *Class and Ideology in the Nineteenth Century* (London: 1972), chapter 5. Neale's evidence shows that the Home Counties and lowland Scotland were the most frequent regions of origin, while Wales and highland Scotland were the least frequent.

[3] Victor Bérard, *L'Angleterre et l'imperialisme* (Paris: 1915), pp. 235–6.

There was a large international market for Welsh and Scottish goods. Denmark, Norway, Russia, Germany, Japan, Belgium and the Netherlands were all buying commercial ships; Japan, Russia, China, Chile, and Portugal were each buying about as many warships as England. Similarly, European and American markets for coal were substantial. A protectionist policy in the British Empire would result in protectionist policies elsewhere and thus in relatively greater tariff barriers against these Scottish and Welsh commodities than against those of England as a whole. The trade Scotland and Wales realized with the colonies and what are now termed the Commonwealth nations was only a fraction of that which would be lost as a result of English monopoly imperialism.

Bérard's argument, then, is that the particular industrial specialization of Welsh and Scottish counties led to antipathy towards protection and thus to opposition to the Conservative Party. The Celtic periphery acted politically in pursuit of economic rationality as did England. However, since the objective market situation differed for the regions, the result could be falsely interpreted as constituting ideological conflict. This is an eminently plausible explanation which also has the virtue of being easily tested.

ESTIMATING THE EFFECT OF ECONOMIC DIVERSITY

If Bérard's hypothesis is sound the dominantly industrial counties of Wales and Scotland should be expected to have voted much more strongly against the Conservative Party and its protectionist policies than the more diversified English industrial counties. Simultaneously, there should be little difference in the voting behavior of the more agricultural counties of all three regions, which should favor the Tories or Liberal Imperialists because protection implied the establishment of higher food prices.

Table 8.2 confirms Bérard's predicted rank-ordering among the industrialized counties.[1] The English industrial counties as a whole are less anti-Conservative than those in Wales and Scotland. During all five elections the English industrial counties have only slightly positive mean voting residuals. In contrast, residuals from comparably industrialized Scottish and Welsh counties generally deviate away

---

[1] Counties were defined as industrial if their percentage of employed adult males in non-agricultural occupations was equal to or exceeded 85 per cent in 1885; and 87·5 per cent for 1892–1924. The basis of this definition is discussed in chapter 5.

TABLE 8.2 Mean voting residuals from multiple regression of Conservative vote on structural variables, in industrial and non-industrial counties*

	1885	N	1892	N	1900	N	1910	N	1924	N
Industrial counties in										
England	+6	(6)	+1	(8)	+1	(10)	+1	(13)	+1	(12)
Wales	−16	(2)	−10	(2)	−3	(2)	−17	(2)	−18	(2)
Scotland	−4	(7)	−3	(6)	+4	(9)	−6	(7)	−6	(8)
Northern Ireland	—		—		—		—		—	
All regions	−2	(15)	−2	(16)	+2	(21)	−3	(22)	−3	(22)
Non-industrial counties in										
England	+4	(34)	+5	(32)	+10	(30)	+10	(27)	+7	(28)
Wales	+3	(11)	−13	(11)	−26	(11)	−19	(11)	−24	(11)
Scotland	−8	(26)	−2	(27)	−6	(24)	−5	(26)	−3	(25)
Northern Ireland	+8	(6)	+11	(6)	+21	(6)	+22	(6)	+30	(6)
All regions	0	(77)	0	(76)	+1	(71)	+1	(70)	+1	(70)

* Source: Adapted from Table 7.5.

from the Conservatives throughout the period. The single exception is Scotland in 1900. In 1900, Scottish and Welsh industrial counties respond somewhat favorably to the sentiments of the Khaki election, but by 1910, they are once more firmly anti-Conservative. It might therefore seem reasonable to infer, as Bérard did, that the specific type of Celtic industrial commodity production resulted in greater opposition to protection than was manifest in England, where industrial development had been more diverse. The evidence from non-industrialized counties (Table 8.2) casts doubt on this interpretation, however. Whereas the English and Northern Irish non-industrial counties remain disproportionately Conservative throughout the period, Welsh and Scottish non-industrial counties are as or more anti-Conservative than their industrialized counterparts. Bérard's supposition that the industrialized portions of the Celtic periphery were responsible for its anti-Conservatism does not seem tenable.

It is quite true that miners, as an occupational group, were more likely to vote Liberal, and later Labor, than any other particular occupational group in Britain.[1] This was a function not only of the nature of export markets for coal, but also of the structural characteristics of the mining villages, which were relatively insulated from bourgeois society and hence favored working-class solidarity. Thus, on the average, English miners were more radical than English textile workers. Despite this, Welsh miners were consistently less Conservative than their English comrades.[2] One of the factors which Pelling claims damped Liberalism among certain English, and to an extent Scottish, workers was their antagonism to the Irish-born in their midst. These Irish workers consistently voted Liberal in support of Home Rule for Ireland. Many English workers expressed their antipathy to the Irish by backing the Tories. This is an excellent example of aristocratic behavior on the part of those English workers who were more interested in emphasizing their status superiority over the Irish, than in creating a viable class solidarity with them. Thus, while material factors such as occupational status and conditions of work were clearly involved in electoral decisions, they do not account for the large deviations from structurally-explained voting demonstrated by the Celtic regions.

[1] Pelling, *Social Geography of British Elections.*
[2] Considering mean percentages for Conservative voting in six elections between 1885 and 1910, mining districts in Yorkshire are 41 per cent while those in Glamorgan and Monmouth are 31 per cent. Data calculated from Pelling, *ibid.* pp. 305, 351.

CONCLUSIONS

The period from 1885 to 1924 witnessed not only the ultimate, if partial, success of Irish nationalism, but a considerable efflorescence of Home Rule movements in Wales and Scotland, in tandem as it were. The chief issues at this stage of the development of Welsh nationalism were expressed in terms of conflict between Celtic and English cultural institutions. There had been an insistent Welsh demand for the disestablishment of the Anglican, English-speaking Church of Wales, and its replacement by a Nonconformist, Welsh-speaking religious institution. This, in turn, led to questions about educational policy with regard to Welsh language instruction. In all the Celtic regions, the rural stratification system had become confounded along cultural lines. The gentry had evolved into an anglicized upper class with little sympathy for their Irish, Welsh, or Scottish tenants. In consequence, rural class conflict had polarized throughout the nineteenth century. The problem of cultural autonomy in the Celtic lands was closely related to the larger issue of political autonomy. To the extent that nationalist political and voluntary associations had developed in the Celtic lands, it would be unlikely that any material benefits accruing to these regions would be attributed to the beneficence of the London government. On the contrary, any concrete gains wrested from the central administration would naturally tend to be explained by the exertion of nationalist, or separatist political pressure—even if, objectively, this were not the case.

Hence the combination of economic and nationalist influences worked against the Conservative Party in the case of Wales. This was true to a much lesser extent in Scotland. Northern Ireland, on the other hand, reacted strongly against Irish separation from the United Kingdom, largely along Protestant-Catholic lines, and voted as a bloc for the Unionists.

The implications of these data for the study of national development are twofold. The hypothesis about the aristocratic behavior of the English working class, at least relative to the Welsh and Scottish proletariat, is lent credence here. Deviations from structurally explained voting in English counties were all towards the Conservative Party. This conclusion directly contradicts Max Weber's assessment of the anti-imperialist proclivities of the working-class. It will be useful to explore his analysis:[1]

[1] Weber, *op. cit.*, vol. II, p. 920.

Nor does labor show an interest in forcibly participating in the exploitation of foreign colonial territories and public commissions. This is a natural outcome of the immediate class situation, on the one hand, and, on the other, of the internal social and political situation of communities in the capitalist era. Those entitled to tribute belong to the opponent class, who dominate the community. Every successful imperialist policy of coercing the outside normally—or at least at first—also strengthens the domestic prestige and therewith the power and influence of those classes, status groups, and parties, under whose leadership the success has been attained.

Weber's argument is that the workers will resist imperialism because it is initiated by, and in the interests of, the bourgeoisie, and will hence lead to a deterioration of the workers' relative class position. Those benefiting from imperialism are precisely the groups which already dominate the community. In this statement Weber neglected to consider that an absolute improvement in the standard of living of the barely subsisting proletariat would have great social import. To the extent that imperial expansion is linked with such material rewards the class consciousness of the metropolitan working class can, in effect, be bought off. Weber was very well aware of the tenuousness of such class consciousness:[1]

Experience shows that the pacifist interests of petty bourgeois and proletarian strata very often and very easily fail. This is partly because of the easier accessibility of all unorganized 'masses' to emotional influences and partly because of the definite notion of some unexpected opportunity somehow arising through war.

This may be an important basis for the much-noted phenomenon of the Tory worker, who—it may be suggested—is very much more likely to be English in national origin, than Celtic.[2] The patriotic ideology of jingoism in this setting serves to strengthen imperial sentiment among metropolitan workers.

But Weber's analysis is only half-wrong. Imperialism may serve to integrate disadvantaged class groups into the metropolitan society but, apparently, not disadvantaged status groups. His suggestion that imperialism functions to increase the social honor of the dominant status group at the expense of subordinate groups is telling. For such expansion tends to be accompanied by the assertion of the cultural superiority of the dominant ethnic group within the metropolis. Such cultural superiority becomes one of the principal

---

[1] *Ibid.*, p. 921.
[2] For some survey data indicating that this is in fact the case, see David Butler and Donald Stokes, *Political Change in Britain* (New York: 1969), chapter 6.

legitimations of imperialism. Halévy notes that the greatest appeal of jingoism was in its appeal to the altruism rather than materialism of its adherents.[1] When Kipling wrote,

> Take up the White Man's burden—
> Send forth the best ye breed—
> Go bind your sons to exile
> To serve your captives' need;
> To wait in heavy harness,
> On fluttered folk and wild—
> Your new caught, sullen peoples,
> Half-devil and half-child.

it may be assumed he was referring to the civilizing mission of the Anglo-Saxons with their particular cultural genius and not that of the British Celts who at this period tended to cling to their traditional language and cultural patterns. In the midst of overseas colonization when the British government turned its sights to domestic problems, it was cultural backwardness which was perceived as lying behind the political intransigence of the Celtic regions.[2] Thus the insistence upon the cultural superiority of the dominant metropolitan ethnic group may serve to exacerbate cultural differences with the periphery, to the extent the periphery is aligned to its traditional culture. I am arguing that the phrase 'No Vietnamese ever called me Nigger!' is a typical, though not a necessary, response on the part of peripheral peoples in the metropolis to demands of support for imperialist policies by a government regarded as representing an ethnically or culturally alien group. Whatever material advantages might accrue to the periphery as a result of imperialist policies may well be offset by a concomitant heightening of cultural intolerance and subsequent discrimination. The stronger the cultural solidarity of the periphery, the greater weight this cultural intolerance will assume in balancing the structural gains. Hence Wales, with a strong historical basis for the development of a Celtic identity, reacts far more vigorously against British imperialism than does

---

[1] 'Far from appealing to the self-interest of their audience, they call upon them to sacrifice their private interests, even their very lives in pursuit of a lofty national ideal.' Halévy, *op. cit.*, p. 21.

[2] Hence a Parliamentary education commission found Welsh culture, in 1846, a definite barrier to the moral and economic progress of the Principality. 'It is not surprising that the commissioners should have swept aside the ancient language of Wales as ruthlessly as Macaulay, a decade earlier, had swept aside the ancient languages of India,' Coupland, *op. cit.*, p. 190. See also L. P. Curtis, Jr, *Anglo-Saxons and Celts* (Bridgeport, Ct: 1968).

Scotland, which was much less ethnically solidary due to a long tradition of conflict between Anglo-Norman and Celtic groups.

More fundamentally, there is no reason to believe that overseas imperialism caused a significant change in the cultural division of labor in the Celtic regions. While it might be argued that Celtic workers in the peripheral regions benefited economically from imperial policies they did not do so at the expense of the anglicized elements of the population. There is no evidence that overseas imperialism directly or indirectly diminished the concentration of most Celts at the bottom of the stratification system in the periphery, nor did it affect residential segregation, or patterns of differential association in general.

This does not, however, imply that the response of servitor imperialism, which is not evident in Wales or Scotland, is empirically rare. If this analysis is sound it would follow that servitor imperialism might occur only among those peripheral groups whose cultural identification lies with the core culture and its central government. Northern Ireland is just such a peripheral region. Far less economically and socially developed than either Wales or Scotland, Northern Ireland and its Protestant majority submerged all class differences in the desperate attempt to keep from being swallowed up in an Ireland with Home Rule, in which they—as Protestants and non-Celts— would be a politically insignificant minority. Identified by the Catholics of Ulster as colonial settlers who had stolen the lands of their ancestors, the Orangemen clung to Union with Great Britain as if it were a lifeline. Had the Partition of Ireland (1921) not occurred, there is little doubt that many Northern Irish Protestants would have left their property and homeland rather than face political domination by the Catholic majority in the south. Thus, even though Northern Ireland was more economically disadvantaged than any other peripheral region, she became the greatest supporter of the Conservatives and their ideology because of this ethnic imperative. Like the white trash of the southern United States—many of whom, by chance, are of Ulster ancestry—the Orangemen were despised by those socially beneath them, and disparaged by the very group they identified with so strongly. Thus they suffered the peculiar disabilities of the man in the middle, who, denied the millenarian eschatology of the truly oppressed, must content himself with a self-definition as merely second-best.

263

CHAPTER 9

TWENTIETH-CENTURY CELTIC NATIONALISM

If we are to sum up the problem of Celtic fringe nationalism, we shall conclude that it provides one of the comparatively rare illustrations of what classical nineteenth century socialist theory hoped for: proletarian nations whose working classes resisted the attractions of nationalist agitation, preferring to organize under the banner of an international ideology based essentially on class interest.

ERIC HOBSBAWM

NATIONALIST sentiment in the Celtic periphery reached a peak in the early part of the twentieth century upon the creation of the Irish Free State, subsequently known as the Republic of Eire. Thereafter, the intensity of Welsh and Scottish nationalism apparently decreased sharply. In 1966 a sudden resurgence of the Scottish and Welsh nationalist parties served notice that the phenomenon of 'Celtic nationalism' could not merely be considered a vestige of the past. The resurgence of Welsh and Scottish nationalism in contemporary Britain is surprising in that most political sociologists have theorized that the social base for such movements would tend to disappear in industrial societies.

However, contrary to this theoretical expectation, the social base of nationalist sentiment has remained significant in the Celtic periphery from 1885 to 1966.[1] As the previous chapter demonstrates each of the Celtic regions, as a whole, remained aloof from jingoism generated by the Boer War. The political distinctiveness of the Celtic lands actually increased markedly in this period, despite material benefits accruing to these regions from 1885 to 1910. This chapter will discuss several aspects of Celtic nationalism in the years 1910 to 1966. This period is characterized by events of major significance for the Celtic lands. The outbreak of World War One, the secession

[1] See chapter 7.

of southern Ireland, and the spatially skewed effects of the Depression all had implications for the continued incorporation of the Celtic regions in the United Kingdom. World War Two resulted in a temporary halt to political argument about national solidarity. And in the post-war years there has been a trend towards political integration in all the British regions, with the notable exception of Northern Ireland.

In particular, this discussion will focus on several related issues: why did the twenty-six counties of Ireland secede from the United Kingdom? Why did Welsh and Scottish nationalism decline in the early twentieth century? What can account for the relatively rapid changes in support for separatist political parties in Wales and Scotland in the face of evidence indicating that these regions have been politically malintegrated throughout the whole period?

These questions bear on the general sociological problem with which this study is concerned: under what conditions do culturally distinct groups occupying specific territories become politically integrated into the wider, national society? There has been much speculation about the role which industrialization plays in the process of national development. Many sociologists have suggested that structural differentiation, which is intensified by industrialization, undermines political association on the basis of commonly held status, or cultural, characteristics in favor of political association on the basis of commonly held market, or class, characteristics. The extensiveness of the division of labor and the high degree of social and geographic mobility in the industrial setting should thus preclude the articulation of political demands on cultural, or on regional grounds.

This chapter reaches somewhat different conclusions. Though the partial industrialization of Wales and Scotland did permit the structural integration of these regions into the national society, principally through the establishment of national trade unions and the Labor Party, persisting economic stagnation in the periphery has shaken much confidence in the class-based political organization. There is a new awareness that no state-wide political party will commit sufficient resources to achieve development in the periphery. Nationalism has reemerged in the Celtic periphery largely as a reaction to this failure of regional development.

THE PROBLEM OF IRISH SECESSION

Why has southern Ireland been the only part of the Celtic periphery to secede from the United Kingdom? To answer this question it is necessary to consider secession in 1921 as an historically problematic event. It will be useful to ask two questions about how this particular historical outcome 'might have been different.' Clearly, it 'might have been different' in a myriad of ways. The present criterion for the selection of these two questions is theoretical, and relates to the conditions under which the political integration of culturally distinct groups occurs. The first historical alternative to be considered is:

In 1921 the movement for national independence and sovereignty in Ireland lost momentum, and thereafter the once thorny 'Irish Question,' which had plagued British politics since the seventeenth century receded into history.

The question then becomes: what general sociological conditions would have had to have been different for Ireland to have remained part of the United Kingdom? The best clues for the solution of this problem may be found by considering a second, alternative, historical outcome:

In 1921, after a state of virtual civil war, the thirty-two counties of the Irish provinces of Leinster, Munster, Connaught, and Ulster seceded from the United Kingdom, and became known as the Irish Free State. Two short months thereafter, similar developments in Wales and Scotland led to the parallel establishment of the Welsh, and Scottish Free States. The British Isles had witnessed a process of almost total national devolution, and the old Liberal party platform of 'Home Rule all Around' was realized, albeit twenty-five years later than it had been initially proposed.

The second question is of the form: what general sociological conditions were different such that Wales, Scotland, and Ulster did not secede from the United Kingdom as had the twenty-six counties? The inclusion of Ulster in the question provides an intermediate case. Although it did not ultimately secede from the United Kingdom, Northern Ireland did achieve considerable local autonomy, far more than Wales or Scotland, in that it came to have its own Parliament and Prime Minister.

Probably the simplest approach to a solution of these problems is to compose a list of the major differentiating factors between Ireland and the other peripheral regions in so far as relations with England are concerned. Perhaps the twenty-six counties may be demonstrated to differ along one particular dimension from Wales and Scotland. It might then be reasonable to suspect that the 'cause' of Irish secession is associated with this specifically different factor. These factors may be grouped under the loose headings of cultural, historical, structural and political differences. Among the cultural differences, religious conflict between Catholic Ireland and Protestant England at once leaps to mind. This initial impression can only be reinforced by a consideration of the recent history of Northern Ireland, which is about two-thirds Protestant, one-third Catholic, and perennially beset by violent conflict between the two religious communities. Hence many writers have stopped at this early point of comparison and exclaimed that the 'real cause' of Irish secession was the persistent Irish adherence to a minority religion.[1] However, it is often

[1] Note the following example: 'The chief general implication of this study is that social divisions are not equal in the strains that they place upon a regime. Economic divisions are pervasive in all societies, including all parts of the United Kingdom. Yet here they have not challenged the authority of the regime ... economic issues are suitable for bargaining politics, for they do not involve zero-sum or all-or-nothing conflicts. By contrast, issues involving national loyalties do not lend themselves to bargaining, because of the either/or nature of national identification at one point in time. Such a conflict can only be avoided in the long run by the creation of a secondary identification, e.g., "Britishness," which complements a primary national identification in ways consistent with the state's boundaries. This did occur in Wales and Scotland, but not in Ireland. Religion is the obstacle to the development of integrated dual loyalties there. Religion is an issue that does not permit bargaining, or even dispute about authorities of this world.' From Richard Rose, 'The United Kingdom as a multi-national state,' *University of Strathclyde, Survey Research Centre*, Occasional Paper No. 6, p. 21. If religious conflict is by its very nature so immutable, then how were the struggles between Anglicans and Dissenters in England; or between Protestants and Catholics in the Netherlands, Germany, or the United States ever peacefully resolved without the necessity of secession? A better explanation for Protestant-Catholic conflict in Northern Ireland emphasizes its peculiar historical fate as a settler colony:

'The religious affiliations of the population of Ulster determine their political leanings to a greater extent than is the case in any part of Europe outside the Balkans. But the manner in which this has developed is also unique. I believe that it is true to say that, politically speaking, the Protestantism of the North of Ireland has no parallel outside this country, and that the Catholicism of the Irish Catholics is, likewise, peculiar in its political trend.

'To explain—I mean that, whereas, Protestantism has in general made for political freedom and political Radicalism, it has been opposed to slavish worship of kings and aristocrats. Here, in Ireland, the word Protestant is almost a convertible term with Toryism, lickspittle loyalty, servile worship of aristocracy and hatred of all that savours of genuine political independence on the part of the "lower classes."

'And in this same manner, Catholicism which in most parts of Europe is synonymous with Toryism, lickspittle loyalty, servile worship of aristocracy and

forgotten that both the Welsh and Scots have historically been committed to minority faiths in the British context—those subsumed under the heading of 'Dissenting religions.' The Welsh came to largely support Calvinistic Methodism, while the Church of Scotland was Presbyterian rather than Episcopalian since its establishment in 1690. Northern Ireland's Protestants are both Presbyterian, of Scottish descent, and Anglican, of English descent, but these internal sectarian differences have paled in the context of political conflict with the Catholic minority. Clearly the case cannot be made that religious difference from England *per se* is sufficient to account for Irish separation, and the continued incorporation of Wales, Scotland, and Northern Ireland in the United Kingdom.

A more sophisticated argument might be made that the English antipathy to Catholicism has far exceeded that directed against Dissenters. There is surely some truth in this position, but not as much as is conventionally assumed. English hostility towards Dissenters was formally institutionalized in the Test and Corporation Acts, which excluded practicing Nonconformists from government and military office in England until their repeal in 1828. These were clearly similar in intent, if not severity, to the Penal Laws directed against Catholics which were terminated in 1829. Furthermore, there was a well-recognized distinction in Stuart Ireland between the so-called 'Old English' settlers (those who had preceded the Reformation), who were Catholic, but civilized and trustworthy, and the 'mere Irish' who were barbarian and subversive.[1]

---

hatred of all that savours of genuine political independence on the part of the lower classes, in Ireland is almost synonymous with rebellious tendencies, zeal for democracy, and intense feeling of solidarity with all strivings towards those who toil.

'Such a curious phenomenon is easily understood by those who know the history of Ireland. Unfortunately for their spiritual welfare ... the Protestant elements of Ireland were, in the main, a plantation of strangers upon the soil from which the owners had been dispossessed by force. The economic dispossession was, perforce, accompanied by a political and social outlawry. Hence every attempt of the dispossessed to attain citizenship, to emerge from their state of outlawry, was easily represented as a tentative step towards reversing the plantation and towards replanting the Catholic and dispossessing the Protestant. Imagine this state of matters persisting for over two hundred years and one realizes at once that the planted population—the Protestants—were bound to acquire insensibly a hatred of political reform, and to look upon every effort of the Catholic to achieve political recognition as an insidious move towards the expulsion of Protestants.' James Connolly, 'British Labour and Irish Politicians' in his *Socialism and Nationalism* (Dublin: 1948), pp. 71, 72.

[1] Aidan Clarke, 'Ireland and the general crisis,' *Past and Present*, 48 (1970), pp. 79–99. Recent studies of anti-Catholicism in England underline the signifi-

This suggests that Irish ethnicity rather than religion may have provided the initial basis of discrimination. The foundation of that ethnicity, Celtic social organization and culture, could equally well be found in Wales and parts of Scotland. As late as the mid-nineteenth century the Parliamentary Commissioners investigating the status of education in Wales made sweeping indictments of the peculiar religious predilections of the Welsh for contributing to the general backwardness of the Principality. The pervasiveness of anti-Celtic racism in the works of prominent nineteenth-century English ethnologists, historians, and literary critics has been amply documented.[1] Finally, the most salient issue in early twentieth-century Welsh politics involved the attempt to disestablish the Anglican Church of Wales, which was seen as an illegitimate institution extending English domination in Wales. The linking of national distinctions with religious differences has occurred in all the Celtic regions since their respective incorporations into the United Kingdom.

With respect to language difference, another cultural factor commonly blamed for inhibiting political integration, Wales was far more culturally distinctive than was Ireland in 1921. The mean proportion speaking Welsh in the thirteen counties of Wales was 50 per cent in that year, while the comparable statistic for Gaelic speaking in Ireland was only 16 per cent. Last, Wales, Ireland, and the highlands of Scotland had a dominantly Celtic social organization,[2] and hence a great many cultural features of these societies were similar. Northern Ireland, on the other hand, began as a new society organized around the establishment of a colony of English and Scottish settlers and many of its cultural traditions and practices were adopted from the core. Thus, on the whole, a case can be made

---

cance of the Irish connection at different historical periods. See William Haller, *Foxe's Book of Martyrs and the Elect Nation* (London: 1963) and Carol Z. Weiner, 'The beleaguered isle. A study of Elizabethan and early Jacobean anti-Catholicism' *Past and Present*, 51 (1971), pp. 27–62, who discusses Elizabethan anti-Catholicism as an ideological response to the perceived threat of a Spanish invasion, which would likely be aided by Catholic support in Ireland. E. R. Norman's *Anti-Catholicism in Victorian England* (New York: 1968) relates that, among the working class of nineteenth-century Britain, anti-Catholicism was a retaliation for the depression of wages which accompanied Irish migration to British cities. Organized interests such as the Church of England mobilized anti-Catholicism among the middle and upper classes in an attempt to deny the political claims of Irish Catholics, who had been incorporated into the Union in 1800.

[1] L. P. Curtis, Jr, *Anglo-Saxons and Celts* (Bridgeport, Ct: 1968).

[2] This is described in H. L. Gray, *English Field Systems* (Cambridge, Mass.: 1915).

that there were as many cultural similarities among Ireland, Wales, and—to a lesser extent, Scotland—as there were differences.

The major historical difference separating Ireland from the other societies in the Celtic periphery along these dimensions is that the nationalist movement there had been much stronger, more organizationally secure, and of longer duration. Whereas Irish antipathy to English rule had been expressed at various times since the seventeenth century through both violent and peaceful means, the movements for Welsh and Scottish independence were primarily nineteenth-century in origin, and marked by much less commitment among both leaders and masses. The causes of the greater intensity of Irish nationalism are in part related to the especially brutal policies perpetrated by the English and Anglo-Irish settlers in Ireland.

English rule in Ireland was symbolically culminated by the disastrous Famine of 1846, during which millions starved as the English continued to export foodstuffs from the island.[1] Although conditions in highland Scotland and parts of north and mid-Wales were similar to those in Ireland, the situation of agrarian laborers in these regions was not quite so desperate. If these conditions led to the greater intensity of the Irish nationalist movement, it might be suggested that they contributed to its organizational strength and commitment as well. However, all of the Celtic lands were similar in that they were relegated to a position of economic dependency within the United Kingdom.[2]

The ultimate success of Irish, as against Welsh and Scottish, nationalism can best be explained by differences in the social structural composition of these regions. The significant differentiating factor is not the great poverty of Ireland relative to England, because Wales, Scotland, and Northern Ireland were likewise materially disadvantaged. However, the functional role played by Ireland in the course of British industrialization differed from that of Wales and Scotland. In the mid-nineteenth century all of the Celtic territories underwent economic transformation. Following the famine, the Irish economy shifted in response to changing English demand from the production of grain to the production of beef cattle.[3] But in Wales, Scotland, and—significantly—Northern Ireland—industrial enclaves arose with the development of heavy

---

[1] Cecil Woodham-Smith, *The Great Hunger* (New York: 1962).
[2] See chapter 5.
[3] Raymond D. Crotty, *Irish Agricultural Production: Its Volume and Structure* (Cork: 1966), pp. 66–83.

industry. The bulk of the territory in all of these regions remained agricultural hinterlands. However, the partial industrialization of Wales and Scotland encouraged the emergence of cultural distinctions between their respective enclaves and hinterlands. For the most part, the industrial enclaves were relatively cosmopolitan and anglicized. Thus these regions proceeded to become split into two separate cultural zones. This cultural differentiation between enclave and hinterland territories interfered with the development of a single regional political identity in Wales and Scotland. Ireland, however, had a comparatively small enclave, since her particular adaptation to the English market was to provide agricultural primary products. Thus territorial political differences could not split the nationalist movement in Ireland as happened in both Wales and Scotland.

This is evident in Table 9.1, which presents enclave-hinterland differences in mean county support for the Liberal Party for England

TABLE 9.1 *Enclave-hinterland differences* in Liberal Party support, by region, 1885–1966*

	England	*Wales*	*Scotland*	*N. Ireland*	*Ireland*
1885	2	19	3	16	6
1892	3	7	2	0	0
1900	3	33	6	2	0
1910	2	39	8	7	0
1924	3	47	17	0	na
1931	11	34	37	0	na
1951	2	26	10	20	na
1966	4	19	20	5	na

* Defined as the absolute difference between $\bar{X}_i$ and $\bar{X}_a$, where $\bar{X}_i$ is the mean percentage of Liberal Party votes in *industrial counties*, and $\bar{X}_a$ is the mean percentage of Liberal Party votes in *non-industrial counties*. Counties are defined as *industrial* if their percentage of employed adult males in non-agricultural occupations was equal to or exceeded 85 per cent for the year 1885; 87·5 per cent for the years 1891–1924, and 90 per cent from 1931 to 1966. (See chapter 5. p. 139)

Wales, Scotland, Northern Ireland, and Ireland. Enclave-hinterland differences in political support for the Liberals (the major Opposition party until 1924 in these statistics) are smallest for Ireland, followed by England. As early as 1901 Scotland exceeds England, while Welsh differentials are higher by a factor of six. Thereafter these differences in political support increased dramatically in Scotland and Wales until 1931; then there is a fall in the post-war years. This should be compared to the English and Irish statistics, where the differences between enclave and hinterland regions are minimal.

The impression to be gained is that Ireland and England were regionally solidary whereas both Wales and Scotland were, at least politically, significantly divided along enclave-hinterland lines. Table 9.2 presents similar data for Labor Party support, and virtually the same conclusions may be drawn.

Together these figures are valuable in determining the course of nationalism in Wales and Scotland in the 1920s in relation to Ireland. In the years 1885 to 1910 both Wales and Ireland show evidence of peripheral sectionalism of similar intensity and direction, while Scotland was relatively less inclined to anti-Conservative

TABLE 9.2 *Enclave-hinterland differences* in Labor Party support, by region, 1885–1966*

	England	Wales	Scotland	N. Ireland	Ireland
1885	1	1	1	0	0
1892	2	0	0	0	0
1900	1	8	0	0	0
1910	8	34	0	0	0
1924	15	42	25	6	na
1931	14	50	27	2	na
1951	9	24	19	14	na
1966	7	26	23	13	na

* As in Table 9.1.

voting in this period. High negative mean residual scores have been interpreted as indicating antipathy towards the center, a low level of political integration, and, consequently a potential social base for nationalist politics. However, while this antipathy to England was channeled into one nationalist party in Ireland, in Wales and Scotland it came to be split among two competing parties, Liberal and Labor, with time.

The development of a nationalist political party in Ireland was itself partially the result of Ireland's particular mode of economic specialization. In the late 1870s the Irish economy experienced severe depression as a consequence of several historically accidental circumstances. These included an economic depression in Britain, which slackened overall demand; the lowering of prices for Irish agricultural exports due to increased foreign competition, while rents remained constant; and a series of bad harvests.[1] This was precisely the period in which the regional economies of Wales and

[1] J. C. Beckett, *The Making of Modern Ireland, 1603–1923* (London: 1966), pp. 384–5.

Scotland were booming: the demise of their specialized economies did not occur until the end of World War One. Given this situation, political organization for secession, as against administrative devolution, could not have appeared nearly so attractive to diverse groups in Wales and Scotland as it did in Ireland.

In Wales and Scotland the Liberal Party remained dominant in the hinterlands, while the new Labor Party made impressive gains in the industrial enclaves of Wales and Scotland after 1911. This affected prospects for separatism in two ways. First, since anti-center sentiments were divided between two formally national political parties, there was no guarantee that members of Parliament representing enclave and hinterland constituencies could act in concert when relevant Welsh and Scottish issues were raised in Parliament. Instead, they were Liberals or Laborites with primary loyalty to their respective national leaderships. The possibility of informal coalitions among the Welsh and Scottish members across party lines was therefore largely dependent on decisions concerning party strategies made in England.[1] Second, in practice the sincere advocacy of political separation for Wales and Scotland would be politically disadvantageous to the Liberal and Labor parties, since disproportionate electoral support for both parties came from the Celtic regions. With the loss of Welsh and Scottish representation in Parliament and the political system, challenges to Conservative dominance would be practically unthinkable.

Therefore the rise of a second opposition party, Labor, had important consequences for the continued incorporation of the Celtic periphery in the United Kingdom. A three-party system offered the prospect of further differentiation of the traditionally anti-English political sentiments of Wales and Scotland. Table 9.3 shows the timing of this decisive shift in the British party system. It is evident that the mean county support for the Conservative Party was relatively unaffected by the rise of Labor, and that Labor's strength appears to be a function of the progressive decay of Liberalism. The problem of the decline of Liberalism has been one of the

---

[1] In Ireland, however, highly disciplined nationalist party organization had emerged under Parnell. Parnell's party was characterized by its rigid independence from both Conservatives and Liberals; by the pledges required of its members and the control exercised over them by the Treasurer of the Party, who paid their salaries; and by its success in forcing Parliament to face the issues in which it was interested. See Conor Cruise O'Brien, 'The machinery of the Irish parliamentary party, 1880–1885,' *Irish Historical Studies*, 5, 17 (1946). The contrast with Wales and Scotland for the period is striking.

great, and only partially studied, issues in British political history.[1] I cannot do the subject much justice here. The most obvious difference between the two parties was that of their respective social bases. The Liberal Party, prior to 1911, was an amalgam of diverse interests and social classes: Noncomformists of all stations, manufacturing interests bent upon the pursuit of Cobdenite policies of free trade as against the protectionist tendencies of the Tories; a heavy sprinkling of industrial workers, most particularly miners and members of the 'aristocracy of labor' in late nineteenth-century

TABLE 9.3 *Major Party support,* Great Britain and Northern Ireland, 1885–1966*

	Conservative Party	Liberal Party	Labor Party
1885	32	44	0
1892	42	37	0
1900	46	31	0
1910	32	41	2
1924	45	28	26
1931	53	26	20
1951	50	8	41
1961	42	14	40

* Mean county proportions.

Britain, and last, those groups in the Celtic periphery who supported Home Rule.

The very heterogeneity of the social base of the Liberal Party in its heyday came to be a liability as the party suffered attack from several quarters. The Irish Nationalists, for their part, refused to align themselves permanently with the Liberals so as to maximize their political power. Hence the Liberals were under constant pressure to maintain the support of the numerous Irish delegation. The greatest threat to the Liberal coalition came from the working classes, who were being increasingly organized into trade unions, to protect their economic interests, and enticed by revolutionary socialist parties, to promote their political interests as a social class. The

[1] On this general theme see G. Dangerfield, *The Strange Death of Liberal England* (New York: 1935); Trevor Wilson, *The Downfall of the Liberal Party* (London: 1966); Paul Thompson, *Socialists, Liberals and Labour: The Struggle for London, 1885–1914* (London: 1967); and Henry Pelling, 'Labour and the downfall of Liberalism' in Henry Pelling, ed., *Popular Politics and Society in Late Victorian Britain* (London: 1968).

great strength of the German Social Democratic Party served as an example to the British Marxist party known as the Social Democratic Federation (SDF), which grew from a small clique in 1883 to a national organization by 1900.

The development of class consciousness among workers stimulated demands for working-class candidates to Parliament. The Liberal Party did not subsidize the electoral expenses of its candidates, and hence only the well-to-do could be nominated for Parliamentary office. The old Liberal strategy had been to put up members of the bourgeoisie to represent working-class constituencies, but this became increasingly unpopular in those constituencies. The growth of class consciousness signalled the impending death knell of the Liberal coalition. If a working-class political party could be formed which would appeal to the vast majority of the British electorate—industrial workers and their families coupled with the remaining urban poor—on class terms rather than on those of relatively vague religious and regional interests, the Liberals could have no future as a distinct party with national political aspirations. Such a class party could attempt to find financial support for working-class candidates for political office.[1] Furthermore, working-class organization, *per se*, tended to split the traditional alliance of bourgeoisie and proletariat which had been forged to wrest power from the landed aristocratic interests. Not only would the proletariat define themselves in opposition to their employers, the reverse would also be likely to occur, and the bourgeoisie would see the Tory camp as the place from which to defend their interests. Similarly, if the workers in the industrial enclaves of Wales and Scotland could be persuaded that class position took precedence over ethnicity in terms of their dominant political identification, then the likelihood of achieving independence from England would correspondingly diminish.

It is evident that the decline of Liberalism did not, however, occur with precipitate speed, and that—at least from this perspective—the striking fact is that the Liberal Party remained the major force in political opposition until the end of the First World War. In large degree this may be accounted for by considering the development of trade union organizations in Britain.[2] Historically, the first type of

[1] See Henry Pelling, *The Origin of the Labour Party* (Oxford: 1965) pp. 2-3, for a discussion of the crucial role of finances in the development of an independent working-men's party.

[2] G. D. H. Cole, *A Short History of the British Working Class Movement, 1789–1947* (London: 1948); E. J. Hobsbawm's articles, 'General Labor unions in Britain, 1889–1914' and 'The Labor aristocracy in nineteenth-century Britain'

labor association to emerge was the 'craft union,' typified by individual grades and sections of workers bargaining independently and separately. The craft union was primarily concerned with skilled labor organization at the local level, most particularly within specific cities though some attempts at national organization were made as well. In contrast, the 'industrial union' sought to unite and coordinate the bargaining of all groups whose bargains affected each other substantially. Industrial unions, which are typical of labor organizations in most advanced capitalist societies today, not only include both skilled and non-skilled labor but more importantly, are organized on a national level. Laborers whom they seek to represent are distributed throughout the national territory. Intermediate between these two historical stages, and their corresponding organizational forms, was the 'general union' which combined features of both the craft and industrial unions in attempting to regulate a regional labor market. To some extent these categories are ideal-typical and contemporary unions conform to a greater or lesser extent to these descriptions.[1] For instance, even today there are unions best described as of the craft type, though the greatest numerical strength of the labor movement is in organizations which are largely industrial, in this special sense. The history of labor-oriented political parties in the Celtic periphery clearly shows that the development of industrial unionism was a prerequisite to their electoral success.

This can best be demonstrated by considering the failure of labor parties in these regions in the pre-World War One period. Wales in the 1880s and 1890s was, according to Kenneth Morgan,[2]

detached from the metropolitan activities of the Fabian Society [and] the Social Democratic Federation. Men felt more immediate loyalty to their village or valley than to their class. Even the Independent Labor Party, in many respects a rebellion of the provinces and intrinsically regional in character, was slow to penetrate into Wales: the Bradford conference of January 1893, which saw the foundation of the Party, contained no delegate from Wales. By the summer of 1897, only four weak branches seem to have been founded in Wales, at Cardiff, Treharris, Merthyr Tydfil, and in

---

in his *Laboring Men* (New York: 1967); and H. A. Clegg, Alan Fox and A. F. Thompson, *A History of British Trade Unions Since 1889* (Oxford: 1964), vol. I, 1889–1910.

[1] See the cautious remarks with respect to these differences by Clegg, Fox and Thompson, *ibid.*, pp. 87–96.

[2] K. O. Morgan, *Wales in British Politics, 1868–1922* (Cardiff: 1963), p. 199.

Wrexham in the North. At the 1895 election, 'Independent Labour' candidates stood at Swansea District and Merthyr Tydfil, but with little success.

This corresponds roughly with a period of the dominance of craft-type unions in Wales. Even these were relatively weak, as the great majority of laborers remained unrepresented by any labor associations. Although attempts to establish militant union organizations among dock workers in South Welsh ports were made, a series of unsuccessful strikes led to setbacks in the number of affiliated workers. Wherever relatively solidary labor associations existed, they were 'hidebound by a cautious attitude towards industrial action and by hostility to unions based in England.'[1]

The single largest body of laborers was the coal miners; they were 'extremely slow to combine and their leaders anxious to compromise.'[2] Wages in the minefields had been regulated according to a sliding scale based on the selling price of coal since 1880. According to this agreement a change of one shilling a ton in price was to lead to a change of $7\frac{1}{2}$ per cent in wages. The agreement was subject to termination on six months notice, and it was administered by a committee of owners' and workers' representatives. The late nineteenth century saw a great rise in Welsh coal exports, and for much of this time miners' wages were rising. The steadiness of work coupled with relatively high wages made mining a relatively attractive occupation in this period.

The further consequence of the sliding scale arrangement was that it encouraged conflict among the various mining unions. The scale itself symbolized the notion of cooperation between labor and capital in the extension of Welsh coal exports. It was recognized in these terms by the very representatives of the miners themselves:[3]

The dominant voice among the Welsh miners was that of William Abraham (Mabon), secretary of the Cambrian Miners Association. A characteristic product of industrial nonconformity, deacon of C[h]apel Nazareth, Pentre, Mabon founded his adherence to the sliding scale essentially on ethical rather than on economic considerations. The apostle of industrial peace, he believed that there was no essential conflict of interest between capital and labour, and that mutual adjustment would secure an agreement satisfactory to both sides. The scale symbolized this harmonious relationship. To Mabon, strikes and lock-outs were primitive and unnecessary. Until the turn of the century, he could command a unique authority over the Welsh mining community. With a homely parable and his fine tenor voice which won fame at the *eisteddfod*, he could enthral multitudes and charm away all dissent.

[1] *Ibid.*   [2] *Ibid.*   [3] *Ibid.*, p. 203.

This was a period of increasing concern with issues of Welsh nationality. Whereas most of the industry in South Wales was controlled by English interests the steam coal industry was exceptional in that Welshmen were prominent in its development.[1] A sizable proportion of the mine owners were born in Wales and shared similar social origins, religion, and language with the workers. On questions relating to Home Rule for Wales and Disestablishment there was no necessary conflict between the native Welsh bourgeoisie and proletariat. The owners of a mine, if Welsh, were locally regarded as paragons of the church and community and usually deferred to in social and political matters. They were also committed Liberals, and were thus natural opposition candidates for Parliament from the mining constituencies. The alliance of the Welsh bourgeoisie and proletariat—for the miners were broadly representative of the Welsh proletariat as a whole—then, was cemented around the notion of separate nationality and attendant cultural distinctiveness from English society in general. Both classes could perceive that they were underdogs, the common victims of the English domination of Wales.

However, this prototypically nationalist solidarity was to prove highly vulnerable to downward shifts in the price of coal in international markets. The sliding scale arrangement provided a direct incentive to employers to under-sell and to over-produce, since it guaranteed that profits would be maintained intact. So long as the selling price of coal would rise both parties would benefit. In the event of a price depression the workers stood to suffer greatly, while owners' profits would be substantially unchanged. Downward wage adjustments were, naturally, a source of conflict between miners and owners. While the selling price of coal had more or less consistently risen in the period 1880–94, in the following four years prices slipped.[2] By 1897 money wages had fallen to a level only 11 per cent higher than that of 1879 and the miners sustained extreme hardship. Both owners and miners developed a heightened class consciousness as their respective interests diverged sharply. In 1898 the owners association terminated all negotiation with the miners' representatives, who argued for a 10 per cent increase in wages plus a minimum wage, and work in the South Wales mines was halted for 100,000 men for a six month period. In this situation

[1] E. D. Lewis, *The Rhondda Valley* (London: 1959), p. 70.
[2] B. R. Mitchell, *Abstract of British Historical Statistics* (Cambridge: 1962), p. 483.

of grinding poverty which could be easily ascribed to the avarice of Welsh mine owners, labor politics made its first headway in Wales. Organizers for the ILP swarmed into the mining valleys, and in 1900 Keir Hardie, a Scot of working-class origin, gained the first Labor (ILP) seat in Parliament from the Welsh mining constituency Merthyr Tydfil. Subsequently, the miners evolved stronger union organization, forming the South Wales Miners Federation (SWMF).[1] The SWMF became more and more militant in its tactics, and in 1910–11 called a strike in the valleys which lasted almost a full year. This strike proved to be a watershed in British labor politics, calling nationwide attention to an impressive display of class consciousness and organization. Two years later the first national miners strike was called.

The most important Celtic nationalist institution in Wales, the Nonconformist church, took a hostile position towards the movement of industrial unionism. Hence the only groups actively promoting industrial unionism in Wales were publicly identified as English in origin. The taint of English leadership was for a time enough to dissuade many Welsh workers from the labor movement in general:[2]

The indifference of Welsh Nonconformity to labour unions meant that the Welsh workers in these parts had no other leadership to follow except that which came from England. This leadership was suspect, as the sermons preached on Chartism showed; and it can be said that there was a latent anti-English feeling in these Welsh industrial communities throughout the nineteenth century, because most of the initiative for working-class unity came from England.

With the worsening conditions in the Welsh mining valleys, however, trade union and socialist propaganda, based upon a principle of the non-nationality of the proletariat, gained increasing impact on Welsh workers. The Nonconformist church became aware of a shift in worker sentiments, and stiffened its attack on union organizations. It perceived that its traditional place at the center of Welsh cultural and institutional affairs could be undermined by this growing social movement:[3]

Nonconformist ministers inveighed against the materialism and atheism of Socialist propaganda, and many young militants left their congregation.

[1] R. Page Arnot, *South Wales Miners: A History of the South Wales Miners Federation (1898–1914)* (London: 1967).
[2] E. T. Davies, *Religion in the Industrial Revolution in South Wales* (Cardiff: 1965), p. 157.   [3] Morgan, *op. cit.*, p. 211.

As nonconformity lost its hold, the new social gospel took its place. Its meetings employed the language and mystique of traditional religion, but it was the miners' agent and not the minister who gained from the new fervour.

Even in the face of depression, however, the labor movement succeeded initially in Wales only to the extent that it identified itself with traditional aspects of Welsh culture. Up until the First World War labor candidates steadily advocated Disestablishment and Home Rule, though the latter came to be justified on socialist principles to distinguish it from earlier nationalist forms. For example, Keir Hardie made a point of attending the *eisteddfod* and learning the Welsh national anthem.[1] In this transitional period the new movement sought the best of both possible worlds in the industrial enclave, nationalist as well as socialist, in order to solidify its social base.

The First World War saw growing labor unrest all over Britain,[2] but especially in Wales and Scotland where there were major concentrations of heavy industry supplying war matériel. In the war period industrial disputes tended to be defined by the government as giving comfort to the enemy. Welsh mines were consolidated into vast cartels, and the owners were increasingly faced by industrial unions whose outlook and organization was national. The socialist image of the forces of labor being dominated by concentrated industrial capital was easily perceived by workers, since it became very closely approximated in reality. The advent of the Russian Revolution provided a new stimulus to industrial unionism, and after 1918 South Wales and the Clydeside were to become the major base of support for the small Communist Party of Great Britain. By the end of the war the Welsh industrial enclave was overwhelmingly in the camp of the Labor Party. But the hinterland, which Labor had never appealed to since few industrial workers were to be found there, continued secure in its Liberalism for want of any alternative. Thus the nationalist sentiments of Wales became divided among two opposition parties.

The Scottish case is similar in many particulars, except that from the early 1880s Scottish skilled workers had played an important role in labor politics, especially in the Social Democratic Federation. The fascinating aspect of this early Scottish involvement

---

[1] David Lowe, *From Pit to Parliament: The Early Life of Keir Hardie* (London: 1923).
[2] Cole, *op. cit.*, pp. 418–22, provides a useful summary.

was that it was so short-lived: center-periphery conflicts erupted even within the very heart of the British revolutionary movement. The SDF had emerged in the 1880s under the leadership of an English bourgeois follower of Marx, H. M. Hyndman.[1] Since Marx and Engels had given scant attention to the question of self-determination for small nations, it is hardly surprising that Hyndman himself would be relatively insensitive to these issues in Britain. In 1880, running as an Independent for the Marylebone constituency in London, Hyndman campaigned against both Home Rule for Ireland and Disestablishment of the Church of England. By 1900 the overwhelmingly metropolitan character of the SDF was evident in its organizational structure, as 50 per cent of the executive committee positions were held by Londoners. This caused great resentment and criticism among the Scottish members of the SDF.[2]

It was no accident that the critics came from Scotland, feeling cut off by distance and impotent before the powerful London executive. Sectional feeling found . . . ground for discontent in the fact that of twenty-four places on the federation executive, twelve were reserved for London, leaving only an equivalent number to the whole remaining membership in the 'provinces.'

Parenthetically, it must be remembered that the greatest new industrial concentration in Britain was to the north and west. Hence the natural political center of gravity for the British revolutionary working-class movement might well have been Manchester, or Liverpool, rather than London, which had a greater proportion of 'old' industries and, thus, relatively more skilled laborers.

Within the internal politics of the SDF the split between the Scottish members, who had formed a Scottish District Council of the SDF in 1898 to consider specifically Scottish problems, and Hyndman's London-based group steadily widened, and soon became mirrored by ideological differences. The Scots were advocates of the development of a revolutionary movement around a base of militant labor organization, and they aligned themselves with de Leonism in the United States. The Hyndman group, on the other hand, was moving to a revisionist position, that working-class power could be gradually won through participation in the political processes of

---

[1] Chushichi Tsuzuki, *H. M. Hyndman and British Socialism* (London: 1961); Pelling, *The Origins of the Labour Party*; Thompson, *op. cit.*; and Walter Kendall, *The Revolutionary Movement in Britain, 1900–1921* (London: 1969).

[2] *Ibid.*, p. 13.

bourgeois states. The issue came to a head at Paris in 1900, with the question of whether the Second International should support the actions of the French socialist, Millerand, who had entered into a bourgeois cabinet. Kautsky advocated a resolution which in effect exonerated Millerand's action; de Leon opposed this resolution. The Hyndman group voted with Kautsky; the Scots supported de Leon. After the Paris meeting open conflict broke out between the rival English and Scottish factions of the SDF.[1]

The English faction began a policy of expelling de Leonist members from the party. Its politics became more and more moderate, in contrast to the Scottish party. On the occasion of the coronation of King Edward VII, the Hyndman forces offered an address which proclaimed:[2]

'That you are very popular, Sir, there can be no doubt whatever'; it excused Edward's notorious 'private peccadilloes' and specifically denied any wish to replace the monarchy with a republic. In an appeal to the new king it pleaded for 'a vigorous initiative in the direction of social reconstruction from the first person in this realm; 'by using your position to improve the well-being of Englishmen [sic] you . . . can secure for yourself a name in history which mankind will look back to with admiration and respect.'

An editorial in the Glasgow *Herald* termed this 'the most remarkable document which traces its origin to the Coronation.' The accuracy of this assessment aside, it cannot be doubted that the sentiments expressed in this address could only have profoundly angered Scots of all political hues. The SDF's later support of the policy of strengthening the British Navy in anticipation of conflict with Germany (1910) was regarded as further evidence of its partiality towards English imperialism. Hence even this bastion of the revolutionary workers movement in Britain was initially dominated by English leadership, primarily organized to promote the interests of English workers, and only incidentally concerned with those of workers in Scotland and Wales. In retaliation, the Scottish wing of the SDF was impelled to found its own organizations, among which was the Socialist Labor Party. Even the ILP, though less Marxist than the SDF, was a refuge for Scottish working-class leaders, and the organiz-

---

[1] This is not to argue that this type of sectionalism was necessarily the major cause of the split within the SDF. Pelling, *The Origins of the Labour Party*, and Thompson, *op. cit.*, place emphasis on factors such as the weakness of its leadership: in part embodied in the personality of Hyndman, which they deem to have been inappropriate to his task.

[2] Kendall, *op. cit.*, p. 19.

ation had distinctive Scottish characteristics: it was religious in its outlook, staunchly Nonconformist and rigidly teetotalist.

Throughout the early years of the twentieth century the trade-union situation in Scotland strongly resembled that of Wales. A Scottish Trades Union Congress had been formed in 1897, but it was concerned with local economic issues, and thus did not take a strong stand on the issue of Home Rule until 1914.[1] The onset of the war greatly strained relations between industrial workers on the one hand, and capitalists and the government on the other, as in Wales. The Clyde was the hotbed of industrial radicalism among all British regions. Since its industries, shipbuilding and the manufacture of munitions, were so critical to the British war effort the government attempted to secure continued production at all costs. Its policies towards workers in essential industries were, therefore, particularly repressive. Partly as a consequence of these conditions, it appears, the STUC began issuing manifestos advocating Home Rule. The labor movement appeared to be moving simultaneously in the direction of class consciousness, on the one hand, and national independence, on the other. The Clyde shop steward's movement, under the effective leadership of John Maclean,[2] an organizer of legendary proportions in Scottish history, remained distant from similar movements in England. In this situation, when the Labor Party, especially with its largely Scottish leadership of Keir Hardie and Ramsay MacDonald, attempted to gather support in industrial Scotland, it came out for Scottish national independence. However it was extremely anxious to confine the nationalist activities of its members to the Party itself. To this end it actively discouraged members from associating with other organizations which were solely dedicated to the realization of independence, such as the Scottish Home Rule Association:[3]

The Scottish executive [of the Labour Party] did its best to prevent its members from becoming active in the Scottish Home Rule Association on the ground that it was established party policy to discountenance the formation or support of overlapping organizations. The executive therefore resolved that 'whilst strongly in favor of Home Rule for Scotland' it was 'of opinion that the people of Scotland can secure this measure by a fuller support of Labour at the polls, and therefore considers it inadvisable for members of the Labour party to associate with members of

[1] H. J. Hanham, *Scottish Nationalism* (London: 1969), pp. 110–11.
[2] In this regard it is most informative to read Hugh MacDiarmid's discussion of Maclean in *The Company I've Kept* (Berkeley: 1967).
[3] Hanham, *op. cit.*, p. 114.

other political parties in special organizations for the purpose of securing Home Rule.'

This was, in effect, a bald attempt to control the potentially divisive effects of nationalism by insisting that the issue be confined to discussion and action within the organizational framework of the British Labor Party, in which Scots members could be but a small minority. To some extent this strategy succeeded, and the nationalist movement was denied a proportion of its potential labor support. After the war, Labor firmly renounced Home Rule for both Scotland and Wales as being impracticable and inadvisable but in this transitional period, when the party sought to supplant Liberalism as well as orthodox Marxism, nationalism was used as a means of attracting new members. It should also be noted that the Communist Party of Great Britain abandoned Scottish independence in its post-war platform, despite its advocacy by John Maclean. Not until 1957 did the CPGB reverse this stand.

In the Irish case, the absence of a significant industrial enclave providing a basis for national affiliations among a majority of the electorate can be seen to contribute significantly to the eventual outcome of secession. The earliest labor associations in Ireland were loosely affiliated with comparable British associations, and had but slight representation at the annual British Trades Union Congresses.[1]

These British Congresses, faced with a multitude of interesting problems, were unable and unwilling to give adequate attention to matters of vital importance to Ireland. Resolutions of mere Irish importance were relegated to the end of the agenda. British labor's interest in Ireland centered more and more in the prevention of the competition, in British labor markets, of Irish labor. Furthermore, the wage scales in Britain were much higher than those for the same jobs in Ireland. For example, in 1891, while nearly 60 per cent of the railway laborers in England and Wales were paid 20s. per week or more and under 1 per cent were paid less than 10s. per week, in Ireland less than a quarter of these workers received more than 20s. per week, and nearly half were paid less than 10s. In response to the virtual neglect of their affairs and concerns Irish trades unionists formed an independent Irish Trades Union Congress in 1894. In retaliation, as it were, the BTUC excluded Ireland from representation on its Parliamentary Committee in the following year.

[1] J. Dunsmore Clarkson, *Labor and Nationalism in Ireland* (New York: 1925), p. 185.

The President of the ITUC explained these developments in the following terms:[1]

Like the Imperial Parliament, the English Congressional machine has become overladen with the multifarious duties and interests committed to its care. It has gone on from year to year, with the rapid growth of the Trade Union movement, gathering largely increased membership with correspondingly increased responsibilities, until it may be said to have outgrown its own strength to cope successfully with the work which pressed upon it from all sides. *Moreover, the industries of England and Scotland, as compared with those of Ireland, being almost entirely of a mining and manufacturing character, it may seem obvious that their representatives should predominate in—as in truth they largely dominate—that Congress.* To expect, then, that a few representatives from Ireland could hope to make any practical impression upon an institution which has already become unwieldy, would be to expect the impossible. I cannot, of course, find fault with our English and Scottish friends in pressing forward their own claims first—that is quite natural seeing that their interests are in the main identical, and the facilities at their disposal favorable; *they cannot be expected to understand the wants of a community largely agricultural, assisting in reviving the languishing manufactures of Ireland.* Our only remedy, our only chance of effectively arresting the attention of the powers that be to the condition of Irish industry and Irish labor, is to maintain our own Annual Congress and our own Parliamentary Committee (applause). Moreover, a further incentive to Irish trade unionists to promote and extend the scope and operations of their own Congress lies in the fact that the Parliamentary Committee of the English Institution recently decided to practically exclude Irish representation henceforth. We are thus thrown upon our own resources, and with that object we are assembled here today.

This is a statement quite remarkable for its restrained and reasonable tone. In essence, the ITUC President was not arguing that the British ITUC took an imperialist position with respect to Ireland— though such a case could probably be made with some justification[2] —but merely that the economic interests of the respective societies were at variance. Ireland's agricultural economy posed for Irish labor problems which were different from those the dominantly industrial economy of Great Britain posed for English, Scottish, and Welsh labor.

[1] *Ibid.*, pp. 187–8, italics added.
[2] There is no doubt that imperialistic attitudes could be found among those of the British left. The Webbs, for instance, could write on the occasion of a visit to Ireland in 1892, 'We will tell you about Ireland when we come back. The people are charming but we detest them, as we should the Hottentots—for their very virtues. Home Rule is an absolute necessity *in order to depopulate the country of this detestable race.*' From Janet Beveridge, *An Epic of Clare Market* (London: 1960), as cited by Curtis, *op. cit.*, p. 63.

Similar localist attitudes were characteristic of the craft and general union organizations in Wales and Scotland as well. The critical departure from British trade unionism came with the development of a militant brand of unionism which emerged under the leadership of James Larkin. It may be thought paradoxical that the tactics of militant industrial unionism should first be developed in largely agricultural Ireland, but this occurrence has a certain internal logic. Since labor organizations were not well established in Ireland there was probably less resistance to strategic innovation, emanating from union leaders fearful of losing their offices if unsuccessful, in this agricultural periphery than in Britain as a whole. Larkin, an organizer for the National Union of Dock Laborers, with headquarters in Liverpool, set to his task with brilliance. In 1907 he led a successful carters' strike at the docks of Belfast, and for six weeks unskilled laborers, both Catholic and Protestant, Unionist and Nationalist, maintained solidarity and withstood attempts by the military to break the strike. After attacks on the massed workers and their sympathizers by the Cameron Highlanders and the Royal Berkshires, handbills went up all over the Falls Road district proclaiming:[1]

Not as Catholics or Protestants, as Nationalists or Unionists, but as Belfast men and workers stand together and don't be misled by the employer's game of dividing Catholic and Protestant.

Such unity between Protestant and Catholic has been infrequent in the history of Northern Ireland, and Larkin received wide attention for his leadership and tactical insight. The strike strategy devised by Larkin and James Connolly, the Irish Marxist leader, has been described by G. D. H. Cole:[2]

(Larkin and Connolly's) methods were the sudden and the sympathetic strike. They did not call great stoppages preceded by long negotiations which gave the employers ample time to prepare. They preferred to call out suddenly the workers at a single establishment, and then, as seemed most helpful, to bring out other workers in sympathy with the original strikers. If, for example, an employer tried to carry on with blackleg labour, they would stop the carmen or the shops in which his goods were sold. Or they would call out the workers in other establishments in which the employer whom they were fighting was known to have an interest.

Although similar methods had earlier been employed in the United States, Larkin was the first to bring them to the United Kingdom.

[1] Clarkson, *op. cit.*, p. 219.   [2] Cole, *op. cit.*, pp. 344–8.

This 1907 strike was halted when Larkin's executive in Liverpool withdrew his financial support, against Larkin's advice, claiming that the action was costing the NUDL a thousand pounds per week.[1] Larkin thereafter resigned from the British union, and formed the Irish Transit Workers Union which carried the tactics of his 'new unionism' to Dublin. In the south of Ireland, which was much less industrial than Belfast, the bulk of the working class was unskilled and correspondingly even less attached to existing labor associations than in Belfast. Larkin and Connolly made steady gains, and the ITWU engaged in bitter and protracted strikes. In Dublin they established a political party, the Irish Socialist Republican Party, which was nationalist and revolutionary and, thus at odds with the bourgeois-led Parliamentary nationalist forces.[2]

While the British Labor Party attempted to win influence in domestic politics, making inroads into Welsh and Scottish nationalism in the industrial enclaves, it devoted less attention to building comparable support in Ireland. Irish representation was excluded at a very early stage from the Labor Party's National Administrative Council:[3]

The Committee did not wish it to be inferred that they wished to do any injustice to Ireland. But their party had no existence in that country. It was true that they were led to believe that there was a very small branch

---

[1] Clarkson, *op. cit.*, p. 219.

[2] James Connolly felt the British Labor Party inadvertently hurt the cause of labor in Ireland by supporting the bourgeois-led Home Rule party:

'I have spent a great portion of my life alternating between interpreting Socialism to the Irish and interpreting the Irish to the Socialists. Of the two tasks, I confess, that while I am convinced that the former has been attended with a considerable degree of success, the latter has not. At least as far as the Socialists of Great Britain are concerned, they always seem to me to exhibit towards the Irish working-class democracy of the Labour movement the same inability to understand their position and to share in their aspirations as the organized British nation, as a whole, has shown to the struggling Irish nation it has so long held in subjection.

'No one, and least of all the present writer, would deny the sympathy of the leaders of the British labour movement towards the Labour and Socialist movements of Ireland, but a sympathy not based on understanding is often more harmful than a direct antagonism. . . . Small wonder that we in Ireland are working to establish a Labour party of our own. We have no fault to find with the Labour Party in Great Britain. We recognize that it has its own problems to face and that it cannot well be expected to turn aside to grapple with ours. And, Heaven knows, these problems are serious enough to require the most earnest study and undivided attention of men on the spot. They require more study and attention than can be given by men absorbed in the urgent problems of the greater population across the water.' Connolly, *op. cit.*, pp. 67–72.

[3] Clarkson, *op. cit.*, pp. 397–8.

somewhere about Belfast, but it had not put itself in evidence. As soon as Ireland had a Labor Party it would be quite right to consider the matter of representation (1893).

By 1907 Ireland was included in ILP plans but only as a part of the Lancashire organizing district. But Labor's lack of success in Ireland was only partially due to this relative neglect. Many Irish workers, for their part, found the Labor Party's strong advocacy of secular education, in combination with its ideological antipathy towards nationalism, to be simply unacceptable. The Roman Catholic church also took an anti-Labor position.[1] Neither of these two political positions was thought to be exceptionable by the bulk of English workers, and while workers of nationalist bent in Wales and Scotland might have been troubled by Labor's militant internationalism, secular education was not a divisive issue in either region. Religious differences never were of much significance in Scottish nationalism, since the Established Church was a Scottish institution. In Wales every gain for secularization was regarded as a defeat for the Established Church of Wales, which was Anglican and not culturally Welsh. However, if these twin policies were received with disfavor in southern Ireland, they were acclaimed by working-class Protestants in Belfast who welcomed the chance to vote against conservative Unionist candidates without thereby voting for candidates of the Irish Nationalist Party. In Northern Ireland, socialism could therefore co-exist with support for the union with Great Britain.

In the south no such possibility existed. The severing of links to the British trade unions precluded the chance that any future advantages would accrue to the Irish working class from continued association with the United Kingdom. Even so, the Irish working class was but a small minority of the population. The peasants, as a whole, perceived no economic interest in maintaining the British connection, and their Catholicism and hatred of the Anglo-Irish landed aristocracy gave them sufficient reason to be ardently nationalistic. Only members of the commercial middle class, who gained as middle-men in the trade between Ireland and Britain, could see their material interests advanced by the British incorporation. However, the development of refrigerator ships at the turn of the century invited competition for the British livestock and dairy market from such distant countries as Argentina, New Zealand, Australia, and Denmark.[2] Under free trade policies there could be

[1] Clarkson *op. cit.*, p. 32.
[2] E. Strauss, *Irish Nationalism and British Democracy* (New York: 1951), p. 197.

no preference for Irish products and hence no incentive on the part of this commercial class to remain part of the United Kingdom. Thus, by the outbreak of the First World War virtually all southern Irish social classes saw continued union as an unnecessary burden, and the nationalist forces had very broad-based support.[1] When the Labor Party reversed its position in Irish nationalism it did so without aiding the socialist faction of the movement. Since bourgeois elements were in control of the nationalist movement, the Labor Party, being opportunistic, supported them as against the weaker ISRP elements. The actions of Labor Party thereby strengthened the anti-revolutionary nationalist forces and weakened the revolutionary nationalist forces. Solidarity under bourgeois leadership was the necessary outcome.[2]

The outbreak of World War One further stimulated the development of Irish nationalism. The war was far more unpopular in Ireland than in Great Britain as a whole. While the war led to higher prices for Irish producers, there were complaints about the cost of living in urban areas and increases in taxation. But clearly the most hated aspect of the war was the attempt to induce Irishmen into military service. Though the government did not apply the Conscription Act to Ireland, 'voluntary enlistment,' derisively known as the 'Enlist or Starve Policy,' was actively encouraged. One of the slogans British recruiters used in their propaganda campaign for Irish enlistment was that 'the trenches are safer than the Dublin slums.' To which James Connolly replied.[3]

---

[1] Among the few remaining supporters of Union in this part of Ireland were the controllers of the small number of export oriented large scale enterprises most of whom, it should be noted, were Protestants. Since this social group was of greater importance in the more industrial north, its attitudes carried great weight '[A]mongst the industrialists of the north-east, directly dependent as they were upon external markets and sources of raw material, membership in the great British free-trade area was vital. For them the nationalist emphasis on tariff autonomy under Home Rule spelt ruin, since it would condemn them—so they believed—to a protectionist regime that would expose them to retaliatory discrimination in the world outside, offering them as recompense only the impoverished Irish hinterland.' F. S. L. Lyons, *Ireland Since the Famine* (London: 1971), p. 288.

[2] 'It is to us a grim comment upon the boasted solidarity of Labour when we see a Labour M.P., in Great Britain, calmly announcing that he prefers to follow the official representatives of Irish capitalism rather than the spokesman of 86,000 organized Irish workers, and that he does so because the latter are yet too weak to protect themselves politically—have no votes to deliver in Parliament, whereas their enemies have.' James Connolly, 'The Solidarity of Labour' in his *Socialism and Nationalism*, p. 121.

[3] Clarkson, *op. cit.*, p. 307.

It is the English idea of wit . . . But you can die honorably in a Dublin slum . . . On every recruiting platform in Dublin you can see the faces of the men who in 1913–14 met together day by day to tell of their plans to murder our women and children by starvation, and who are now appealing to the men of those women and children to fight in order to save the precious skins of the gangs that conspired to starve and outrage them. . . . These are the recruiters. Every Irish man or boy who joins at their call gives these carrion a fresh victory over the Dublin Working Class—over the Working Class of all Ireland. 'The trenches are safer than the Dublin slums.' We may yet see the day that the trenches will be safer for these gentry than any part of Dublin.

Parallel to, and interacting with, these specifically political developments had been a profoundly rich Gaelic revival in the early-twentieth century. Though it was most noted for its literary lights— this was the period of Yeats, Joyce, O'Casey, Lady Gregory, Synge and others—many other sectors of Irish cultural life were similarly affected. The Gaelic Athletic Association set about creating 'ancient' Irish sports like hurling, in place of English ones like football. This provided remote sections of the countryside with their first taste of nationalist ideology. And, in the urban areas, the Gaelic League actively encouraged the speaking of Irish, by then (and in contrast to Welsh) almost a forgotten language.

A very small group of the most militant nationalists had by this time concluded that independence would come about only through the use of violence. When it was evident that England would be imbroiled in a continental war, this group conceived a plan for an armed insurrection to occur in Dublin. The Easter Rising of 1916 was a peculiar event in that it was, in the eyes of many of its participants, doomed to failure. The worst of their predictions came to pass; many of the leaders were captured, including James Connolly, and put to death. Nevertheless, in the long run the Rising probably served to legitimate the violent tactics of the Irish Republican Army in its struggle with the government and the troops of the Royal Irish Constabulary. The IRA continued to develop into an effective guerilla force with mass support, and by 1921 London estimated that the cost of pacifying Ireland would be excessive. Thereafter negotiation between the parties led to the Partition settlement.

What then seems to account best for the secession of the twenty-six counties of southern Ireland? In general terms the following argument may be proposed. Increasingly difficult working conditions, in part due to fluctuations in prices and wages in the late nineteenth and early twentieth century, led to a heightening of class consciousness among all industrial workers in the United Kingdom. Class consciousness arose as a consequence of the declining importance of stratification within the early labor movement, particularly the gradual erosion of the social distinction between skilled workers and unskilled, or general laborers. The organizational structure of trade unions shifted from the craft association, which was typically concerned with a local or regional labor market, to the militant, all-grade industrial union, which attempted to bargain for many different kinds of workers spatially dispersed throughout the national economy. The establishment of a labor-oriented political party linked to the Trades Union Congress gave a financial base to working-class candidates for national political office enabling them to compete effectively with Liberals and Tories alike at general elections. In the period between 1910 and 1924 the Labor Party gained substantial support from industrial workers in England, Wales, and Scotland primarily (see Table 9.4). Since the political (and financial)

TABLE 9.4   *The association between manufacturing occupations and Labor Party support, by region, 1885–1966**

	England	Wales	Scotland	N. Ireland	All regions
1885	0·030	0·016	0·008	0·000	0·015
1892	0·023	0·000	0·007	0·000	0·011
1900	0·034	0·131	0·000	0·000	0·022
1910	0·264	0·470	0·062	0·000	0·176
1924	0·463	0·576	0·687	0·161	0·609
1931	0·509	0·793	0·432	0·046	0·532
1951	0·463	0·556	0·291	0·332	0·392
1966	0·500	0·354	0·302	0·445	0·408

*Unstandardized regression coefficients.

base of the Labor Party was so closely tied to the trade unions, there were no attempts to seek electoral support in predominantly agricultural constituencies. Thus there was no strong appeal on behalf of Labor in Ireland. The development of class consciousness in the industrial areas of Wales and Scotland led ultimately to growing political differentiation between the enclaves, which came to support Labor, and the hinterlands, which remained—for want of an alternative—in the camp of the Liberal Party. A potential social base for nationalism, however, remained in both enclave and hinterland regions of the periphery. This is suggested by the evidence of the mean regional voting residuals. Welsh and Scottish counties continued to differ in voting behavior from structurally similar English counties. Thus the effect of enclave-hinterland differences was to divert potential nationalist sentiment into two segments, one part going to the Labor Party, the other part which was expressed through support of the Liberals. Neither of these organizations was ultimately committed to the national independence for Wales and Scotland, since the Celtic lands were the strongest bases of support for the Parliamentary ambitions of these national political parties. In effect, then, the Labor Party contributed to the continued incorporation of Wales and Scotland, while simultaneously campaigning on a platform of regional devolution. In this sense Labor served to 'negatively integrate' the British Isles.[1]

There are four lessons which might be drawn from this case history. (1) The secession of Ireland was not in any ultimate sense due to the existence of prior cultural differences between England and Ireland. (2) Similarly, its secession was not fundamentally a result of the peculiar treatment afforded Ireland, e.g., its particular 'historical legacy,' relative to the other Celtic regions in the period 1642 to 1846. (3) Nor was it due to backward material conditions caused by Ireland's dependent development as an internal colony. It has already been remarked that Wales, Scotland, and Northern Ireland share many of these economic features with Ireland, and can also be conceivably regarded as internal colonies. (4) Irish secession is best explained, rather, by the particular mode of dependent development which emerged in Ireland during the period 1846–1921. This involved the evolution of a relatively capital-intensive agrarian regional economy which did not lead to substantial interregional organizational affiliations as occurred following the highly restricted industrial development of Wales and Scotland. What inhibited comparable Irish industrialization? Perhaps, in part, historical accident: Ireland did not have natural resources as useful in early industrial

---

[1] I borrow this useful term from Guenther Roth. In *The Social Democrats in Imperial Germany* (Totowa, N.J.; 1963), he illustrates how the working class in Germany became organizationally affiliated with the Social Democratic movement, thereby providing social integration, albeit on an anti-capitalist basis, in the German national society: 'The sub-culture was "negatively" integrated into the dominant system because by its very existence it provided an important means for the controlled expression and dissipation of conflict and thus contributed, for decades of peacetime, to the stability of the Empire,' p. 315. In this chapter it is argued that the Labor Party similarly served to integrate important sectors of the Celtic periphery, while ostensibly promoting the special interests of these regions and their peoples.

development as coal, which provided the major stimulus for the partial industrialization of both Wales and Scotland. However, the relative industrial development of Belfast suggests that this is, at best, an incomplete explanation.

Thus the lack of enclave-hinterland differences in southern Ireland permitted the development of a solidary and broad-based political party capable of effecting independence. The relatively moderate development of an industrial enclave in Northern Ireland, coupled with the special political cleavages characteristic of settler colonies, helps account for the high level of regional autonomy which has existed there since 1921, despite its cultural affinities to England.

THE INTER-WAR YEARS: SOLIDIFICATION OF CLASS-BASED VOTING

Popular support for Welsh and Scottish nationalism virtually disappeared in the period 1921 to 1964. Electoral statistics show that class-based voting increased sharply in both regions. While the Disestablishment of the Anglican church in Wales (1920) temporarily alleviated anti-English sentiment in that region, this event should not be regarded as having lasting importance for the political integration of Wales.

At the end of World War One the regional economies of Wales, Scotland, and Northern Ireland—along with several older industrial areas of England—were plunged into depression. Nineteenth-century British prosperity and economic growth had been primarily based on exports of textiles, iron, steel, ships, and coal, mostly to industrializing countries. As the first industrial society, Britain initially had no competitors in the international economy. By the 1920s however, the British industrial plant, once revolutionary, had become obsolescent.[1] Coal resources had been seriously depleted. More recently industrialized states began underselling British exports in world markets. All of the by then 'traditional' export industries underwent secular decline. Since these industries, except textiles, were disproportionately located in the enclaves of Wales, Scotland, and, to a lesser extent Northern Ireland, unemployment quickly soared in these areas. The world wide depression of 1929 only served to intensify the state of depression in the Celtic periphery. For

[1] D. H. Aldcroft, ed., *The Development of British Industry and Foreign Competition, 1875–1914* (Toronto: 1968), contains several studies on this general theme.

example, by January, 1933, 72 per cent were out of work at the Scottish port of Stornoway, 60 per cent at Wishaw, and 43 per cent at Clydebank. In Wales, 82 per cent were unemployed at Taff Wells, 72 per cent at Pontycymmer, 68 per cent at Merthyr and 66 per cent at Abertillery.[1] Throughout the period Wales, Scotland, and Northern Ireland had markedly the highest levels of unemployment of all British regions, on the average ranging between 20 and 30 per cent of the respective regional labor forces.

The Board of Inland Revenue did not publish income statistics by region or county during this period and, therefore, indicators of relative county wealth are unavailable. One attempt to measure the change in Scottish national income relative to that of the United Kingdom as a whole shows that the Scottish income *per capita* decreases from about 96 per cent of the United Kingdom average in 1924 to 87 per cent in 1932–5, then increases to about 95 per cent by World War Two.[2] No comparable figures are available for Wales and Northern Ireland.

Table 9.5 shows that Wales and Northern Ireland continued to

TABLE 9.5 *The level of peripheral sectionalism in regions, 1885–1966* [*England =0*]*

Region	1885	1892	1900	1910	1924	1931	1951	1966
Wales	−4	−16	−30	−26	−28	−27	−16	−15
Scotland	−11	−6	−11	−12	−8	−4	+2	−2
Northern Ireland	4	7	13	15	31	23	11	12

* Source: Figure 7.1.

have high levels of peripheral sectionalism in this period, while Scotland appears to become more politically integrated over time. While peripheral sectionalism indicates a potential basis for nationalist support, the evidence shows that the bulk of votes continued to be split between the Labor and Liberal parties. If anything, as Tables 9.1 and 9.2 demonstrate, the 1931 election resulted in the highest enclave-hinterland political differences of any of the eight elections sampled. Not surprisingly, class-based support for the Labor Party also reached its apex in 1931, save in Scotland. If this is regarded as a crude indicator of the level of class conscious voting behavior,

[1] Gavin McCrone, *Regional Policy in Britain* (London: 1969), p. 91.
[2] A. D. Campbell, 'Changes in Scottish incomes, 1924–49,' *Economic Journal*, 62, 2 (1955), pp. 225–40.

Table 9.4 suggests that there were dramatic increases in class consciousness which occurred during the depression in England, Wales, and Scotland (but significantly not in Northern Ireland, which only begins to show class voting in 1951), though it appears that it was highest in Wales. This may be a reflection of the organizational effectiveness of the South Wales Miners Federation, which was the most left-wing branch of the British miners federation—itself the most radical of all the large national unions.

The labor conditions of the mining valleys had been steadily deteriorating. Much of the time those who were not unemployed were out on strike. But the British labor movement had gained much solidarity both at local and national levels since the end of the war. The so-called 'General Strike' called in support of coal workers in 1926 gives impressive evidence of the effectiveness of national organization in the labor movement. In this action workers in four other unions—railway and transport workers, iron and steel workers, builders, and printers—went off their jobs all over Britain along with the coal miners. The full extent of national labor solidarity was largely unanticipated: 'There can be no doubt that the completeness of the stoppage astonished, not only the government, but scarcely less the strike leaders themselves.'[1] Working-class antagonism to the Conservative-dominated government was stimulated further, all over Britain, when in 1932 a means test was required in order to receive unemployment benefits.

In consequence, the industrial enclaves of Wales and Scotland were centers of radical politics, both Parliamentary and extra-Parliamentary:[2]

What was unique and significant about the mid-1930s in the South Wales coalfield was the emergence of 'extra-Parliamentary' popular protest movements. These became steadily more coherent, unified, and politically oriented by 1935–6, and ultimately were harnessed in many spheres to the Communist readiness to participate in social disturbances. Having lost their economic power, they reverted to seemingly pre-industrial tactics of 'collective bargaining by riot.' These were not merely reflex actions against the prevailing conditions. There were disturbances at Mardy Bedwas (1933) and Bedlinog (1935) against company unionism; at Merthyr (1934), Abertillery, Nantyglo, and Blaina (1935) against the Means Test; at Ammanford (1935) during a transport dispute; and at Tonypandy (1935) against fascism.

---

[1] Cole, *op. cit.*, pp. 418–22.
[2] Hywel Francis, 'Welsh miners and the Spanish Civil War,' *Journal of Contemporary History*, 5, 3 (1970), p. 178.

The only long-term Communist Member of Parliament, William Gallacher, was a Scot regularly elected from west Fife. Much of the leadership of the CPGB was Scottish and Welsh. Similarly, the CPGB made strong inroads in small communities all over south Wales, and gained particular influence in the miners federation. It is important to understand that this radicalism was, however, expressly internationalist in ideology. This can be demonstrated by the following example. There were one hundred and seventy Welsh volunteers to the International Brigade during the Spanish Civil War, most of them associated with mining occupations. The SWMF, in its propaganda, equated strike-breaking in Britain with German and Italian support of the Fascist forces in Spain.[1]

Table 9.6 indicates that the Welsh voting patterns in 1924 and 1931 are about equally anti-Conservative in both the enclave and hinterland. The Scottish means are much closer to the English norm. After the war, rural Wales underwent significant changes.[2] During the post-war price inflation many of the Welsh gentry sold off their large estates in parcels to their tenants. By and large this marked the end of the anglophile Welsh gentry as a dominant social group in the hinterland. But the newly won ownership of land was not entirely in the interests of the farmers. Although they were relieved of the various indignities they had suffered at the hands of land agents and gamekeepers, they bought their land at inflated prices. This required, in most instances, heavy mortgages. Hence the real landlords of the Welsh hinterland were English banks. Further economic difficulties, for both the Welsh and Scottish hinterlands, were caused by the 1921 repeal of the Corn Production Act, which had guaranteed British producers artificially high prices for cereals.

In another sense, however, the disproportionate economic burden of the Celtic periphery in the depression was not conducive to popular support for schemes of Home Rule. The demise of the Welsh and Scottish economies and the high unemployment which reflected it led to greater dependence on England for financial support. This was true not only at the organizational level—where various local branches of national organizations such as labor unions might have required aid from the central bureaus—but also at the level of the individual. Unemployment benefits, no matter how meager, came ultimately from the connection with England. Programs of regional

---

[1] *Ibid.*
[2] David Williams, *A History of Modern Wales* (London: 1969), p. 286.

TABLE 9.6 *The level of peripheral sectionalism in enclave and hinterland areas, within regions**

	1885	1892	1900	1910	1924	1931	1951	1966
Industrial counties in								
England	+6 (6)	+1 (8)	+1 (10)	+1 (13)	+1 (12)	+2 (10)	-2 (16)	+1 (16)
Wales	-16 (2)	-10 (2)	-3 (2)	-17 (2)	-18 (2)	-30 (2)	-9 (2)	-9 (2)
Scotland	-19 (7)	-3 (6)	+4 (9)	-6 (6)	-6 (8)	+4 (6)	0 (8)	-7 (8)
Northern Ireland	—	—	—	—	—	—	—	+19 (1)
All regions	-2 (15)	-2 (16)	+2 (21)	-3 (22)	-3 (22)	-1 (18)	-2 (26)	-2 (27)
Non-industrial counties in								
England	+4 (34)	+5 (52)	+10 (30)	+10 (27)	+7 (28)	+4 (30)	+2 (24)	+3 (24)
Wales	+3 (11)	-13 (11)	-26 (11)	-19 (11)	-24 (11)	-21 (11)	-16 (11)	-13 (11)
Scotland	-8 (26)	-2 (27)	-6 (24)	-5 (26)	-3 (25)	-2 (27)	+4 (25)	+3 (25)
Northern Ireland	+8 (6)	+11 (6)	+21 (6)	+22 (6)	+36 (6)	+27 (6)	+12 (6)	+13 (5)
All regions	0 (77)	0 (76)	0 (71)	1 (70)	1 (70)	0 (74)	1 (66)	1 (65)

* Source: Table 7.5.

development—such as the Special Areas Act of 1934[1]—which were clearly necessary to alter the vicious circle of poverty, unemployment, and declining industry could come only from continued association with England. The fact that the Celtic economies were in a collapsed state meant that separation from England could not be easily countenanced.

Even so, during this period a Scottish literary revival was spearheaded by both serious and popular writers. 'The Scottish newspapers, the reviews, the little magazines, became the equivalent of the Czech drawingrooms before 1848 and of the literary salons for Young Ireland in the 1830s.'[2] Much of the popularity of contemporary Scottish nationalism derives from this historical source. It is of note that the Scottish National Party was formed in 1934, but that it attained minimal support for a platform of federal devolution. Similarly, Plaid Cymru (The Party of Wales), the Welsh Nationalist political party, was established in 1925, but foundered until the 1960s.

The onset of World War Two marked the nadir of nationalist political activity in Wales and Scotland. In 1937 the SNP drafted a resolution to the effect that[3]

the Scottish National Party is strongly opposed to the manpower of Scotland being used to defend an Empire in the government of which she has no voice, and all male members of the Scottish National Party of military age hereby pledge themselves to refuse to serve with any section of the Crown Forces until the programme of the Scottish National Party has been fulfilled.

But when the war came the great majority of SNP members ignored these sentiments and supported the war. To some extent the war stimulated those heavy industries in Wales and Scotland which had flagged for twenty years: new ships had to be built; new guns and munitions produced; steel production and coal consumption increased. This prosperity lasted, however, only as long as the war and the demand it created. Given a choice of domination by Nazi Germany or Westminster, most of the British Celts unhesitatingly chose the latter. In contrast Eire remained formally neutral during the war.

THE PARADOX OF CELTIC RESURGENCE

Since the middle 1960s the electoral strength of the two nationalist political parties, the SNP and Plaid Cymru, has taken a sharp

[1] See McCrone, *op. cit.*, pp. 91–105.
[2] Hanham, *op. cit.*, p. 148.　　　　　　　　　　　　[3] *Ibid.*

upturn in both national and local contests.[1] Both regional parties won unexpected seats in Parliament as a consequence of by-election victories over candidates from the national parties. Substantial gains in county and municipal elections followed these Parliamentary successes. Party membership increased markedly. Celtic nationalism showed every sign of becoming a factor to be reckoned with in British politics. While the 1970 General Election did not result in further Parliamentary representation for the nationalists, the meaning of the poll may be ambiguous with respect to nationalist sentiment in the Celtic periphery. Both by-election seats were lost; however, the SNP picked up another in the remote Western Isles constituency. The SNP and Plaid Cymru contested a far greater number of seats than ever before. In consequence, their percentage of the total vote increased substantially. Thus while there were no spectacular triumphs which might herald increasing nationalist momentum, the results could none the less be seen as evidence of some gain for the nationalist forces.

This recent trend towards a resurgence of Celtic nationalism is in some respects paradoxical when considered in conjunction with evidence from the voting residual data. Table 9.5 demonstrates that the degree of peripheral sectionalism in Wales and Northern Ireland in 1966 is as high as it was in 1892. Clearly, regionalism has persisted in peripheral politics from 1892 to 1966. To reiterate, these mean regional voting residuals indicating peripheral sectionalim are a parameter of structurally unexplained county voting patterns. Differences between such regional means indicate a dissimilarity of political contexts in so far as the relationship between social structural factors and conservative voting is concerned. A high positive or negative mean residual is evidence of a political context characterized by status group rather than class solidarity. At this point no attempt will be made to specify the basis of this type of political solidarity. That is, for the moment it does not matter whether this difference in regional voting patterns is associated with, or perhaps caused by, relative poverty or cultural distinctiveness, to give but two possible examples. What is important is that these differences may be demonstrated to exist, whatever their basis.

In order to describe the Celtic counties as being political contexts definitely different from English counties, it must be demonstrated that the differences between these mean residuals are statistically

---

[1] For the most general recent developments, see the articles on Wales and Scotland in O. D. Edwards, et al., *Celtic Nationalism* (London: 1968).

significant, and not merely the result of random error. Table 9.7 summarizes the results of a test based on one-way analysis of variance for statistical significance between the individual means. The null hypothesis is that the differences between these populations with respect to structurally-explained voting is zero. Hence, if the null hypothesis cannot be rejected it is likely that the populations have political contexts which are essentially homogeneous. The results indicate that the Welsh mean is significantly different at the level of 0·05 or greater from the mean for England at each of the seven elections examined from 1891 to 1966. While the absolute difference between Welsh and English voting residuals declines following the 1931 election, nevertheless as late as 1966 differences in the level of peripheral sectionalism remain significantly large.

The trend in Scotland is clearly towards convergence with English voting patterns, and by 1931 the difference between means has become insignificant. Northern Ireland presents virtually a mirror image to the Scottish trend. Whereas the hypothesis of contextual similarity to England cannot be rejected for elections from 1885 through 1910, in the period 1924 to 1966 Northern Ireland's political behavior differed from England's.

These data on statistically significant differences between national means provide a more precise interpretation of Table 9.5. It may be seen that there are really three separate trends in peripheral sectionalism occurring from 1885 to 1966. Wales has remained politically distinctive from England throughout the social and economic changes of the twentieth century, though this distinctiveness is less in 1966 than 1931. Scotland, by this measure, grew increasingly more politically integrated. And Northern Ireland became successively more differentiated from England with time.

The paradox of Celtic resurgence, then, is that it has occurred precisely during a period in which peripheral sectionalism has declined from its peak in 1924 and 1931: why do the nationalist parties suddenly gain strength in 1966? More fundamentally, why is there no apparent correlation between the measure of peripheral sectionalism and the level of support for the nationalist parties?

I suggest that part of the explanation is that there has been a profound shift in the legitimate rationale for regional autonomy, i.e., in the terms in which the demand for separation has been couched, which has occurred from the nineteenth to the mid-twentieth century. The demand for Celtic nationalism in the nineteenth century was largely expressed in cultural terms: it was to an extent

TABLE 9.7 *t-values* of differences between English and peripheral mean voting residuals

		1885	1892	1900	1910	1924	1931	1951	1966
Wales	t	1·00	3·41†	5·05‡	4·29‡	4·16‡	3·23‡	4·15‡	4·05‡
Scotland	t	3·64‡	1·90	2·49†	2·64‡	2·21†	0·70	0·82	0·63
Northern Ireland	t	0·72	0·94	1·62	1·81	4·01‡	2·09†	2·34†	2·30†

* The t-test for planned comparisons of differences between means is described by the following formula:

$$t = \frac{c_1(R_e) + c_2(R_p)}{\sqrt{\dfrac{\text{MS error} \sum \dfrac{c_j^2}{n_j}}{2}}}$$

where R_e = mean English Voting Residual
R_p = mean Peripheral Voting Residual
$c_1 = 1$
$c_2 = -1$
MS error = mean squared error
n = number of counties within groups, e and p
† Significant at 0·05 (2-tailed test)
‡ Significant at 0·01 (2-tailed test)

a romantic plea. In most of the multinational states on the continent movements arose to assert the rights of cultural minorities during this period. Many of these peripheral groups, like those in the Celtic fringe, were at that time substantially culturally differentiated from the dominant groups in these respective states. As industrialization proceeded much of this peripheral cultural distinctiveness, especially linguistic distinctiveness, began to be muted. However the sense of separate peripheral identity persisted on two accounts. In the first place, the initial penetration of the national economy into peripheral regions created a cultural division of labor. Individuals maintaining their adherence to the peripheral culture probably were clustered at the bottom of the stratification system in these regions. Furthermore, it is likely that this cultural division of labor has not significantly changed. In the second place, at an aggregate level, economic development in peripheral regions was retarded as a function of economic dependence. At some point peripheral élites decided that the only means of stimulating economic growth was to attract new investment and other resources to these disadvantaged regions. Their attempts to influence the central government to transfer such resources to peripheral regions tended to fall short of achieving full equality and the old nationalist solution once more appeared viable in some sectors. Thus the perception of regional economic distress brought a new salience to peripheral identity. The triumph of functional, class-based political orientations, in combination with continued depression in the Scottish and Welsh regional economies, has led not to a passive acceptance of integration in the United Kingdom on any terms, but rather has stimulated interest in national independence precisely on economic grounds.

In large part this development is the result of earlier promises of regional economic development by successive central governments, promises which have not been kept. The Conservatives, who were continuously in power from 1951 to 1964, had in the past advocated *laissez-faire* policies with regard to regional development in Scotland and Wales. But by the early 1960s the government sponsored several reports and development plans, particularly for Scotland:[1]

In Scotland a series of reports were produced which seemed to promise great things for the future. The Toothill *Report on the Scottish Economy* prepared for the Scottish Council (Development and Industry) in 1960–61 was published in 1962. The government White Paper *Central Scotland: a*

[1] Hanham, *op. cit.*, pp. 181–2.

Programme for Development and Growth was published in November 1963. And the great Forth Road Bridge started in 1958 was completed in 1964. But the outstanding feature of the period was the gap between the expectations of the people and what was actually happening. Led to expect prosperity, most Scots found instead that they were little better off, or that they were actually worse off. For although new industries were planned, or had actually been started, as was the case with the new Scottish motor industry, there was a time lag. Old industries were everywhere closing down—mining, shipping, iron and steel—but there was for many people no obvious replacement. Moreover, in many parts of the country the closure of railways amid the decay of small-scale agriculture were affecting the character of rural and small-town life.

The Conservatives might have raised expectations about Scottish prosperity, but even their failure to live up to these goals could not have seemed extraordinary. Of all the national parties, the Conservatives have found it least necessary to appeal to regional support in the Celtic periphery. As a consequence of its antipathy to national devolution, the Conservatives had long been resigned to the loss of most Welsh seats, and of many Scottish seats as well. Their continued electoral success was achieved mainly within England. Hence, it could be argued that these plans for regional economic development in the traditionally depressed areas of Britain were only half-hearted to begin with.

But the Celtic vote was a mainstay of Labor's social base. With the accelerated decline of the Liberal Party, Labor began actively contesting seats from hinterland constituencies in the Celtic periphery on the basis of ambitious plans for industrial relocation to spur economic growth. So long as Labor remained an opposition party, it could not be blamed for the continued regional depression. The argument that a Labor government would promote development in Wales and Scotland was plausible, and gained much support. After Labor took over the government in 1964 it became clear that its schemes for regional development[1] were insufficient to make much headway. In this situation the nationalist parties began to make greater impact as early as 1966. Their argument was a simple one. Neither the Conservatives nor the Laborites will solve the problems of Scotland and Wales because they are insufficiently committed to these areas. They are in essence English parties for the English electorate:[2]

---

[1] McCrone, *op. cit.*, pp. 120–48.
[2] *SNP and You: Aims and Policy of the Scottish National Party* (Edinburgh and Glasgow: 1968), pp. 4, 5.

The unionist parties talk and plan and talk some more, in office and out of office, but our needs are never met. Why? Because the Tory and Labour unionist parties who have had it in their power to act for Scotland are UK parties, and they will never deal with Scottish problems except in a manner which suits London's policies for England, which constitutes ninety per cent of the UK. . . . We have been deceived by the propaganda of Anglo-Scottish unionist parties and their mouthpieces for generations. Instead of asking us to put our own country first the Labour, Tory and Liberal parties divide Scotland against herself. These parties ask us Scots to give our prime loyalty to their outdated Anglo-Scottish sectional and class interests. Put Scotland First politically—vote SNP.

This reference to the deceitful appeal to Celtic voters in the past also may be found in a recent Plaid Cymru manifesto:[1]

Nothing displays the callousness of the Labour Party as much as its lack of concern for the coal and slate areas of Wales. It is on the backs of miners and quarrymen that the Labour Party came to power. Once in power, the welfare of these areas had no place in its governing priorities.

The theme of betrayal by the Labor party is frequent in the nationalist literature and propaganda. Repeatedly, the peripheral voter is urged to deny his traditional protest vote against the Conservatives to an English opposition party, and to affirm, instead, support of the nationalist party as the best means of satisfying his immediate interests:[2]

The Labour Party's attitude to a meaningful degree of legislative devolution in Scotland is a comment on that party's desertion of its radical origins. Before, and during, the Second World War the Labour Party supported home rule for Scotland. But after Labour's runaway victory at the end of the war, the matter was quietly dropped, probably for no better reason than that in party political terms Labour needs the Scottish vote. The ageing placemen who make up a majority of the Scottish Labour MPs are the natural product of the stultifying of a once genuinely radical and Scottish movement. The two-party system acts, and is bound to act, so as to cut across the interests of Scotland and to substitute political squabbling between right and left, which is the chief *raison d'être* of the English-based parties.

For the nationalist parties the issue is not so much one of 'capitalism' versus 'socialism' as it is economic development by any and all means. If socialism is necessary to bring such development about, well and good. H. J. Hanham's judgment that the SNP is unrealistically committed to everything 'except a frank acceptance of the modern state and of modern bureaucratized industrial, political,

[1] *Action for Wales* (Denbigh: n.d.), p. 17.
[2] *SNP and You*, p. 4.

304

trade union, and commercial empires'[1] is, I think, unusually severe. The nationalist parties are questioning the necessity of continual regional imbalance in the large nation-state. They are challenging the persistence of English domination of the British Isles from a basically decentralist position. Finally, they are openly committed to the building of more diversified economies within these relatively small areas. A 1970 plan for economic development in Wales sponsored by Plaid Cymru makes this last point explicitly:[2]

This plan has concentrated its attention on the provision of secure employment for all the people of Wales within about twenty miles of their homes. It has dealt mainly with manufacturing industry together with its ancillary services because we believe that it is by strengthening and diversifying the manufacturing sector that a strong economic base can be built.

This is in no way to decry the value of the primary industries—mining, quarrying, and agriculture—nor of the tertiary sector, the service industries and the tourist trade. It is merely to face the facts that these industries are unlikely to provide the large number of additional full-time jobs we need in Wales in the immediate future.

Only by concentrating on economic development as an immediate and urgent need can the distinctiveness of Welsh culture— to the extent it remains—be safe-guarded and preserved for future generations:[3]

We do not apologize in any way for concentrating our attention on the need to provide work for the people of Wales. Employment is fundamental to the very survival of the towns and communities of our country. Without employment, we have the familiar features of depopulation, the ageing of the residual population and the gradual decay of the fabric of that community. Without work we can neither maintain the social and cultural life of the towns and villages of Wales, nor can we provide the level of services and investment which can make Wales a better place for our children.

Thus both the SNP and Plaid Cymru devote much attention to complaints about continual unemployment; the 'forced migration' from the periphery to alien lands; worsening industrial squalor; and the decay of the agricultural sector. Both parties maintain that, contrary to the views of Labor Party economists, net contributions to Westminster tax rolls from Scotland and Wales exceed government transfers to these regions. Hence, Scotland and Wales are

---

[1] Hanham, *op. cit.*, p. 175.
[2] Plaid Cymru Research Group, *An Economic Plan for Wales* (Cardiff: 1970), mimeographed, p. 284.
[3] *Ibid.*, p. 286.

portrayed as actually subsidizing, to an extent, the governance of England. Further, there have been repeated objections to various United Kingdom foreign policies on the grounds that they do not reflect the interests of Scotland and/or of Wales. Much of the taxation siphoned into the British defense forces, it is argued, could be better spent on health and welfare services. Similarly, Scotland and Wales could be exempted from unpopular foreign policy decisions made in Westminster such as support for the United States role in the war in Indochina, or aid to the Federal Nigerian government in its conflict with secessionist Biafra. Finally, an independent Wales and Scotland could resist inclusion into the European Common Market, while if the regions were to remain incorporated such decisions would be made according to different interests.

The nub of the argument has therefore come around to the position that self-determination is the only means to realize economic development and diversification in the peripheral regions. The authors of the Plaid Cymru economic plan for Wales, who incidentally point out that theirs is the first such plan to be written in the history of Wales, emphasize the point:[1]

It can be argued that much of this plan could be put into operation without the full self-government which we in Plaid Cymru envisage for Wales. Perhaps this is so; but if this is the case, it is strange that successive London Governments, whatever their colour, have failed completely to not only implement but even to plan a coherent economic strategy for Wales. At no time has this been borne out more emphatically than during the period of office of this Labour Government [1964–70], when the need in Wales has been so apparent, and Welshmen of ability and influence so numerous in the corridors of power.

We believe that self-government is a prerequisite to Welsh economic growth, not because Welshmen are any more able than Englishmen or Scotsmen in these matters, but because only a government serving Wales and Wales alone can give the unqualified commitment and unwavering attention to the problems of Wales that is necessary to solve our problems.

Edward Nevin, an economist who has initiated pioneering studies of the regional economy of Wales, states the problem more metaphorically, 'the Welsh economy is drifting not because the crew are fast asleep, but because the boat has no engine and the navigator no map. The Welsh economy is drifting because no one knows where it

---

[1] Plaid Cymru Research Group, *An Economic Plan for Wales* (Cardiff: 1970), mimeographed, p. 286. This bears a striking resemblance to James Connolly's sentiments as expressed in note 2, p. 287.

is, or should be going.'[1] Similarly, an SNP economist echoes these sentiments:[2]

Self-government is good, not just because it may lead to greater efficiency in running the Scottish economy: self-government is good as an end in itself because it means that people are learning by doing. This means that, if we take the responsibility for running our own affairs, then we as producers are likely to benefit from this responsibility, because in exercising it we make ourselves more efficient and become better able to do the job. I think that few people would disagree with this idea of the value of running one's own affairs. . . . A further advantage of political independence from the economic point of view is the fact that it would give us the instruments of control of our economy. For a long time now we have had inflicted on us various policies such as taxation of employment in services, and periodic restrictions on bank lending which, however appropriate they may have been for the south-east of England, have certainly never been appropriate for the Scottish economy. They have simply accelerated the trends in emigration and unemployment. In fact, the medicine which has been applied to the Scottish economy, so far from effecting a cure, has actually made the patient worse. . . . It seems that only the achievement of political independence will bring about a situation in which measures appropriate to the needs of the Scottish economy—that is the need for more jobs and not fewer jobs, for more investment and not less investment—will be satisfied by Scottish economic policies which are relevant to the Scottish economy.

Much of the nationalist literature attempts to convince peripheral voters that small states such as Wales or Scotland can be economically viable societies. They point to Norway, Denmark, and Switzerland as examples. The Labor Party, which has felt most threatened by the revitalization of Celtic nationalism of the national parties, has countered these arguments by insisting that peripheral development could best be achieved through an increased allocation of resources from the central government to these depressed areas.[3] It is not necessary to go into the economic details of this question: a serious lack of relevant data will prevent an adequate analysis of the problem for some time.

The fact that there is no strong appeal to the separate cultural identity of Scotland in the program of the SNP has important consequences for the party's social base. It should be noted that

[1] *Ibid.*, p. 288.

[2] David Simpson, 'Independence: the economic issues' in Neil MacCormick, ed., *The Scottish Debate: Essays on Scottish Nationalism* (London: 1970), pp. 121–31.

[3] For the Labor Party view see Gavin McCrone, *Scotland's Future: The Economics of Nationalism* (Oxford: 1969). David Simpson has written a rebuttal for the SNP: *Scottish Independence: An Economic Analysis* (West Calder: 1969).

Plaid Cymru, though it too gives major emphasis in its platform to economic development, insists, however, on the maintenance of Welsh cultural distinctiveness by such policies as the advocacy of a bilingual state. If the sole criterion for the need for political independence is to be measured by statistics such as regional GDP or GNP; if input-output tables are the likely battlefield determining incorporation or secession, it is clear that any reasonably successful economic policy for Scotland will do away with the major rationale for national independence. The SNP tacitly admits the cultural indistinguishability of Scotland from England by resorting to this justification for national independence. Scottish nationalism therefore makes itself available for co-optation with appropriate ceremony and rewards. The SNP is, in this sense, anything but a revolutionary party.

This is of importance in considering the future of Celtic nationalism. The hypothesis that support for the nationalist parties could be interpreted as a kind of populist discontent with encroaching modernization among the politically isolated self-employed does not appear to hold.[1] The success of the SNP and Plaid Cymru in the late 1960s was, on the contrary, concentrated in largely industrial constituencies. The by-election victories occurred at Hamilton in industrial Lanarkshire, and Carmarthenshire, one of the more industrialized Welsh counties, and not in the hinterland regions. Furthermore, some recent, if skimpy, survey data suggest that the highest occupational support for the SNP has come from skilled and unskilled manual laborers, rather than from the self-employed petit bourgeoisie.[2] The voters of Hamilton and Carmarthen seemed to be demonstrating that the Parliamentary seats of the industrial enclaves could no longer be automatically presumed to be safely in the Labor camp. The reasons for the waning of attachments to Labor are evident from this description of the Hamilton constituency:[3]

Hamilton is in many ways typical of central Scotland. Once the seat of the Duke of Hamilton and still the judicial centre for much of Lanarkshire,

[1] See. J. Kellas, 'Scottish nationalism' in D. Butler and M. Pinto-Duschinsky, eds, *The British General Election of 1970* (London: 1971), p. 450.

[2] J. M. Bochel and D. T. Denver, 'The decline of the SNP—an alternative view,' *Political Studies*, 20, 3 (September, 1972) pp. 311–16. Richard W. Mansbach, 'The Scottish National Party: a revised political portrait,' *Comparative Politics*, 5, 2 (1973) shows, however, that the SNP is growing fastest in non-industrial areas of Scotland. The party also seems to have different social bases in different Scottish regions. For a study of the leadership of the SNP see John E. Schwarz, 'The Scottish National Party: nonviolent separatism and theories of violence,' *World Politics*, 27, 4, (1970).   [3] Hanham, *op. cit.*, p. 186.

it was long the centre of a coal-mining district and just across the valley from it lie the great steel mills of Motherwell. But Lanarkshire is no longer what it was. By the time of the by-election all mining had ceased. The town of Hamilton was being modernized. There was a regular electric train service to Glasgow, and since the by-election a new motorway on the edge of the constituency has formed a fast new road-link with Glasgow and other neighboring industrial towns. Hamilton is being slowly sucked into the new industrial system of greater Glasgow. Meanwhile, it is an area which is visibly in course of transition from the nineteenth century cottage life of the coalfield to the twentieth century life of the working-class suburbia. Inevitably the old loyalties are slackening. The claim of the miners to dominate the constituency Labour party no longer makes economic sense. And the old mining communities no longer vote Labour as a matter of course now that their mines have closed. Hamilton is still the sort of place that requires a jolt before it will cease to vote Labour as a matter of course, . . . but it is no longer the sort of place it was in the old days.

The gradual extinction of the initial industrial base of the peripheral enclaves, the closing down of the Welsh and Scottish coal mines, the decay of shipbuilding on the Clyde, has lessened the ties of the electorate to industrial trade unions, and simultaneously to the Labor Party. The years of depression in Scotland and Wales have begun to erode the strong class-conscious links of the peripheral working class to national institutions (Table 9.4). The failure of these traditional industries leaves the votes of the originally displaced workers and succeeding generations open for the competition of other political parties. Labor can no longer be counted on to protect their jobs, because, in large measure, traditional employment in heavy industries has gradually disappeared. To the extent that alternative employment is made available in the service sector of the economy, or in white collar occupations, Labor will stand to suffer further, unless its image and appeal to the electorate can be correspondingly changed. The SNP, in its present tack, can only hope for electoral support on the issue of the Scottish economy and its future prospects. If the economic situation does not substantially improve, and it appears unlikely to change in the near future, the SNP may continue to gain strength. But any other political party which succeeds in aiding Scottish development will be rewarded handsomely at the polls. While similar issues have been raised by Plaid Cymru in Wales, there the nationalist movement is more closely identified with the cultural traditions of the Principality. This is undoubtedly because a sizable minority of the population continues to be Welsh-speaking. Plaid Cymru is committed to the survival of Welsh culture and language, and sees economic development as the best means by which to accomplish this end. The SNP really cannot take a similar position because it is difficult to make the case that Scotland is a single 'nation.' For centuries Scotland has contained three separate cultural groups, Celts in the Highlands, Norwegians in the northern counties, and English-speaking groups in the Lowlands and Border counties; hence the SNP shies away from the designation of Scotland as a Celtic land. Since Plaid Cymru's platform is based upon both economic and cultural demands, it is likely to be a somewhat more resilient political party.[1]

The most recent crystallization of Celtic nationalism may ultimately be understood as a trenchant critique of the principle of bureaucratic centralism. This principle has increasingly come under attack in organizations varying in size from universities to entire states. Dissatisfaction in such organized systems tends to arise when the distribution of resources among socially heterogeneous groups is made according to criteria which are held to be universalistic. However the specific symbols upon which the definition of group boundaries is made are always subject to change. Group consciousness among the Welsh and Scottish in the nineteenth century arose around cultural symbols which differentiated these regions from England; whereas in the twentieth century such consciousness has been stimulated by an awareness of persisting regional underdevelopment. Bureaucratic administration seldom seems to enable less advantaged groups to achieve resources equal to those of dominant groups. Hence disadvantaged groups are likely to demand that decision-making be 'localized' so that their special problems might become appreciated and therefore taken into account in the allocation process. The extent to which these types of popular political pressures can succeed in limiting or transforming central bureaucratic power is one of the most significant themes for future sociological research.

[1] This chapter was written before the discovery of substantial deposits of oil in Scottish coastal water. This unanticipated stroke of good fortune conceivably might give new strength to the SNP, which can now argue that the revenues from these new resources need not be shared with England.

CHAPTER 10

THE POLITICAL ECONOMY OF ETHNIC CHANGE

The term 'ethnic' is one of the vaguest known to sociology. We use it here merely to designate a state of fact, going in no sense into the question of explaining the fact.

VILFREDO PARETO

THE social origins of ethnic solidarity and change have remained obscure since Pareto's day. This obscurity derives partly from conceptual, and partly from empirical considerations. In the first place, there is no standard definition of ethnicity, let alone much agreement on its explanation. In the second place, there is a serious lack of evidence about changes in the ethnic solidarity of particular groups over time. This chapter will make a preliminary attempt to elucidate the process of ethnic change. To this end, it offers a definition of ethnicity, presents two simple theories of ethnic change, and, finally, evaluates these theories in the light of historical data on the relationship between England and the Celtic fringe.

ETHNICITY AND CULTURE: PROBLEMS OF DEFINITION

Social scientists have often been content to consider ethnicity less as a phenomenon to be explained than as a given, a defining attribute of particular social groups.[1] Every society has observable customs, styles of life, and institutions—in short, a distinctive set of cultural forms—through which meanings are ascribed, goals are enumerated, and social life is regulated. The totality of these cultural forms is often considered to make up the 'ethnicity' of a particular group. In this conception, ethnicity becomes indistinguishable from culture.

[1] Two exceptions which prove this rule are Frank W. Young, 'Reactive subsystems,' *American Sociological Review*, 35, 2 (1970), and Edward H. Spicer, 'Persistent cultural systems,' *Science*, 174 (1971), pp. 795–800. Neither writer, however, attempts an empirical investigation of these issues.

These specific cultural forms are conceived to have their origins in unique historical circumstances. Ecological conditions, patterns of migration and conquest, relations of various types with other groups, and variations in systems of production are all potentially responsible for the development of distinctive ethnicity. Therefore, in one part of Europe large numbers of people became either 'French,' 'German,' or 'English.' To the extent that in-group interactions predominate in a society, its specific cultural forms will largely be maintained. Since most Englishmen interact with other Englishmen, rather than Kurds, or even Frenchmen, English culture persists.

However, it is likely that all the individuals observed to practice a particular set of cultural forms do not identify to the same degree with others who may share those practices. Hence, the tendency to conflate the terms culture and ethnicity should be resisted. Let culture refer to a set of observable behaviors which occur independent of a group's relationship to the means of production and exchange. Thus variables describing religious affiliation or linguistic behavior may be considered to be cultural variables. On the other hand, let ethnicity refer to the sentiments which bind individuals into solidary groups on some cultural basis. Ethnicity therefore alludes to the quality of relations existing between individuals sharing certain cultural behaviors.

This distinction has an important methodological consequence: cultural variables, as I have defined them, cannot be used to indicate the strength of ethnic solidarity within groups. Thus, changes in a group's cultural practices have no necessary bearing on changes in the extent of its ethnic solidarity. The study of ethnic change does not, therefore, rely upon evidence concerning cultural change. It is, however, a much easier task to generate data on the latter process than it is on the former.

TWO THEORIES OF ETHNIC CHANGE

Due to the paucity of existing systematic evidence, there is some theoretical argument surrounding the explanation of ethnic change. Two very different approaches may be distinguished. A functionalist theory, which is incorporated in the diffusion model of national development, suggests that ethnic solidarity should wane among groups having long experience in the industrial setting. In contrast, a reactive theory, which forms a key element of the internal colonial model, suggests that ethnic solidarity is likely to persist in industrial society given the existence of a cultural division of labor.

312

According to the functional theory, ethnic identification is considered a primordial sentiment,[1] emanating in relatively undifferentiated social settings. Grounded in the structures of the *Gemeinschaft*, ethnic ties are, therefore, seen to be threatened by the process of structural differentiation. To a greater or lesser degree, these essentially parochial ties should be superseded by attachments of more universalistic scope. Because of this tendency, ethnicity should come to lose much of its salience in the system of stratification and in the determination of political behavior—barring, of course, the entry of new ethnic groups into society through conquest or voluntary immigration. The allocation of roles and resources in society becomes increasingly universalistic, at least in so far as cultural criteria are concerned.[2] Political associations come to be formed by individuals of similar market situation, rather than cultural commonality, acting in concert.

Although these expectations were held by nearly all the classical theorists, perhaps the clearest statement of this theory of ethnic change was made by Max Weber. Weber described the process as involving a shift from affinity on the basis of status groups (*Stände*) to affinity on the basis of classes.[3] The decline of status group solidarity is assumed to occur for various structural reasons: the modern economic system requires a public order which functions promptly and predictably; the expansion of markets favors the monopolization of all legitimate coercive power by the state; and the interests of classes tend to diverge more sharply as industrialization proceeds.[4]

[1] This term was first used by Edward Shils, 'Primordial, personal, sacred and civil ties,' *British Journal of Sociology*, 8, 2 (1957). Shils's use of the term primordial sentiment is closely parallel to the concept of ʿaṣabîyah employed by Ibn Khaldûn in the fourteenth century: '[Respect for] blood ties is something natural among men, with the rarest exceptions. It leads to affection for one's relations and blood relatives, [the feeling that] no harm ought to befall them nor any destruction come upon them.' (Ibn Khaldûn, *The Muqaddmah: An introduction to History* (Princeton: 1967), p. 264).

While Shils feels that such sentiments are strongest in the *Gemeinschaft*, he assumes them to be highly salient in the *Gesellschaft* as well. Hence, for Shils, primordial sentiments are functionally necessary at all levels of societal development. This position is somewhat less evolutionary than that taken by Geertz in 'The Integrative Revolution: Primordial Sentiments and Civil Politics in the New States' in C. Geertz, ed., *Old Societies and New States* (New York: 1963), despite his adoption of similar terminology.

[2] Talcott Parsons, *Societies: Evolutionary and Comparative Perspectives* (Englewood Cliffs, N.J.: 1966), pp. 22–3.

[3] Max Weber, *Economy and Society*, ed. by Guenther Roth and Claus Wittich (New York: 1968), pp. 927–36.

[4] *Ibid.*, pp. 336–7.

As a consequence of these trends, tradition-determined relationships disintegrate, along with the belief in their sacredness. All told, the influence of the market should gain relative to that of cultural distinctions in social interactions of all kinds.

This hypothesis was stated more explicitly by Ferdinand Tönnies;[1] his treatment was subsequently elaborated in Talcott Parsons's conception of the pattern variables.[2] In this highly generalized form, it was brought into the heart of functionalist sociological theory. Other sociologists, T. H. Marshall[3] and S. M. Lipset[4] among them, adapted elements of this theory to the study of political change in developed societies. And Clifford Geertz extended the theory to account for the prevalence of ethnic cleavages in less developed societies.[5]

However, the resurgence of ethnic political conflict in the most highly differentiated societies appears to challenge the generality of the functionalist theory. It is becoming evident that this is a most inadequate account of ethnic identification and change, at least among cultural minorities in developed societies. Among many such minorities, ethnicity must be maintained in the face of considerable pressure for assimilation which arises from dominant cultural groups. Far from being threatened by the intensification of intergroup contact, ethnicity is sometimes created, and at other times strengthened, as a consequence of interaction. Political movements arise to champion minority languages; cultural revivals, such as has occurred in Ireland, emerge to legitimate new cultural forms in the guise of old ones. In the functionalist theory, ethnicity is considered to be a relatively passive element in social life, a set of values and predispositions acquired during socialization. But among some cultural minorities, ethnic solidarity appears to be maintained as a result of much effort at organization. In this sense, ethnic solidarity might have a good deal in common with the phenomenon of political mobilization.

The reactive theory of ethnic change suggests that ethnicity arises from the salience of cultural distinctions in the system of stratification. When individuals are assigned to specific types of occupations

---

[1] Ferdinand Tönnies, *Gemeinschaft and Gesellschaft* (East Lansing: 1957).

[2] Talcott Parsons, *The Social System* (New York: 1953).

[3] T. H. Marshall, *Class, Citizenship and Social Development* (New York: 1964), pp. 135–57.

[4] S. M. Lipset and Stein Rokkan, 'Cleavage Structures, Party Systems, and Voter Alignments: An Introduction' in S. M. Lipset and S. Rokkan, eds, *Party Systems and Voter Alignments* (New York: 1967).

[5] Clifford Geertz, *op cit*.

and other social roles on the basis of observable cultural traits, or markers, this may be appropriately termed a cultural division of labor. Further in contradiction to functionalist assumptions, the reactive theory postulates that the cultural division of labor may exist regardless of the level of structural differentiation in the society.

Here, then, are two very simple theories purporting to explain variations in ethnic solidarity among groups. Their predictions differ markedly. The functionalist theory emphasizes structural differentiation as the principal cause of declining ethnic solidarity. Differentiation should also mute the importance of cultural distinctions in the system of stratification. On the other hand, the reactive theory of ethnic change suggests that ethnic solidarity arises from the cultural division of labor, and that neither factor is necessarily related to processes of structural differentiation.

The simplest way to evaluate the adequacy of these models is to pose three separate questions. First, can it be shown that ethnic solidarity weakens as structural differentiation proceeds? Second, does the significance of the cultural division of labor decline with increasing differentiation? Finally, is it possible to detect any relationship between the cultural division of labor and ethnic solidarity? The first two questions bear directly on the functional theory of ethnic change, while the last is the critical test of the reactive theory.

While these might appear to be easy questions to answer, in reality they are not. It is very difficult to construct adequate indicators for some of these concepts, even at a single point in time. If, as in this case, the analysis is to be historical, the evidential problems increase at an exponential rate. Since historical data cannot be generated anew, one is forced to select indicators which are, to say the least, imprecise and ungainly.

In this study, evidence is drawn from a set of social, electoral, and demographic data which have been collected for the counties of England, Wales, Scotland, and Northern Ireland. It must be admitted at the outset that the county is a very heterogeneous unit of social analysis; though, in this respect, it is far more adequate than the nation-state. In this case study the problem of heterogeneity is somewhat vitiated because the cultural groups under consideration are largely concentrated within clusters of counties, that is to say, within regions.

The variables employed as indicators of these concepts are of uneven quality. Structural differentiation is easiest to estimate; it may be presumed to vary directly with the level of industrialization in counties. Hence, agrarian counties are less differentiated than their industrial counterparts. The seven structural variables discussed in chapter 5 provide excellent multiple indicators of industrialization. Measurement of the other two concepts is considerably more tenuous. Ethnic solidarity is particularly troublesome due to its intersubjective nature. As has been previously explained, status groups (including ethnic groups) tend to enforce closure from the free social interaction of the marketplace. The exercise of closure may occur in any number of social contexts. Hence, ethnic solidarity may be indicated by the extent to which objective cultural distinctions account for the aggregate voting behavior of groups.[1] The cultural variables used in making this indicator are measures of religious affiliation and language distribution in counties.

Finally, the cultural division of labor refers to the salience of objective cultural distinctions in the distribution of occupations and rewards. If occupational or income categories were cross-tabulated by appropriate cultural categories in the British censuses, this concept could easily be measured by constructing an index of dissimilarity. However, no such data exist in time series. This makes it necessary to approach the problem in a more indirect fashion, through statistics of *per capita* income. The cultural division of labor may be roughly indicated by the extent to which cultural variables determine levels of *per capita* income within counties.

Great Britain is an ideal research site to observe long-term trends in ethnic solidarity. Britain became the first modern society, and has been among the most politically stable states in modern history. It is usually considered to have achieved great progress in national development, and class, rather than cultural, cleavages are frequently held to be of dominant importance in British politics.[2] Further, the salience of local attachments has been significantly eroded by the social changes of the past two centuries. National institutions, both voluntary (trade unions, political parties) and compulsory (educa-

[1] See chapter 7.
[2] This tendency is carried to almost absurd lengths by David Butler and Donald Stokes, *Political Change in Britain* (New York: 1969), pp. 144–50. Noting that their survey data showed regional differences in party support by social class, Butler and Stokes attempt to explain these differences by 'the contextual effect of class.' While controlling for industrial context does seem to diminish regional political differences *within England*, they are forced to admit that it does not reduce the political distinctiveness of Wales. Yet, Wales must not count for much, since this does not keep Butler and Stokes from stating that 'the explanation of regional differences therefore involves a number of variations on the theme of class' (p. 150).

tional, health and welfare), have penetrated all territorial space, thereby providing an organizational basis for the development of a comprehensively national politics. Despite these conditions favoring the decline in significance of cultural distinctions for political behavior, however, there are indications that there is something about the Celtic periphery which continues to distinguish it from England.

Given the imprecision of some of these indicators, the results of the data analysis should be regarded as tentative at best. Nevertheless, if the processes of long-term social change are ever to be elucidated, there must be an effort to collect and analyze the existing evidence, however inadequate, which bears on these large questions.

TESTING THE FUNCTIONALIST THEORY: TRENDS IN STATUS GROUP SOLIDARITY

It has previously been shown that deviations in the prediction of Conservative voting from seven structural indicators of industrialization[1] had substantially different means in England, Wales, and Scotland in the period 1885 to 1966. The results suggested that these structural factors alone were insufficient to account for the determination of voting in the society as a whole. In particular, it seemed likely that an unspecified factor in the regression model was contributing to lower propensities towards Conservative voting in the Celtic fringe than was expected on the basis of social structural considerations.

From external evidence, it was surmised that this missing element in the predictive model would be found not in the domain of social structure, but in the cultural peculiarities of the Celtic fringe. Hence, deviations from unexpected Conservative voting on the basis of the structural variables were interpreted as indicating the presence of status group orientations towards politics rather than the functional orientations characteristic of class solidarity. It was assumed that these deviations from structurally explained political behavior were a function of the salience of ethnicity as a factor promoting closure

[1] These variables are: manufacturing, agricultural, commercial and professional occupations, decennial population growth, proportion living in cities over 20,000 marriage rate, and proportion of population aged sixty-five and over. See chapter 7.

among groups in the periphery. By and large, Celtic ethnicity has traditionally been associated with religious and linguistic differences from England. The Celtic areas have been largely Nonconformist, in Wales and Scotland, and Roman Catholic in Ireland, whereas England has been, of course, dominantly Episcopalian. While these religious differences have remained temporally stable, the incidence of Gaelic and Welsh speaking has, in contrast, declined with time.

It is, of course, possible that the residuals from actual and expected levels of Conservative voting represented randomly distributed error in the measurement of the variables, or in their coding, or simply reflect the inappropriateness of the regression model to behaviors in the real world. If this were the case there could be no empirical basis for the previous hypotheses. In each of these examples such error terms would be uncorrelated with any variables which might serve to differentiate the Celtic regions from England. However, since the voting residuals were generally correlated with cultural variables at each point in time, these error terms could not be assumed to be random.

In this chapter the significance of these cultural factors on voting behavior in counties will be evaluated in a more direct fashion. In fact it can be shown that, at certain times, the independent effect of the cultural variables on the determination of voting behavior actually exceeds that of the social structural variables. This can be estimated through the technique of stagewise multiple regression.[1] During this procedure each of the cultural variables is regressed in turn on the set of structural variables. The aim is to eliminate the joint effect of structural and cultural variables. To give an example, it has long been known that industrialization led to the rapid expansion of Nonconformity in nineteenth-century Britain on the part of both bourgeoisie and proletariat.[2] Thus, a county's social structural composition—such as the proportion of its workers engaged in manufacturing occupations—would tend to influence the distribution of Nonconformist strength in the county as a whole. Part of the effect of Nonconformity would be due to the hidden influence, as it were, of structural factors.

From statistics on marriage, indicators were found for four cul-

---

[1] N. R. Draper and H. Smith, *Applied Regression Analysis* (New York: 1966), pp. 173–7.
[2] J. and B. C. Hammond, *The Town Laborer* (New York: 1968), pp. 231–45, E. P. Thompson, *The Making of the English Working Class* (New York: 1963), pp. 350–400.

tural variables, each of which varied considerably between regions. They are Established Church affiliation, Nonconformity, Celtic language speaking, and religiosity.[1] All these variables are proportional to the total country population. In the analysis, the regression equations predict for every county an expected value for each of the four cultural variables (c_i), on the basis of the structural factors. This procedure was repeated at each point in time for which data were available. If each estimate $\hat{c}_i$ is subtracted from the actual value of the county score on a specific cultural variable, a residual term $(c_i - \hat{c}_i)$ is obtained with the structural effects minimized. The independent effect of cultural factors on county voting behavior may then be estimated by the coefficients of determination (R^2) from the regression of the Conservative vote on the set of cultural residuals determined separately at each point in time.

Table 10.1 presents the independent effect of the set of four cul-

TABLE 10.1   *Independent effects of structural and cultural factors on the determination of conservative voting in counties of Great Britain and Northern Ireland (N = 92)*

| | Coefficients of determination (R^2) for the regression of voting on | |
Year	Structural Variables*	Cultural Residuals†
1885	0·279	0·218
1892	0·178	0·222
1900	0·277	0·294
1910	0·285	0·274
1924	0·147	0·459
1931	0·091	0·214
1951	0·250	0·251
1966	0·155	0·429

* decennial population growth; proportion 65 and over; marriage rate; proportion of employed males in agricultural occupations; proportion of males in manufacturing occupations, proportion of males in professional and commercial occupations, proportion living in cities over 20,000.
† *1851–1881:* residual Nonconformity; residual Established church affiliation; residual religiosity. *1891 on*—a fourth variable. residual Celtic language speaking, has been added to the regression model.

tural variables on Conservative voting, as compared with the effect of the seven structural variables. It should be noted that these structural variables have not been similarly purified of cultural covariation.

[1] For the derivation of these indicators see chapter 6.

This is because it has been assumed that in the relationship between social structure and culture, the direction of causality runs from structure to culture. This assumption provides the most inclusive definition of the structural factor, as well as the most conservative estimate of the cultural factor.

For six of the eight points in time at which data are available, the cultural factors explain more of the variance in voting than the structural factors. Yet, the British social structure clearly underwent continual differentiation in this period. Industrialization made great headway in the Celtic fringe, in particular. That there is no evidence of a secular trend towards structurally explained voting calls the functionalist theory into question. The persisting salience of cultural distinctions in British political behavior conflicts with the functionalist expectations—that industrialization brings class politics to the fore. This, in turn, must lead to a reconsideration of the meaning of the distinction between class and status group orientations towards political behavior. If status group solidarity is, in reality, the manifestation of a group's primordial sentiments then these data are apparently paradoxical.

One meaning of the term primordial is that such attachments are characteristic of relatively early stages of social organization. How and why do these 'primordial sentiments' not only exist in the modern industrial social system, but remain constantly influential through seventy years of extraordinarily rapid social change? How can it be explained that the distribution of votes within a British county is better predicted, on the whole, from knowledge of its religious composition than from knowledge of its social structural composition? Finally, the fact that this persistent political significance of culture can be demonstrated in Great Britain, of all societies, is in itself remarkable. For, in Britain, the intrusiveness of the central government into the lives of all citizens is relatively great even among developed societies. Here it should be expected *a fortiori* that 'national unity is maintained not by calls to blood and land but by a vague, intermittent, and routine allegiance to a civil state, supplemented to a greater or lesser extent by governmental use of police powers and ideological exhortation.'[1]

These data present strong evidence that political demands are made both on the basis of status group and class criteria within Britain. That is to say, voting is explained by the independent effects of cultural variables as well as by structural variables. Hence, accord-

[1] Geertz, *op. cit.*, p. 110.

ing to these results, status group solidarity has not noticeably declined in the period from 1885 to 1966. The functionalist expectation appears not to be supported.

TESTING THE FUNCTIONALIST THEORY: THE INFLUENCE OF CULTURAL FACTORS ON INCOME

While the independent effect of cultural factors in the determination of Conservative voting persists over time, the same cannot be said for their contribution to the explanation of *per capita* income. Table 10.2 presents a comparison of the independent effect of the set of

TABLE 10.2   *Independent effects of structural and cultural factors on the determination of county income in Great Britain* (N = 86)

Year	Coefficients of determination (R^2) for the regression of income on	
	Structural Variables*	Cultural Residuals*
1851	0·275	0·155
1861	0·172	0·200
1871	0·208	0·215
1881	0·119	0·164
1891	0·270	0·062
1901	0·260	0·040
1951	0·448	0·035
1961	0·252	0·086

* As in Table 10.1.

four cultural variables on county *per capita* income as compared with the effect of the seven structural variables.

From 1851 through 1881, it is apparent that the cultural variables explain roughly the same amount of variance in county income distribution as the structural variables. Furthermore, the regression coefficients for the Nonconformity residual, which is to be found disproportionately in the Celtic lands (see Map 6), are negative. This means that to the extent a British county is Nonconformist, its *per capita* income will be decreased by varying degrees at different times. It must be stressed that this relationship holds while the effects of the industrialization variables are being accounted for. These results are somewhat surprising for two reasons.

Although the effects of cultural factors on differential economic

321

Map 6 Relatively Nonconformist counties, 1851–1961 (Great Britain and Northern Ireland)

development have long been discussed, at least since the time of Weber's essay on Protestantism and capitalism, relatively little systematic empirical evidence, as opposed to illustration, has been presented which lends credence to these notions. Second, the Weber thesis held Roman Catholicism responsible for economic backwardness in Western Europe, whereas ascetic Protestantism was thought to be a progressive force in development. Catholic traditionalistic values were conceived to act as an endogenous constraint on economic development. Yet, here is evidence that the Nonconformist counties—Nonconformity being closest in the British context to Weber's ascetic ideal-type—are precisely those having lower incomes than counties with Established Church strength.

The early data might be interpreted to indicate the existence of a cultural division of labor. The force of this interpretation is that collectivities are ultimately denied opportunities for development on the basis of their ethnicity by the actions of exogenous controlling institutions. Ethnic status *per se* rather than traditional religious values would therefore be responsible for Celtic economic backwardness. The socioeconomic position of Blacks in America or that of Amerindians in Latin American societies are cases which illustrate these patterns.

However, the explanatory power of the cultural variables appears to drop off sharply after 1881. Thereafter, the independent effect of culture on county income in Great Britain is virtually negligible. This suggests there is some validity to this part of the functionalist theory. Apparently, cultural distinctions cease to significantly determine *per capita* income within British counties after 1881. However, the data are somewhat ambiguous in two respects. First, why should the effect of cultural factors have been so great between 1851 and 1881? Second, despite the drop in importance of the cultural factors after 1881, it should be noted that there is only a slight increase in the amount of variance explained by the set of structural variables after this date.

SOME FURTHER CONSIDERATIONS

Can the functionalist theory account for the general significance of cultural factors in the determination of wealth and voting behavior? If particular elements of Celtic culture, as indicated by the incidence of Nonconformity and Celtic language speaking, in some way cause lower county income, then the relative economic disadvantages of the Celtic regions could be explained as a consequence of the prevalence of this culture. Assume, for the moment, that there is a 'traditional' component to British Nonconformity which leads to a low need for achievement and, hence, to low labor productivity. This is, of course, a familiar kind of explanation in the literature on economic development, ultimately a throwback to the Weber thesis. The implication of the argument is that in certain areas development is curtailed because the dominant cultural values do not reward individuals for economically efficient behavior. If this were the case with respect to Nonconformity in Britain, then the Celtic regions would be relatively poor because they are in fact disproportionately Nonconformist.

A similar argument can be made that Nonconformists have an 'historical legacy' of anti-Conservatism, and that, consequently, the cause of Celtic political distinctiveness is the disproportionate strength of Nonconformity in these areas. Both arguments are similar to many types of explanations frequently utilized in comparative sociological studies.

One way of empirically testing these questions is to analyze the independent importance of cultural factors on the determination of income and voting behavior separately in England, Wales, and Scotland. Are the effects of cultural distinctions equally important within these different regions? According to the general thesis sketched above, the concentration of traditional cultural values is ultimately responsible for the relatively low income and high propensity to anti-Conservative voting characteristic of the Celtic regions. England is presumably different because its cultural values are progressive. Over all, however, according to the functionalist perspective, the effect of the cultural factors (in other words, the size of the coefficients of determination) on income and voting distributions should be approximately equal in all parts of Great Britain, once differences of social structural composition have been accounted for. On the other hand, the regression coefficients for Celtic and English cultural indicators should be of opposite sign.

Tables 10.3 and 10.4 summarize the results of the regression of income and conservative voting on the set of cultural residuals within the three regions. In the explanation of *per capita* income, Table 10.3 clearly indicates that Wales is a very different place from England and Scotland. Cultural factors are consistently more significant for the determination of income in Wales than in England and Scotland at each point in time. Second, even as late as 1951 and 1961, the set

324

TABLE 10.3   *Effects of cultural residuals on the determination of county income within England, Wales and Scotland*

Year	Coefficients of determination (R^2) for the regression of income on cultural residuals in		
	England (N = 40)	*Wales* (N = 13)	*Scotland* (N = 33)
1851	0·112	—	0·193
1861	0·231	0·286	0·174
1871	0·082	0·608	0·101
1881	0·191	0·628	0·072
1891	0·100	—	0·078
1901	0·067	0·277	0·065
1951	0·144	0·689	0·114
1961	0·211	0·496	0·151

TABLE 10.4   *Effects of cultural residuals on the determination of Conservative voting within England, Wales, and Scotland*

Year	Coefficients of determination (R^2) for the regression of proportion Conservative voting on cultural residuals in		
	England (N = 40)	*Wales* (N = 13)	*Scotland* (N = 33)
1892	0·106	—	0·334
1900	0·088	0·431	0·119
1910	0·235	0·801	0·134
1924	0·207	0·684	0·283
1931	0·291	0·137	0·224
1951	0·121	0·316	0·187
1966	0·357	0·744	0·243

of cultural variables explains, respectively, 69 and 50 per cent of the variance of income among Welsh counties. Hence, the data in Table 10.2, which indicate the waning importance of culture as a determinant of income, are shown to be misleading when this relationship is studied within the various parts of Britain. The effects of culture on income in England and Scotland are very closely paralleled. In general, the set of cultural variables explains somewhat more income in 1861 and 1961 than at those points of time in between. But on the whole, culture is a far less significant factor in England and Scotland than in Wales.

A very similar picture emerges in Table 10.4. Here, too, the independent effect of culture on Conservative voting is greatest in Wales, while the Scottish and English coefficients of determination are generally lower. The curve of the Welsh R^2s over time is also subject to greater fluctuation than that of England or Scotland. Particularly noticeable is the decline in the importance of culture during the 1931 election in Wales. This may, in some way, be a consequence of the Depression. However, in 1951 and 1966 the salience of cultural factors once again rises significantly there. These data lead to the conclusion that no theory emphasizing the causality of cultural factors can satisfactorily explain English–Welsh differences in county wealth and voting patterns. Clearly the importance, and perhaps social meaning, of these cultural variables changes within the regional contexts of Wales, Scotland, and England.

These results raise the following questions. Why are cultural variables still serving as major determinants of income and political behavior in Wales, and, to a much lesser extent, in Scotland? Why are cultural distinctions less important in these respects within England? The problem is to account for the differential significance of cultural factors within various regions of a developed society.

Here, it will be useful to take the reactive theory of ethnic change into consideration. To do this, it will be necessary to distinguish *objective cultural differences*, such as the existence of religious distinctions between individuals or groups, from the socially constructed boundaries which ultimately define *ethnic groups*. The reactive theory suggests that only when such objective cultural differences are linked to structural inequities between groups will they assume enduring significance in complex societies. For, according to this theory, it is precisely under the conditions of a cultural division of labor that ethnic boundaries are maintained, despite social interaction between groups. Gaining an understanding of the conditions under which ethnicity persists in developed societies will *pari passu* elucidate the process of ethnic change.

ON THE PRECONDITIONS OF STATUS GROUP SOLIDARITY

Within Great Britain the differential intensity of status group solidarity in Wales, Scotland, and England has been indicated. By and large, such solidarity has been strongest in Wales, and weakest in England. I shall now seek to account for these differences in the relative salience of cultural variables in the voting behavior of these regions. Part of the explanation of these differences must be that something about the past history and present reality of the respective regions lends ethnicity its distinctive place in the social order. As it stands, this statement is a truism. It is necessary to learn what specific aspect of this history; exactly which present conditions affect the place of ethnicity in regional politics. Here, one cannot be satisfied with a solution of the type: it is because the traditional cultural forms are more institutionalized in Wales than in England. Clearly this too must be true. But what factors are responsible for such institutionalization and its perpetuation? What are the objective conditions which result in the creation and maintenance of status group solidarity?

While there has been much discussion of these questions with regard to complex societies, relatively little of it has been informed by empirical research. The Celtic periphery has been measurably distinct from England basically in two ways. First, at comparable levels of industrialization the Celtic counties have generally had lower *per capita* incomes than those in England. Second, despite many centuries of contact between these regions, the Celtic lands have remained objectively culturally different from England. In the main, the Celtic counties, taken as an aggregate, have been economically disadvantaged and culturally subordinate relative to the aggregate of English counties. Much of the argument about the societal underpinnings of ethnicity involves disputes about the relative contribution of these two elements to the emergence of ethnic solidarity.

It is generally expected that the existence of significant material inequalities between culturally similar groups in industrial society—such as between the English bourgeoisie and proletariat—will encourage the subordinate group to become class conscious in its attempts to affect change in the distribution of resources. Class consciousness is by no means a certainty in this situation, but its development may be regarded as likely given the presence of other, exogenous, conditions. With Marx, it is useful to use the category *Klasse an sich*—which implies that the emergence of class consciousness in such circumstances always exists as a potentiality.

Much less is known about types of political solidarity adopted in culturally heterogeneous settings, where stratification on the basis of economic and cultural differences can be analytically separated from one another. It is certainly possible to speculate how a culturally distinctive but materially advantaged group might press its political demands in such a society. A plausible case can be made that, since the group is not placed in an inferior market position its demands will be made on the basis of its culture, or precisely that element which serves to differentiate it from other similarly situated groups in the society. To this extent it might be expected to engage in ethnic politics. This has an intuitively pleasing logic.

However, among economically disadvantaged groups the extent of ethnic solidarity is quite unpredictable from such theoretical principles. If a given group is both materially disadvantaged, that is, a proletariat, and subject to cultural discrimination as well, its political demands might be expressed either in class or in ethnic terms. There is no *a priori* reason to believe that one or the other factor will tend to dominate. This is a problem of far from academic interest, for many developed societies are presently faced with political challenges from groups bearing these twin burdens.

How such dissident groups may become integrated into the polity as normal participants in the social order is quite problematic. The basic theoretical issue concerns the relative dominance of economic or cultural factors in the persistence of ethnically based demands. The policy implications of these alternatives are very different. If material factors are conceived to be primary, then policies promoting occupational and income equality between groups will perforce be seen to lead to the effacement of ethnic distinctions with time. On the other hand, the dominance of cultural factors in varying economic contexts would imply that the state should direct its efforts towards promoting more effective acculturation of the distinctive group in the hope of easing the divisiveness of ethnic conflict in society.[1]

In order to sort out whether ethnic politics is determined largely by economic or cultural factors, or a combination of both, the following typology of counties (which should be seen, in this sense, as groups) may be constructed (see Figure 5).

Type I counties will be termed 'core,' for they are both culturally and materially advantaged and may be presumed to be politically dominant in the society. Type II may be described as 'provincial' counties: though they share the dominant culture, they are economically disadvantaged. Type III counties may be considered 'dissenting' in that they are culturally separate but materially equal. And last, counties are 'peripheral' (Type IV) when cultural subordination is

---

[1] These alternative policy implications surround much of the current debate on the so-called 'culture of poverty' in urban sociology. Those subscribing to the cultural dominance position have advocated the establishment of institutional arrangements which will enable disadvantaged children to be socialized into equality, such as Project Head Start. It is sometimes assumed that the adults are beyond the reach of all such help. The structural solution to problems of integration is to provide equal employment opportunities and wages for members of the disadvantaged group.

superimposed upon economic disadvantage.

Relative economic and cultural advantages among counties may be estimated as follows. In the regression of *per capita* income on the seven industrialization variables, the value of the residual term for each county can be either positive or negative. Thus, a county with an actual income *per capita* of £2,000 could, in comparison with all other British counties at that time, be expected to have had an income of £1,900 as a function of its level of industrialization. In this example the residual value for this county would be +£100. Its actual income was underestimated by the regression equation. Hence, at this point in time, the county is economically advantaged relative to all other British counties. On the other hand, when a county's

		Economically	
		Advantaged	Disadvantaged
Culturally	Dominant	I 'Core'	II 'Provincial'
	Subordinate	III 'Dissenting'	IV 'Peripheral'

Figure 5   A typology of counties

income is overestimated by the set of structural variables, it may be regarded as relatively economically disadvantaged.

Similarly, in the generation of cultural residuals from the regression of cultural variables on the indicators of industrialization, the estimated proportion of Nonconformists for some counties is greater than the actual proportion. Since the Nonconformist sects are minority religions of low prestige relative to Anglicanism in Britain (or to Presbyterianism in Scotland), these counties may be considered culturally advantaged. Those counties where the extent of Nonconformity is underestimated by the regression equation are, given their degree of industrialization, culturally subordinate. All eighty-six counties in England, Wales, and Scotland may therefore be placed in one of these four categories in the typology for the years when data are available: 1885, 1891, 1901, 1951 and 1965.

To begin with, it should be noted that these relative cultural and economic advantages apparently do not occur independent of one another. This can be seen in Table 10.5, which presents the distribution of counties in these four categories. Note that the likelihood of any county appearing in either categories I, II, or IV, that is to say, the core, provincial, and peripheral types, is more than twice as great as the likelihood of its appearance in category III, the dissenting type. Thus, to the extent a county has adherents linked to a culture of low prestige, it will also probably be inordinately economically disadvantaged. The inverse relationship does not hold: economically disadvantaged counties are about equally likely to be culturally dominant or subordinate.

Within these contexts, it is necessary to examine the relationship between social structural and cultural factors as determinants of

TABLE 10.5 *Number of counties in each context* (N = 86)

Year	Core I	Provincial II	Dissenting III	Peripheral IV
1885	29	22	11	24
1892	23	25	10	28
1900	20	25	8	33
1951	26	21	11	28
1966	22	28	14	22

county income and voting patterns respectively. The aim is to estimate the extent of culturally as against structurally determined voting occurring in each of these types of contexts. Since the number of cases in each cell of the typology is relatively small—never exceeding thirty-three, to be precise—it will be difficult to resort to multiple indicators of the structural and cultural factors. Measurement error cannot be statistically estimated without introducing greater complexity in the analysis. Because of the constraints of small sample size, it will be useful to employ a simple version of path analysis wherein the structural and cultural factors are represented by single variable indicators. A good indicator of the structural factor is the proportion of occupied males in the manufacturing sector. For the cultural factor Nonconformity will serve as the single indicator. Nonconformity is strongly negatively correlated with Established church affiliation and equally strongly positively associated with Celtic language speaking. Both income and voting are single variables. The path model will relate these four variables in each context—that is, in core, provincial, dissenting, and peripheral counties—according to the model presented in Figure 6.[1]

[1] Note that in these models income is seen to be causally dependent on industrialization and culture. It might be argued, however, that culture should be

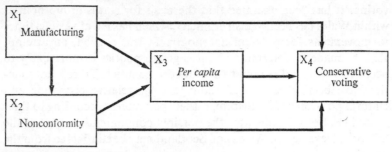

Figure 6   The voting determination model

TESTING THE REACTIVE THEORY: CONTEXTUAL FOUNDATIONS FOR THE EMERGENCE OF STATUS GROUP POLITICS

Collectivities, as was suggested, may in general be disposed towards two kinds of orientations to political action. If the political behavior of a group is largely determined by its relationship to markets for capital, commodities, and labor, this gives evidence of class orientations towards politics. The extent of such class orientations in a given historical situation will be roughly indicated by the degree to which political behavior, such as voting, can be accounted for by the social structural composition of the group. In such a case, it would be possible to predict the voting responses of groups (or areas) according to their respective concentrations of industrial workers, for example. Alternatively, status group orientations (including ethnic orientations), may be inferred when objective cultural differences assume a dominant independent effect on such political behavior. In this case a group's (or area's) voting patterns might best be predicted from knowledge of its religious, or linguistic, composition.

While the functionalist theory anticipates that, in the polity as a whole, class solidarity would steadily gain over status solidarity with time, largely as a consequence of ongoing modernization, it has already been demonstrated that this did not occur in Great Britain from 1885 to 1966. Cultural differences within counties, particularly in Wales, have continued to account for much of the variance in

---

dependent on income as well as the indicator of industrialization. In England particularly Nonconformity might be expected to be a negative function of county income during certain years. However, since I am most interested in testing the possibility that Celtic counties have low income *as a function of their ethnicity* the causal arrow goes from culture to income in this model.

voting. It has been assumed that the basis for status group politics within Wales has been Welsh ethnicity, which has led at various times to movements for political autonomy. In this section, an attempt shall be made to determine if status group politics is more likely to occur in peripheral counties than in core counties. To repeat, counties have been grouped according to their relative economic and cultural position within Britain, rather than merely according to their spatial relations. In this way, the possibly contaminating effect of the 'historical legacies' of Wales and Scotland may be eliminated from the analysis.

In Table 10.6, the relationship between class and status group

TABLE 10.6 *Determinants of Conservative voting from path models, by type of context**

		Determinant		
Year/Context	Manufacturing	Per capita *income*	Nonconformity	$R^2(4\cdot123)$
1885				
Core	−0·204 (−0·173)	+0·311 (0·012)	−0·699 (−0·951)	0·707
Provincial	−0·346 (−0·306)	+0·375 (+0·012)	−0·388 (−0·306)	0·484
Dissenting	−0·470 (−0·475)	ns	−0·937 (−0·934)	0·549
Peripheral	ns	ns	−0·766 (−0·763)	0·495
1892				
Core	ns	ns	−0·475 (−0·771)	0·355
Provincial	−0·510 (−0·493)	+0·252 (+0·206)	−0·349 (−0·689)	0·388
Dissenting	ns	ns	ns	0·266
Peripheral	ns	ns	−0·391 (−0·266)	0·153
1900				
Core	ns	ns	−0·615 (−1·177)	0·356
Provincial	−0·256 (−0·262)	ns	−0·762 (−1·980)	0·556
Dissenting	ns	ns	ns	0·310
Peripheral	−0·347 (−0·578)	ns	−0·590 (−0·983)	0·298
1951				
Core	−0·547 (−0·285)	−0·270 (−0·001)	ns	0·513
Provincial	ns	ns	ns	0·108
Dissenting	ns	ns	ns	0·274
Peripheral	−0·500 (−0·423)	ns	−0·693 (−0·717)	0·494
1966				
Core	−0·647 (−0·468)	ns	ns	0·449
Provincial	−0·636 (−0·411)	ns	ns	0·480
Dissenting	ns	ns	ns	0·301
Peripheral	ns	ns	−0·513 (−0·380)	0·376

*All results are significant to the 0·20 level (2-tailed test). Numbers not in parentheses are standardized path coefficients. These are appropriate for comparing the effects on voting within each context at each point in time. Unstandardized coefficients appear in parentheses. These are appropriate for comparisons of the effects of the same variables in different contexts or periods of time (Hubert M. Blalock, Jr, 'Causal inferences, closed populations, and measures of association,' *American Political Science Review*, 61, 1 (1967), pp. 130–6).

political orientations may be estimated by the relative size of path coefficients linking manufacturing occupations, the social structural indicator, and Nonconformity, the cultural indicator, to aggregate voting results in each context. It should be emphasized that the four-fold typology was constructed not on the basis of absolute structural and cultural differences among counties, but according to the relative differences in these dimensions *between counties of comparable levels of industrialization.* Thus, agrarian and industrial counties are equally likely to be found among both the relatively wealthy and poor categories. Since the confounding effects of social structural differences have been removed from the categorization of counties as being 'advantaged' or 'disadvantaged,' within each of the four cells of the typology there is a set of structurally heterogeneous counties. Therefore, according to the functionalist theory, it should be expected that social structural considerations within these contexts—particularly on rural–urban or agricultural–industrial dimensions—should outweigh cultural factors in the determination of Conservative voting. Hence, this theory would predict that industrial workers in all contexts would vote largely against the Conservative Party, whereas in rural counties, Conservative strength should increase. Finally, there is no *a priori* reason to suspect that the relationship between these variables should significantly vary among the different groups of counties.

Nevertheless, important differences in the determination of voting behavior can be shown among these types of counties. Clearly, some types of counties are favorable to the articulation of political demands along status group rather than class lines. This can be seen by ranking all four country contexts according to the frequency with which the cultural factor largely determines voting behavior. In the peripheral context, this occurs at all five observations; in the core, in three of five; it occurs not at all in the provincial counties. The high instability of voting patterns in dissenting counties should be noted, in this respect. In four of five periods, neither class nor status group voting patterns may be discerned, since in these years no paths to voting are statistically significant. The rank order of contexts for the prevalence of class voting is, of course, reversed.

Thus, in counties where economic disadvantages are superimposed upon objective cultural differences, political demands are most likely to be made on a status group basis. This does not rule out the formulation of political demands on class lines as well. At certain times in the peripheral context, 1901 and 1951, there is evidence of *both* class and status group orientations towards voting. However, in every case status group orientations are stronger. Since the majority of counties in the peripheral context are located in Wales and Scotland (see Table 10.7), it seems likely that sentiments of Welsh and Scottish

TABLE 10.7 *Number of counties in each context, by region*

	England (N = 40)	*Wales (N = 13)*	*Scotland (N = 33)*
1885			
Core	20	2	7
Provincial	16	1	5
Dissenting	2	1	8
Peripheral	2	9	13
1892			
Core	15	2	6
Provincial	21	0	4
Dissenting	1	5	4
Peripheral	3	6	19
1900			
Core	12	1	7
Provincial	22	0	3
Dissenting	1	1	6
Peripheral	5	11	17
1951			
Core	12	0	14
Provincial	13	0	8
Dissenting	3	4	4
Peripheral	12	9	7
1961			
Core	11	0	11
Provincial	18	0	10
Dissenting	7	3	4
Peripheral	4	10	8

ethnic solidarity, or nationalism, lie at the basis of these status group orientations, an assumption which the consistency of the pattern over all of the years observed helps support. However, the inverse of this proposition does not appear to hold, at least for all points in time. The core counties have not always been characterized by the salience of their class political orientations. In fact, status group politics is evident in the years 1885, 1891, and 1901. Not until 1951 and 1966 does the effect of culture totally drop out of the voting models in the core and provincial contexts.

334

What can account for the strength of such status group orientations in the core during 1885–1901? Clearly there is no counterpart to Celtic nationalism among core counties. That is to say, the question of English ethnicity cannot have been at stake within the core, in the same fashion as it most certainly was in the periphery. If ethnicity cannot explain this pattern of political behavior, what can? The basis of political affiliation has changed in the core not on account of the shifting salience of ethnicity, but because the entire British party system was transformed after World War One. In the late nineteenth century, the Liberals, who had been the leading party in opposition to the Tories, were far from a socially homogeneous political party. The Liberal coalition was, in retrospect, a curious amalgam of capitalists and proletarians; Nonconformists and Celtic Home Rulers all united under the standard of a single political party.[1] The Conservatives were perhaps somewhat less heterogeneous with respect to social class. But the rise of the Labor Party, with its appeal to the class consciousness of the proletariat, reoriented the British party system. Status-based parties gradually evolved into class-based parties. Here, then, is evidence for the evolutionary trend from status group to class politics so frequently described in the literature. *But it can be seen only in the core and provincial contexts.* In these contexts, as the functionalist theory would predict, the triumph of functional cleavages in the polity has indeed become virtually complete. However, in the periphery, status group orientations have continued to persist.

Thus, some factor within the peripheral counties themselves must account for the persistent salience of status group solidarity there. Since cultural distinctions in the periphery continue to have significance in the articulation of political demands, patterns of social interaction in these counties must be different in some way from those occurring in the other types of counties. The peripheral context is made up of both relatively poor and culturally disadvantaged counties in Great Britain. Of all British counties, these, in particular, should be expected to have a cultural division of labor.

For evidence concerning the cultural division of labor, it is necessary to delve into processes occurring within the different contexts. Table 10.8 indicates there is, to some extent, an association between the cultural division of labor and the emergence of status group politics. When cultural distinctions are salient in the allocation of

[1] Henry Pelling, *Popular Politics and Society in Late Victorian Britain* (London: 1968), chapter 6.

TABLE 10.8 *Determinants of county* per capita *income from path models, by type of context**

Year/Context	Manufacturing	Nonconformity	$R^2(3.12)$
1881			
Core	−0·292 (−6·501)	ns	0·084
Provincial	ns	−0·482 (−12·095)	0·228
Dissenting	−0·480 (−13·594)	−0·602 (−16·814)	0·620
Peripheral	+0·312 (+3·632)	−0·333 (−4·087)	0·314
1892			
Core	ns	ns	0·058
Provincial	ns	ns	0·040
Dissenting	ns	ns	0·041
Peripheral	+0·601 (+9·755)	ns	0·447
1900			
Core	+0·496 (+25·247)	−0·334 (−25·165)	0·326
Provincial	ns	−0·596 (−15·483)	0·355
Dissenting	ns	ns	0·199
Peripheral	+0·411 (+3·795)	−0·391 (−6·734)	0·451
1951			
Core	ns	+0·303 (+191·592)	0·225
Provincial	ns	ns	0·056
Dissenting	ns	ns	0·251
Peripheral	+0·537 (+92·503)	−0·240 (−50·600)	0·453
1961			
Core	ns	ns	0·018
Provincial	ns	+0·364 (+331·321)	0·134
Dissenting	ns	−0·432 (−221·306)	0·461
Peripheral	+0·657 (+99·594)	−0·263 (−51.075)	0·629

* As in Table 10.6.

resources (here indicated by levels of county *per capita* income) status group politics is likely to occur. This table presents the path co-efficients leading from structural and cultural variables to *per capita* income in counties of all types at each point in time. Here, too, since the categories are heterogeneous with regard to levels of industrialization, it would be expected, on the basis of conventional assumptions, that structural considerations within these contexts will outweigh cultural factors in the determination of *per capita* income. In general, a positive association between county income and industrialization would be expected, if only because wages and the standard of living in the urban-industrial setting are typically higher than in the agricultural sector. In this situation, as well, there are no *a priori* reasons to suspect the relationship between these factors to vary among the different contexts.

Nevertheless, striking differences in the determination of income emerge both across time, and among the various types of counties. In the *core* counties, both structural and cultural factors predominantly account for the distribution of income at different periods. In 1881 industrialization leads to lower county income, but the direction of influence changes by 1901, such that the more a county is industrialized, the higher will be its income. Thereafter, the effect of structural considerations on the determination of income in the model is insignificant. The relative importance of culture on the level of income in the core counties also changes with time. In 1901, Nonconformity has a somewhat weaker effect on income than industrialization, and it is in a negative direction. But by 1951, Nonconformity assumes a greater importance than industrialization and actually causes an increase in county income. On the whole, then, the core counties manifest two separate trends over time. The effect of industrialization on income shifts from being negative to positive, and thereafter becomes insignificant. Alternatively the effect of Nonconformity on income fluctuates over time, but the nature of its influence shifts as well, from a negative to a positive direction.

If this is compared with the situation in *peripheral* counties, major differences emerge. First, the factors leading to the determination of income among peripheral counties do not change across time. Industrialization continually leads to higher income; Nonconformity consistently lowers county income in this context. But, in 1951 when the effects of Nonconformity on income in the core and peripheral counties are compared, the direction of the effect actually differs. Thus, among core counties, the independent effect of Nonconformity *raises* county income, whereas the effect of the same variable actually *lowers* income in the set of peripheral counties. Hence, any explanation of the relative poverty of the periphery on the basis of development constraints which derive from traditional cultural values must apparently be rejected. The same cultural element in one context is associated with lowered incomes, whereas in the other it serves to heighten them. This can be accounted for only by assuming that there is a context-level effect which is itself more important for the distribution of income than the relationship between the structural and cultural variables. The social meaning of the Nonconformity variable, in so far as the determination of income is concerned, must shift from one context to the other.

But which element—economic disadvantage or cultural subordination—is most responsible for these contextual differences? Since both the core and peripheral counties are consistently ranked on both of these dimensions, some idea of the differentiating element between these contexts may be gathered by looking at income determination models in the *provincial* and *dissenting* types of counties. These counties are, so to speak, inconsistently stratified according to their structural and cultural position in the society. Hence, the determination of income in these two contexts may be similar to the other contexts on either structural or cultural terms. If contextual differences in the determination of county income are a function of structural dimensions in the society as a whole, then the provincial context would be most similar to that of the peripheral counties, and dissenting counties would tend to resemble the core, in so far as the causes of income are concerned. Likewise, if cultural dimensions are largely responsible for the difference between contexts, then the determinants of income in the provincial counties would be similar to those in the core, while dissenting counties would have more affinity with the peripheral group.

Table 10.8 indicates that the contextual similarity, in so far as the determination of income is concerned, occurs along cultural dimensions. This is so because the influence of Nonconformity on income is positive in the provincial context in 1961 (and, hence, similar to the core in 1951); while it is negative in the dissenting counties (and, thus, is similar to the periphery). Therefore, the situation is as follows. Among culturally dominant counties, during the years 1951 and 1961, Nonconformity leads to higher income. In culturally subordinate counties, during these years, Nonconformity leads to lower income. Two-thirds of the counties placed in the 'culturally subordinate' category in these years are Welsh and Scottish. In these counties, Nonconformity has traditionally served as the cultural marker of Celtic ethnicity. Therefore, in the peripheral and dissenting contexts Nonconformity masks the effect of an ethnic factor—the strength of Welsh and Scottish ethnicity—whereas in the core and provincial counties no such ethnic meaning goes with Nonconformity, where it is purely a religious condition. Some Englishmen are Methodist, others Anglican, but they share a common ethnicity despite these religious differences. Thus, economic disadvantages have been associated with cultural distinctions throughout the period studied in the peripheral context. Peripheral counties are not only poorer and culturally distinctive relative to all British counties, but within these counties as well it appears that the distribution of material assets is systematically related to ethnicity. It must be presumed that when collectivities become aware that the distribution of occupational roles, wages, and incomes are a function of ethnic differences—such as when Welshmen earn less than Englishmen for work in collieries—that this is a powerful inducement to the pursuit of ethnic politics. Even in cultural dominant settings, Nonconformity was sometimes associated with lower income in the early period. Cultural distinctions are related to economic disadvantages in three of the six cases where status group voting patterns can be observed.

CONCLUSIONS

If reservations about the quality of these data are temporarily suspended, the following conclusions may be drawn from this case study.

Ongoing industrialization has not been associated with a shift from status group to class political cleavages throughout Great Britain as a whole. Instead, this process has been limited solely to those contexts which have been culturally dominant in the polity. Peripheral counties, that is those which are relatively poor and culturally subordinate, have continually manifested status group political orientations over time. The basis of these orientations appears to have been the sense of Celtic ethnic identity.

The evidence tends to indicate that the persistence of such status group political orientations among collectivities is, at least in part, a function of the salience of cultural distinctions in the distribution of resources, and, hence, in the general system of stratification. Objective cultural differences between groups typically do not assume major significance in the articulation of political demands in the absence of this condition. In historical circumstances where the national party system is not established along lines of class cleavage, these conclusions are subject to some modification. Hence, in the core counties during the early elections (1885–1901) Nonconformity assumed political significance because cultural distinctions were, in effect, institutionalized in the party system.

The emergence of status group politics may, therefore, be explained apart from reference to differential historical legacies, national traditions, or party loyalty among particular groups. The salience of these differentiating factors is ultimately a function of objective conditions operating within the society as a whole.

Hence, it follows that the political integration of minority ethnic groups will be facilitated to the extent that systematic structural differences between such groups are progressively effaced. This conclusion is indirectly supported by two separate pieces of evidence. First, contexts which are culturally dominant but economically disadvantaged are typified by the strongest extent of class political orientations. Second, in those relatively few counties which are culturally subordinate, but economically advantaged, no constant pattern of status group political emerges.

Last, since the manifestation of ethnic solidarity appears to be a response to the perception of patterns of structural discrimination in the society at large, it is not useful to conceive of it as a traditional, or primordial sentiment. On the contrary, such solidarity represents high political consciousness on the part of groups seeking to alter the cultural division of labor.

However, given ecological data on the level of county units, it is difficult to accept these conclusions with anything approaching certainty. Rather, they should be regarded as a first approximation of a theoretical explanation of ethnic solidarity and change. In this light, these conclusions may prove to be of some use. If even a few writers may be induced to study the relationship between the cultural division of labor and the emergence of ethnic solidarity, in greater detail than has been possible here, then this chapter will have clearly served its purpose.

CHAPTER 11

CONCLUSION

'O words are lightly spoken,'
Said Pearse to Connolly,
'Maybe a breath of politic words
Has withered our Rose Tree;
Or maybe but a wind that blows
Across the bitter sea.'

'It needs to be but watered,'
James Connolly replied,
'To make the green come out again
And spread on every side,
And shake the blossom from the bud
To be the garden's pride.'

'But where can we draw water,'
Said Pearse to Connolly,
'When all the wells are parched away?
O plain as plain can be
There's nothing but our own red blood
Can make a right Rose Tree.'

WILLIAM BUTLER YEATS

IT is time for a reckoning. This book has tried to account for the bitter sea which separates England from the Celtic fringe by discussing the types of conditions which promote national development in culturally heterogeneous societies. The critical process in national development has been termed ethnic change; this refers, in a two-group system, to the willingness of the culturally subordinate group to redefine its ethnic identity to be congruent with that of the culturally dominant group. To the extent that a society is composed of different ethnic groups, it will tend to be plagued by conflicts which may ultimately threaten its territorial, as well as its moral integrity. While this study has sought to characterize the specific

341

pattern of English–Celtic interaction in modern history, it has utilized categories and explanatory schemes applying generally to all industrial societies. Hence, England has been referred to as the national core; and each of the Celtic lands has been termed a peripheral region. From the theoretical literature, it was possible to select two quite different sets of expectations about the relationship between core and peripheral regions, particularly as it was affected by industrialization. The diffusion model of social change, as applied to the study of national development, predicts that ethnic change in the periphery will occur as a long-term consequence of structural differentiation (industrialization). On the other hand, the internal colonial model of national development suggests that peripheral ethnic identity will persist following differentiation, given the institutionalization of a cultural division of labor.

The adequacy of these alternative models was then considered with respect to this case study. Part II discussed the essentially colonial process by which English institutions and markets expanded into the regions of the Celtic fringe. This expansion occurred simultaneous to the strengthening of central political authority in England, and on the heels of the Reformation, which asserted English sovereignty from Rome. While all the evidence is not yet in, it seems reasonable to suggest that the rulers of England initiated overland expansion to secure coastal boundaries and discourage foreign invasion, to promote political stability at England's (rather than Britain's) geographic extremities, and to provide for new sources of foodstuffs. In common with colonialism overseas, the English state attempted to rule the Celtic lands for instrumental ends.

From the seventeenth century on, English military and political control in the peripheral regions was buttressed by a racist ideology which held that Norman Anglo-Saxon culture was inherently superior to Celtic culture. English denigration of the Celts and their culture survives today in at least one form, the ethnic joke.[1] While the colonial basis of England's domination of Ireland and Wales is clearest, the situation of Scotland is somewhat more complex. Because the rulers of the Scottish state were, themselves, culturally

---

[1] 'In the golden days of Oxford, when Balliol was remarkable for the number of niggers it took, and drunken Trinity louts had a chant which challenged Balliol to "bring out its white men," one scoffed at Jesus [College] for its connections with Wales. It was said that if you walked into the front quad of the college and called out "Jones," a face would appear at every window; if you then added "I mean, the Jones with the toothbrush," all the faces would disappear.' From a review of *The Welsh Extremist*, *New Statesman*, 81, 2101 (1971), p. 884.

anglicized, their English counterparts felt it unnecessary to insist upon total control over Scottish cultural institutions, as they had done in Wales and Ireland. Of course, the 'auld alliance' with France provided Scotland with an additional lever in the negotiations leading to the Union of 1707. But the persistent concern of the English and lowland Scots to neutralize Celtic culture in Scotland is evidenced by their policies in the highlands following the Jacobite Risings of the eighteenth century.

The colonial incursion of England into the Celtic lands raised the problem of culture in yet another way. The English connection stimulated anglicization among the agrarian ruling class in the Celtic regions. Wider horizons beckoned to the Celtic gentry, if these men could but shed their provincial languages and *mores* to become Englishmen in fact, as well as in name. Many took advantage of this new opportunity, and soon the agrarian social structure became confounded by parallel cultural and class distinctions. However, such ethnic re-identification was a possibility for only a small élite within the periphery. The bulk of the inhabitants of these regions adhered to Celtic cultural forms by default, rather than by design. However, by the nineteenth century, the existence of Celtic culture had become a weapon, in that it could be used as a basis for anti-English political mobilization in these traditionally disadvantaged regions. For this reason alone, it should be recognized that cultural differences between groups are fundamental for the study of social change. Analyses of collective behavior which ignore the presence of such factors, when they are in fact salient, are, therefore, incomplete.

This description of core-periphery relations in the pre-industrial era is not inconsistent with either model of national development. Indeed, many writers of the diffusionist persuasion are aware of the explicitly imperial nature of early nation-building.[1] For them, the social structure of peripheral regions undergoes a decisive transformation only in the course of industrialization. This is because industrialization stimulates economic, cultural, and political interactions of all kinds between the core and the periphery. Even if it is conceded that the peripheral social structure is initially colonial, the long-term effects of industrialization should change this social structure into the mirror image of that of the core. This is because heightened core–periphery interaction, and ongoing structural differentiation, should encourage the development of regional economic equality, national cultural homogeneity, and a national

[1] S. N. Eisenstadt, *The Political Systems of Empires* (New York: 1963).

politics dominated by functional, rather than status group, orientations to political action.

The internal colonial model posits altogether different consequences resulting from heightened core–periphery interaction. According to this model, structural inequalities between the regions should increase, as the periphery develops in a dependent mode. Individuals of the core culture are expected to dominate high prestige roles in the social structure of the peripheral regions, as is the situation in overseas colonies. The bulk of the peripheral population will be confined to subordinate positions in the social structure. In sum, a cultural division of labor will tend to arise.

Because they are limited to a range of subordinate social roles, individuals in the periphery will tend to maintain their cultural institutions and identity. This culture maintenance results from the importance of culture in the system of stratification, and the consequent tendencies towards ecological segregation in the work and residential settings. But the salience of the peripheral culture is also strengthened by making demands for the allocation of greater resources to the peripheral regions. In these circumstances, separatism is seen either as a viable solution to the problem of regional dependency, or as an effective bargaining stance *vis-à-vis* the central government.[1]

Therefore, the consequences of industrialization are critical for evaluating the adequacy of these two models. The bulk of the quantitative evidence in this study attempted to describe these general consequences. Within their limitations, which are considerable, the findings tended to support the predictions of the internal colonial model, at least with respect to Wales, Scotland and Ireland. Specific-

[1] This principle is expressed in more abstract terms by A. O. Hirschman: 'Loyalty is a key concept in the battle between exit and voice not only because, as a result of it, members may be locked into their organizations a little longer and thus use the voice option with greater determination and resourcefulness than would otherwise be the case. It is helpful also because it implies the possibility of disloyalty, that is, exit. Just as it would be impossible to be good in a world without evil, so it makes no sense to speak of being loyal to a firm, a party, or an organization with an unbreakable monopoly. While loyalty postpones exit its very existence is predicated on the possibility of exit. That even the most loyal member can exit is often an important part of his bargaining power *vis-à-vis* the organization. The chances for voice [i.e., protest] to function effectively as a recuperation mechanism are appreciably strengthened if voice is backed up by the *threat of exit*, whether it is made openly or whether the possibility of exist is merely well understood to be an element in the situation by all concerned.' *Exit, Voice and Loyalty: Responses to Decline in Firms, Organization, and States* (Cambridge, Mass.: 1970), p. 82.

ally, the expectations of the diffusion model were not upheld with respect to long-term trends in aggregate regional inequalities. Industrialization did not diffuse into the peripheral areas in the same form as it had developed in the core. When industrialization did penetrate the periphery, it was in a dependent mode; consequently, production was highly specialized and geared for export. Regional economic inequalities persisted despite industrialization: the *per capita* income of the Celtic industrial counties has been lower than those of comparably industrial English counties for over a century.

Similarly, industrialization did not lead to the establishment of a national culture, particularly in so far as religious adherence is concerned. It is true that language maintenance in peripheral regions has faded with time, but a group's ethnic identity need not rest solely on its linguistic distinctiveness.[1] Finally, there has been no clear trend towards the development of functional political cleavages within the peripheral areas. Aggregate voting patterns in the Celtic lands continued to be largely determined by cultural rather than social structural factors. Each of these findings is inconsistent with the expectations of the diffusion model, but consistent with its alternative. However, within England itself, the diffusion model appears to have general relevance.

As a whole these findings remain merely suggestive. They do not provide much insight into the more micro-sociological processes which are specified in the internal colonial model. In large part, the ecological data collected for this study can *never* adequately describe the detailed social structures of local communities, and, hence, the political sentiments of their inhabitants. The rather complex statistical analysis of chapter 10 is, at best, an approximation of such a description. By measuring whether a county's aggregate vote is best explained by its cultural or its social structural composition, I have attempted to infer something about its collective political sentiments. The conclusions of this chapter also tend to support the internal colonial thesis, because they show that in those counties where Nonconformity has a significant negative effect on *per capita* income, cultural variables explain more of the variance in voting than structural variables. It is possible to interpret these findings to mean that, in those areas where there is a cultural division of labor, political demands will largely be formulated in ethnic terms, rather than those of social class. For ethnic solidarity may be said to occur whenever

[1] However, as was pointed out in chapter 6, regional dialectical differences continue to have great salience in the social life of these islands.

345

a group defines its boundaries in cultural terms. But, whereas these data are certainly consistent with such an interpretation, they are hardly detailed enough to strongly support it. There are no ready-made ecological data which cross-tabulate ethnic and occupational variables, in time series, for any society. Perhaps this study will stimulate the collection of such data, since they are invaluable for studies of ethnicity and for a greater understanding of social change in general.

It is probably true that, at any given time, a sense of ethnic identification need not rest on any structural basis whatever. This is because ethnic identity is very likely to be transmitted in the course of socialization. If ethnicity is a salient part of a father's identity, it may remain so for his children. But, unless it corresponds with significant categories in the social structure, there is no reason to expect ethnic identity to persist in succeeding generations. Hence, there is a need for some structural explanation, such as the cultural division of labor, of the persistence of ethnic identification within given groups.

The cultural division of labor must not be regarded as a binary variable; rather, it exists in any society to a greater or lesser degree. If progress is to be made in the systematic study of ethnicity, adequate indicators of the extensiveness of the cultural division of labor must be developed. This may not be an easy task, but it is far from an impossible one. It should also be noted that cultural distinctions may have salience in other domains of social life than the work-place: for example, in neighborhoods, educational institutions, and voluntary associations of all kinds. I have assumed that, over the long run, the existence of cultural stratification in the occupational structure will determine the significance of culture in these other domains of social life. Whether this assumption may be justified is, of course, an empirical question. At any given time, however, cultural stratification in one of these other domains, such as in the distribution of housing, may independently lead to the development of ethnic solidarity.[1]

In the absence of systematic evidence on the cultural division of labor, it is necessary to turn to scattered ethnographies of rural and urban communities in peripheral areas. Several excellent works of this kind have been published, though they typically concern the agricultural village as a social setting. By and large, the conclusions

---

[1] John Rex and Robert Moore, *Race, Community, and Conflict* (London: 1967).

of these field studies are wholly consistent with the interpretations presented above.[1] But there is little published evidence bearing on intergroup relations in the enclave cities of the Celtic periphery, particularly for the earlier industrial period. Hence, many relevant details about the extensiveness of the cultural division of labor in these areas remain cloudy. There is much fruitful work to be done on these themes by social scientists interested in both historical and contemporary societies.

Another large body of inference concerns the mode of England's domination of the Celtic periphery, particularly by its financial and political institutions. That London has exerted great influence on the economy of the peripheral regions, through its banks and Ministries, is obvious. Yet very little is known about the actual mechanisms of such control, or about the prevalence of ethnocentric attitudes towards inhabitants of the peripheral regions on the part of key decision-makers. This kind of information may be worth pursuing.

This study raises implicitly at least one more research question. For the sake of simplicity, the models of national development introduced in chapter 2 concerned only two interacting groups, a core, and a periphery. But there are probably few actual situations where such a simple model is justified and this, of course, is not one of them. If England may be considered the core, then at least four separate peripheries must be distinguished in the British Isles, namely, Wales, Scotland, Ireland, and Ulster. Hardly any attention has been paid to the interaction of these multiple peripheries both with each other, and with respect to the core. To take the extreme possibilities, these separate peripheral groups can either band together as one solidary group (the Pan–Celtic movement is an illustration),[2] or they can compete for scarce resources at each other's expense (the fate of Irish immigrants in Scotland is an illustration).[3] It is likely that the actual relations between these peripheral groups varied between these poles in different circumstances. The specification of these circumstances awaits further investigation.

However, even if it is granted that the internal colonial model does a better job of explaining the relationship between England and the

---

[1] Few ethnographic studies, however, have been predominantly concerned with such questions. An interesting exception is Isabel Emmett, *A North Wales Village* (London: 1964). In this study there is explicit reference to the colonial analogy.

[2] F. S. L. Lyons, *Ireland Since the Famine* (London: 1971), p. 223.

[3] J. E. Handley, *The Irish in Scotland* (Cork: 1943), and J. E. Handley, *The Irish in Modern Scotland* (Cork: 1947).

Celtic fringe than the diffusion model, is it justly named? Readers having extensive knowledge of colonial societies could argue that the description of Wales as an internal colony is overstated. They might suggest that there are qualitative differences existing between the extremely high levels of regional inequality and inter-ethnic conflict in Third World societies, and the moderate, perhaps even quaint, differences separating the Celts from their English cousins. Perhaps Wales should rather be termed a peripheral region within the metropolis.

To this objection I would disagree on two counts. First, this argument is manifestly ahistorical. Most societies of the Third World have, in the main, only begun the process of national development. Since there is no real disagreement that national development must occur in stages of one kind or another, the logic of comparing Ghana's present situation to that of the contemporary United Kingdom is dubious. In those ex-colonial societies which have already undergone some experience in national development—notably in Latin America—the concept of internal colonialism has begun to enjoy wide usage. The precise form of internal colonialism in Latin America differs from that in the United Kingdom. There, the Amerindians are more deprived of civil and political liberties, and far more destitute in relation to the ruling *mestizos*, than are the Celts in relation to the English. The reasons behind this variation in patterns of internal colonialism have scarcely ever been discussed, but I hazard the guess that these contrasts relate, in some way, to the different positions these respective societies have within the world system. The Amerindians are an internal colony within a peripheral part of the world system. The Celts, on the other hand, are an internal colony within the very core of this world system. To paraphrase Orwell, all internal colonies are equal, but some are more equal than others.

My second objection to this criticism is that it is manifestly asociological. Groups must define their situations in the social structure as being legitimate, or non-legitimate, within the context of their own society. The knowledge that an Irishman, though the victim of discrimination in Britain, is far better off than all but a small élite in India is not likely to satisfy his yearning for dignity and equality. So long as states serve to demarcate societies, they will be the relevant arenas in which justice, and, consequently, injustice will be determined for better or for worse.

In fact, there is no hard and fast line which can be drawn between the three multi-dimensional concepts colony, internal colony, and peripheral region. Yet, the term internal colony has been selected here not for its possible dramatic appeal, but for its analytic utility. These three concepts of peripherality may tentatively be sorted out by their relationship to five particular variables: (1) the degree of administrative integration,[1] (2) the extensiveness of citizenship in the periphery,[2] (3) the prestige of the peripheral culture, (4) the existence of geographical continguity, and (5) the length of the association between the periphery and the core. The absence of economic dependency from this list is due to the fact that it is a common feature of all three concepts. If each of these variables is assigned a high or low rank, then a *colony* is a region generally ranked low on all five variables; an *internal colony* is given a high rank on (1), (2), and (4), and a medium rank on (5); and a *peripheral region* is ranked highly on all the variables. From this exercise, it is easy to see that the situation of the internal colony has more in common with that of a peripheral region than with an (overseas) colony. Yet, the existence of a culture of low prestige within a peripheral region is justification enough for the establishment of an internal colonial category: without it, there can be no cultural division of labor.

The persistence of ethnic solidarity in the peripheral regions of the United Kingdom has general implications for comparative sociology. Most, if not all, of the historical nation-states had their beginnings in culturally distinctive core regions, where national bureaucratic administrations first appeared. 'Administrative revolutions' in the core were almost always followed by forays into peripheral areas. Thus, there is reason to believe that the pattern of state-building in the British Isles was not, by any means, idiosyncratic in Western European history. For a very long time the United Kingdom has been described as one of a small group of nation-states having greatest success in the establishment of a fully national economy, culture, and political system. Indeed, even among the Anglo-American democracies—a sample of societies consistently highly

[1] This may be defined as the extent to which laws passed for the core apply in the periphery.
[2] Citizenship, as defined by T. H. Marshall, *Class, Citizenship and Social Development* (New York: 1964), pp. 71–134, involves three separate components: civil, political and social rights. For the most part, colonies were placed at a disadvantage with respect to all these rights. However, in the late stages of colonialization, civil and political rights were extended in some colonies. However, social rights (welfare, security and education) in colonies always lagged behind those in the metropolis.

ranked on dimensions of national development—the United Kingdom stands out as a model national society. Regional cleavages are less severe in the British Isles than they are in most other developed areas of the world.

It is against this comparative backdrop that the book's conclusions must be considered. On the basis of these findings, it should no longer be surprising that the uneven pattern of development termed internal colonialism should have developed in the first industrial society. That it has survived the rise and fall of the most extensive overseas colonial empire in the history of the world also makes sense. Further research might establish that internal colonialism is, in fact, the *modal* form of national development in industrial societies.

What can be said of the future? If, as I have argued, internal colonialism tends to arise naturally in the course of industrialization, can it ever be mediated? Any answer must, at this point, be largely speculative. This analysis proposes that, to the extent a culturally distinct group gains equal access to the full range of social roles within society, it will undergo ethnic change. The state can play a central role in promoting national development, by transferring resources from the core to the periphery, as well as by legislating against the perpetuation of the cultural division of labor.[1] Both of these policies represent an interference with the normal workings of civil society.[2] For this reason, it may be expected that socialist states are placed at an advantage, relative to capitalist states, in coping with the problems of internal colonialism. This is not to suggest that internal colonialism is any less likely to develop in these societies; but, rather, that once these patterns occur, they may be more easily addressed by socialist regimes.[3]

The prospects for achieving such equality for individuals of Celtic social origins in the United Kingdom seem relatively good, in the long run. The continuation of Celtic nationalist ferment can only serve to increase the awareness of the plight of these regions, and

[1] Recent federal laws passed in the United States requiring that 'Affirmative Action' be taken to employ various minorities, at least in the public sector, serve as an example.

[2] For the classic distinction between the state and civil society, see Karl Marx, 'On the Jewish question' in T. B. Bottomore, ed., *Karl Marx: Early Writings* (New York: 1964).

[3] However, this expectation does not appear to be borne out by the evidence. See I. S. Koropeckyj, 'Equalization of regional development in socialist countries: an empirical study,' *Economic Development and Cultural Change*, 21, 1 (1972).

their citizens, to England's government and status-conferring institutions, most importantly, perhaps, the universities.

For their part, the Celts themselves may be more willing to identify with England as immigration from Asia, Africa, and the West Indies proceeds. In relation to these non-white immigrants, even the desperately poor Irish in Britain appear privileged. Already these most recent immigrant groups in Britain have adopted the political analyses of radical American Black groups. It is only a matter of time before they lay claim to the mantle of being internal colonies. How the Celtic peoples will react to English racism directed, for a change, against other internal minorities remains, of course, to be determined.

INDEX

Abraham, William ('Mabon'), 277
Acculturation, see Culture and cultural differences
Agriculture, 79–80, 82, 131; capital-intensive, 151; grain, 85, 270; Highland Line, 134; restraints on productivity, 156
Ake, Claude, 26
Aldcroft, D. H., 293
Alford, Robert, 213, 218
Allardt, Erik, 16, 28
Allport, Gordon W., 24
Allum, P. A., 119
Almond, Gabriel, 25, 132
Alonso, William, 29, 129
Amery, L. S., 213
Anglicanism, see Church of England
Anglo-Saxons, 47
Apter, David, 22, 25
Arnold, Matthew, 127
Arnot, R. Page, 279
Assimilation, xvii, 24, 64, 314
Authority, centralization of, 61–2
Autonomy, 62–3

Bacon, Sir Francis, 76, 237
Baer, Werner, 29, 131
Bagehot, Walter, 213, 241
Balandier, Georges, 30, 69
Banfield, Edward C., 29
Banks, 88; Irish, 88; Scottish, 89; Welsh, 88–9
Barth, Frederik, 36, 37–8, 207
Bateman, John, 119
Beard, C. A., 122
Beckett, J. C., 84, 94, 102, 184, 272
Beer, Samuel, 213
Belfast, 186, 286
Bell, Daniel, 16

Bendix, Reinhard, 18, 231
Bérard, Victor, 256, 257, 259
Berg, Elliott J., 23
Bettelheim, Charles, 243
Beveridge, Janet, 285
Birnie, Arthur, 54
Black communities, xiv–xvi
Blair, P. H., 53
Blalock, Hubert M., 178, 332
Blau, P. M., 247
Blauner, Robert, 33
Blewett, Neal, 252
Bloch, Marc, 56
Blom, Jan-Petter, 192
Blondel, Jean, 213
Bochel, J. M., 230, 308
Boer War, 244–6, 253
Bolton, G. C., 73
Bottigheimer, Karl S., 103
Boudon, Raymond, 247
Bourgeoisie, 127, 238
Boyne, Battle of the, 108
Braudel, Fernand, 32, 47, 49, 67, 69, 234, 235
Brazil, 29
Brehon Laws, 77
Brenner, Robert, 98
British Isles, see Great Britain
Brittany, 31, 63
Brooke, Christopher, 78, 112
Brown, A. J., 149, 158, 159, 160
Buckatsch, E. J., 138
Budge, Ian, 214
Butler, David, 214, 261, 316

Calvinism, 97
Cameron, Rondo, 88, 89
Campbell, A. D., 294
Campbell, Angus, 248
Campbell, R. H., 83, 84, 88, 115

353

Capital and capitalists, 98, 100, 114, 115, 150
Carmichael, Stokely, 40, 133
Carus-Wilson, E. M., 136
Catholics and Catholicism, 33, 61, 97, 100, 103, 104, 108, 109, 168, 180, 288, 323; Emancipation, 77; English antipathy to, 268; in Ireland, 183, 184, 267; merchant classes, 90; Penal Laws, 184, 268; prohibitions against, 76–7
Cattle trade: Ireland, 84–5, 87, 93–4, 270, 288; Scotland, 83, 84
Celts and Celtic fringe, xiv, xvi, 10–11, 47, 87, 100, 127, 317–29 passim; anglicization, 164–217 passim; assimilation, 64, 65; counties of, 123, wealth of, 151; culture of, 48–9, 74, 76, 109, 161, 327; economic dependency and disadvantages, 90, 130, 161; industrialization in, 139, 148, 149, 150, 320, 327; investment in, 88; languages, 195, 330 (see also Gaelic, Wales); nationalism in twentieth century, 264–310; political control and incorporation, 67–8, 79–123, 212; social organization, 52, 58, 59; sovereignty, loss of, 68, 90–5, 119; trade with England, 89; see also Ireland, Scotland, Wales
Chamberlain, Joseph, 246
Charles I, 103, 107
Charles II, 107
Chartism, 279
Church of England, 66, 74, 96–7, 100, 102, 168, 170, 171, 172, 177, 206; Disestablishment, 281
Churches, Established: adherence, 173, 190; see also Scotland (Church), Wales (Church)
Cities, location, 31
Civil War (England), 113
Clapham, Sir John, 70
Clark, G. N., 99
Clarke, Aidan, 268
Clarkson, J. Dunsmore, 284, 286, 287, 288, 289
Class, 217, 218, 242, 313; consciousness, 275, 291, 295, 327; solidarity, 37; War, 16
Clegg, A. H., 276
Coate, Mary, 65
Cole, G. D. H., 275, 280, 286
Coleman, D. C., 91

Collins, Randall, 17
Collison-Black, R. B., 86, 87
Colonialism, internal, xvi, 8–9, 10, 13, 39, 80, 133, 166, 185–6, 212, 243, 342–51 passim; defining features of, 33, 73; in Latin America, 32, 348
Colonies, 91, 262; 'colonial situation,' 30, 31; development, 147–8; expansion, 31–2, 100
Commerce: centers, 139; occupations, 141
Communist Party, 280, 284, 296
Connell, K. H., 170
Conner, Walker, 25
Connolly, James, 268, 286, 287, 289–90
Conservative Party, 219, 221, 229, 246, 251, 252, 253, 273, 302–3, 319, 325, 332–3, 335; opposition to, 257, 260
Core regions, 4, 5, 6, 12, 18, 26, 32, 36, 342, 347; domination of periphery, 9, 10; incorporation with periphery, 118; interaction with periphery, 7, 8, 9, 14, 22–3, 27, 34, 118; 166; modernized, 23; monopoly of commerce and trade, 33
Corn Laws, 85, 86–7
Cornwall, 64–5, 101; boroughs, 120
Costigan, Giovanni, 77
Counties, typology of, 328–30
Coupland, Reginald, 75, 183, 214, 244, 245, 262
Cox, Kevin R., 214
Cromwell, Oliver, 103, 107, 108
Cromwell, Thomas, 66, 96
Crotty, Raymond D., 87, 148, 270
Crown, The, 96, 98–100
Cullen, L. M., 68, 84, 86, 88, 92, 94
Culloden, Battle of, 113
Cultural division of labor, 9, 38–41 passim, 43, 90, 133, 263, 302, 312, 315, 316, 335, 344, 346–7
Cultural groups, 4, 10; migrating 47; minority, 194; 'segmented pluralism,' 48
Culture and cultural differences, 7, 11, 21, 23, 24, 43, 118, 329; acculturation, 9, 10, 24, 40, 48; between groups, 34–9; homogenization, 164–167; and income, 325; indigenous, 73; integration, 18–19; traditional, 28, 29; variables, 312, 317, 318, 319, 321, 326; and voting, 325
Culture of poverty, xv, 328

Cuming, G. J., 97
Curtis, Edmund, 77, 184
Curtis, L. Perry, 77, 161, 184-5, 262, 269
Customs barriers, 135
Czarnowski, Stefan, 104

Dahl, Robert A., 16
Dahrendorf, Ralf, 43
Daiches, David, 225
Danegeld, 54
Dangerfield, G., 274
Darien expedition, 71
Davies, Christopher S. L., 97, 143
Davies, E. T., 279
Davies, Sir John, 76
Davis, Horace B., 236
De Maistre, Joseph, 15
Deane, Phyllis, 161, 254
Denver, D. T., 230, 308
Depression, World, 293-6
Deutsch, Karl W., 12, 25, 132, 142, 192, 211, 216
Devine, T. M., 94, 105
Dibble, Vernon K., 122
Dickens, A. G., 97
Diffusion theory, 6, 7, 10, 13, 22, 28, 166, 167, 210, 342, 343; definition, 7; inadequacies of, 26, 30
Dobb, Maurice, 66, 91
Dodd, A. H., 89, 143, 201
Dogan, Mattei, 13, 245
Domar, Evsey, 80
Donaldson, Gordon, 94, 105, 107, 108, 186, 188, 256
Dos Santos, Theotonio, 81, 130
Dow, J., 105
Draper, N. R., 318
Dublin, 143; Pale of, 72, 76, 186
Duby, Georges, 33, 50, 62, 79
Duncan, Otis Dudley, 200
Durkheim, Emile, 23-4, 34, 164; conscience collective, 4, 20; 'osmosis,' 24, 29

Eckstein, Harry, 213
Ecology, 13; in British history, 49-59; cultural, 36; ecological analysis, 245
Edie, Carolyn A., 93
Edinburgh, 186
Education, 27; compulsory, 195, 204; literacy, 165; Scottish and English, 116
Edward VII, 282

Edwards, Otis Dudley, 214, 299
Eire (Irish Free State), 266, 298
Eisenstadt, S. N., 60, 64, 65, 343
Elite groups, 26; regional, 122
Ellis, P. B., 73
Elton, G. R., 27, 66, 96
Emery, Frank, 59, 134
Emmanuel, Arghiri, 243
Emmett, Isabel, 347
Enclosures, 82, 134, 185
Engels, Friedrich, 127, 164, 176, 238
England and the English, 32, 253; commerce, 67; political unification, 55; social organizations, 58; state expansion, 47-8; in Wales, 188-90, 203-4; see also Great Britain
Episcopalianism, 97, 100, 107, 109, 168, 268
Ethnicity, 16-17; change, xiii, 6, 15-43, 311-41, 350, politics of, 39-43; cleavage, 11; and culture, 311-17; ethnocentrism, 159, 160; functional theory of ethnic change, 312, 314, 317-23, 324; groups, xiv-xvi, 36-7; identification, xiii, 11, 34, 38, 40, 41, 346; political integration, 340; prejudice and discrimination, 160; as primordial sentiment, 313, 320, 340; reactive theory of ethnic change, 312, 314-15, 326, 331-9; solidarity, 6, 315, 316, 345-6, 349

Fabian Society, 276
Fanon, Frantz, xv
Fascism, 295
Feinstein, C. H., 162
Feldman, Arnold, 23
Ferguson, William, 83, 93, 244
Feudalism, 31, 61; vassals, 62
Finer, S. E., 213
Fisher, F. J., 82, 136
Fishman, Joshua A., 191, 194, 196, 205
Food: markets, 82; supply, 69-70
Forman, Shepard, 29
France, 32-3, 71
Francis, Hywel, 295, 296
Frank, Andre Gunder, 31
Freeman, T. W., 143
Freud, Sigmund, 237
Friedlander, Dov, 138, 139, 186
Friedmann, John, 29
Furtado, Celso, 146
Fustel de Coulanges, N. D., 3

355

Gaelic language, 109, 167, 168; in
Ireland, 76, 77, 168, 184, 193, 198;
revival, 290; speaking, decline of,
191–207 *passim*
Gallacher, John, 246
Gallacher, William, 296
Gamson, William A., 41
Gay, John D., 168, 171
Geertz, Clifford, 15, 22, 36, 313, 314,
320
Gellner, Ernest, 36–7
General Strike (1926), 295
Genovese, Elizabeth F., 117
Gerth, Hans, 28
Giglioli, Pier Paolo, 191
Glasgow, 186
Gonzáles-Casanova, P., 32, 133
Gordon, David C., 39
Government: central, 27, legitimacy,
19–20; local, 122
Gramsci, Antonio, 9, 236, 239
Grant, I. F., 94, 104
Gray, H. L., 134, 269
Gray, M., 143
Great Britain, 68, 213, 316–17; cul-
tural groups, 10–11; geographical
areas, 51–2; immigrant groups,
351; as model national society, 350;
religious affiliations, 167–91; Ro-
man occupation, 52, 53; Union of,
61, Ireland, 68, 72, Scotland, 67–8,
motives behind, 69–73; *see also*
England
Griffin, Keith, 147
Gross National Product, 242
Gumperz, John J., 191, 192, 195, 206

Haas, Ernst, 26
Habsburg Empire, 61
Hadrian's Wall, 53
Halévy, Elie, 169, 176, 255, 262
Haller, William, 269
Hamilton (Scotland), 308–9
Hamilton, Charles V., 40, 133
Hammond, Edwin, 129, 142, 158
Hammond, J. L., and Barbara, 168,
318
Handley, J. E., 347
Hanham, H. J., 116, 118, 172, 214,
283, 298, 302, 304, 305
Hardie, Keir, 279, 280, 283
Harmon, Harry, 151
Harris, Walter, 184
Harriss, G. L., 66

Hartwell, R. M., 177
Hassall, C., 189
Hatcher, John, 65
Haug, Marie R., 167
Hechter, Michael, 12, 90, 136, 142,
214
Hecksher, Eli F., 26, 91, 135, 136
Henry VIII, 66, 96, 101, 102, 104, 168
Heslinga, M. W., 134, 195
Hicks, J. R., 129
Highlands, 50, 52–3, 57; highland
societies, 51
Hill, Christopher, 66, 78, 90, 93, 98,
100, 108, 120
Hintze, Otto, 61
Hirschman, A. O., 159, 160, 344
History and historiography, 5–6, 13
Hobsbawm, Eric J., 96, 117, 168, 177,
214, 238, 240, 254, 275
Hodges, T. Mansel, 89
Homans, George C., 24, 35, 59, 132
Hoskins, W. G., 181
Hyndman, H. M., 281, 282

Imperialism, 244, 245, 282; Cecil
Rhodes on, 239; expansion, 60, 63,
64, conditions for, 65–6; jingoism,
241–2; preference, 253; servitor
imperialism, 234–63 *passim*; and
standard of living, 255
Income, *per capita*, 130, 152, 157,
161–3, 211, 316, 323, 329, 330–1,
336–7, 345; cultural factors and, 321,
323, 324; National, 254; Scottish,
294
Independent Labor Party, 276, 279,
282–3, 288
Industrialization, 7, 8, 14, 17, 22, 61,
127–163, 167, 204, 211, 214, 249,
251, 270, 271, 337, 343, 345; and
Anglicanism, 185; and Celtic languages, 198, 199–203; consequences
of, 128–30, 143, 231–3; counties,
139–41, disadvantaged, 154, 159–60;
factor of, 151, 152, 153; indicators
of, 201, 251–2, 316, 317; industrial
enclaves, 143, 145, 147, 149, 186,
196, 198, 270–1, 291; Industrial
Revolution, 27; level, by counties,
187; peripheral, 9; and political
centralization, 211; and regionalism,
208; and religious affiliation, 173,
176–80 *passim*, 190; spatial con-
finement of, 150

Inglehart, R. F., 166
Inglis, K. S., 171
Inheritance customs, 81; *gavelkind*, 82, 83, 110, 134; partible inheritance, 82, 134; primogeniture, 110
Integration: economic, 19; national, measurement, 216–17, 233, counties, 228, 229; 'negative,' 292; political, 19, 228, 235; of societies, 22
Intellectuals, 98
Ireland, Northern, xvi, 129, 152, 226, 227, 254, 263, 265, 269, 288, 293, 300; Catholics in, 180; local autonomy in, 266; Protestants in, 77
Ireland and the Irish, xiii, xvi–xvii, 11, 33, 56, 67, 84–7, 100, 102–4, 244, 269, 284–93 *passim*; anglicization, 117, 185, 343; Civil War (1641), 103; culture, 76, 77; Easter Rising (1916), 290; Famine (1846), 270; gentry, 116, 123; Home Rule, 214, 253, 259, 260, 263, 281, 296; industrial development, 92; migration to Britain, 137, 186, 196; Nationalism, 270, 272, 274, 289; Parliament, 68, 72–3, 84, 94; Partition and Secession of, 263, 290, 292–3; Plantations, 72, 76, 103, 184, 268; social groups, 103; Union with England, 68, 72, 114; wage scales in, 284–5; *see also* Eire
Irish Republican Army, 290
Irish Socialist Republican Party, 287, 289
Irish Transit Workers Union, 287
Iron industry, 138

Jacobitism, 113, 120
James I (and VI), 71, 94
James, M. E., 97
Jaszi, Oscar, 61
Jesus College, Oxford, 111, 342
John, A. H., 189
Jones, E. Terrence, 219
Jones, W. R., 161
Justices of the Peace, 122–3, 136

Kellas, J., 308
Kendall, P. L., 247
Kendall, Walter, 281
Kennedy, Robert E., 170
Key, V. O., 248
Keyfitz, N., 170
Kiernan, V. G., 31, 87
Kingsley, Charles, xvi–xvii

Kinnear, Michael, 253
Kipling, Rudyard, 262
Knox, Ronald, 176
Koropeckyj, I. S., 350
Kroeber, A. L., 7, 22, 24
Kuznets, S., 132

'Labor, aristocracy of,' 236, 238, 239–240, 255
Labor Party, xvii, 205, 219, 221, 230, 259, 265, 280, 284, 287–8, 289, 303, 304, 305, 307, 308, 309, 335; support, 272, 273, 291
Labor supply curve, 23
Labov, William, 206
Ladurie, Emmanuel Le Roy, 49
Laissez-faire policy, 91
Landlords and tenants, 85, 117, 118, 182, 185, 296; absentee, 85, 116; Catholic, 103; land tenure, 54, 86, 119; rents, 85
Langholm, Sivert, 5
Language, 165–6, 191–207; bilingualism, 192, 193, 194, 201, 205; change, 192, 206; *see also* Gaelic, Scotland, Wales
Lanternari, Vittorio, 177
Larkin, James, 286, 287
Lasuén, J. R., 29, 131
Lazarsfeld, P. F., 247
Leadership, 25–6
Lee, J., 150
Lee, Maurice, 94
Legitimacy, 60, 61, 63
Lenin, V. I., 8, 236, 238, 239
Lewis, E. D., 189, 204, 278
Lewis, George R., 65
Liberal Party, 219, 221, 230, 246, 254, 259, 273, 280, 291, 335; decline of, 273–4, 275, 303; support, 271
Lieberson, Stanley, 192
Linen Trade, 92–3
Lipset, Seymour M., 16, 25, 63, 210, 212, 230, 231, 249, 314
Lofchie, Michael F., 11
London, 150
Londonderry Plantation, 72, 76, 103, 184, 186, 268
Lorwin, Val R., 48, 194
Lowe, David, 280
Lowlands, 50, 57
Lutheranism, 97
Lyons, F. S. L., 143, 148, 214, 289, 347
Lythe, S. G. E., 94, 95, 105

McCracken, Eileen, 84
McCrone, Gavin, 158, 294, 298 303, 307
MacDiarmid, Hugh, 283
MacDonald, J. Ramsay, 283
Machiavelli, Niccolò, 62
Mackinder, Halford, 51, 134
Mackintosh, J. P., 214
Maclean, John, 283, 284
Macnamara, J., 193
Madison, James, 237-8
Maine, Sir Henry, 52
Mannheim, Karl, 177
Mansbach, Richard W., 308
Marriage: rate, 142, 170, 252, Irish, 170; registers, 169, analysis, 169-72; Registry Offices, 171
Marshall, T. H., 18, 212, 314, 349
Marx, Karl, 15, 20, 42, 87, 88, 128, 164, 236, 327, 350
Mary of Guise, 71, 104, 106
Mason, Phillip, 73
Maxwell, Constantia, 76, 237
Medieval societies, 62, 64
Memmi, Albert, 73
Mendenhall, Thomas C., 89, 136
Mercantilism, 26, 91, 135
Merton, Robert K., 160
Methodism and Methodists, 110, 177
Michels, Robert, 216, 239, 255
Migrants and migration, 87; group, 132; internal and interregional, 137, 176, 188-90, 200, 204
Mills, C. Wright, 28
Minchinton, W. E., 67
Miners and mining, 114, 259; coal, 131, 139, 147, 148, 188, 200, 277-9, 293, 309, wages, 277, 278; South Wales Miners Federation, 279, 295, 296
Mitchell, B. R., 278
Mitchison, Rosalind, 113
Montesquieu, Robert de, 117
Moody, T. W., 103, 184
Moore, Wilbert E., 23, 128
Morgan, Kenneth O., 183, 214, 245, 276, 277
Mosca, Gaetano, 79
Myrdal, Gunnar, 17, 43, 133, 148

Namier, Lewis, 67, 120
Nation, concept of, 60
National development, 5, 6-7, 11, 17-30 passim; definition of, 17-18; expansion, 60, 63; intermediate, 22

National Union of Dock Laborers, 286, 287
Nationalism, xvii, 3-4, 214, 215, 230, 256, 270; see also Ireland, Scotland, Wales
Nationality, 19; development of, 48
Navigation Acts, 93, 100, 256
Neale, R. S., 256
Nef, John U., 98
Nevin, Edward, 306
Nobility, 97
Nonconformism, 74, 75, 168, 170, 171, 174, 185, 206, 279, 280, 318, 321-4 passim, 329, 330, 337, 338, 339, 345; in industrial areas, 176-80, 181; rural, 182; Test and Corporation Acts, 268; and Welsh nationality, 183, 190-1
Norman, E. R., 269
Norman Conquest, 54, 56
North, Douglass C., 80

O'Brien, Conor Cruise, 77, 273
Ostrogorski, Moisei, 27

Palma, Giuseppe di, 119
Palmer, Norman D., 85
Pares, Richard, 121
Pareto, Vilfredo, 311
Parnell, Charles Stewart, 273
Parsons, Talcott, 23, 24, 28, 211, 217, 313, 314
Pelling, Henry, 171, 219, 221, 229, 246, 250, 253, 259, 274, 275, 282, 335
Periphery and peripheral regions, 5, 7, 18, 26, 28, 32, 342, 347; collectivity, 43; control, 114; cultures in, 27, 64, 166; in developing countries, 15-16; economic dependence, 81; emigration to, 188-9; interaction with core, 7, 8, 9, 14, 22-3, 27, 34, 118, 166; as internal body, 30-4; isolation of, 29; political position, 40; segregation in, 42; traditional orientation of, 23, 28
Perkin, Harold, 123, 128, 172
Perroux, François, 131
Petit-Dutaillis, Charles, 56
Pettigrew, Thomas F., 24
Phillips, C. H., 256
Pickering, W. S. F., 171
Pierce, T. Jones, 82
Plumb, J. H., 120, 122

Poggi, Gianfranco, 4
Polanyi, Karl, 238
Politics: centralization, 27, 106, 128; cleavage, 16; contextual effects, 247–8; corruption, 120; elections and electoral returns, 219, 253, analysis, 245, 247; franchise, 235; General Election (1970), 290; incorporation, 79–123; integration, 19, 20, 21, 43, 265; parties, 212, 218, 219, 220, 250, 251, 274 (*see also* Communist, Conservative, Labor, Liberal); responses, measurement, 243–51; 'stable unrepresentation,' 40–1; structures, 7; voting behavior and patterns, 218, 222, 223, 224, 248, 253, 257–9, 271, 272, 292, 294, 296, 297, 300, 301, 308, 317, 319, 324, 325, 330–3 *passim*
Pomfret, John E., 85
Pool, Jonathan, 167
Population, 252
Portugal, 32
Potatoes, 85, 86
Pounds, N. J. G., 5
Poyning's Law, 84
Presbyterianism, 78, 100, 106, 109, 168, 268
Price, Richard, 245
Protestants and Protestantism, 72, 73, 77, 106, 108, 168, 267, 268, 289
Pryde, G. S., 188
Pye, Lucian, 25

Quinn, D. B., 102

Racism, xvii, 16; anti-Celtic, 269, 342; institutionalized, 130, 133; inverse, xv
Railways, 149
Read, Donald, 138, 226
Rebellions, 97, 99, 113
Redfield, Robert, 24
Rees, Alwyn D., 182
Rees, Thomas, 190
Rees, William, 57, 69, 114
Reform Act (1832), 120
Reformation, 66, 95–109 *passim*, 168
Regions and regional differences, 7, 8, 211, 213; autonomy, 300–1; backward, 29; coefficient of variation, 144–6; cultural differences, 95–109; development (special areas), 298, 303; economic specialization, 18,

82; growth differentials, 129, 132; inequality, 129–33 *passim*, 137, 139, 141–63 *passim*; integration, economic, 136; political differences, 208, 209, 214; stagnant, 133; structural differences, 251–7; variations in income, 128, 155, 156, 158
Regression analysis, linear, 155; coefficient, 178; multiple, 152, 157, 200–1, 223, 252, 258, 318
Renouard, Yves, 63
Rex, John, 346
Rhodes, Cecil, 239
Richards, E. S., 149
Richardson, W. C., 66
Riegelhaupt, J. F., 29
Roads (highland), 113, 114
Roberts, R. D., 89
Robinson, Ronald, 246
Rokkan, Stein, 13, 16, 231, 245, 314
Romans in Britain, 53–4
Rose, Richard, 95, 210, 213, 267
Roth, Guenther, 60, 292
Rowe, John, 65
Rowse, A. L., 63, 65, 101

Schermerhorn, R. A., 18
Schmitter, Philippe, 26
Schramm, Wilbur, 25
Schumpeter, Joseph, 241
Schwarz, John E., 308
Scotland and the Scottish, xvii, 11, 32, 53, 67, 83–4, 100, 104–6, 121–2, 129, 159, 244, 246, 253, 256, 263, 280–1, 300, 310, 326; alliance with France, 71, 95, 104, 105, 343; anglicization, 77, 112, 115, 343; aristocracy and gentry, 105, 115, 123; Church of Scotland, 105–6, 168, 172, 268; clans, 113, 114; exports and foreign trade, 71–2, 95, 105, 257, trade with England, 105; heavy industry, 93, 148, 298; highland territories, 52, 112, Risings, 113; language, 115–16, 168, 198; linguistic groups, 78; Literary Revival, 298; Nationalism, 188, 214, 264, 283–4, 288, 293, 334; Nationalist Party, 298, 299, 303–5, 307–10 *passim*; Parliament and MPs, 67, 71, 112, 121; patronage, 121, 122; Union with England, 67–8, 71, 83
Sectionalism, 208–33; functional, 209, 210; peripheral, 209, 210, 248, 294,

Sectionalism—*contd.*
297, 299, 300, measurement of, 215–16, 221, 225–33 *passim*
Semmel, Bernard, 239, 249, 253
Shannon, R. T., 244
Shils, Edward, 211, 217, 313
Simmel, Georg, 200
Simms, J. G., 103
Simpson, David, 307
Skeel, Caroline, 83
Smelser, Neil J., 8
Smith, Adam, 135
Smout, T. C., 71, 78, 83, 108, 113–14, 256
Snyder, Edward D., 161
Social Democratic Federation, 275, 276, 280–1, 283; Scottish Wing, 282, 283
Social mobilization, 25
Social organizations: allocations of social roles, 38; British, 57; geography and, 50; relationships, closed and open, 217; structural differences, 106
Solidary groups, 3, 4; bases of solidarity, 209; collective solidarity, 42; party solidarity, 218
Solow, Barbara L., 86
Spain, 32, 71; Civil War in, 296
Spengler, Joseph J., 92
Spicer, Edward H., 24, 311
Stamp, J. C., 162
State, The, 60; economic development and, 91–2; expansion, 62
Status groups, 37, 40, 211, 217–18, 236, 242, 261, 313; orientations, 334, 335; politics of, 95, 212, 331–9 *passim*; solidarity, 320, 321, 326–31
Stavenhagen, Rodolfo, 32
Steward, Julian, 36
Stinchcombe, Arthur, 117
Stokes, Donald, 214, 261
Stone, Lawrence, 27, 142
Stratification, *see* Cultural division of labor
Strauss, E., 85, 86, 288
Strayer, Joseph R., 61
Swift, Jonathan, 86
Switzerland, 21

Tabouret-Keller, A., 192
Tachi, M., 29, 132
Tariffs, 249, 250, 253, 256, 257

Textile industry, 106, 138, 139
Third World societies, 11, 21, 23, 26, 30, 33, 128, 147, 348
Thirsk, Joan, 57, 58, 59, 70, 82, 134
Thomas, Brinley, 188, 198
Thompson, E. P., 117, 177, 318
Thompson, F. M. L., 118, 181
Thompson, Paul, 274
Tilly, Charles, 66, 69, 70, 234
Tilly, Louise A., 117
Tocqueville, Alexis de, 20, 117, 118
Tönnies, Ferdinand, 314
Trade, 51; balance of, 91; Free, 92–3, 135, 233; protectionist measures, 93–4; *see also* Cattle trade, Wool trade
Trade unions, 37, 275, 277, 279; congresses, 283, 284, 285, 291; craft, 276, 291; industrial, 276, 280, 291
Trevor-Roper, H. R., 96, 104
Tsuzuki, Chushichi, 281
Turkish Massacre, 243–4
Turner, F. J., 238

Ullman, Edward, 31
Unemployment, 293–6 *passim*
United Kingdom, *see* Great Britain
Universalism, 217
Urbanization, 252
Urwin, Derek, 95, 210, 214

Verba, Sidney, 25, 132

Wales and the Welsh, xvii, 11, 53, 69–71, 82, 100, 129, 133, 152, 159, 180, 244–6, 251, 256, 262, 276–80, 300, 316, 326; anglicization, 110–11, 189–90, 204, 254, 343; annexation and Union, 67, 69, 82; Church of Wales, 74, 100–1, 110, 168, 172, 183, 253, 260, 268, 288; gentry, 82, 101, 110, 111, 123, 182, 189, political domination of, 120; heavy industry, 298; highland territories, 52; Home Rule, 278, 280; language, 74, 75, 109, 110, 167, 168, 182–3, 193, 260, 269, 308, 309, decline of, 191–207 *passim*, 262; Marcher Lords, 56, 57, 70, 101; Marches, 56, 57; mercenary soldiers, 87; Nationalism, 205, 214, 264, 278, 284, 293, 334, Plaid Cymru, 298, 299, 304, 305, 306, 308, 309; Penal Laws, 74; self-government for, 306–7; trade, international, 257

Wall, Maureen, 77, 90, 104, 186
Wallerstein, Immanuel, 36, 99, 234
Webb, Sidney and Beatrice, 122, 123, 285
Weber, Max, 23, 28, 37, 59–60, 62, 211, 212, 217, 218, 241, 260–1, 313, 323
Weiner, Carol Z., 269
Weiner, Myron, 17
Wessex, 54, 55, 56
Wilensky, Harold, 220
William of Orange, 108
Williams, David, 74, 101, 102, 110, 111, 120, 189, 296
Williams, Glanmor, 101, 188, 204, 214
Williams, Penry, 66
Williams, Robin M., 24
Williams, W. Ogwen, 111, 198

Williamson, Jeffrey G., 19, 128, 145, 163, 211
Wilson, Charles, 91, 93
Wilson, Trevor, 274
Wolsey, Thomas, 66
Woodham-Smith, Cecil, 270
Woodward, M., 166
Woodward, V. H., 163
Wool trade, 82, 83, 136; Welsh, 89–90
World War One, 264, 280, 289
World War Two, 265, 298
Wriggins, W. H., 22

Young, Frank W., 64, 311

Zagorin, Perez, 99
Zipf, G. K., 129

Routledge Social Science Series

Routledge & Kegan Paul   London and Boston

68–74 Carter Lane   London EC4V 5EL
9 Park Street   Boston   Mass 02108

Contents

International Library of Sociology 3
General Sociology 3
Foreign Classics of Sociology 4
Social Structure 4
Sociology and Politics 4
Foreign Affairs 5
Criminology 5
Social Psychology 5
Sociology of the Family 6
Social Services 7
Sociology of Education 7
Sociology of Culture 8
Sociology of Religion 9
Sociology of Art and Literature 9
Sociology of Knowledge 9
Urban Sociology 9
Rural Sociology 10
Sociology of Industry and Distribution 10
Documentary 11
Anthropology 11
Sociology and Philosophy 12
International Library of Anthropology 12
International Library of Social Policy 12
International Library of Welfare and Philosophy 13
Primary Socialization, Language and Education 13
Reports of the Institute of Community Studies 13
Reports of the Institute for Social Studies in Medical Care 14
Medicine, Illness and Society 14
Monographs in Social Theory 14
Routledge Social Science Journals 15

*Authors wishing to submit manuscripts for any series in
this catalogue should send them to the Social Science Editor,
Routledge & Kegan Paul Ltd, 68–74 Carter Lane,
London EC4V 5EL*

●*Books so marked are available in paperback
All books are in Metric Demy 8vo format (216 × 138mm approx.)*

International Library of Sociology

General Editor John Rex

GENERAL SOCIOLOGY

Barnsley, J. H. The Social Reality of Ethics. *464 pp.*
Belshaw, Cyril. The Conditions of Social Performance. *An Exploratory Theory. 144 pp.*
Brown, Robert. Explanation in Social Science. *208 pp.*
● Rules and Laws in Sociology. *192 pp.*
Bruford, W. H. Chekhov and His Russia. *A Sociological Study. 244 pp.*
Cain, Maureen E. Society and the Policeman's Role. *326 pp.*
Gibson, Quentin. The Logic of Social Enquiry. *240 pp.*
Glucksmann, M. Structuralist Analysis in Contemporary Social Thought. *212 pp.*
Gurvitch, Georges. Sociology of Law. *Preface by Roscoe Pound. 264 pp.*
Hodge, H. A. Wilhelm Dilthey. *An Introduction. 184 pp.*
Homans, George C. Sentiments and Activities. *336 pp.*
Johnson, Harry M. Sociology: *a Systematic Introduction. Foreword by Robert K. Merton. 710 pp.*
Mannheim, Karl. Essays on Sociology and Social Psychology. *Edited by Paul Keckskemeti. With Editorial Note by Adolph Lowe. 344 pp.*
   Systematic Sociology: *An Introduction to the Study of Society. Edited by J. S. Erös and Professor W. A. C. Stewart. 220 pp.*
Martindale, Don. The Nature and Types of Sociological Theory. *292 pp.*
●**Maus, Heinz.** A Short History of Sociology. *234 pp.*
Mey, Harald. Field-Theory. *A Study of its Application in the Social Sciences. 352 pp.*
Myrdal, Gunnar. Value in Social Theory: *A Collection of Essays on Methodology. Edited by Paul Streeten. 332 pp.*
Ogburn, William F., and **Nimkoff, Meyer F.** A Handbook of Sociology. *Preface by Karl Mannheim. 656 pp. 46 figures. 35 tables.*
Parsons, Talcott, and **Smelser, Neil J.** Economy and Society: *A Study in the Integration of Economic and Social Theory. 362 pp.*
●**Rex, John.** Key Problems of Sociological Theory. *220 pp.*
   Discovering Sociology. *278 pp.*
   Sociology and the Demystification of the Modern World. *282 pp.*
●**Rex, John** (Ed.) Approaches to Sociology. *Contributions by Peter Abell, Frank Bechhofer, Basil Bernstein, Ronald Fletcher, David Frisby, Miriam Glucksmann, Peter Lassman, Herminio Martins, John Rex, Roland Robertson, John Westergaard and Jock Young. 302 pp.*
Rigby, A. Alternative Realities. *352 pp.*
Roche, M. Phenomenology, Language and the Social Sciences. *374 pp.*
Sahay, A. Sociological Analysis. *220 pp.*
Urry, John. Reference Groups and the Theory of Revolution. *244 pp.*
Weinberg, E. Development of Sociology in the Soviet Union. *173 pp.*

FOREIGN CLASSICS OF SOCIOLOGY

● **Durkheim, Emile.** Suicide. *A Study in Sociology. Edited and with an Introduction by George Simpson. 404 pp.*
   Professional Ethics and Civic Morals. *Translated by Cornelia Brookfield. 288 pp.*
● **Gerth, H. H.,** and **Mills, C. Wright.** From Max Weber: *Essays in Sociology. 502 pp.*
● **Tönnies, Ferdinand.** Community and Association. (*Gemeinschaft und Gesellschaft.*) *Translated and Supplemented by Charles P. Loomis. Foreword by Pitirim A. Sorokin. 334 pp.*

SOCIAL STRUCTURE

Andreski, Stanislav. Military Organization and Society. *Foreword by Professor A. R. Radcliffe-Brown. 226 pp. 1 folder.*
Coontz, Sydney H. Population Theories and the Economic Interpretation. *202 pp.*
Coser, Lewis. The Functions of Social Conflict. *204 pp.*
Dickie-Clark, H. F. Marginal Situation: *A Sociological Study of a Coloured Group. 240 pp. 11 tables.*
Glaser, Barney, and **Strauss, Anselm L.** Status Passage. *A Formal Theory. 208 pp.*
Glass, D. V. (Ed.) Social Mobility in Britain. *Contributions by J. Berent, T. Bottomore, R. C. Chambers, J. Floud, D. V. Glass, J. R. Hall, H. T. Himmelweit, R. K. Kelsall, F. M. Martin, C. A. Moser, R. Mukherjee, and W. Ziegel. 420 pp.*
Jones, Garth N. Planned Organizational Change: *An Exploratory Study Using an Empirical Approach. 268 pp.*
Kelsall, R. K. Higher Civil Servants in Britain: *From 1870 to the Present Day. 268 pp. 31 tables.*
König, René. The Community. *232 pp. Illustrated.*
● **Lawton, Denis.** Social Class, Language and Education. *192 pp.*
McLeish, John. The Theory of Social Change: *Four Views Considered. 128 pp.*
Marsh, David C. The Changing Social Structure of England and Wales, 1871-1961. *288 pp.*
Mouzelis, Nicos. Organization and Bureaucracy. *An Analysis of Modern Theories. 240 pp.*
Mulkay, M. J. Functionalism, Exchange and Theoretical Strategy. *272 pp.*
Ossowski, Stanislaw. Class Structure in the Social Consciousness. *210 pp.*
Podgórecki, Adam. Law and Society. *About 300 pp.*

SOCIOLOGY AND POLITICS

Acton, T. A. Gypsy Politics and Social Change. *316 pp.*
Hechter, Michael. Internal Colonialism. *The Celtic Fringe in British National Development, 1536–1966. About 350 pp.*
Hertz, Frederick. Nationality in History and Politics: *A Psychology and Sociology of National Sentiment and Nationalism. 432 pp.*

Kornhauser, William. The Politics of Mass Society. *272 pp. 20 tables.*
Laidler, Harry W. History of Socialism. *Social-Economic Movements: An Historical and Comparative Survey of Socialism, Communism, Co-operation, Utopianism; and other Systems of Reform and Reconstruction. 992 pp.*
Lasswell, H. D. Analysis of Political Behaviour. *324 pp.*
Mannheim, Karl. Freedom, Power and Democratic Planning. *Edited by Hans Gerth and Ernest K. Bramstedt. 424 pp.*
Mansur, Fatma. Process of Independence. *Foreword by A. H. Hanson. 208 pp.*
Martin, David A. Pacifism: *an Historical and Sociological Study. 262 pp.*
Myrdal, Gunnar. The Political Element in the Development of Economic Theory. *Translated from the German by Paul Streeten. 282 pp.*
Wootton, Graham. Workers, Unions and the State. *188 pp.*

FOREIGN AFFAIRS: THEIR SOCIAL, POLITICAL AND ECONOMIC FOUNDATIONS

Mayer, J. P. Political Thought in France from the Revolution to the Fifth Republic. *164 pp.*

CRIMINOLOGY

Ancel, Marc. Social Defence: *A Modern Approach to Criminal Problems. Foreword by Leon Radzinowicz. 240 pp.*
Cain, Maureen E. Society and the Policeman's Role. *326 pp.*
Cloward, Richard A., and Ohlin, Lloyd E. Delinquency and Opportunity: *A Theory of Delinquent Gangs. 248 pp.*
Downes, David M. The Delinquent Solution. *A Study in Subcultural Theory. 296 pp.*
Dunlop, A. B., and McCabe, S. Young Men in Detention Centres. *192 pp.*
Friedlander, Kate. The Psycho-Analytical Approach to Juvenile Delinquency: *Theory, Case Studies, Treatment. 320 pp.*
Glueck, Sheldon, and Eleanor. Family Environment and Delinquency. *With the statistical assistance of Rose W. Kneznek. 340 pp.*
Lopez-Rey, Manuel. Crime. *An Analytical Appraisal. 288 pp.*
Mannheim, Hermann. Comparative Criminology: *a Text Book. Two volumes. 442 pp. and 380 pp.*
Morris, Terence. The Criminal Area: *A Study in Social Ecology. Foreword by Hermann Mannheim. 232 pp. 25 tables. 4 maps.*
Rock, Paul. Making People Pay. *338 pp.*
●**Taylor, Ian, Walton, Paul, and Young, Jock.** The New Criminology. *For a Social Theory of Deviance. 325 pp.*

SOCIAL PSYCHOLOGY

Bagley, Christopher. The Social Psychology of the Epileptic Child. *320 pp.*
Barbu, Zevedei. Problems of Historical Psychology. *248 pp.*
Blackburn, Julian. Psychology and the Social Pattern. *184 pp.*

●**Brittan, Arthur.** Meanings and Situations. *224 pp.*
Carroll, J. Break-Out from the Crystal Palace. *200 pp.*
●**Fleming, C. M.** Adolescence: Its Social Psychology. *With an Introduction to recent findings from the fields of Anthropology, Physiology, Medicine, Psychometrics and Sociometry. 288 pp.*
● The Social Psychology of Education: *An Introduction and Guide to Its Study. 136 pp.*
Homans, George C. The Human Group. *Foreword by Bernard DeVoto. Introduction by Robert K. Merton. 526 pp.*
● Social Behaviour: *its Elementary Forms. 416 pp.*
●**Klein, Josephine.** The Study of Groups. *226 pp. 31 figures. 5 tables.*
Linton, Ralph. The Cultural Background of Personality. *132 pp.*
●**Mayo, Elton.** The Social Problems of an Industrial Civilization. *With an appendix on the Political Problem. 180 pp.*
Ottaway, A. K. C. Learning Through Group Experience. *176 pp.*
Ridder, J. C. de. The Personality of the Urban African in South Africa. *A Thematic Apperception Test Study. 196 pp. 12 plates.*
●**Rose, Arnold M.** (Ed.) Human Behaviour and Social Processes: *an Interactionist Approach. Contributions by Arnold M. Rose, Ralph H. Turner, Anselm Strauss, Everett C. Hughes, E. Franklin Frazier, Howard S. Becker, et al. 696 pp.*
Smelser, Neil J. Theory of Collective Behaviour. *448 pp.*
Stephenson, Geoffrey M. The Development of Conscience. *128 pp.*
Young, Kimball. Handbook of Social Psychology. *658 pp. 16 figures. 10 tables.*

SOCIOLOGY OF THE FAMILY

Banks, J. A. Prosperity and Parenthood: *A Study of Family Planning among The Victorian Middle Classes. 262 pp.*
Bell, Colin R. Middle Class Families: *Social and Geographical Mobility. 224 pp.*
Burton, Lindy. Vulnerable Children. *272 pp.*
Gavron, Hannah. The Captive Wife: *Conflicts of Household Mothers. 190 pp.*
George, Victor, and **Wilding, Paul.** Motherless Families. *220 pp.*
Klein, Josephine. Samples from English Cultures.
1. Three Preliminary Studies and Aspects of Adult Life in England. *447 pp.*
2. Child-Rearing Practices and Index. *247 pp.*
Klein, Viola. Britain's Married Women Workers. *180 pp.*
The Feminine Character. *History of an Ideology. 244 pp.*
McWhinnie, Alexina M. Adopted Children. *How They Grow Up. 304 pp.*
● **Myrdal, Alva,** and **Klein, Viola.** Women's Two Roles: *Home and Work. 238 pp. 27 tables.*
Parsons, Talcott, and **Bales, Robert F.** Family: Socialization and Interaction Process. *In collaboration with James Olds, Morris Zelditch and Philip E. Slater. 456 pp. 50 figures and tables.*

SOCIAL SERVICES

Bastide, Roger. The Sociology of Mental Disorder. *Translated from the French by Jean McNeil. 260 pp.*

Carlebach, Julius. Caring For Children in Trouble. *266 pp.*

Forder, R. A. (Ed.) Penelope Hall's Social Services of England and Wales. *352 pp.*

George, Victor. Foster Care. *Theory and Practice. 234 pp.*
Social Security: *Beveridge and After. 258 pp.*

George, V., and **Wilding, P.** Motherless Families. *248 pp.*

●**Goetschius, George W.** Working with Community Groups. *256 pp.*

Goetschius, George W., and **Tash, Joan.** Working with Unattached Youth. *416 pp.*

Hall, M. P., and **Howes, I. V.** The Church in Social Work. *A Study of Moral Welfare Work undertaken by the Church of England. 320 pp.*

Heywood, Jean S. Children in Care: *the Development of the Service for the Deprived Child. 264 pp.*

Hoenig, J., and **Hamilton, Marian W.** The De-Segregation of the Mentally Ill. *284 pp.*

Jones, Kathleen. Mental Health and Social Policy, 1845-1959. *264 pp.*

King, Roy D., Raynes, Norma V., and **Tizard, Jack.** Patterns of Residential Care. *356 pp.*

Leigh, John. Young People and Leisure. *256 pp.*

Morris, Mary. Voluntary Work and the Welfare State. *300 pp.*

Morris, Pauline. Put Away: *A Sociological Study of Institutions for the Mentally Retarded. 364 pp.*

Nokes, P. L. The Professional Task in Welfare Practice. *152 pp.*

Timms, Noel. Psychiatric Social Work in Great Britain (1939-1962). *280 pp.*

● Social Casework: *Principles and Practice. 256 pp.*

Young, A. F. Social Services in British Industry. *272 pp.*

Young, A. F., and **Ashton, E. T.** British Social Work in the Nineteenth Century. *288 pp.*

SOCIOLOGY OF EDUCATION

Banks, Olive. Parity and Prestige in English Secondary Education: a Study in Educational Sociology. *272 pp.*

Bentwich, Joseph. Education in Israel. *224 pp. 8 pp. plates.*

●**Blyth, W. A. L.** English Primary Education. *A Sociological Description.*
1. Schools. *232 pp.*
2. Background. *168 pp.*

Collier, K. G. The Social Purposes of Education: *Personal and Social Values in Education. 268 pp.*

Dale, R. R., and **Griffith, S.** Down Stream: *Failure in the Grammar School.* *108 pp.*

Dore, R. P. Education in Tokugawa Japan. *356 pp. 9 pp. plates.*

Evans, K. M. Sociometry and Education. *158 pp.*

●**Ford, Julienne.** Social Class and the Comprehensive School. *192 pp.*

Foster, P. J. Education and Social Change in Ghana. *336 pp. 3 maps.*

Fraser, W. R. Education and Society in Modern France. *150 pp.*

Grace, Gerald R. Role Conflict and the Teacher. *About 200 pp.*

Hans, Nicholas. New Trends in Education in the Eighteenth Century. *278 pp. 19 tables.*

● Comparative Education: *A Study of Educational Factors and Traditions.* *360 pp.*

Hargreaves, David. Interpersonal Relations and Education. *432 pp.*

● Social Relations in a Secondary School. *240 pp.*

Holmes, Brian. Problems in Education. *A Comparative Approach. 336 pp.*

King, Ronald. Values and Involvement in a Grammar School. *164 pp.*

School Organization and Pupil Involvement. *A Study of Secondary Schools.*

●**Mannheim, Karl,** and **Stewart, W. A. C.** An Introduction to the Sociology of Education. *206 pp.*

Morris, Raymond N. The Sixth Form and College Entrance. *231 pp.*

●**Musgrove, F.** Youth and the Social Order. *176 pp.*

●**Ottaway, A. K. C.** Education and Society: An Introduction to the Sociology of Education. *With an Introduction by W. O. Lester Smith. 212 pp.*

Peers, Robert. Adult Education: *A Comparative Study. 398 pp.*

Pritchard, D. G. Education and the Handicapped: *1760 to 1960. 258 pp.*

Richardson, Helen. Adolescent Girls in Approved Schools. *308 pp.*

Stratta, Erica. The Education of Borstal Boys. *A Study of their Educational Experiences prior to, and during, Borstal Training. 256 pp.*

Taylor, P. H., Reid, W. A., and **Holley, B. J.** The English Sixth Form. *A Case Study in Curriculum Research. 200 pp.*

SOCIOLOGY OF CULTURE

Eppel, E. M., and **M.** Adolescents and Morality: *A Study of some Moral Values and Dilemmas of Working Adolescents in the Context of a changing Climate of Opinion. Foreword by W. J. H. Sprott. 268 pp. 39 tables.*

●**Fromm, Erich.** The Fear of Freedom. *286 pp.*

● The Sane Society. *400 pp.*

Mannheim, Karl. Essays on the Sociology of Culture. *Edited by Ernst Mannheim in co-operation with Paul Kecskemeti. Editorial Note by Adolph Lowe. 280 pp.*

Weber, Alfred. Farewell to European History: *or The Conquest of Nihilism. Translated from the German by R. F. C. Hull. 224 pp.*

SOCIOLOGY OF RELIGION

Argyle, Michael and **Beit-Hallahmi, Benjamin.** The Social Psychology of Religion. *About 256 pp.*

Nelson, G. K. Spiritualism and Society. *313 pp.*

Stark, Werner. The Sociology of Religion. *A Study of Christendom.*
Volume I. *Established Religion. 248 pp.*
Volume II. *Sectarian Religion. 368 pp.*
Volume III. *The Universal Church. 464 pp.*
Volume IV. *Types of Religious Man. 352 pp.*
Volume V. *Types of Religious Culture. 464 pp.*

Turner, B. S. Weber and Islam. *216 pp.*

Watt, W. Montgomery. Islam and the Integration of Society. *320 pp.*

SOCIOLOGY OF ART AND LITERATURE

Jarvie, Ian C. Towards a Sociology of the Cinema. *A Comparative Essay on the Structure and Functioning of a Major Entertainment Industry. 405 pp.*

Rust, Frances S. Dance in Society. *An Analysis of the Relationships between the Social Dance and Society in England from the Middle Ages to the Present Day. 256 pp. 8 pp. of plates.*

Schücking, L. L. The Sociology of Literary Taste. *112 pp.*

Wolff, Janet. Hermeneutic Philosophy and the Sociology of Art. *About 200 pp.*

SOCIOLOGY OF KNOWLEDGE

Diesing, P. Patterns of Discovery in the Social Sciences. *262 pp.*

● **Douglas, J. D.** (Ed.) Understanding Everyday Life. *370 pp.*

● **Hamilton, P.** Knowledge and Social Structure. *174 pp.*

Jarvie, I. C. Concepts and Society. *232 pp.*

Mannheim, Karl. Essays on the Sociology of Knowledge. *Edited by Paul Kecskemeti. Editorial Note by Adolph Lowe. 353 pp.*

Remmling, Gunter W. (Ed.) Towards the Sociology of Knowledge. *Origin and Development of a Sociological Thought Style. 463 pp.*

Stark, Werner. The Sociology of Knowledge: *An Essay in Aid of a Deeper Understanding of the History of Ideas. 384 pp.*

URBAN SOCIOLOGY

Ashworth, William. The Genesis of Modern British Town Planning: *A Study in Economic and Social History of the Nineteenth and Twentieth Centuries. 288 pp.*

Cullingworth, J. B. Housing Needs and Planning Policy: *A Restatement of the Problems of Housing Need and 'Overspill' in England and Wales. 232 pp. 44 tables. 8 maps.*

Dickinson, Robert E. City and Region: *A Geographical Interpretation* *608 pp. 125 figures.*
The West European City: *A Geographical Interpretation. 600 pp. 129 maps. 29 plates.*
● The City Region in Western Europe. *320 pp. Maps.*
Humphreys, Alexander J. New Dubliners: *Urbanization and the Irish Family. Foreword by George C. Homans. 304 pp.*
Jackson, Brian. Working Class Community: *Some General Notions raised by a Series of Studies in Northern England. 192 pp.*
Jennings, Hilda. Societies in the Making: *a Study of Development and Redevelopment within a County Borough. Foreword by D. A. Clark. 286 pp.*
●**Mann, P. H.** An Approach to Urban Sociology. *240 pp.*
Morris, R. N., and **Mogey, J.** The Sociology of Housing. *Studies at Berinsfield. 232 pp. 4 pp. plates.*
Rosser, C., and **Harris, C.** The Family and Social Change. *A Study of Family and Kinship in a South Wales Town. 352 pp. 8 maps.*

RURAL SOCIOLOGY

Chambers, R. J. H. Settlement Schemes in Tropical Africa: *A Selective Study. 268 pp.*
Haswell, M. R. The Economics of Development in Village India. *120 pp.*
Littlejohn, James. Westrigg: *the Sociology of a Cheviot Parish. 172 pp. 5 figures.*
Mayer, Adrian C. Peasants in the Pacific. *A Study of Fiji Indian Rural Society. 248 pp. 20 plates.*
Williams, W. M. The Sociology of an English Village: *Gosforth. 272 pp. 12 figures. 13 tables.*

SOCIOLOGY OF INDUSTRY AND DISTRIBUTION

Anderson, Nels. Work and Leisure. *280 pp.*
●**Blau, Peter M.,** and **Scott, W. Richard.** Formal Organizations: *a Comparative approach. Introduction and Additional Bibliography by J. H. Smith. 326 pp.*
Eldridge, J. E. T. Industrial Disputes. *Essays in the Sociology of Industrial Relations. 288 pp.*
Hetzler, Stanley. Applied Measures for Promoting Technological Growth. *352 pp.*
Technological Growth and Social Change. *Achieving Modernization. 269 pp.*
Hollowell, Peter G. The Lorry Driver. *272 pp.*
Jefferys, Margot, *with the assistance of Winifred Moss.* Mobility in the Labour Market: *Employment Changes in Battersea and Dagenham. Preface by Barbara Wootton. 186 pp. 51 tables.*

Millerson, Geoffrey. The Qualifying Associations: *a Study in Professionalization. 320 pp.*

Smelser, Neil J. Social Change in the Industrial Revolution: *An Application of Theory to the Lancashire Cotton Industry, 1770-1840. 468 pp. 12 figures. 14 tables.*

Williams, Gertrude. Recruitment to Skilled Trades. *240 pp.*

Young, A. F. Industrial Injuries Insurance: *an Examination of British Policy. 192 pp.*

DOCUMENTARY

Schlesinger, Rudolf (Ed.) Changing Attitudes in Soviet Russia.
  2. The Nationalities Problem and Soviet Administration. *Selected Readings on the Development of Soviet Nationalities Policies. Introduced by the editor. Translated by W. W. Gottlieb. 324 pp.*

ANTHROPOLOGY

Ammar, Hamed. Growing up in an Egyptian Village: *Silwa, Province of Aswan. 336 pp.*

Brandel-Syrier, Mia. Reeftown Elite. *A Study of Social Mobility in a Modern African Community on the Reef. 376 pp.*

Crook, David, and **Isabel.** Revolution in a Chinese Village: *Ten Mile Inn. 230 pp. 8 plates. 1 map.*

Dickie-Clark, H. F. The Marginal Situation. *A Sociological Study of a Coloured Group. 236 pp.*

Dube, S. C. Indian Village. *Foreword by Morris Edward Opler. 276 pp. 4 plates.*

  India's Changing Villages: *Human Factors in Community Development. 260 pp. 8 plates. 1 map.*

Firth, Raymond. Malay Fishermen. *Their Peasant Economy. 420 pp. 17 pp. plates.*

Firth, R., Hubert, J., and **Forge, A.** Families and their Relatives. *Kinship in a Middle-Class Sector of London: An Anthropological Study. 456 pp.*

Gulliver, P. H. Social Control in an African Society: a Study of the Arusha, Agricultural Masai of Northern Tanganyika. *320 pp. 8 plates. 10 figures.*

  Family Herds. *288 pp.*

Ishwaran, K. Shivapur. *A South Indian Village. 216 pp.*

  Tradition and Economy in Village India: *An Interactionist Approach. Foreword by Conrad Arensburg. 176 pp.*

Jarvie, Ian C. The Revolution in Anthropology. *268 pp.*

Jarvie, Ian C., and **Agassi, Joseph.** Hong Kong. *A Society in Transition. 396 pp. Illustrated with plates and maps.*

Little, Kenneth L. Mende of Sierra Leone. *308 pp. and folder.*

  Negroes in Britain. *With a New Introduction and Contemporary Study by Leonard Bloom. 320 pp.*

Lowie, Robert H. Social Organization. *494 pp.*

Mayer, Adrian, C. Caste and Kinship in Central India: *A Village and its Region. 328 pp. 16 plates. 15 figures. 16 tables.*

Peasants in the Pacific. *A Study of Fiji Indian Rural Society. 248 pp.*

Smith, Raymond T. The Negro Family in British Guiana: *Family Structure and Social Status in the Villages. With a Foreword by Meyer Fortes. 314 pp. 8 plates. 1 figure. 4 maps.*

SOCIOLOGY AND PHILOSOPHY

Barnsley, John H. The Social Reality of Ethics. *A Comparative Analysis of Moral Codes. 448 pp.*

Diesing, Paul. Patterns of Discovery in the Social Sciences. *362 pp.*

●**Douglas, Jack D.** (Ed.) Understanding Everyday Life. *Toward the Reconstruction of Sociological Knowledge. Contributions by Alan F. Blum. Aaron W. Cicourel, Norman K. Denzin, Jack D. Douglas, John Heeren, Peter McHugh, Peter K. Manning, Melvin Power, Matthew Speier, Roy Turner, D. Lawrence Wieder, Thomas P. Wilson and Don H. Zimmerman. 370 pp.*

Jarvie, Ian C. Concepts and Society. *216 pp.*

Pelz, Werner. The Scope of Understanding in Sociology. *Towards a more radical reorientation in the social humanistic sciences. 283 pp.*

Roche, Maurice. Phenomenology, Language and the Social Sciences. *371 pp.*

Sahay, Arun. Sociological Analysis. *212 pp.*

Sklair, Leslie. The Sociology of Progress. *320 pp.*

International Library of Anthropology

General Editor Adam Kuper

Brown, Paula. The Chimbu. *A Study of Change in the New Guinea Highlands. 151 pp.*

Lloyd, P. C. Power and Independence. *Urban Africans' Perception of Social Inequality. 264 pp.*

Pettigrew, Joyce. Robber Noblemen. *A Study of the Political System of the Sikh Jats. 284 pp.*

Van Den Berghe, Pierre L. Power and Privilege at an African University. *278 pp.*

International Library of Social Policy

General Editor Kathleen Jones

Bayley, M. Mental Handicap and Community Care. *426 pp.*

Butler, J. R. Family Doctors and Public Policy. *208 pp.*

Holman, Robert. Trading in Children. *A Study of Private Fostering. 355 pp.*

Jones, Kathleen. History of the Mental Health Service. *428 pp.*

Thomas, J. E. The English Prison Officer since 1850: *A Study in Conflict. 258 pp.*

Woodward, J. To Do the Sick No Harm. *A Study of the British Voluntary Hospital System to 1875. About 220 pp.*

International Library of Welfare and Philosophy

General Editors Noel Timms and David Watson

● **Plant, Raymond.** Community and Ideology. *104 pp.*

Primary Socialization, Language and Education

General Editor Basil Bernstein

Bernstein, Basil. Class, Codes and Control. *2 volumes.*
1. *Theoretical Studies Towards a Sociology of Language. 254 pp.*
2. *Applied Studies Towards a Sociology of Language. About 400 pp.*

Brandis, W., and **Bernstein, B.** Selection and Control. *176 pp.*

Brandis, Walter, and **Henderson, Dorothy.** Social Class, Language and Communication. *288 pp.*

Cook-Gumperz, Jenny. Social Control and Socialization. *A Study of Class Differences in the Language of Maternal Control. 290 pp.*

● **Gahagan, D. M.,** and **G. A.** Talk Reform. *Exploration in Language for Infant School Children. 160 pp.*

Robinson, W. P., and **Rackstraw, Susan D. A.** A Question of Answers. *2 volumes. 192 pp. and 180 pp.*

Turner, Geoffrey J., and **Mohan, Bernard A.** A Linguistic Description and Computer Programme for Children's Speech. *208 pp.*

Reports of the Institute of Community Studies

Cartwright, Ann. Human Relations and Hospital Care. *272 pp.*

● Parents and Family Planning Services. *306 pp.*

Patients and their Doctors. *A Study of General Practice. 304 pp.*

● **Jackson, Brian.** Streaming: *an Education System in Miniature. 168 pp.*

Jackson, Brian, and **Marsden, Dennis.** Education and the Working Class: *Some General Themes raised by a Study of 88 Working-class Children in a Northern Industrial City. 268 pp. 2 folders.*

Marris, Peter. The Experience of Higher Education. *232 pp. 27 tables.*

Loss and Change. *192 pp.*

Marris, Peter, and Rein, Martin. Dilemmas of Social Reform. *Poverty and Community Action in the United States. 256 pp.*

Marris, Peter, and Somerset, Anthony. African Businessmen. *A Study of Entrepreneurship and Development in Kenya. 256 pp.*

Mills, Richard. Young Outsiders: *a Study in Alternative Communities. 216 pp.*

Runciman, W. G. Relative Deprivation and Social Justice. *A Study of Attitudes to Social Inequality in Twentieth-Century England. 352 pp.*

Willmott, Peter. Adolescent Boys in East London. *230 pp.*

Willmott, Peter, and Young, Michael. Family and Class in a London Suburb. *202 pp. 47 tables.*

Young, Michael. Innovation and Research in Education. *192 pp.*

●Young, Michael, and McGeeney, Patrick. Learning Begins at Home. *A Study of a Junior School and its Parents. 128 pp.*

Young, Michael, and Willmott, Peter. Family and Kinship in East London. *Foreword by Richard M. Titmuss. 252 pp. 39 tables.*
The Symmetrical Family. *410 pp.*

Reports of the Institute for Social Studies in Medical Care

Cartwright, Ann, Hockey, Lisbeth, and Anderson, John L. Life Before Death. *310 pp.*

Dunnell, Karen, and Cartwright, Ann. Medicine Takers, Prescribers and Hoarders. *190 pp.*

Medicine, Illness and Society

General Editor W. M. Williams

Robinson, David. The Process of Becoming Ill. *142 pp.*

Stacey, Margaret, *et al.* Hospitals, Children and Their Families. *The Report of a Pilot Study. 202 pp.*

Monographs in Social Theory

General Editor Arthur Brittan

●Barnes, B. Scientific Knowledge and Sociological Theory. *About 200 pp.*

Bauman, Zygmunt. Culture as Praxis. *204 pp.*

● Dixon, Keith. Sociological Theory. *Pretence and Possibility. 142 pp.*

●Smith, Anthony D. The Concept of Social Change. *A Critique of the Functionalist Theory of Social Change. 208 pp.*

Routledge Social Science Journals

The British Journal of Sociology. *Edited by Terence P. Morris. Vol. 1, No. 1, March 1950 and Quarterly. Roy. 8vo. Back numbers available. An international journal with articles on all aspects of sociology.*

Economy and Society. *Vol. 1, No. 1. February 1972 and Quarterly. Metric Roy. 8vo. A journal for all social scientists covering sociology, philosophy, anthropology, economics and history. Back numbers available.*

Year Book of Social Policy in Britain, The. *Edited by Kathleen Jones. 1971. Published annually.*

Printed in Great Britain by Unwin Brothers Limited
The Gresham Press Old Woking Surrey
A member of the Staples Printing Group